Older Americans

A CHANGING MARKET

Older Americans

A CHANGING MARKET

4th EDITION

BY THE NEW STRATEGIST EDITORS

New Strategist Publications, Inc.
Ithaca, New York

New Strategist Publications, Inc.
P.O. Box 242, Ithaca, New York 14851
800/848-0842; 607/273-0913
www.newstrategist.com

ISBN 1-885070-50-0

Printed in the United States of America

Table of Contents

Chapter 4. Income

Chapter 5. Labor Force

Chapter 6. Living Arrangements

Chapter 7. Population

Chapter 8. Spending

Chapter 9. Wealth

Tables

Chapter 3. Housing

Chapter 4. Income

Chapter 5. Labor Force

Chapter 6. Living Arrangements

Chapter 7. Population

Chapter 8. Spending

Chapter 9. Wealth

Illustrations

Introduction

A revolution has begun. In 2004, the oldest members of the Baby-Boom generation turn 58, accelerating the radical transformation of the 55-or-older age group.

No segment of the population will change as much as older Americans during the next two decades. Not only is the age group becoming increasingly sophisticated as it fills with well-educated Boomers, but the number of older Americans is expanding rapidly. And because older men and women are more likely to vote than younger adults, the number-one priority of politicians, policymakers, and businesses in the years ahead will be catering to the wants and needs of people aged 55 or older.

The fourth edition of *Older Americans: A Changing Market* (formerly titled *Americans 55 & Older: A Changing Market*) reveals the characteristics of the older population today and tomorrow. It shows the lifestyles, incomes, and spending patterns of fifty-, sixty-, and seventy-year-olds. Those who peruse these pages will become aware of the changes that lie ahead as Boomers increasingly dominate the age group. The characteristics of 55-to-59-year-olds, an age group now almost entirely filled with the oldest Boomers, reveals the shape of things to come.

Older Americans have crossed most of life's milestones. More than 90 percent have married, had children, and become grandparents, according to an AARP survey. Most have experienced the death of their mother and father and are now the oldest members of their extended family. But some milestones still lie ahead. Fewer than half (46 percent) have experienced a major illness and about half (49 percent) have made a major career change.

Those two issues—health care and work/retirement—will be the top concerns of older Americans in the years ahead. Businesses and politicians are already wrestling with the problems of health care cost and coverage. As Boomers age and confront serious health problems for the first time, health care policy will become even more important, a political firestorm for the unwary. Older Americans are already postponing retirement, and Boomers will join those ranks soon. Most Boomers will be forced to work well into their sixties, frustrating those who hoped to retire early. Some will enjoy a second career, however, as they supplement their retirement income.

Perhaps the most important story told by *Older Americans: A Changing Market* is that the stereotypes of aging—poverty, ill health, and an unwillingness to do or spend—must be put to rest. The majority of older Americans are healthy, happy, and comfortably well off. A small minority is sick or poor. For decades the nation's social policies have focused on improving living conditions for the elderly, and they have succeeded in lifting older Ameri-

Critical Life Events among Older Americans, 2002

(percent of people aged 57 or older who have ever experienced selected life events, 2002)

	percent of people aged 57 or older who have ever
Gotten married for the first time	95%
Become a parent for the first time	90
Gotten a divorce	27
Remarried	23
Had last child move out of the house	86
Had spouse die	29
Become a grandparent	91
Had an adult child move back home	34
Moved back into parents' home	9
Provided child care or daycare to a grandchild on a regular basis	26
Had father die	93
Had mother die	86
Experienced a midlife crisis	27
Survived a major illness	46
Made major changes in your diet because of a medical condition	42
Made a major career change	49
Lost a job	37

Source: © 2002, AARP. Reprinted with permission. **Boomers at Midlife: The AARP Life Stage Study,** *A National Survey Conducted for AARP by Princeton Survey Research Associates, November 2002; Internet site http://www.aarp.org*

cans out of poverty and adding years to their lives—making the 55-or-older age group a political and economic powerhouse. As the older population grows in size and sophistication, it will become an even more potent force in politics and business. Those who understand the changing wants and needs of the older population will be prepared for the future. *Older Americans: A Changing Market* will help prepare you for what lies ahead.

How to use this book

Older Americans: A Changing Market is designed for easy use. It is divided into nine chapters, organized alphabetically: Education, Health, Housing, Income, Labor Force, Living Arrangements, Population, Spending, and Wealth.

This edition of *Older Americans* includes the latest statistics on the health, living arrangements, incomes, spending, and wealth of the 55-or-older age group. The socioeconomic estimates presented here reflect 2000 census results, which counted 6 million more Americans than demographers had estimated. This book contains the latest data on the health of the population, including updated estimates of the overweight and the obese. It presents labor force data for 2003, including the government's updated occupational classifications. The Census Bureau's latest population projections—the first released by the bureau in years—are also included in the book, revealing the enormous expansion of the 55-or-older age group during the next two decades. *Older Americans* presents the latest data on wealth from the Survey of Consumer Finances. And because the government now breaks out the Asian population separately in its estimates, most of the racial and ethnic breakdowns include Asians for the first time, along with blacks, Hispanics, and non-Hispanic whites.

Most of the tables in *Older Americans* are based on data collected by the federal government, in particular the Census Bureau, the Bureau of Labor Statistics, the National Center for Education Statistics, the National Center for Health Statistics, and the Federal Reserve Board. The federal government is the best source of up-to-date, reliable information on the changing characteristics of Americans.

While most of the tables in this book are based on data collected by the federal government, they are not simply reprints of government spreadsheets—as is the case in many reference books. Instead, each table is individually compiled and created by New Strategist's editors, with calculations designed to reveal the trends. Each chapter of *Older Americans* includes the demographic and lifestyle data most important to researchers. Each table tells a story about older Americans, a story amplified by the accompanying text and chart, which analyze the data and highlight future trends. If you need more information than tables and text provide, you can plumb the original source listed at the bottom of each table.

The book contains a lengthy table list to help you locate the information you need. For a more detailed search, see the index at the back of the book. Also at the back of the book is the glossary, which defines the terms and describes the surveys commonly used in the tables and text. A list of telephone and Internet contacts also appears at the end of the book, allowing you to access government specialists and web sites.

With *Older Americans: A Changing Market* in hand, you can position your organization to benefit from the coming revolution.

1

Education

■ One of the most dramatic changes of the past half-century is the rise in the educational attainment of the older population. Even as recently as 1970, a minority of men and women aged 55 or older were high school graduates. Today, three out of four have a high school diploma.

■ The older population is educationally diverse. Eighty-five percent of men aged 55 to 59 have a high school diploma versus only 66 percent of men aged 75 or older.

■ Among men aged 55 or older, 80 percent of Asians and non-Hispanic whites are high school graduates compared with only 59 percent of blacks and a 44 percent minority of Hispanics.

■ Thirty-eight percent of people aged 55 to 64 took part in adult education in 2001, 15 percentage points more than the 23 percent of 1991.

Big Gains in Educational Attainment

Until 1980, the majority of older Americans had not completed high school.

Of all the social revolutions that have occurred over the past half-century, one of the most dramatic is the rise in the educational attainment of the nation's older population. Even as recently as 1970, a minority of men and women aged 55 or older were high school graduates. Today, three out of four have a high school diploma.

Twenty-six percent of men aged 55 or older are college graduates today, up from only 4 percent in 1940 and 9 percent in 1970. Among women, the figure has grown from 2 percent in 1940 to 16 percent today. The gap in the educational attainment of men and women will close in the years ahead as better-educated generations enter the age group.

■ The health and wealth of older Americans are improving because of their rising educational attainment. As well-educated Baby Boomers enter the age group, the sophistication of the 55-or-older population will continue to grow.

There has been a revolution in the educational attainment of older Americans

(percent of people aged 55 or older who are high school graduates, by sex, 1970 and 2002)

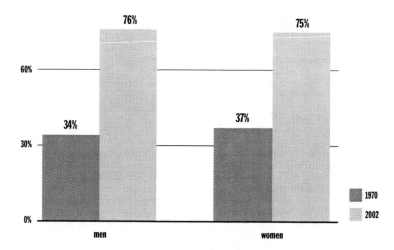

Table 1.1 Educational Attainment of People Aged 55 or Older, 1940 to 2002

(percent distribution of men and women aged 55 or older by educational attainment, 1940 to 2002)

	total	not a high high school graduate	high school graduate or more	some college or more	college, four years or more
Men					
2002	100.0%	23.7%	76.3%	46.0%	26.2%
2000	100.0	24.9	75.1	43.9	24.3
1990	100.0	38.5	61.5	30.2	18.1
1980	100.0	50.4	49.6	22.5	12.6
1970	100.0	65.9	34.1	15.8	8.9
1960	100.0	79.2	20.8	11.1	5.3
1950	100.0	78.4	17.8	8.7	4.6
1940	100.0	84.2	13.6	6.9	3.7
Women					
2002	100.0	24.6	75.4	37.1	16.3
2000	100.0	25.8	74.2	34.6	14.6
1990	100.0	38.2	61.8	22.9	10.6
1980	100.0	49.4	50.6	17.7	7.9
1970	100.0	62.8	37.2	14.0	6.3
1960	100.0	75.4	24.6	11.1	4.0
1950	100.0	76.4	20.5	8.4	3.3
1940	100.0	82.2	16.0	6.0	2.2

Source: Bureau of the Census, Educational Attainment in the United States: March 2002, *detailed tables (PPL-169); Internet site http://www.census.gov/population/www/socdemo/education/ppl-169.html; calculations by New Strategist*

The Oldest Men Are the Least Educated

Men aged 55 to 59 are far better educated than those aged 75 or older.

The older population is educationally diverse. At the younger end are the most educated men in the nation. At the older end are the least educated.

Eighty-five percent of men aged 55 to 59 (the age group now filling with the oldest Boomers) have a high school diploma versus only 66 percent of men aged 75 or older. The majority of men in their late fifties have college experience, and 33 percent have a college degree. In contrast, only 37 percent of men aged 75 or older have been to college and just 20 percent have a bachelor's degree.

■ Better health is linked with greater educational attainment. As better-educated men replace older men with little education, the older population is becoming increasingly healthy and active.

Men in their late fifties have the most college experience

(percent of men aged 55 or older who are college graduates, 2002)

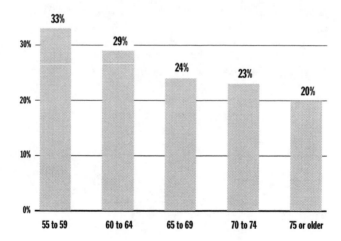

55 to 59	60 to 64	65 to 69	70 to 74	75 or older
33%	29%	24%	23%	20%

Table 1.2 Educational Attainment of Men Aged 55 or Older, 2002

(number and percent distribution of men aged 25 or older, and aged 55 or older in five-year age groups, by highest level of education, 2002; numbers in thousands)

	total aged 25 or older	aged 55 or older						
		total	55 to 59	60 to 64	aged 65 or older			
					total	65 to 69	70 to 74	75+
Total men	**86,996**	**26,609**	**7,091**	**5,282**	**14,236**	**4,451**	**3,794**	**5,991**
Not a high school graduate	14,095	6,313	1,048	974	4,291	1,115	1,131	2,045
High school graduate	26,947	8,064	2,067	1,694	4,303	1,436	1,150	1,717
Some college, no degree	14,661	3,903	1,141	792	1,970	634	520	816
Associate's degree	6,466	1,353	504	309	540	216	119	205
Bachelor's degree	15,925	3,924	1,298	811	1,815	609	527	679
Master's degree	5,595	1,808	678	432	698	234	187	277
Professional degree	1,795	617	186	135	296	85	76	135
Doctoral degree	1,514	627	169	136	322	122	85	115
High school graduate or more	72,903	20,296	6,043	4,309	9,944	3,336	2,664	3,944
Some college or more	45,956	12,232	3,976	2,615	5,641	1,900	1,514	2,227
Bachelor's degree or more	24,829	6,976	2,331	1,514	3,131	1,050	875	1,206
Total men	**100.0%**	**100.0%**	**100.0%**	**100.0%**	**100.0%**	**100.0%**	**100.0%**	**100.0%**
Not a high school graduate	16.2	23.7	14.8	18.4	30.1	25.1	29.8	34.1
High school graduate	31.0	30.3	29.1	32.1	30.2	32.3	30.3	28.7
Some college, no degree	16.9	14.7	16.1	15.0	13.8	14.2	13.7	13.6
Associate's degree	7.4	5.1	7.1	5.9	3.8	4.9	3.1	3.4
Bachelor's degree	18.3	14.7	18.3	15.4	12.7	13.7	13.9	11.3
Master's degree	6.4	6.8	9.6	8.2	4.9	5.3	4.9	4.6
Professional degree	2.1	2.3	2.6	2.6	2.1	1.9	2.0	2.3
Doctoral degree	1.7	2.4	2.4	2.6	2.3	2.7	2.2	1.9
High school graduate or more	83.8	76.3	85.2	81.6	69.9	74.9	70.2	65.8
Some college or more	52.8	46.0	56.1	49.5	39.6	42.7	39.9	37.2
Bachelor's degree or more	28.5	26.2	32.9	28.7	22.0	23.6	23.1	20.1

Source: Bureau of the Census, Educational Attainment in the United States: March 2002, *detailed tables (PPL-169); Internet site http://www.census.gov/population/www/socdemo/education/ppl-169.html; calculations by New Strategist*

Educated Women Will Reinvent Old Age

Women aged 55 to 59 are more than twice as likely to be college graduates as those aged 75 or older.

The educational diversity of older women is striking. Women in their late fifties are much more likely to have finished high school than women aged 75 or older, 85 versus 66 percent. While half of women aged 55 to 59 have some college experience, the proportion is just 28 percent among the oldest women. And while only 11 percent of women aged 75 or older are college graduates, nearly one in four women aged 55 to 59 has a bachelor's degree.

Women comprise the great majority of the older population. As the well-educated Baby-Boom generation ages into the 55-or-older age group, the educational attainment of older women will continue to climb. This ongoing socioeconomic revolution will transform what it means to be old in America.

■ The stereotypical image of the elderly as frail and vulnerable will give way to a more active and demanding view of old age.

One in four women aged 55 to 59 is a college graduate

(percent of women aged 55 or older who are college graduates, 2002)

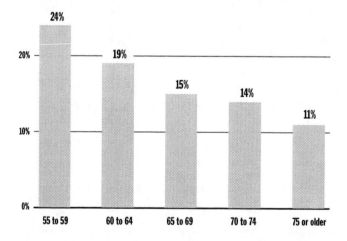

Table 1.3 Educational Attainment of Women Aged 55 or Older, 2002

(number and percent distribution of women aged 25 or older, and aged 55 or older in five-year age groups, by highest level of education, 2002; numbers in thousands)

	total aged 25 or older	aged 55 or older						
					aged 65 or older			
		total	55 to 59	60 to 64	total	65 to 69	70 to 74	75+
Total women	95,146	33,035	7,575	5,926	19,534	5,146	4,732	9,656
Not a high school graduate	14,854	8,112	1,114	1,119	5,879	1,285	1,279	3,318
High school graduate	31,509	12,664	2,666	2,375	7,623	2,088	1,893	3,641
Some college, no degree	16,330	4,828	1,332	961	2,535	714	630	1,190
Associate's degree	8,585	2,033	674	358	1,001	286	254	461
Bachelor's degree	16,357	3,428	1,055	695	1,678	509	436	733
Master's degree	5,893	1,539	582	306	651	197	200	254
Professional degree	942	226	79	54	93	35	24	34
Doctoral degree	676	206	75	57	74	32	17	25
High school graduate or more	80,292	24,924	6,463	4,806	13,655	3,861	3,454	6,338
Some college or more	48,783	12,260	3,797	2,431	6,032	1,773	1,561	2,697
Bachelor's degree or more	23,868	5,399	1,791	1,112	2,496	773	677	1,046
Total women	100.0%	100.0%	100.0%	100.0%	100.0%	100.0%	100.0%	100.0%
Not a high school graduate	15.6	24.6	14.7	18.9	30.1	25.0	27.0	34.4
High school graduate	33.1	38.3	35.2	40.1	39.0	40.6	40.0	37.7
Some college, no degree	17.2	14.6	17.6	16.2	13.0	13.9	13.3	12.3
Associate's degree	9.0	6.2	8.9	6.0	5.1	5.6	5.4	4.8
Bachelor's degree	17.2	10.4	13.9	11.7	8.6	9.9	9.2	7.6
Master's degree	6.2	4.7	7.7	5.2	3.3	3.8	4.2	2.6
Professional degree	1.0	0.7	1.0	0.9	0.5	0.7	0.5	0.4
Doctoral degree	0.7	0.6	1.0	1.0	0.4	0.6	0.4	0.3
High school graduate or more	84.4	75.4	85.3	81.1	69.9	75.0	73.0	65.6
Some college or more	51.3	37.1	50.1	41.0	30.9	34.5	33.0	27.9
Bachelor's degree or more	25.1	16.3	23.6	18.8	12.8	15.0	14.3	10.8

Source: Bureau of the Census, Educational Attainment in the United States: March 2002, *detailed tables (PPL-169); Internet site http://www.census.gov/population/www/socdemo/education/ppl-169.html; calculations by New Strategist*

Asians Are the Best-Educated Older Americans

Most older Hispanics have not even graduated from high school.

Among people aged 55 or older, Asians and non-Hispanic whites are far better educated than blacks and Hispanics. Among men aged 55 or older, 80 percent of Asians and non-Hispanic whites are high school graduates compared with only 59 percent of blacks and a 44 percent minority of Hispanics. Fully 42 percent of Asian men aged 55 or older are college graduates versus 28 percent of non-Hispanic whites, 12 percent of blacks, and 9 percent of Hispanics.

Among older women, Asians are less likely than non-Hispanic whites to be high school graduates (71 versus 80 percent). But 28 percent of Asian women aged 55 or older are college graduates versus a smaller 17 percent of non-Hispanic whites, 12 percent of blacks, and just 6 percent of Hispanics.

■ The educational attainment of older blacks will rise as black Boomers with much more education enter the age group. In contrast, the educational attainment of older Hispanics will not rise much because Hispanic Boomers lag in education.

A minority of older Hispanics are high school graduates

(percent of men aged 55 or older with a high school diploma, by race and Hispanic origin, 2002)

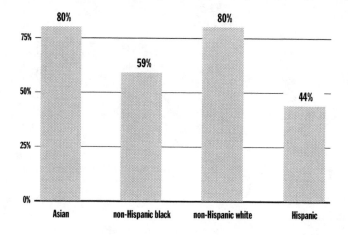

Table 1.4 Educational Attainment of Men Aged 55 or Older by Race and Hispanic Origin, 2002

(number and percent distribution of men aged 55 or older by educational attainment, race, and Hispanic origin, 2002; numbers in thousands)

		non-Hispanic		
	Asian	black	white	Hispanic
Total men	**819**	**2,129**	**21,759**	**1,727**
Not a high school graduate	163	861	4,276	957
High school graduate	200	633	6,801	385
Some college, no degree	77	284	3,351	159
Associate's degree	35	90	1,148	61
Bachelor's degree	212	145	3,442	108
Master's degree	62	68	1,638	29
Professional degree	30	17	557	13
Doctoral degree	36	25	550	10
High school graduate or more	652	1,262	17,487	765
Some college or more	452	629	10,686	380
Bachelor's degree or more	340	255	6,187	160
Total men	**100.0%**	**100.0%**	**100.0%**	**100.0%**
Not a high school graduate	19.9	40.4	19.7	55.4
High school graduate	24.4	29.7	31.3	22.3
Some college, no degree	9.4	13.3	15.4	9.2
Associate's degree	4.3	4.2	5.3	3.5
Bachelor's degree	25.9	6.8	15.8	6.3
Master's degree	7.6	3.2	7.5	1.7
Professional degree	3.7	0.8	2.6	0.8
Doctoral degree	4.4	1.2	2.5	0.6
High school graduate or more	79.6	59.3	80.4	44.3
Some college or more	55.2	29.5	49.1	22.0
Bachelor's degree or more	41.5	12.0	28.4	9.3

Note: Numbers will not add to total because not all races are shown and Hispanics may be of any race.
Source: Bureau of the Census, Educational Attainment in the United States: March 2002, detailed tables (PPL-169); Internet site http://www.census.gov/population/www/socdemo/education/ppl-169.html; calculations by New Strategist

Table 1.5 Educational Attainment of Women Aged 55 or Older by Race and Hispanic Origin, 2002

(number and percent distribution of women aged 55 or older by educational attainment, race, and Hispanic origin, 2002; numbers in thousands)

		non-Hispanic		
	Asian	black	white	Hispanic
Total women	**1,016**	**3,094**	**26,575**	**2,112**
Not a high school graduate	291	1,216	5,237	1,258
High school graduate	309	936	10,812	524
Some college, no degree	70	361	4,240	133
Associate's degree	63	197	1,689	66
Bachelor's degree	217	218	2,901	91
Master's degree	39	124	1,336	33
Professional degree	12	20	185	9
Doctoral degree	13	13	173	4
High school graduate or more	723	1,869	21,336	860
Some college or more	414	933	10,524	336
Bachelor's degree or more	281	375	4,595	137
Total women	**100.0%**	**100.0%**	**100.0%**	**100.0%**
Not a high school graduate	28.6	39.3	19.7	59.6
High school graduate	30.4	30.3	40.7	24.8
Some college, no degree	6.9	11.7	16.0	6.3
Associate's degree	6.2	6.4	6.4	3.1
Bachelor's degree	21.4	7.1	10.9	4.3
Master's degree	3.8	4.0	5.0	1.6
Professional degree	1.2	0.6	0.7	0.4
Doctoral degree	1.3	0.4	0.7	0.2
High school graduate or more	71.2	60.4	80.3	40.7
Some college or more	40.7	30.2	39.6	15.9
Bachelor's degree or more	27.7	12.1	17.3	6.5

Note: Numbers will not add to total because not all races are shown and Hispanics may be of any race.
Source: Bureau of the Census, Educational Attainment in the United States: March 2002, *detailed tables (PPL-169); Internet site http://www.census.gov/population/www/socdemo/education/ppl-169.html; calculations by New Strategist*

Few Older Americans Are in School

Of the nation's 74 million students, only 292,000 are aged 55 or older.

Just 0.5 percent of people aged 55 or older are currently enrolled in school. This figure is much smaller than the proportion of middle-aged Americans in school, but it is likely to grow as the well-educated Baby-Boom generation enters the age group. The more educated the person, the more likely he or she is to return to school to get even more education.

Among older students, women outnumber men 165,000 to 127,000. In the 55-or-older age group, those aged 55 to 59 are most likely to be students, 1 percent being enrolled in school.

■ As well-educated Boomers age into their sixties, expect to see school enrollment rise among older Americans.

Older women outnumber older men in school

(number of people aged 55 or older enrolled in school, by sex, 2002)

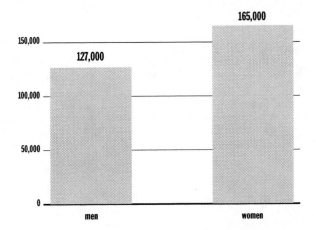

Table 1.6 School Enrollment by Sex and Age, 2002

(total number of people aged 3 or older, and number and percent enrolled in school by sex and age, 2002; numbers in thousands)

		enrolled	
	total	number	percent
Total people	**270,919**	**74,046**	**27.3%**
Under age 55	210,303	73,754	35.1
Aged 55 or older	60,616	292	0.5
Aged 55 to 59	15,150	153	1.0
Aged 60 to 64	11,609	58	0.5
Aged 65 or older	33,857	81	0.2
Total females	**139,061**	**37,266**	**26.8**
Under age 55	105,589	37,101	35.1
Aged 55 or older	33,472	165	0.5
Aged 55 to 59	7,807	97	1.2
Aged 60 to 64	6,061	29	0.5
Aged 65 or older	19,604	39	0.2
Total males	**131,858**	**36,779**	**27.9**
Under age 55	104,714	36,652	35.0
Aged 55 or older	27,144	127	0.5
Aged 55 to 59	7,343	56	0.8
Aged 60 to 64	5,548	29	0.5
Aged 65 or older	14,253	42	0.3

Source: Bureau of the Census, School Enrollment—Social and Economic Characteristics of Students: October 2002, *detailed tables; Internet site http://www.census.gov/population/www/socdemo/school/cps2002.html; calculations by New Strategist*

Most Older Students Attend College Part-time

More than eight out of ten older college students are part-timers.

As the number of older college students has grown over the past few decades, so has the number of students attending college part-time. Many of the older Americans enrolled in college work during the day and take classes at night. Others are actively pursuing a college degree while also enjoying retirement.

Overall, 253,000 people aged 55 or older are in college, accounting for just 1.5 percent of total college enrollment. The age group represents 3 percent of part-time undergraduates and 6 percent of part-time graduate students.

■ Look for college enrollment among people aged 55-or-older to rise as the well-educated Baby-Boom generation enters the age group.

Older students are part-timers

(percent of total college students and college students aged 55 or older who attend school part-time, 2002)

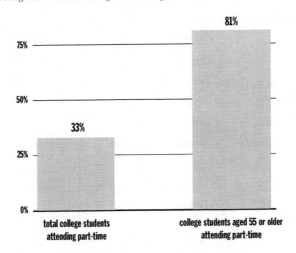

Table 1.7 College Students by Age and Attendance Status, 2002

(number and percent distribution of people aged 15 or older enrolled in institutions of higher education, by age and full- or part-time attendance status, 2002; numbers in thousands)

	total	undergraduate			graduate		
		total	full-time	part-time	total	full-time	part-time
Total enrolled	**16,497**	**13,425**	**9,735**	**3,690**	**3,072**	**1,406**	**1,666**
Under age 55	16,244	13,295	9,705	3,590	2,949	1,389	1,560
Aged 55 or older	253	130	30	100	123	17	106
Aged 55 to 59	146	78	20	58	68	9	59
Aged 60 to 64	33	17	4	13	16	2	14
Aged 65 or older	74	35	6	29	39	6	33

PERCENT DISTRIBUTION BY ATTENDANCE STATUS

	total	undergraduate			graduate		
Total enrolled	**100.0%**	**81.4%**	**59.0%**	**22.4%**	**18.6%**	**8.5%**	**10.1%**
Under age 55	100.0	81.8	59.7	22.1	18.2	8.6	9.6
Aged 55 or older	100.0	51.4	11.9	39.5	48.6	6.7	41.9
Aged 55 to 59	100.0	53.4	13.7	39.7	46.6	6.2	40.4
Aged 60 to 64	100.0	51.5	12.1	39.4	48.5	6.1	42.4
Aged 65 or older	100.0	47.3	8.1	39.2	52.7	8.1	44.6

PERCENT DISTRIBUTION BY AGE

	total	undergraduate			graduate		
Total enrolled	**100.0%**	**100.0%**	**100.0%**	**100.0%**	**100.0%**	**100.0%**	**100.0%**
Under age 55	98.5	99.0	99.7	97.3	96.0	98.8	93.6
Aged 55 or older	1.5	1.0	0.3	2.7	4.0	1.2	6.4
Aged 55 to 59	0.9	0.6	0.2	1.6	2.2	0.6	3.5
Aged 60 to 64	0.2	0.1	0.0	0.4	0.5	0.1	0.8
Aged 65 or older	0.4	0.3	0.1	0.8	1.3	0.4	2.0

Source: Bureau of the Census, School Enrollment—Social and Economic Characteristics of Students: October 2002, detailed tables; Internet site http://www.census.gov/population/www/socdemo/school/cps2002.html; calculations by New Strategist

Adult Education Is Increasingly Popular

Even the oldest Americans are going back to the classroom.

Forty-seven percent of people aged 16 or older participated in an adult education course in 2001, up from only 32 percent in 1991. While people under age 55 are more likely to participate in adult education, those aged 55 and older are increasingly likely to go back to school.

Thirty-eight percent of people aged 55 to 64 took part in adult education in 2001, 15 percentage points more than the 23 percent of 1991. Among people aged 65 or older, more than one in five participated in adult education in 2001—up from just 10 percent in 1991.

■ As well-educated younger generations age into the 55-or-older age group, the proportion of older Americans participating in adult education will continue to rise.

More than one-third of 55-to-64-year-olds participated in adult education

(percent of people aged 16 or older participating in adult education, by age, 2001)

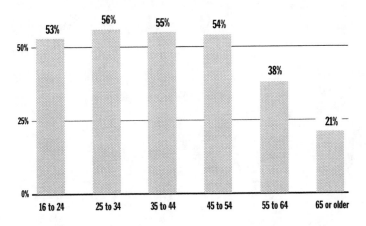

Table 1.8 Participation in Adult Education by Age, 1991 and 2001

(percent of people aged 16 or older participating in adult education activities, by age, 1991 and 2001; percentage point change, 1991–2001)

	2001	1991	percentage point change 1991–01
Total people	**47%**	**32%**	**15**
Aged 16 to 24	53	33	20
Aged 25 to 34	56	37	19
Aged 35 to 44	55	44	11
Aged 45 to 54	54	32	22
Aged 55 to 64	38	23	15
Aged 65 or older	21	10	11

Note: Adult education activities include apprenticeships, courses for basic skills, personal development, English as a second language, work-related courses, and credential programs in organizations other than postsecondary institutions. Excludes full-time participation in postsecondary institutions leading to a college degree, diploma, or certificate.
Source: National Center for Education Statistics, Adult Education and Lifelong Learning Survey of the National Household Education Surveys Program; Internet site http://nces.ed.gov/programs/coe/2003/section1/tables/t08_2.asp; calculations by New Strategist

2

Health

■ The percentage of people who rate their health as good to excellent declines with age as chronic conditions become common. Nevertheless, fully 70 percent of people aged 65 or older report good to excellent health.

■ Americans have a weight problem, and it peaks in the older age groups. Among men, those aged 65 to 74 are most likely to be overweight (77 percent), 33 percent being obese. Among women, those aged 55 to 64 are most likely to be overweight (73 percent), 43 percent being obese.

■ Older Americans spent a median of $695 on prescription drugs in 2000, with 57 percent of the cost paid for out-of-pocket.

■ Forty-nine percent of people aged 65 or older have hypertension, making it the most common health condition in the age group. Arthritis is second, affecting 35 percent.

■ According to the 2000 census, 19 percent of the U.S. population is disabled in some way. Among people aged 65 or older, the figure stands at 42 percent.

■ People aged 65 or older account for 26 percent of doctor visits, 16 percent of visits to hospital outpatient departments, and 15 percent of visits to emergency rooms.

■ In 1900, the average 65-year-old could expect to live 12 more years. By 2002, the remaining life expectancy for 65-year-olds had increased to 18 years.

Most Older Americans Say Their Health Is Good to Excellent

The proportion falls with age, however.

Fully 85 percent of Americans aged 18 or older say their health is good, very good, or excellent. The figure peaks at 92 percent in the 18-to-34 age group, then declines with age as chronic conditions become more common. The percentage of people who report good to excellent health bottoms out at 70 percent in the 65-or-older age group. Even in the oldest age group, the proportion of people reporting excellent health (11 percent) surpasses those reporting poor health (9 percent).

As people age, the percentage of those who have experienced poor physical health in the past 30 days rises from 1.5 percent in the 18-to-24 age group to 12 percent among people aged 65 or older. Interestingly, the percentage reporting poor mental health peaks in the 45-to-54 age group at 5.7 percent, then falls slightly with age. Only 5 percent of the oldest Americans say they have been unable to do their normal activities because of poor health during the past 30 days.

■ Medical advances that allow people to manage their chronic conditions more easily should boost the proportion of older Americans who report excellent health.

Regardless of age, the majority of people say their health is good to excellent

(percentage of people aged 18 or older who say their health is good, very good, or excellent, by age, 2002)

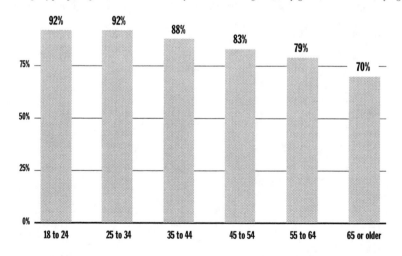

Table 2.1 Health Status by Age, 2002

(percent distribution of people aged 18 or older by self-reported health status, 2002)

	excellent	very good	good	fair	poor
Total people	**21.4%**	**33.8%**	**29.8%**	**10.4%**	**3.9%**
Aged 18 to 24	25.4	37.0	29.5	6.0	0.8
Aged 25 to 34	26.6	37.5	27.4	5.8	1.2
Aged 35 to 44	24.8	35.8	27.6	8.1	2.4
Aged 45 to 54	21.1	32.6	29.6	10.7	4.1
Aged 55 to 64	18.8	30.0	30.2	13.5	6.5
Aged 65 or older	11.4	25.0	33.6	19.7	8.7

Source: Centers for Disease Control and Prevention, Behavioral Risk Factor Surveillance System Prevalence Data, 2002; Internet site http://apps.nccd.cdc.gov/brfss/index.asp

Table 2.2 Health Problems in Past 30 Days by Age, 2001

(percent of people aged 18 or older reporting one or more days of poor physical or mental health during the past 30 days or activity limitations due to poor health, by age, 2001)

	poor physical health	poor mental health	activity limitations due to poor health
Total people	**5.9%**	**4.7%**	**3.2%**
Aged 18 to 24	1.5	4.4	0.8
Aged 25 to 34	2.4	4.1	1.3
Aged 35 to 44	4.0	4.9	2.4
Aged 45 to 54	6.2	5.7	3.8
Aged 55 to 64	9.0	4.9	5.3
Aged 65 or older	12.2	3.8	5.4

Source: Centers for Disease Control and Prevention, Behavioral Risk Factor Surveillance System Prevalence Data, 2001; Internet site http://apps.nccd.cdc.gov/brfss/

Weight Problems Are the Norm for Older Americans

Many are trying to lose weight.

Americans have a weight problem. The 64 percent majority of people aged 20 or older are overweight, and 30 percent are obese, according to the latest data from the National Center for Health Statistics. Weight problems peak in the older age groups. Fully 77 percent of men aged 65 to 74 are overweight, with 33 percent being obese. Among women, those aged 55 to 64 are most likely to be overweight (73 percent), with 43 percent being obese. The percentage of people who are overweight declines in the 75-or-older age group, but remains the majority.

Not surprisingly, many Americans are trying to lose weight. Nationally, 38 percent are trying to shed pounds, and the figure stands at 43 percent among people aged 55 to 64. Among people aged 65 or older, a smaller 31 percent are trying to lose weight.

Eighteen percent of 55-to-64-year-olds have been advised by a health professional to lose weight. Among 55-to-64-year-olds trying to lose or maintain weight, the majority say they are using physical activity or exercise. Among people aged 65 or older, a smaller 43 percent are using physical activity or exercise to lose or maintain their weight.

■ Although most Americans are overweight, surprisingly few have been advised by the medical community to lose weight.

The percentage of Americans who are overweight declines in the oldest age group

(percent of people aged 55 or older who are overweight, by sex and age, 1999–2000)

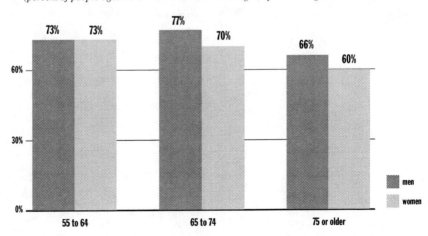

Table 2.3 Overweight and Obese by Sex and Age, 1999–2000

(percent of people aged 20 or older who are overweight or obese, by sex and age, 1999–2000)

	overweight	obese
TOTAL PEOPLE*	**64.3%**	**30.3%**
Total men*	**66.5**	**27.5**
Aged 20 to 34	58.0	24.1
Aged 35 to 44	67.6	25.2
Aged 45 to 54	71.3	30.1
Aged 55 to 64	72.5	32.9
Aged 65 to 74	77.2	33.4
Aged 75 or older	66.4	20.4
Total women*	**62.0**	**34.0**
Aged 20 to 34	51.5	25.8
Aged 35 to 44	63.6	33.9
Aged 45 to 54	64.7	38.1
Aged 55 to 64	73.1	43.1
Aged 65 to 74	70.1	38.8
Aged 75 or older	59.6	25.1

* Aged 20 to 74.
Note: Being overweight is defined as having a body mass index of 25 or higher. Obesity is defined as having a body mass index of 30 or higher. Body mass index is calculated by dividing weight in kilograms by height in meters squared.
Source: National Center for Health Statistics, Health, United States, 2003, *Internet site http://www.cdc.gov/nchs/hus.htm*

Table 2.4 Weight Loss Behavior by Age, 2000

(percent of people aged 18 or older engaging in selected weight loss behaviors, by age, 2000)

	total	18 to 24	25 to 34	35 to 44	45 to 54	55 to 64	65 or older
Trying to lose weight	38.0%	30.2%	38.0%	40.4%	44.7%	42.6%	30.6%
Trying to maintain weight	58.9	51.9	56.9	59.8	63.1	60.8	58.4
Eating fewer calories to lose/maintain weight*	13.5	11.4	12.1	13.9	15.2	13.2	12.0
Eating less fat to lose/maintain weight*	27.4	25.3	25.8	27.7	28.3	29.1	29.4
Eating fewer calories and less fat to lose/maintain weight*	29.6	25.5	27.0	30.1	32.6	33.0	29.0
Using physical activity or exercise to lose/maintain weight*	60.7	74.7	67.7	64.0	60.5	55.4	43.3
Advised by health professional to lose weight	11.7	4.0	8.4	11.3	16.0	17.7	11.2

* Among those trying to lose or maintain weight.
Source: Centers for Disease Control and Prevention, Behavioral Risk Factor Surveillance System Prevalence Data, 2000; Internet site http://apps.nccd.cdc.gov/brfss/index.asp

Few Older Americans Are Physically Active

The majority of those aged 75 or older are physically inactive.

Although many people claim to exercise, few older Americans participate in regular leisure-time physical activities. Forty-seven percent of people aged 65 to 74 are physically inactive during their leisure time. Among those aged 75 or older, the 61 percent majority are inactive. Only 26 percent of people aged 65 to 74 participate regularly in leisure-time physical activities. The figure falls to just 16 percent among those aged 75 or older.

The most popular physical activities among people aged 55 or older are fitness walking, stretching, and treadmill exercises. More than 3 million older people play golf at least 25 times a year. Day hiking, resistance machines, stationary cycling, and free weights are frequent pursuits of at least 1 million people aged 55 or older, according to the Sporting Goods Manufacturers Association.

■ As active Baby Boomers enter the 55-or-older age group, the proportion of older Americans who regularly exercise might increase.

Most older people do not exercise regularly

(percent of people aged 18 or older who participate regularly in leisure-time physical activity, by age, 1999–2001)

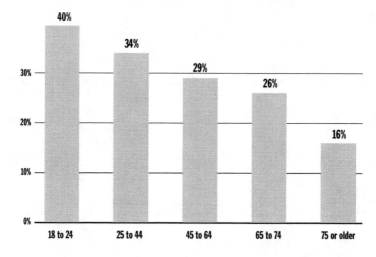

Table 2.5 Leisure-Time Physical Activity Level by Sex and Age, 1999–2001

(percent distribution of people aged 18 or older by leisure-time physical activity level, percent participating in regular leisure-time physical activity by level, and percent participating in strengthening activities, by sex and age, 1999–2001)

	total	physically inactive	at least some physical activity	regular physical activity			strengthening activities
				any	light-moderate	vigorous	
Total people	**100.0%**	**38.4%**	**61.6%**	**31.4%**	**15.5%**	**22.6%**	**23.2%**
Aged 18 to 24	100.0	29.9	70.1	39.7	17.8	31.7	36.5
Aged 25 to 44	100.0	33.7	66.3	34.3	15.4	26.6	27.2
Aged 45 to 64	100.0	40.5	59.5	29.3	15.1	19.9	18.6
Aged 65 to 74	100.0	46.6	53.4	26.3	17.0	13.4	12.4
Aged 75 or older	100.0	60.8	39.2	15.6	11.2	6.2	9.2
Total men	**100.0**	**35.4**	**64.6**	**35.1**	**16.8**	**26.6**	**27.5**
Aged 18 to 24	100.0	25.3	74.7	46.6	20.6	39.1	45.3
Aged 25 to 44	100.0	31.4	68.6	37.0	16.3	29.9	31.6
Aged 45 to 64	100.0	39.8	60.2	31.5	15.7	22.5	20.5
Aged 65 to 74	100.0	42.1	57.9	30.4	18.7	16.9	14.3
Aged 75 or older	100.0	54.4	45.6	20.7	14.5	9.4	11.9
Total women	**100.0**	**41.2**	**58.8**	**28.0**	**14.3**	**18.9**	**19.3**
Aged 18 to 24	100.0	34.4	65.6	32.8	15.1	24.5	27.8
Aged 25 to 44	100.0	36.0	64.0	31.7	14.6	23.3	23.0
Aged 45 to 64	100.0	41.3	58.7	27.3	14.5	17.4	16.9
Aged 65 to 74	100.0	50.3	49.7	22.9	15.6	10.6	10.9
Aged 75 or older	100.0	65.0	35.0	12.3	9.1	4.2	7.4

Note: "Physically inactive" means no light-moderate or vigorous leisure-time physical activity. "At least some" includes light-moderate or vigorous leisure-time physical activities. "Regular physical activity" includes activities done at least three to five times per week. Regular "light-moderate" activity is defined as engaging in light-moderate activity at least five times per week for at least 30 minutes each time. Regular "vigorous" activity is defined as engaging in vigorous activity at least three times per week for at least 20 minutes each time. "Any" regular activity is defined as meeting either criterion or both critera. Light-moderate activity is leisure-time physical activity that causes only light sweating or a light to moderate increase in breathing or heart rate and is done for at least 10 minutes per episode. Vigorous activity is leisure-time physical activity that causes heavy sweating or large increases in breathing or heart rate and is done for at least 10 minutes per episode. "Strengthening" activities are those designed to strengthen muscles such as weight lifting or calisthenics. Minimum duration and frequency were not asked. Those engaging in strengthening activities may be included in the physically inactive if they did not engage in any other type of physical activity. Numbers will not add to 100 because people may be in more than one category.
Source: National Center for Health Statistics, Health Behaviors of Adults: United States, 1999–2001, Vital and Health Statistics, Series 10, No. 219, 2004

Table 2.6 Recreational Activities among People Aged 55 or Older, 2002

(fifteen most popular recreational activities among people aged 55 or older, 2002; ranked by number participating frequently; numbers in thousands)

1.	Fitness walking (100 or more days/year)	6,515
2.	Stretching (100 or more days/year)	4,107
3.	Treadmill exercise (100 or more days/year)	3,887
4.	Golf (25 or more days/year)	3,646
5.	Freshwater fishing (15 or more days/year)	1,903
6.	Recreational vehicle camping (15 or more days/year)	1,736
7.	Free weights (hand weights, 100 or more days/year)	1,735
8.	Bowling (25 or more days/year)	1,725
9.	Day hiking (15 or more days/year)	1,545
10.	Weight/resistance machines (100 or more days/year)	1,513
11.	Stationary cycling: upright bike (100 or more days/year)	1,298
12.	Abdominal machine/device (100 or more days/year)	1,185
13.	Free weights: dumbbells (100 or more days/year)	1,040
14.	Running/jogging (100 or more days/year)	870
15.	Calisthenics (100 or more days/year)	827

Source: Sporting Goods Manufacturers Association, Internet site http://www.sgma.com

Smoking Declines Sharply with Age

Only 10 percent of people aged 65 or older smoke cigarettes.

The percentage of Americans who smoke cigarettes is sharply lower than what it was a few decades ago. Nevertheless, in 2002, 23 percent of people aged 18 or older were current smokers. The figure peaks among 18-to-24-year-olds at 31 percent. Among people aged 55 to 64, a smaller 21 percent smoke, and the figure is only half that (10 percent) among people aged 65 or older. More than 40 percent of smokers aged 55 or older have tried to quit in the past twelve months.

Drinking alcoholic beverages is more popular than smoking among older Americans. Overall, 63 percent of people aged 18 or older are current drinkers, with men being much more likely than women to drink (69 versus 57 percent). The proportion of people who drink alcohol peaks in the 25-to-44 age group, then declines with age. A minority of people aged 65 or older are drinkers.

Few older Americans have ever used illicit drugs, but that's about to change. Among people aged 55 to 59, a substantial 35 percent admit to having used illicit drugs at some time during their lives, a figure that will climb above 50 percent in the next few years as Boomers enter the age group. The proportion of older Americans who have used illicit drugs recently—during the past year or month—is less than 5 percent.

■ As health problems increase with age, smoking and drinking become less common.

Many older Americans have tried to quit smoking

(percent of people aged 55 or older who smoke cigarettes and share of smokers who have tried to quit in the past 12 months, by age, 2002)

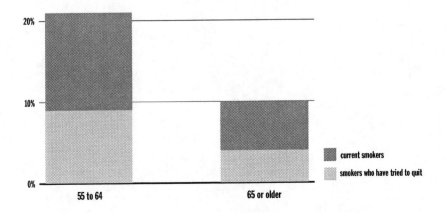

current smokers

smokers who have tried to quit

55 to 64

65 or older

Table 2.7 Cigarette Smoking and Attempts to Quit by Age, 2002

(percent of people aged 18 or older who currently smoke cigarettes and percent of smokers who quit smoking for at least one day in the past 12 months, by age, 2002)

	current smokers	smokers who quit on one or more days
Total people	**23.0%**	**51.8%**
Aged 18 to 24	31.2	65.4
Aged 25 to 34	25.9	56.9
Aged 35 to 44	27.2	49.3
Aged 45 to 54	24.8	47.9
Aged 55 to 64	20.8	44.2
Aged 65 or older	10.0	42.0

Source: Centers for Disease Control and Prevention, Behavioral Risk Factor Surveillance System Prevalence Data, 2002; Internet site http://apps.nccd.cdc.gov/brfss/index.asp

Table 2.8 **Alcohol Use by Age, 2001**

(percent of people aged 18 or older who are current drinkers, by age and sex, 2001)

	total	men	women
Total people	**62.5%**	**68.8%**	**56.8%**
Aged 18 to 24	63.6	57.7	57.7
Aged 25 to 44	70.8	66.1	65.0
Aged 45 to 54	65.6	60.7	61.2
Aged 55 to 64	57.6	49.4	51.6
Aged 65 or older	42.0	36.6	35.5
Aged 65 to 74	45.8	42.0	38.2
Aged 75 or older	37.6	30.2	32.6

Source: National Center for Health Statistics, Health, United States, 2003

Table 2.9 Drug Use by Age, 2002

(percent of people aged 12 or older who ever used any illicit drug, who used an illicit drug in the past year, and who used an illicit drug in the past month, by age, 2002)

	ever used	used in past year	used in past month
Total people	**46.0%**	**14.9%**	**8.3%**
Aged 12 to 17	30.9	22.2	11.6
Aged 18 to 25	59.8	35.5	20.2
Aged 26 to 29	57.4	22.4	12.8
Aged 30 to 34	59.0	17.2	8.8
Aged 35 to 39	61.0	15.5	8.6
Aged 40 to 44	66.4	14.4	7.8
Aged 45 to 49	60.9	12.3	7.5
Aged 50 to 54	51.1	6.5	3.4
Aged 55 to 59	35.0	3.3	1.9
Aged 60 to 64	23.7	4.1	2.5
Aged 65 or older	9.2	1.3	0.8

Note: Illicit drugs include marijuana/hashish, cocaine (including crack), heroin, hallucinogens, inhalants, or any prescription-type psychotherapeutic used nonmedically.
Source: SAMHSA, Office of Applied Studies, National Survey on Drug Use and Health, 2002; Internet site http://www.samhsa.gov/

Many 55-to-64-Year-Olds Lack Health Insurance

More than 3 million 55-to-64-year-olds are uninsured.

Among all Americans, 44 million lacked health insurance in 2002—or 15 percent of the population. While the figure is a smaller 13 percent among 55-to-64-year-olds, the chance of illness in that age group is much greater than average. Nearly everyone aged 65 or older has health insurance through the federal government's Medicare program.

Two-thirds of 55-to-64-year-olds have employment-based health insurance coverage. Only 18 percent have government health insurance, including 6 percent with Medicaid coverage and 5 percent with military insurance. While 34 percent of people aged 65 or older have employment-based health insurance coverage, fully 95 percent are covered by Medicare—meaning many older people are covered by more than one health insurance policy.

Older Americans without health insurance are vulnerable to financial catastrophe. Chronic illness is common among people aged 55 to 64. With nearly one in eight lacking insurance, a financial crisis threatens many.

■ With the huge Baby-Boom generation approaching the age of Medicare eligibility, it will become increasingly difficult to reform the system.

Thirteen percent of 55-to-64-year-olds lack health insurance

(percent of people aged 18 or older without health insurance coverage, by age, 2002)

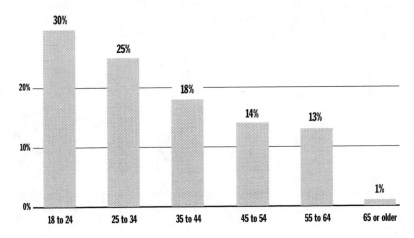

Table 2.10 Health Insurance Coverage by Age, 2002

(number and percent distribution of people by age and health insurance coverage status, 2002; numbers in thousands)

		covered by private or government health insurance							not
		private health insurance			government health insurance				
	total	total	total	employment based	total	Medicaid	Medicare	military	covered
Total people	**285,933**	**242,360**	**198,973**	**175,296**	**73,624**	**33,246**	**38,448**	**10,063**	**43,574**
Under age 18	73,312	64,781	49,473	46,182	19,662	17,526	524	2,148	8,531
Aged 18 to 24	27,438	19,310	16,562	13,429	3,738	2,909	183	779	8,128
Aged 25 to 34	39,243	29,474	26,492	24,800	3,944	2,801	455	922	9,769
Aged 35 to 44	44,074	36,292	33,240	31,180	4,240	2,728	881	1,121	7,781
Aged 45 to 54	40,234	34,648	31,724	29,617	4,345	2,227	1,382	1,351	5,586
Aged 55 to 64	27,399	23,879	20,797	18,505	4,882	1,773	2,392	1,482	3,521
Aged 65 or older	34,234	33,976	20,685	11,583	32,813	3,283	32,631	2,259	258
PERCENT DISTRIBUTION BY AGE									
Total people	**100.0%**	**100.0%**	**100.0%**	**100.0%**	**100.0%**	**100.0%**	**100.0%**	**100.0%**	**100.0%**
Under age 18	25.6	26.7	24.9	26.3	26.7	52.7	1.4	21.3	19.6
Aged 18 to 24	9.6	8.0	8.3	7.7	5.1	8.7	0.5	7.7	18.7
Aged 25 to 34	13.7	12.2	13.3	14.1	5.4	8.4	1.2	9.2	22.4
Aged 35 to 44	15.4	15.0	16.7	17.8	5.8	8.2	2.3	11.1	17.9
Aged 45 to 54	14.1	14.3	15.9	16.9	5.9	6.7	3.6	13.4	12.8
Aged 55 to 64	9.6	9.9	10.5	10.6	6.6	5.3	6.2	14.7	8.1
Aged 65 or older	12.0	14.0	10.4	6.6	44.6	9.9	84.9	22.4	0.6
PERCENT DISTRIBUTION BY TYPE OF COVERAGE									
Total people	**100.0%**	**84.8%**	**69.6%**	**61.3%**	**25.7%**	**11.6%**	**13.4%**	**3.5%**	**15.2%**
Under age 18	100.0	88.4	67.5	63.0	26.8	23.9	0.7	2.9	11.6
Aged 18 to 24	100.0	70.4	60.4	48.9	13.6	10.6	0.7	2.8	29.6
Aged 25 to 34	100.0	75.1	67.5	63.2	10.1	7.1	1.2	2.3	24.9
Aged 35 to 44	100.0	82.3	75.4	70.7	9.6	6.2	2.0	2.5	17.7
Aged 45 to 54	100.0	86.1	78.8	73.6	10.8	5.5	3.4	3.4	13.9
Aged 55 to 64	100.0	87.2	75.9	67.5	17.8	6.5	8.7	5.4	12.9
Aged 65 or older	100.0	99.2	60.4	33.8	95.8	9.6	95.3	6.6	0.8

Note: Numbers may not add to total because some people have more than one type of health insurance coverage.
Source: Bureau of the Census, 2003 Current Population Survey, Internet site http://www.census.gov/hhes/hlthins/historic/hihistt2.html; calculations by New Strategist

Older Americans Spend Big on Health Care

Some expenses are covered by Medicare, but many are not.

Medical expenses are the norm for Americans regardless of age. But people aged 65 or older, because they have more medical problems, spend much more than younger adults on medical care—although most are covered by the government's Medicare health insurance program.

In 2000, the median amount people aged 65 or older spent on medical care stood at a hefty $2,278, according to the federal government's Medical Expenditure Panel Survey. Only 55 percent of those expenses were covered by Medicare, while 18 percent were paid for out-of-pocket.

People under age 65 spent a median of $136 on prescription drugs in 2000, paying 41 percent of the cost out-of-pocket and 42 percent through private insurance. Americans aged 65 or older spent a median of $695 on prescription drugs in 2000, with 57 percent of that amount paid for out-of-pocket and only 17 percent paid for by private insurance.

■ It remains to be seen how the new Medicare prescription drug plan will change the spending of older Americans on drugs.

Out-of-pocket spending on health care by older Americans varies by service

(percent of spending on medical care by people aged 65 or older paid for out-of-pocket, by type of service, 2000)

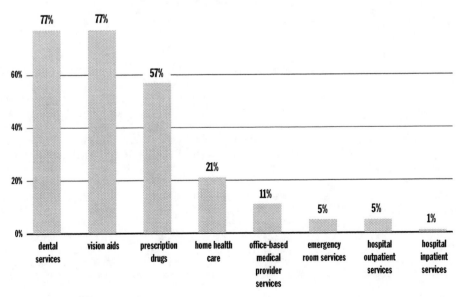

dental services	vision aids	prescription drugs	home health care	office-based medical provider services	emergency room services	hospital outpatient services	hospital inpatient services
77%	77%	57%	21%	11%	5%	5%	1%

Table 2.11 Health Care Expenditures by Age, Type, and Source of Payment, 2000

(percent of people with health care expense, median amount spent by those with expense, total expenses, and percent distribution of total by source of payment, by age, 2000)

	percent with expense	median amount spent by those with expense (in $)	total expenses (in $ million)	percent distribution of total expenses by source of payment					
				total	out-of-pocket	private insurance	Medicare	Medicaid	other
TOTAL PEOPLE									
Any health care expenses	83.5%	$721	$627,897	100.0%	19.4%	40.5%	20.9%	9.8%	9.5%
Prescription medicine	62.3	186	102,992	100.0	46.1	33.9	4.6	11.2	4.2
Dental services	40.1	168	55,551	100.0	49.3	42.2	0.5	4.0	3.9
Vision aids	15.6	180	9,287	100.0	76.4	16.5	1.1	4.2	1.7
Other medical equip., services	3.7	121	4,124	100.0	59.6	14.8	7.3	12.4	6.0
Hospital inpatient services	7.6	5,195	230,229	100.0	2.2	40.7	35.9	9.8	11.4
Emergency room services	11.6	315	19,248	100.0	12.2	46.1	17.9	8.4	15.3
Hospital outpatient services	13.1	555	54,880	100.0	7.5	52.9	22.2	5.0	12.4
Office-based medical provider services	68.8	243	125,946	100.0	17.8	48.5	16.8	5.8	11.1
Home health care	1.8	1,710	25,640	100.0	12.4	4.2	25.6	48.2	9.6
UNDER AGE 65									
Any health care expenses	81.8	586	423,933	100.0	20.3	52.8	4.6	12.3	10.0
Prescription medicine	58.5	136	69,171	100.0	41.0	42.4	0.9	12.9	2.8
Dental services	40.2	164	48,209	100.0	45.2	46.3	–	4.6	3.9
Vision aids	15.2	180	7,914	100.0	76.3	17.7	–	4.2	1.7
Other medical equip., services	2.7	80	2,123	100.0	52.0	22.0	–	19.6	4.5
Hospital inpatient services	5.9	4,372	136,609	100.0	2.9	59.4	8.6	15.7	13.4
Emergency room services	10.9	312	14,781	100.0	14.6	55.1	3.0	10.4	16.9
Hospital outpatient services	11.0	528	36,767	100.0	8.6	68.0	5.3	6.3	11.8
Office-based medical provider services	66.1	212	95,400	100.0	19.9	58.1	3.2	6.6	12.2
Home health care	0.8	1,507	12,960	100.0	–	–	–	68.0	–
AGED 65 OR OLDER									
Any health care expenses	95.5	2,278	203,964	100.0	17.5	15.0	54.7	4.5	8.3
Prescription medicine	88.3	695	33,821	100.0	56.6	16.6	12.1	7.7	7.0
Dental services	39.5	196	7,341	100.0	76.7	15.2	3.6	0.4	4.1
Vision aids	18.5	183	1,373	100.0	77.4	9.6	6.5	–	2.0
Other medical equip., services	10.5	220	2,002	100.0	67.5	7.1	13.0	–	–
Hospital inpatient services	19.0	9,160	93,620	100.0	1.2	13.3	75.7	1.3	8.5
Emergency room services	16.8	341	4,467	100.0	4.6	16.4	67.3	2.1	–
Hospital outpatient services	28.3	615	18,113	100.0	5.4	22.2	56.5	2.4	13.5
Office-based medical provider services	87.6	490	30,546	100.0	11.4	18.6	59.0	3.3	7.7
Home health care	8.7	1,800	12,680	100.0	21.2	4.7	38.4	28.1	7.6

Note: Other medical equipment and services includes expenses for ambulance services, orthopedic items, hearing devices, prostheses, bathroom aids, medical equipment, disposable supplies, and other miscellaneous items or services that were obtained, purchased, or rented during the year. Hospital inpatient services include room and board and all hospital diagnostic and laboratory expenses associated with the basic facility charge. They also include payments for separately billed physician inpatient services and emergency room expenses incurred immediately prior to inpatient stays. Expenses for newborns who left the hospital on the same day as the mother are included in the mother's record. (–) means sample is too small to make a reliable estimate.
Source: Agency for Healthcare Research and Quality, Medical Expenditure Panel Survey, 2000; Internet site http://www.meps.ahrq.gov/Data_Public.htm

Health Problems Are Common in the 65-or-Older Age Group

Hypertension is the most common health condition among people aged 65 or older, with arthritis not far behind.

Forty-nine percent of Americans aged 65 or older have hypertension, making it the most common health condition in the age group. Arthritis is second, affecting 35 percent of people aged 65 or older. Thirty-two percent had lower back pain during the past three months, and 20 percent have had cancer.

The percentage of people experiencing health problems rises steeply with age for most conditions. The percentage of people with hypertension rises from just 7 percent of 18-to-44-year-olds to more than half of those aged 75 or older. Similarly, the percentage of Americans with arthritis rises from 12 to 37 percent. Forty percent of people aged 65 or older have at least some trouble hearing, and 14 percent have visual problems.

As Americans became more aware of the problems associated with high cholesterol over the past few decades, rates have dropped in most age groups. The same cannot be said for high blood pressure. The majority of men aged 65 or older and women aged 55 or older had high blood pressure in 1999–2000, a significantly larger share than in 1988–94.

■ As the Baby-Boom generation ages into the 65-or-older age group, the number of people with hypertension, arthritis, and hearing problems will surge.

The percentage of people with arthritis rises with age

(percent of people with arthritis, by age, 2001)

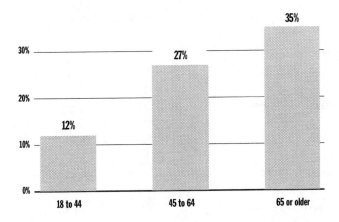

Table 2.12 Number of People Aged 18 or Older with Selected Health Conditions, 2001

(number of people aged 18 or older with selected health conditions, by type of condition and age, 2001; numbers in thousands)

	total	18 to 44	45 to 64	aged 65 or older total	65 to 74	75 or older
Total people	**203,832**	**108,436**	**62,531**	**32,864**	**17,742**	**15,122**
Heart disease	23,482	4,996	8,173	10,313	4,731	5,582
Coronary	12,719	1,057	4,748	6,914	3,137	3,777
Hypertension	41,764	7,604	17,900	16,260	8,325	7,935
Stroke	4,836	478	1,416	2,942	1,224	1,718
Emphysema	2,984	200	1,100	1,684	837	847
Asthma	22,169	12,795	6,508	2,866	1,661	1,205
Hay fever	20,405	10,834	7,218	2,353	1,325	1,028
Sinusitis	35,462	17,203	13,281	4,979	3,048	1,931
Chronic bronchitis	11,199	4,913	4,074	2,211	1,177	1,034
Cancer	14,003	2,379	5,151	6,473	3,201	3,272
Breast cancer	2,256	176	987	1,092	517	575
Cervical cancer	1,172	597	423	151	117	34
Prostate cancer	1,499	3	225	1,274	612	662
Diabetes	13,006	2,167	5,834	5,005	2,954	2,051
Ulcers	18,901	7,025	7,211	4,665	2,413	2,252
Kidney disease	3,301	1,019	1,124	1,158	535	623
Liver disease	2,697	927	1,337	432	264	168
Arthritic symptoms	41,185	12,987	16,850	11,348	5,691	5,657
Migraines or severe headaches	33,899	21,616	10,027	2,255	1,470	785
Pain in neck	34,084	15,801	13,117	5,167	2,725	2,442
Pain in lower back	63,253	30,783	22,010	10,460	5,511	4,949
Pain in face or jaw	10,789	5,991	3,657	1,141	676	465
Hearing						
Good	168,207	99,096	49,678	19,433	11,546	7,887
A little trouble	28,411	8,199	10,822	9,389	4,719	4,670
A lot of trouble or deaf	6,996	1,116	1,988	3,893	1,441	2,452
Vision						
No trouble	183,272	101,587	54,778	26,907	15,218	11,689
Trouble	20,378	6,786	7,675	5,917	2,520	3,397
Absence of teeth	17,211	2,370	5,793	9,047	4,357	4,690
Sadness						
All or most of the time	6,862	3,455	2,337	1,070	503	567
Some of the time	19,529	9,692	6,319	3,519	1,769	1,750
Hopelessness						
All or most of the time	4,377	2,275	1,491	611	336	275
Some of the time	9,038	4,937	2,900	1,202	672	530
Worthlessness						
All or most of the time	3,850	1,824	1,432	594	333	261
Some of the time	7,031	3,516	2,442	1,073	525	548
Everything is an effort						
All or most of the time	11,464	6,319	3,596	1,549	773	776
Some of the time	18,362	10,285	5,455	2,622	1,370	1,252
Nervousness						
All or most of the time	9,147	4,540	3,177	1,431	764	667
Some of the time	28,279	15,921	8,671	3,687	2,056	1,631
Restlessness						
All or most of the time	11,171	6,187	3,563	1,421	797	624
Some of the time	26,962	15,001	8,387	3,573	2,021	1,552

Note: From heart disease through arthritic symptoms, respondents were asked whether they had been told by a doctor or other health professional in the past twelve months that they had the condition; from migraines through pain in face or jaw, respondents were asked whether they had experienced pain for one full day or more during the past three months; from sadness through restlessness, respondents were asked how often they had the feeling in the past thirty days; numbers will not add to total because people may have more than one condition.
Source: National Center for Health Statistics, Summary Health Statistics for U.S. Adults: National Health Interview Survey, 2001, Series 10, No. 218, 2004

Table 2.13 Percent of People Aged 18 or Older with Selected Health Conditions, 2001

(percent of people aged 18 or older with selected health conditions, by type of condition and age, 2001)

				aged 65 or older		
	total	18 to 44	45 to 64	total	65 to 74	75 or older
Total people	**100.0%**	**100.0%**	**100.0%**	**100.0%**	**100.0%**	**100.0%**
Heart disease	11.5	4.6	13.1	31.4	26.7	36.9
Coronary	6.2	1.0	7.6	21.0	17.7	25.0
Hypertension	20.5	7.0	28.6	49.5	46.9	52.5
Stroke	2.4	0.4	2.3	9.0	6.9	11.4
Emphysema	1.5	0.2	1.8	5.1	4.7	5.6
Asthma	10.9	11.8	10.4	8.7	9.4	8.0
Hay fever	10.0	10.0	11.5	7.2	7.5	6.8
Sinusitis	17.4	15.9	21.2	15.2	17.2	12.8
Chronic bronchitis	5.5	4.5	6.5	6.7	6.6	6.8
Cancer	6.9	2.2	8.2	19.7	18.0	21.6
Breast cancer	1.1	0.2	1.6	3.3	2.9	3.8
Cervical cancer	0.6	0.6	0.7	0.5	0.7	0.2
Prostate cancer	0.7	0.0	0.4	3.9	3.4	4.4
Diabetes	6.4	2.0	9.3	15.2	16.6	13.6
Ulcers	9.3	6.5	11.5	14.2	13.6	14.9
Kidney disease	1.6	0.9	1.8	3.5	3.0	4.1
Liver disease	1.3	0.9	2.1	1.3	1.5	1.1
Arthritic symptoms	20.2	12.0	26.9	34.5	32.1	37.4
Migraines or severe headaches	16.6	19.9	16.0	6.9	8.3	5.2
Pain in neck	16.7	14.6	21.0	15.7	15.4	16.1
Pain in lower back	31.0	28.4	35.2	31.8	31.1	32.7
Pain in face or jaw	5.3	5.5	5.8	3.5	3.8	3.1
Hearing						
Good	82.5	91.4	79.4	59.1	65.1	52.2
A little trouble	13.9	7.6	17.3	28.6	26.6	30.9
A lot of trouble or deaf	3.4	1.0	3.2	11.8	8.1	16.2
Vision						
No trouble	89.9	93.7	87.6	81.9	85.8	77.3
Trouble	10.0	6.3	12.3	18.0	14.2	22.5
Absence of teeth	8.4	2.2	9.3	27.5	24.6	31.0
Sadness						
All or most of the time	3.4	3.2	3.7	3.3	2.8	3.7
Some of the time	9.6	8.9	10.1	10.7	10.0	11.6
Hopelessness						
All or most of the time	2.1	2.1	2.4	1.9	1.9	1.8
Some of the time	4.4	4.6	4.6	3.7	3.8	3.5
Worthlessness						
All or most of the time	1.9	1.7	2.3	1.8	1.9	1.7
Some of the time	3.4	3.2	3.9	3.3	3.0	3.6
Everything is an effort						
All or most of the time	5.6	5.8	5.8	4.7	4.4	5.1
Some of the time	9.0	9.5	8.7	8.0	7.7	8.3
Nervousness						
All or most of the time	4.5	4.2	5.1	4.4	4.3	4.4
Some of the time	13.9	14.7	13.9	11.2	11.6	10.8
Restlessness						
All or most of the time	5.5	5.7	5.7	4.3	4.5	4.1
Some of the time	13.2	13.8	13.4	10.9	11.4	10.3

Note: From heart disease through arthritic symptoms, respondents were asked whether they had been told by a doctor or other health professional in the past twelve months that they had the condition; from migraines through pain in face or jaw, respondents were asked whether they had experienced pain for one full day or more during the past three months; from sadness through restlessness, respondents were asked how often they had the feeling in the past thirty days; numbers will not add to total because people may have more than one condition.

Source: National Center for Health Statistics, Summary Health Statistics for U.S. Adults: National Health Interview Survey, 2001, *Series 10, No. 218, 2004*

Table 2.14 Percent Distribution of People Aged 18 or Older with Selected Health Conditions, 2001

(percent distribution of people aged 18 or older with selected health conditions, by type of condition and age, 2001)

	total	18 to 44	45 to 64	aged 65 or older total	65 to 74	75 or older
Total people	**100.0%**	**53.2%**	**30.7%**	**16.1%**	**8.7%**	**7.4%**
Heart disease	100.0	21.3	34.8	43.9	20.1	23.8
Coronary	100.0	8.3	37.3	54.4	24.7	29.7
Hypertension	100.0	18.2	42.9	38.9	19.9	19.0
Stroke	100.0	9.9	29.3	60.8	25.3	35.5
Emphysema	100.0	6.7	36.9	56.4	28.1	28.4
Asthma	100.0	57.7	29.4	12.9	7.5	5.4
Hay fever	100.0	53.1	35.4	11.5	6.5	5.0
Sinusitis	100.0	48.5	37.5	14.0	8.6	5.4
Chronic bronchitis	100.0	43.9	36.4	19.7	10.5	9.2
Cancer	100.0	17.0	36.8	46.2	22.9	23.4
Breast cancer	100.0	7.8	43.8	48.4	22.9	25.5
Cervical cancer	100.0	50.9	36.1	12.9	10.0	2.9
Prostate cancer	100.0	0.2	15.0	85.0	40.8	44.2
Diabetes	100.0	16.7	44.9	38.5	22.7	15.8
Ulcers	100.0	37.2	38.2	24.7	12.8	11.9
Kidney disease	100.0	30.9	34.1	35.1	16.2	18.9
Liver disease	100.0	34.4	49.6	16.0	9.8	6.2
Arthritic symptoms	100.0	31.5	40.9	27.6	13.8	13.7
Migraines or severe headaches	100.0	63.8	29.6	6.7	4.3	2.3
Pain in neck	100.0	46.4	38.5	15.2	8.0	7.2
Pain in lower back	100.0	48.7	34.8	16.5	8.7	7.8
Pain in face or jaw	100.0	55.5	33.9	10.6	6.3	4.3
Hearing						
Good	100.0	58.9	29.5	11.6	6.9	4.7
A little trouble	100.0	28.9	38.1	33.1	16.6	16.4
A lot of trouble or deaf	100.0	16.0	28.4	55.6	20.6	35.1
Vision						
No trouble	100.0	55.4	29.9	14.7	8.3	6.4
Trouble	100.0	33.3	37.7	29.0	12.4	16.7
Absence of teeth	100.0	13.8	33.7	52.6	25.3	27.3
Sadness						
All or most of the time	100.0	50.3	34.1	15.6	7.3	8.3
Some of the time	100.0	49.6	32.4	18.0	9.1	9.0
Hopelessness						
All or most of the time	100.0	52.0	34.1	14.0	7.7	6.3
Some of the time	100.0	54.6	32.1	13.3	7.4	5.9
Worthlessness						
All or most of the time	100.0	47.4	37.2	15.4	8.6	6.8
Some of the time	100.0	50.0	34.7	15.3	7.5	7.8
Everything is an effort						
All or most of the time	100.0	55.1	31.4	13.5	6.7	6.8
Some of the time	100.0	56.0	29.7	14.3	7.5	6.8
Nervousness						
All or most of the time	100.0	49.6	34.7	15.6	8.4	7.3
Some of the time	100.0	56.3	30.7	13.0	7.3	5.8
Restlessness						
All or most of the time	100.0	55.4	31.9	12.7	7.1	5.6
Some of the time	100.0	55.6	31.1	13.3	7.5	5.8

Note: From heart disease through arthritic symptoms, respondents were asked whether they had been told by a doctor or other health professional in the past twelve months that they had the condition; from migraines through pain in face or jaw, respondents were asked whether they had experienced pain for one full day or more during the past three months; from sadness through restlessness, respondents were asked how often they had the feeling in the past thirty days; numbers will not add to total because people may have more than one condition.
Source: National Center for Health Statistics, Summary Health Statistics for U.S. Adults: National Health Interview Survey, 2001, *Series 10, No. 218, 2004*

Table 2.15　High Cholesterol by Age, 1988–1994 and 1999–2000

(percent of people aged 20 or older who have high serum cholesterol, by sex and age, 1988–1994 and 1999–2000; percentage point change, 1988–1994 to 1999–2000)

	1999–00	1988–94	percentage point change
TOTAL PEOPLE	**17.8%**	**19.6%**	**–1.8**
Total men	**16.7**	**17.7**	**–1.0**
Aged 20 to 34	11.0	8.2	2.8
Aged 35 to 44	21.1	19.4	1.7
Aged 45 to 54	22.9	26.6	–3.7
Aged 55 to 64	16.5	28.0	–11.5
Aged 65 to 74	19.2	21.9	–2.7
Aged 75 or older	10.1	20.4	–10.3
Total women	**18.7**	**21.3**	**–2.6**
Aged 20 to 34	9.3	7.3	2.0
Aged 35 to 44	12.8	12.3	0.5
Aged 45 to 54	23.7	26.7	–3.0
Aged 55 to 64	26.2	40.9	–14.7
Aged 65 to 74	37.4	41.3	–3.9
Aged 75 or older	27.6	38.2	–10.6

Note: High cholesterol is defined as 240 mg/dL or more.
Source: National Center for Health Statistics, Health, United States, 2003, *Internet site http://www.cdc.gov/nchs/hus.htm; calculations by New Strategist*

Table 2.16 High Blood Pressure by Age, 1988–1994 and 1999–2000

(percent of people aged 20 or older who have hypertension, by sex and age, 1988–1994 and 1999–2000; percentage point change, 1988–1994 to 1999–2000)

	1999–00	1988–94	percentage point change
TOTAL PEOPLE	**28.9%**	**24.1%**	**4.8**
Total men	**27.4**	**23.8**	**3.6**
Aged 20 to 34	9.8	7.1	2.7
Aged 35 to 44	17.1	17.1	0.0
Aged 45 to 54	32.3	29.2	3.1
Aged 55 to 64	44.1	40.6	3.5
Aged 65 to 74	59.9	54.4	5.5
Aged 75 or older	68.8	60.4	8.4
Total women	**30.3**	**24.4**	**5.9**
Aged 20 to 34	–	2.9	–
Aged 35 to 44	16.0	11.2	4.8
Aged 45 to 54	30.5	23.9	6.6
Aged 55 to 64	53.0	42.5	10.5
Aged 65 to 74	70.3	56.1	14.2
Aged 75 or older	84.1	73.5	10.6

Note: A person with hypertension is someone with systolic pressure of at least 140 mmHg or diastolic pressure of at least 90 mmHg, or who takes antihypertensive medication. (–) means sample is too small to make reliable estimate.
Source: National Center for Health Statistics, Health, United States, 2003 (updated tables), Internet site http://www.cdc.gov/nchs/hus.htm; calculations by New Strategist

Millions of Older Americans Are Disabled

More than one in three people aged 65 or older is severely disabled.

Population surveys and censuses measure disability in many different ways. But the results are the same. The percentage of Americans who are disabled rises with age. According to the 2000 census, 19 percent of the U.S. population is disabled in some way. Among people aged 65 or older, the figure stands at 42 percent.

A survey by the National Center for Health Statistics finds the percentage of people who are limited in their physical functioning to be 19 percent among those aged 18 to 44, to rise to 40 percent in the 45-to-64 age group, and to reach the 64 percent majority among those aged 65 or older. Fully 72 percent of people aged 75 or older are disabled in some way and 46 percent are severely disabled.

The Census Bureau's Current Population Survey reports that 21 to 25 percent of people aged 55 or older had a work disability in 2002—meaning a health problem that prevented them from working or limited the amount or kind of work they can do. The more educated the worker, the less likely he or she is to have a work disability, however.

People with AIDS are often counted among the nation's disabled. As of mid-2002, more than 800,000 people had been diagnosed with AIDS. Only 11 percent were aged 50 or older at the time of diagnosis.

■ Although disability statistics vary depending on survey questions and respondents' attitudes, it's clear that older Americans are far more likely to be disabled than younger ones.

Older Americans have a variety of disabilities

(percent of people aged 65 or older with disabilities, by type, 2000)

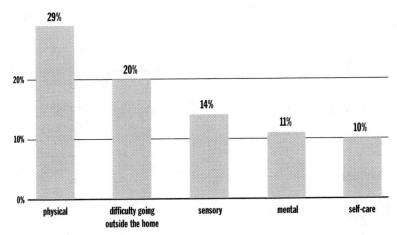

Table 2.17 Disability Status of People by Age, 2000 Census

(total number of people aged 5 or older and number and percent with disabilities, by age and type of disability, 2000)

	total		female		male	
	number	percent	number	percent	number	percent
TOTAL PEOPLE	257,167,527	100.0%	132,530,702	100.0%	124,636,825	100.0%
With any disability	49,746,248	19.3	25,306,717	19.1	24,439	19.6
TOTAL AGED 5–15	45,133,667	100.0	22,008,343	100.0	23,125,324	100.0
With any disability	2,614,919	5.8	948,689	4.3	1,666,230	7.2
Sensory	442,894	1.0	200,689	0.9	242,706	1.0
Physical	455,461	1.0	203,609	0.9	251,852	1.1
Mental	2,078,502	4.6	691,109	3.1	1,387,393	6.0
Self-care	419,018	0.9	174,194	0.8	244,824	1.1
TOTAL AGED 16–64	178,687,234	100.0	91,116,651	100.0	87,570,583	100.0
With any disability	33,153,211	18.6	16,014,192	17.6	17,139,019	19.6
Sensory	4,123,902	2.3	1,735,781	1.9	2,388,121	2.7
Physical	11,150,365	6.2	5,870,634	6.4	5,279,731	6.0
Mental	6,764,439	3.8	3,329,808	3.7	3,434,631	3.9
Self-care	3,149,875	1.8	1,686,691	1.9	1,463,184	1.7
Difficulty going outside the home	11,414,508	6.4	5,845,146	6.4	5,569,362	6.4
Employment disability	21,287,570	11.9	9,913,784	10.9	11,373,786	13.0
TOTAL AGED 65+	33,346,626	100.0	19,405,708	100.0	13,940,918	100.0
With any disability	13,978,118	41.9	8,343,836	43.0	5,634,282	40.4
Sensory	4,738,479	14.2	2,561,263	13.2	2,177,216	15.6
Physical	9,545,680	28.6	5,955,541	30.7	3,590,139	25.8
Mental	3,592,912	10.8	2,212,852	11.4	1,380,060	9.9
Self-care	3,183,840	9.5	2,138,930	11.0	1,044,910	7.5
Difficulty going outside the home	6,795,517	20.4	4,456,389	23.0	2,339,128	16.8

Note: Sensory disabilities are long-lasting impairments of vision and hearing; physical disabilities are limitations such as difficulty walking or climbing stairs; mental disabilities are difficulty with cognitive tasks such as learning, remembering, and concentrating; self-care disabilities are difficulty taking care of personal needs like dressing and bathing; employment disabilities are physical, mental, or emotional conditions making it difficult for people to work at a job; difficulty going outside the home is difficulty shopping or visiting the doctor.
Source: Bureau of the Census, Disability Status: 2000, *Census 2000 Brief, 2003*

Table 2.18   People with Limitations in Physical Functioning by Age, 2001

(number and percent distribution of people aged 18 or older with limitations in physical functioning, by type of limitation and age, 2001; numbers in thousands)

	total	18 to 44	45 to 64	aged 65 or older total	65 to 74	75 or older
TOTAL PEOPLE	203,832	108,436	62,531	32,864	17,742	15,122
Total with any difficulty	66,214	20,460	24,728	21,026	10,156	10,870
Moderate	37,024	14,473	13,402	9,150	5,291	3,859
Severe	29,190	5,987	11,326	11,876	4,865	7,011
Mobility difficulty	45,586	11,786	17,097	16,704	7,776	8,928
Moderate	25,173	8,303	9,308	7,562	4,147	3,415
Severe	20,413	3,483	7,789	9,142	3,629	5,513
Flexibility/strength difficulty	56,048	15,834	21,704	18,509	8,890	9,619
Moderate	32,842	11,251	12,549	9,042	5,001	4,041
Severe	23,206	4,583	9,155	9,467	3,889	5,578
Social/leisure difficulty	22,170	7,320	8,995	5,856	2,923	2,933
Moderate	16,180	5,761	6,210	4,210	2,081	2,129
Severe	5,990	1,559	2,785	1,646	842	804
PERCENT DISTRIBUTION BY AGE						
TOTAL PEOPLE	100.0%	53.2%	30.7%	16.1%	8.7%	7.4%
Total with any difficulty	100.0	30.9	37.3	31.8	15.3	16.4
Moderate	100.0	39.1	36.2	24.7	14.3	10.4
Severe	100.0	20.5	38.8	40.7	16.7	24.0
Mobility difficulty	100.0	25.9	37.5	36.6	17.1	19.6
Moderate	100.0	33.0	37.0	30.0	16.5	13.6
Severe	100.0	17.1	38.2	44.8	17.8	27.0
Flexibility/strength difficulty	100.0	28.3	38.7	33.0	15.9	17.2
Moderate	100.0	34.3	38.2	27.5	15.2	12.3
Severe	100.0	19.7	39.5	40.8	16.8	24.0
Social/leisure difficulty	100.0	33.0	40.6	26.4	13.2	13.2
Moderate	100.0	35.6	38.4	26.0	12.9	13.2
Severe	100.0	26.0	46.5	27.5	14.1	13.4
PERCENT DISTRIBUTION BY TYPE OF LIMITATION						
TOTAL PEOPLE	100.0%	100.0%	100.0%	100.0%	100.0%	100.0%
Total with any difficulty	32.5	18.9	39.5	64.0	57.2	71.9
Moderate	18.2	13.3	21.4	27.8	29.8	25.5
Severe	14.3	5.5	18.1	36.1	27.4	46.4
Mobility difficulty	22.4	10.9	27.3	50.8	43.8	59.0
Moderate	12.3	7.7	14.9	23.0	23.4	22.6
Severe	10.0	3.2	12.5	27.8	20.5	36.5
Flexibility/strength difficulty	27.5	14.6	34.7	56.3	50.1	63.6
Moderate	16.1	10.4	20.1	27.5	28.2	26.7
Severe	11.4	4.2	14.6	28.8	21.9	36.9
Social/leisure difficulty	10.9	6.8	14.4	17.8	16.5	19.4
Moderate	7.9	5.3	9.9	12.8	11.7	14.1
Severe	2.9	1.4	4.5	5.0	4.7	5.3

Note: Mobility activities include walking a quarter of a mile or three city blocks; standing for two hours; and climbing 10 steps without resting. Flexibility/strength activities include stooping/bending/kneeling; reaching over one's head; using one's fingers to grasp or handle small objects; lifting or carrying a 10-pound object; and pushing or pulling a large object. Social/leisure activities include sitting for two hours; going shopping, to the movies, or attending sporting events; participating in social activities such as visiting friends, attending clubs or meeting; and activities to relax at home or for leisure (such as reaching, watching TV, etc.). Moderate difficulty includes the response categories "only a little difficult" or "somewhat difficult." Severe difficulty includes the categories "very difficult" or "can't do at all."
Source: National Center for Health Statistics, Summary Health Statistics for U.S. Adults: National Health Interview Survey, 2001, Series 10, No. 218, 2004

Table 2.19 People Aged 55 or Older with a Work Disability, 2002

(number and percent of people aged 16 to 74 and aged 55 or older with a work disability, by education and severity of disability, 2002; numbers in thousands)

| | | with a work disability | | | | | |
| | | total | | not severe | | severe | |
	total	number	percent	number	percent	number	percent
Total aged 16 to 74	**201,141**	**22,425**	**11.1%**	**8,357**	**4.2%**	**14,067**	**7.0%**
Not a high school graduate	37,992	6,712	17.7	1,728	4.5	4,984	13.1
High school graduate	61,243	8,061	13.2	2,931	4.8	5,130	8.4
Associate's degree or some college	53,493	5,136	9.6	2,295	4.3	2,841	5.3
Bachelor's degree or more	48,413	2516	5.2	1,404	2.9	1,112	2.3
Total aged 55 to 64	**25,869**	**5,678**	**21.9**	**1,556**	**6.0**	**4,122**	**15.9**
Not a high school graduate	4,254	1,775	41.7	239	5.6	1,536	36.1
High school graduate	8,799	1,984	22.5	541	6.1	1,444	16.4
Associate's degree or some college	6,070	1,189	19.6	426	7.0	763	12.6
Bachelor's degree or more	6,743	730	10.8	350	5.2	380	5.6
Total aged 65 to 69	**9,597**	**2,166**	**22.6**	**1,325**	**13.8**	**841**	**8.8**
Not a high school graduate	2,399	817	34.1	395	16.5	422	17.6
High school graduate	3,524	758	21.5	489	13.9	269	7.6
Associate's degree or some college	1,851	359	19.4	259	14.0	100	5.4
Bachelor's degree or more	1,823	231	12.7	181	9.9	50	2.7
Total aged 70 to 74	**8,526**	**2,139**	**25.1**	**1,545**	**18.1**	**594**	**7.0**
Not a high school graduate	2,407	853	35.4	532	22.1	321	13.3
High school graduate	3,043	724	23.8	564	18.5	160	5.3
Associate's degree or some college	1,524	335	22.0	260	17.1	76	5.0
Bachelor's degree or more	1,551	227	14.6	191	12.3	36	2.3

Note: A person is considered to have a work disability if one or more of the following conditions are met: 1) identified by the March supplement question "Does anyone in this household have a health problem or disability which prevents them from working or which limits the kind or amount of work they can do?"; 2) identified by the March supplement question "Is there anyone in this household who ever retired or left a job for health reasons?"; 3) identified by the core questionnaire as currently not in the labor force because of a disability; 4) identified by the March supplement as a person who did not work at all in the previous year because of illness or disability; 5) under 65 years old and covered by Medicare in previous year; 6) under 65 years old and received Supplemental Security Income (SSI) in previous year; 7) received VA disability income in previous year. If one or more of conditions 3, 4, 5, and 6 are met, the person is considered to have a severe work disability.
Source: Bureau of the Census, 2002 Current Population Survey Annual Demographic Supplement, Internet site http://www .census.gov/hhes/www/disable/cps/cps102.html

Table 2.20 AIDS Cases by Sex and Age, through June 2002

(cumulative number and percent distribution of AIDS cases by age at diagnosis and sex for those aged 13 or older, through June 2002)

	number	percent of total cases
Total cases	**831,112**	**100.0%**
Under age 1	3,249	0.4
Aged 1 to 12	5,558	0.7
Aged 13 to 19	4,627	0.6
Aged 20 to 29	134,170	16.1
Aged 30 to 39	365,924	44.0
Aged 40 to 49	223,467	26.9
Aged 50 to 59	68,988	8.3
Aged 60 or older	25,129	3.0
Females		
Aged 13 or older	145,696	17.5
Aged 13 to 19	1,995	0.2
Aged 20 to 29	29,996	3.6
Aged 30 to 39	63,504	7.6
Aged 40 to 49	35,168	4.2
Aged 50 to 59	10,243	1.2
Aged 60 or older	4,790	0.6
Males		
Aged 13 or older	676,609	81.4
Aged 13 to 19	2,632	0.3
Aged 20 to 29	104,174	12.5
Aged 30 to 39	302,420	36.4
Aged 40 to 49	188,299	22.7
Aged 50 to 59	58,745	7.1
Aged 60 or older	20,339	2.4

Source: National Center for Health Statistics, Health, United States, 2003; *calculations by New Strategist*

Older Americans Account for More than One in Four Physician Visits

Most of those visiting a doctor are women.

In 2001, Americans visited physicians a total of 880 million times. People aged 65 or older accounted for 26 percent of visits. Women account for the great majority of physician visits by the age group because women outnumber men among older Americans.

People aged 65 or older account for a much smaller 16 percent of visits to hospital outpatient departments. Most older Americans visiting outpatient departments are there because of chronic problems rather than acute conditions. The 65-or-older age group accounts for just 15 percent of visits to emergency rooms. But among emergency room visitors, those aged 65 or older are most likely to be classified as having an "emergent" problem, which means a true emergency—a condition that needs to be addressed within 15 minutes.

People aged 65 or older accounted for nearly 12 million discharges from short-stay hospitals in 2001, women being the 62 percent majority of those being discharged. Heart disease is the most common first-listed diagnosis for those discharged from the hospital, followed by cancer among men and injuries (primarily fractures) among women.

■ As the Baby-Boom generation ages, older Americans will become an even larger share of health care consumers, boosting demand for physicians trained in geriatric medicine.

People aged 65 or older go to the doctor six to seven times a year

(average number of physician visits per person per year, by age, 2001)

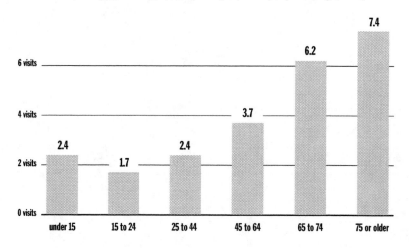

Table 2.21 Physician Office Visits by Sex and Age, 2001

(total number, percent distribution, and number of physician office visits per person per year, by sex and age, 2001; numbers in thousands)

	total	percent distribution	average visits per year
Total visits	**880,487**	**100.0%**	**3.1**
Under age 15	146,683	16.7	2.4
Aged 15 to 24	65,632	7.5	1.7
Aged 25 to 44	200,636	22.8	2.4
Aged 45 to 64	239,106	27.2	3.7
Aged 65 to 74	112,978	12.8	6.2
Aged 75 or older	115,452	13.1	7.4
Visits by females	**520,110**	**59.1**	**3.6**
Under age 15	69,614	7.9	2.4
Aged 15 to 24	42,071	4.8	2.2
Aged 25 to 44	131,664	15.0	3.1
Aged 45 to 64	142,657	16.2	4.3
Aged 65 to 74	64,029	7.3	6.5
Aged 75 or older	70,075	8.0	7.3
Visits by males	**360,377**	**40.9**	**2.6**
Under age 15	77,069	8.8	2.5
Aged 15 to 24	23,562	2.7	1.2
Aged 25 to 44	68,971	7.8	1.7
Aged 45 to 64	96,449	11.0	3.1
Aged 65 to 74	48,950	5.6	6.0
Aged 75 or older	45,376	5.2	7.6

Source: National Center for Health Statistics, National Ambulatory Medical Care Survey: 2001 Summary, *Advance Data No. 337, 2003*

Table 2.22 Hospital Outpatient Department Visits by Age and Reason, 2001

(number and percent distribution of visits to hospital outpatient departments by age and major reason for visit, 2001; numbers in thousands)

	total	acute problem	chronic problem, routine	chronic problem, flare-up	pre- or post-surgery	preventive care	unknown
					major reason for visit		
Total visits	**83,715**	**31,738**	**26,017**	**6,619**	**3,230**	**12,969**	**3,142**
Under age 15	18,319	7,970	4,258	1,106	588	3,936	460
Aged 15 to 24	9,834	3,881	1,977	663	272	2,737	304
Aged 25 to 44	20,576	8,790	5,243	1,643	795	3,267	838
Aged 45 to 64	21,590	7,128	8,750	2,033	911	1,831	938
Aged 65 to 74	7,299	2,190	3,044	665	376	661	363
Aged 75 or older	6,097	1,779	2,745	510	288	536	238
PERCENT DISTRIBUTION BY AGE							
Total visits	**100.0%**	**100.0%**	**100.0%**	**100.0%**	**100.0%**	**100.0%**	**100.0%**
Under age 15	21.9	25.1	16.4	16.7	18.2	30.3	14.6
Aged 15 to 24	11.7	12.2	7.6	10.0	8.4	21.1	9.7
Aged 25 to 44	24.6	27.7	20.2	24.8	24.6	25.2	26.7
Aged 45 to 64	25.8	22.5	33.6	30.7	28.2	14.1	29.9
Aged 65 to 74	8.7	6.9	11.7	10.1	11.6	5.1	11.6
Aged 75 or older	7.3	5.6	10.6	7.7	8.9	4.1	7.6
PERCENT DISTRIBUTION BY MAJOR REASON							
Total visits	**100.0%**	**37.9%**	**31.1%**	**7.9%**	**3.9%**	**15.5%**	**3.8%**
Under age 15	100.0	43.5	23.2	6.0	3.2	21.5	2.5
Aged 15 to 24	100.0	39.5	20.1	6.7	2.8	27.8	3.1
Aged 25 to 44	100.0	42.7	25.5	8.0	3.9	15.9	4.1
Aged 45 to 64	100.0	33.0	40.5	9.4	4.2	8.5	4.3
Aged 65 to 74	100.0	30.0	41.7	9.1	5.2	9.1	5.0
Aged 75 or older	100.0	29.2	45.0	8.4	4.7	8.8	3.9

Source: National Center for Health Statistics, National Hospital Ambulatory Medical Care Survey: 2001 Outpatient Department Summary, *Advance Data No. 338, 2003*

Table 2.23 Emergency Department Visits by Age and Urgency of Problem, 2001

(number of visits to emergency rooms and percent distribution by age and urgency of problem, 2001; numbers in thousands)

	number	percent distribution	percent distribution by urgency of problem					
			total	emergent	urgent	semiurgent	nonurgent	unknown
Total visits	**107,490**	**100.0%**	**100.0%**	**19.2%**	**31.7%**	**16.3%**	**9.1%**	**23.6%**
Under age 15	22,245	20.7	100.0	14.9	31.2	17.6	8.7	27.6
Aged 15 to 24	17,371	16.2	100.0	15.7	31.4	18.5	11.4	22.9
Aged 25 to 44	32,732	30.5	100.0	17.9	32.2	17.1	10.2	22.6
Aged 45 to 64	19,260	17.9	100.0	22.6	31.5	14.8	8.6	22.5
Aged 65 to 74	6,551	6.1	100.0	26.7	31.3	13.4	6.4	22.1
Aged 75 or older	9,332	8.7	100.0	29.0	32.0	11.4	5.0	22.6

Note: Emergent is a visit in which the patient should be seen in less than 15 minutes; urgent is a visit in which the patient should be seen within 15 to 60 minutes; semiurgent is a visit in which the patient should be seen within 61 to 120 minutes; nonurgent is a visit in which the patient should be seen within 121 minutes to 24 hours; unknown is a visit with no mention of immediacy or triage or the patient was dead on arrival.
Source: National Center for Health Statistics, National Hospital Ambulatory Medical Care Survey: 2001 Emergency Department Summary, *Advance Data No. 335, 2003*

Table 2.24 Hospital Care by Sex, Diagnosis, and Age, 2001

(hospital discharges, rate of discharge, and average length of stay for people aged 65 or older in nonfederal, short-stay hospitals by sex, selected first-listed diagnosis, and age, 2001)

	number of discharges (in thousands)		rate of discharge (per 1,000 population)		average length of stay (in days)	
	65 to 74	75 or older	65 to 74	75 or older	65 to 74	75 or older
Total women	**2,527**	**4,867**	**252.3**	**455.2**	**5.7**	**5.9**
Malignant neoplasms	147	192	14.7	18.0	7.3	7.6
Large intestine and rectum	21	34	2.1	3.2	8.9	9.3
Trachea, bronchus, lung	23	19	2.3	1.8	7.2	7.7
Breast	22	28	2.2	2.6	2.4	3.7
Diabetes	59	67	5.9	6.3	6.1	5.2
Serious mental illness	47	45	4.7	4.2	12.8	10.9
Diseases of heart	489	1,010	48.8	94.4	4.9	5.0
Ischemic heart disease	222	363	22.1	34.0	4.9	4.7
Acute myocardial infarction	80	181	8.0	16.9	7.4	6.0
Congestive heart failure	111	336	11.1	31.4	5.7	5.6
Cerebrovascular diseases	118	301	11.7	28.2	5.3	5.2
Pneumonia	115	286	11.5	26.7	6.5	6.8
Osteoarthritis	100	107	10.0	10.0	4.7	4.4
Injuries and poisoning	189	503	18.9	47.1	6.2	6.1
Fracture, all sites	79	322	7.9	30.1	5.3	6.0
Fracture of neck of femur (hip)	34	190	3.4	17.8	5.9	6.4
Total men	**2,268**	**2,203**	**260.9**	**471.9**	**5.6**	**5.9**
Malignant neoplasms	220	189	18.0	24.8	7.6	6.9
Large intestine and rectum	24	25	2.8	4.3	8.7	9.1
Trachea, bronchus, lung	50	25	2.8	4.1	8.4	7.1
Prostate	40	45	3.4	4.3	4.6	4.2
Diabetes	34	21	4.9	6.1	5.1	6.5
Serious mental illness	20	12	2.9	3.1	–	9.1
Diseases of heart	547	489	68.2	115.6	4.6	5.1
Ischemic heart disease	331	226	38.6	49.5	4.4	5.0
Acute myocardial infarction	110	106	12.1	21.1	5.8	6.4
Congestive heart failure	90	143	12.9	33.5	5.8	5.1
Cerebrovascular diseases	108	139	13.1	24.9	4.7	5.2
Pneumonia	90	178	13.3	39.5	5.6	6.4
Hyperplasia of prostate	113	82	4.2	7.2	2.4	3.5
Osteoarthritis	39	27	7.8	8.2	4.5	4.4
Injuries and poisoning	139	144	17.3	31.6	7.4	6.5
Fracture, all sites	36	63	5.0	13.7	7.8	7.3
Fracture of neck of femur (hip)	12	39	2.0	7.9	7.8	7.1

Note: (–) means sample is too small to make a reliable estimate.
Source: National Center for Health Statistics, Health, United States, 2003, *Internet site http://www.cdc.gov/nchs/hus.htm*

More than 1 Million Use Home Health Care

But more of the elderly are in nursing homes than receiving home health care.

Home health care surged during the 1990s as insurance companies pressured hospitals to discharge patients sooner. But growth in home health care has slowed as government cost-cutters and insurance companies have asked families to shoulder more of the patient care burden. In 2000, 1.4 million people—most of them aged 65 or older—received home health care services. Diseases of the circulatory system are the most common reason for receiving home health care.

The latest census of the nursing home population counted 1.5 million people aged 65 or older living in nursing homes, 74 percent of them women. More than half the elderly in nursing homes are aged 85 or older. Eighty percent of the elderly in nursing homes are mobility dependent, 66 percent are incontinent, and 47 percent cannot eat independently.

Hospice care has received much attention in the media, but only slightly more than 100,000 people took advantage of it in 2000. Eighty-one percent of hospice care patients are aged 65 or older, and cancer is the primary diagnosis for the 52 percent majority.

■ As home health care services are curtailed to save health care costs, a larger burden falls on family caregivers. For the elderly living alone, this can mean institutionalization.

Among the elderly in nursing homes, most are very old

(percent distribution of nursing home residents aged 65 or older, by age, 1999)

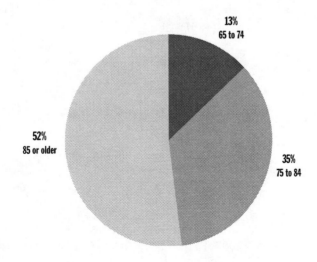

13%
65 to 74

52%
85 or older

35%
75 to 84

Table 2.25 Home Health Care Patients, 2000

(number and percent distribution of home health care patients by sex, age, and primary admission diagnosis, 2000)

	number	percent
Total home health care patients	**1,355,290**	**100.0%**
Females	878,228	64.8
Males	477,062	35.2
Under age 65	399,811	29.5
Aged 65 or older	955,479	70.5
Aged 65 to 74	234,465	17.3
Aged 75 to 84	424,206	31.3
Aged 85 or older	296,809	21.9
Primary admission diagnosis		
Malignant neoplasms	66,409	4.9
Diabetes	105,713	7.8
Diseases of the nervous system and sense organs	82,673	6.1
Diseases of the circulatory system	319,848	23.6
Diseases of heart	147,727	10.9
Cerebrovascular diseases	98,936	7.3
Diseases of the respiratory system	92,160	6.8
Decubitus ulcers	25,751	1.9
Diseases of the musculoskeletal system and connective tissue	132,818	9.8
Osteoarthritis	47,435	3.5
Fractures, all sites	55,567	4.1
Fracture of neck of femur (hip)	20,329	1.5
Other	472,996	34.9

Source: National Center for Health Statistics, **Health, United States, 2003,** *Internet site http://www.cdc.gov/nchs/hus.htm; calculations by New Strategist*

Table 2.26 Nursing Home Residents Aged 65 or Older, 1999

(number and percent distribution of nursing home residents aged 65 or older, residents per 1,000 population, and percent with functional problems, by sex and age, 1999)

	number	percent distribution	residents per 1,000 population	percent with functional problems			
				dependent mobility	incontinent	dependent eating	dependent eating, mobility, incontinent
Total residents aged 65 or older	**1,469,500**	**100.0%**	**42.9**	**80.4%**	**65.7%**	**47.4%**	**37.0%**
Aged 65 to 74	194,800	13.3	10.8	73.9	58.5	43.1	31.7
Aged 75 to 84	517,600	35.2	43.0	77.8	64.2	46.6	35.4
Aged 85 or older	757,100	51.5	182.5	83.8	68.6	49.0	39.4
Female residents	**1,091,700**	**74.3**	**54.6**	**81.9**	**65.6**	**48.1**	**37.7**
Aged 65 to 74	110,700	7.5	11.2	76.4	57.7	41.6	29.3
Aged 75 to 84	368,100	25.1	51.2	78.2	62.2	47.4	35.6
Aged 85 or older	612,900	41.7	210.5	85.2	69.0	49.7	40.4
Male residents	**377,800**	**25.7**	**26.5**	**75.9**	**66.0**	**45.1**	**35.0**
Aged 65 to 74	84,100	5.7	10.3	70.5	59.6	45.0	34.8
Aged 75 to 84	149,500	10.2	30.8	76.9	68.9	44.7	35.2
Aged 85 or older	144,200	9.8	116.5	78.1	66.8	45.7	34.9

Source: National Center for Health Statistics, Health, United States, 2003, *Internet site http://www.cdc.gov/nchs/hus.htm; calculations by New Strategist*

Table 2.27 Hospice Patients, 2000

(number and percent distribution of hospice patients by sex, age, and primary admission diagnosis, 2000)

	number	percent
Total hospice patients	**105,496**	**100.0%**
Females	68,361	57.4
Males	37,135	42.6
Under age 65	19,622	18.6
Aged 65 or older	85,874	81.4
Aged 65 to 74	18,145	17.2
Aged 75 to 84	39,034	37.0
Aged 85 or older	28,800	27.3
Primary admission diagnosis		
Malignant neoplasms	54,752	51.9
Large intestine and rectum	5,169	4.9
Trachea, bronchus, and lung	12,976	12.3
Breast	5,064	4.8
Prostate	8,123	7.7
Diseases of heart	13,504	12.8
Diseases of the respiratory system	6,857	6.5
Other	30,383	28.8

Source: National Center for Health Statistics, **Health, United States, 2003,** *Internet site http://www.cdc.gov/nchs/hus.htm; calculations by New Strategist*

Heart Disease and Cancer Are the Biggest Killers

Cancer is the leading cause of death among people aged 55 to 74.

Among the 2.4 million Americans who died in 2001, 85 percent were aged 55 or older. More than half (57 percent) were aged 75 or older. The 55-or-older age group accounts for 92 percent of deaths from heart disease, 94 percent of deaths from influenza and pneumonia, and nearly 100 percent of deaths from Alzheimer's disease. But the age group accounts for only 25 percent of motor vehicle accident deaths, 28 percent of suicides, and 10 percent of homicides.

While heart disease is the number-one cause of death among people aged 75 or older, cancer is the leading cause of death among 55-to-74-year-olds. Together, the two diseases account for 55 percent of all deaths in the 55-or-older age group. Among the oldest Americans, aged 85 or older, heart disease causes 38 percent of deaths while cancer accounts for only 12 percent.

■ With most Americans living to old age, growing numbers must cope with the disabilities of aging. The demands of the disabled drive up health care costs, but they provide opportunities for the health care industry.

Heart disease overtakes cancer as a cause of death in old age

(percent of deaths from heart disease and cancer, by age, 2001)

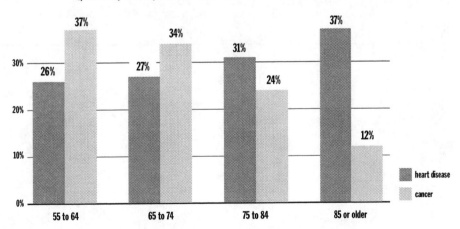

Table 2.28 Deaths from the Fifteen Leading Causes of Death, 2001: Number of Deaths

(number of deaths from the fifteen leading causes of death, by age, 2001; ranked by total number of deaths)

	total	aged 55 or older total	55 to 64	65 to 74	75 to 84	85+
Total deaths	**2,416,425**	**2,042,559**	**244,139**	**430,960**	**701,929**	**665,531**
Diseases of heart	700,142	645,216	62,486	116,299	216,992	249,439
Malignant neoplasms	553,768	480,437	90,223	147,018	165,445	77,751
Cerebrovascular diseases	163,538	154,094	9,608	22,598	55,822	66,066
Chronic lower respiratory diseases	123,013	118070	11166	30,751	47,762	28,391
Accidents	101,537	40,370	7,658	7,835	12,688	12,171
Motor vehicle accidents	43,788	10,990	3,465	2,990	3,312	1,223
Diabetes mellitus	71,372	63,277	9,570	16,731	22,805	14,171
Influenza and pneumonia	62,034	58,222	2,704	6,650	18,677	30,191
Alzheimer's disease	53,852	53,774	529	3,422	18,542	31,281
Nephritis, nephrotic syndrome, and nephrosis	39,480	36,405	3,284	7,356	13,097	12,668
Septicemia	32,238	28,529	3,111	5,998	10,351	9,069
Suicide	30,622	8,710	3,317	2,432	2,192	769
Chronic liver disease and cirrhosis	27,035	16,016	5,750	5,486	3,801	979
Homicide	20,308	1,967	1,018	532	312	105
Essential hypertension and hypertensive disease	19,250	17,859	1,462	2,832	5,993	7,572
Pneumonia due to solids and liquids	17,301	16,590	659	1,830	5,759	8,342

Note: Numbers will not add to total because "age not stated" is not shown.
Source: National Center for Health Statistics, Deaths: Final Data for 2001, National Vital Statistics Report, Vol. 52, No. 3, 2003

Table 2.29 Deaths from the Fifteen Leading Causes of Death, 2001: Distribution by Cause

(percent distribution of deaths by cause for total people and people aged 55 or older, 2001; ranked by total number of deaths)

	total	aged 55 or older				
		total	55 to 64	65 to 74	75 to 84	85+
Total deaths	**100.0%**	**100.0%**	**100.0%**	**100.0%**	**100.0%**	**100.0%**
Diseases of heart	29.0	31.6	25.6	27.0	30.9	37.5
Malignant neoplasms	22.9	23.5	37.0	34.1	23.6	11.7
Cerebrovascular diseases	6.8	7.5	3.9	5.2	8.0	9.9
Chronic lower respiratory diseases	5.1	5.8	4.6	7.1	6.8	4.3
Accidents	4.2	2.0	3.1	1.8	1.8	1.8
Motor vehicle accidents	1.8	0.5	1.4	0.7	0.5	0.2
Diabetes mellitus	3.0	3.1	3.9	3.9	3.2	2.1
Influenza and pneumonia	2.6	2.9	1.1	1.5	2.7	4.5
Alzheimer's disease	2.2	2.6	0.2	0.8	2.6	4.7
Nephritis, nephrotic syndrome, and nephrosis	1.6	1.8	1.3	1.7	1.9	1.9
Septicemia	1.3	1.4	1.3	1.4	1.5	1.4
Suicide	1.3	0.4	1.4	0.6	0.3	0.1
Chronic liver disease and cirrhosis	1.1	0.8	2.4	1.3	0.5	0.1
Homicide	0.8	0.1	0.4	0.1	0.0	0.0
Essential hypertension and hypertensive disease	0.8	0.9	0.6	0.7	0.9	1.1
Pneumonia due to solids and liquids	0.7	0.8	0.3	0.4	0.8	1.3

Source: National Center for Health Statistics, Deaths: Final Data for 2001, *National Vital Statistics Report, Vol. 52, No. 3, 2003; calculations by New Strategist*

Table 2.30 Deaths from the Fifteen Leading Causes of Death, 2001: Distribution by Age

(percent distribution of deaths by age for total people and people aged 55 or older, 2001; ranked by total number of deaths)

| | total | aged 55 or older | | | | |
		total	55 to 64	65 to 74	75 to 84	85+
Total deaths	**100.0%**	**84.5%**	**10.1%**	**17.8%**	**29.1%**	**27.5%**
Diseases of heart	100.0	92.2	8.9	16.6	31.0	35.6
Malignant neoplasms	100.0	86.8	16.3	26.5	29.9	14.0
Cerebrovascular diseases	100.0	94.2	5.9	13.8	34.1	40.4
Chronic lower respiratory diseases	100.0	96.0	9.1	25.0	38.8	23.1
Accidents	100.0	39.8	7.5	7.7	12.5	12.0
Motor vehicle accidents	100.0	25.1	7.9	6.8	7.6	2.8
Diabetes mellitus	100.0	88.7	13.4	23.4	32.0	19.9
Influenza and pneumonia	100.0	93.9	4.4	10.7	30.1	48.7
Alzheimer's disease	100.0	99.9	1.0	6.4	34.4	58.1
Nephritis, nephrotic syndrome, and nephrosis	100.0	92.2	8.3	18.6	33.2	32.1
Septicemia	100.0	88.5	9.7	18.6	32.1	28.1
Suicide	100.0	28.4	10.8	7.9	7.2	2.5
Chronic liver disease and cirrhosis	100.0	59.2	21.3	20.3	14.1	3.6
Homicide	100.0	9.7	5.0	2.6	1.5	0.5
Essential hypertension and hypertensive disease	100.0	92.8	7.6	14.7	31.1	39.3
Pneumonia due to solids and liquids	100.0	95.9	3.8	10.6	33.3	48.2

Source: National Center for Health Statistics, Deaths: Final Data for 2001, National Vital Statistics Report, Vol. 52, No. 3, 2003; calculations by New Strategist

Table 2.31 Leading Causes of Death for People Aged 55 to 64, 2001

(number and percent distribution of deaths for the ten leading causes of death for people aged 55 to 64, 2001)

		number	percent
All causes		**244,139**	**100.0%**
1.	Malignant neoplasms (2)	90,223	37.0
2.	Diseases of heart (1)	62,486	25.6
3.	Chronic lower respiratory diseases (4)	11,166	4.6
4.	Cerebrovascular diseases (3)	9,608	3.9
5.	Diabetes mellitus (6)	9,570	3.9
6.	Accidents (5)	7,658	3.1
7.	Chronic liver disease and cirrhosis (12)	5,750	2.4
8.	Suicide (11)	3,317	1.4
9.	Nephritis (9)	3,284	1.3
10.	Septicemia (10)	3,111	1.3
All other causes		37,966	15.5

Note: Number in parentheses shows rank for all age groups if the cause of death is among top fifteen.
Source: National Center for Health Statistics, Deaths: Leading Causes for 2001, *National Vital Statistics Report, Vol. 52, No. 9, 2003; calculations by New Strategist*

Table 2.32 Leading Causes of Death for People Aged 65 to 74, 2001

(number and percent distribution of deaths for the ten leading causes of death for people aged 65 to 74, 2001)

		number	percent
All causes		**430,960**	**100.0%**
1.	Malignant neoplasms (2)	147,018	34.1
2.	Diseases of heart (1)	116,299	27.0
3.	Chronic lower respiratory diseases (4)	30,751	7.1
4.	Cerebrovascular diseases (3)	22,598	5.2
5.	Diabetes mellitus (6)	16,731	3.9
6.	Accidents (5)	7,835	1.8
7.	Nephritis (9)	7,356	1.7
8.	Influenza and pneumonia (7)	6,650	1.5
9.	Septicemia (10)	5,998	1.4
10.	Chronic liver disease and cirrhosis (12)	5,486	1.3
All other causes		64,238	14.9

Note: Number in parentheses shows rank for all age groups if the cause of death is among top fifteen.
Source: National Center for Health Statistics, Deaths: Leading Causes for 2001, National Vital Statistics Report, Vol. 52, No. 9, 2003; calculations by New Strategist

Table 2.33 Leading Causes of Death for People Aged 75 to 84, 2001

(number and percent distribution of deaths for the ten leading causes of death for people aged 75 to 84, 2001)

		number	percent
All causes		**701,929**	**100.0%**
1.	Diseases of heart (1)	216,992	30.9
2.	Malignant neoplasms (2)	165,445	23.6
3.	Cerebrovascular diseases (3)	55,822	8.0
4.	Chronic lower respiratory diseases (4)	47,762	6.8
5.	Diabetes mellitus (6)	22,805	3.2
6.	Influenza and pneumonia (7)	18,677	2.7
7.	Alzheimer's disease (8)	18,542	2.6
8.	Nephritis (9)	13,097	1.9
9.	Accidents (5)	12,688	1.8
10.	Septicemia (10)	10,351	1.5
All other causes		119,748	17.1

Note: Number in parentheses shows rank for all age groups if the cause of death is among top fifteen.
Source: National Center for Health Statistics, Deaths: Leading Causes for 2001, *National Vital Statistics Report, Vol. 52, No. 9, 2003; calculations by New Strategist*

Table 2.34 Leading Causes of Death for People Aged 85 or Older, 2001

(number and percent distribution of deaths for the ten leading causes of death for people aged 85 or older, 2001)

		number	percent
All causes		**665,531**	**100.0%**
1.	Diseases of heart (1)	249,439	37.5
2.	Malignant neoplasms (2)	77,751	11.7
3.	Cerebrovascular diseases (3)	66,066	9.9
4.	Alzheimer's disease (8)	31,281	4.7
5.	Influenza and pneumonia (7)	30,191	4.5
6.	Chronic lower respiratory diseases (4)	28,391	4.3
7.	Diabetes mellitus (6)	14,171	2.1
8.	Nephritis (9)	12,668	1.9
9.	Accidents (5)	12,171	1.8
10.	Septicemia (10)	9,069	1.4
All other causes		134,333	20.2

Note: Number in parentheses shows rank for all age groups if the cause of death is among top fifteen.
Source: National Center for Health Statistics, Deaths: Leading Causes for 2001, *National Vital Statistics Report, Vol. 52, No. 9, 2003; calculations by New Strategist*

Life Expectancy Has Grown at Older Ages

The biggest gains have been made since 1950.

Between 1900 and 2002, life expectancy at age 65 grew by 6.3 years. In 1900, the average 65-year-old could expect to live 12 more years. In 2001, a 65-year-old could expect to live 18 more years. The gain in life expectancy results primarily from the success of medical science at curtailing deaths from heart disease, the biggest killer of Americans.

Life expectancy at birth stood at 74.7 years for males and 79.9 years for females in 2002. At all ages, the life expectancy of females is greater than that of males. Among people aged 85, men can expect to live another 5.9 years, while women can expect 7.0 more years of life.

■ Perhaps more important than length of life is quality of life, particularly in very old age. While medical science has made great strides in lengthening life, older Americans are now demanding improved quality of life as well.

More years remain at the end of life

(number of years of life remaining for people aged 65 or older, 1900 and 2002)

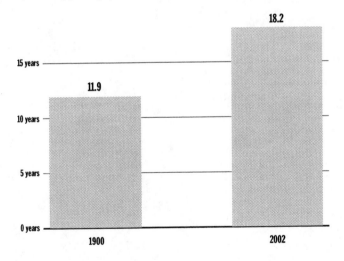

Table 2.35 Life Expectancy by Age, 1900 to 2002

(years of life remaining at birth and age 65, 1900 to 2002; change in years of life remaining for selected years)

	at birth	age 65
2002	77.4	18.2
2001	77.2	18.1
2000	76.9	17.9
1999	76.7	17.7
1998	76.7	17.8
1997	76.5	17.7
1996	76.1	17.5
1995	75.8	17.4
1994	75.7	17.4
1993	75.5	17.3
1992	75.8	17.5
1991	75.5	17.4
1990	75.4	17.2
1980	73.7	16.4
1970	70.8	15.2
1960	69.7	14.3
1950	68.2	13.9
1900	47.3	11.9
Change in years		
1990–02	2.0	1.0
1900–02	30.1	6.3

Source: National Center for Health Statistics, Health, United States, 2003; *and* Deaths: Preliminary Data for 2002, *National Vital Statistics Report, Vol. 52, No. 13, 2004; calculations by New Strategist*

Table 2.36 Life Expectancy by Age and Sex, 2002

(years of life remaining at selected ages, by sex, 2002)

	total	females	males
At birth	77.4	79.9	74.7
Aged 1	76.9	79.4	74.3
Aged 5	73.0	75.5	70.4
Aged 10	68.1	70.6	65.4
Aged 15	63.1	65.6	60.5
Aged 20	58.3	60.7	55.8
Aged 25	53.6	55.9	51.1
Aged 30	48.8	51.0	46.5
Aged 35	44.1	46.2	41.8
Aged 40	39.4	41.5	37.2
Aged 45	34.9	36.8	32.7
Aged 50	30.4	32.2	28.4
Aged 55	26.2	27.8	24.2
Aged 60	22.0	23.5	20.3
Aged 65	18.2	19.5	16.6
Aged 70	14.7	15.8	13.3
Aged 75	11.6	12.5	10.4
Aged 80	8.9	9.5	8.0
Aged 85	6.7	7.0	5.9
Aged 90	4.9	5.1	4.4
Aged 95	3.7	3.8	3.3
Aged 100	2.8	2.8	2.6

Source: National Center for Health Statistics, **Deaths: Preliminary Data for 2002,** *National Vital Statistics Report, Vol. 52, No. 13, 2004*

3

Housing

■ The percentage of householders who own their home is at a record high, thanks to the aging of the population and low mortgage interest rates. In 2003, 68.3 percent of the nation's householders owned their home.

■ According to the 2000 census, most householders aged 65 or older are homeowners, regardless of race or Hispanic origin. The homeownership rate ranges from a high of 81 percent for non-Hispanic whites to a low of 62 percent for Asians.

■ Sixty-nine percent of householders aged 65 or older live in single-family detached homes. Nineteen percent live in apartment buildings, while 7 percent live in mobile homes.

■ Older Americans are just as likely as the average household to have a home outfitted with amenities. Fully 84 percent have a porch, deck, balcony, or patio, 56 percent have central air conditioning, and most have a dishwasher.

■ When asked how they would rate their housing unit on a scale of 1 (worst) to 10 (best), 81 percent of householders aged 65 or older rate their home an 8 or higher. Seventy-five percent rate their neighborhood an 8 or higher.

■ Homeowners aged 65 or older have the lowest housing costs. Median monthly housing costs for married homeowners aged 65 or older were just $383 in 2001.

Older Americans Are Most Likely to Own a Home

People aged 60 to 74 have the highest homeownership rate.

The percentage of householders who own their home is at a record high, thanks to the aging of the population and low mortgage interest rates. In 2003, 68.3 percent of the nation's householders owned their home—including 80 percent of householders aged 65 or older.

Between 1982 and 2003, householders aged 65 or older experienced big gains in homeownership, their rate rising 6 percentage points, from 74 to 80 percent. Behind the increase was the entry of a more affluent generation into the age group. Between 2000 and 2003, however, the homeownership rate fell slightly among 65-to-74-year-olds, although it continued to rise among those aged 75 or older. Only 42 percent of householders under age 35 are homeowners.

■ Since older Americans are most likely to own a home, the nation's homeownership rate will continue to climb as the population ages.

Homeownership rate is highest in the 60-to-74 age group

(percent of householders aged 55 or older who own their home, by age, 2003)

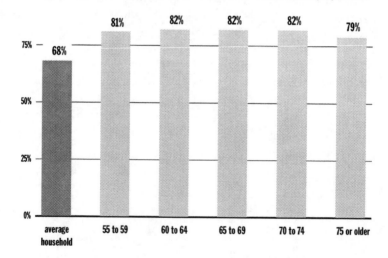

Table 3.1 Homeownership by Age of Householder, 1982 to 2003

(percentage of householders who own their home by age of householder, 1982 to 2003; percentage point change for selected years)

	2003	2000	1990	1982	percentage point change 2000–03	1990–03	1982–03
Total households	68.3%	67.4%	63.9%	64.8%	0.9	4.4	3.5
Under age 35	42.2	40.8	38.5	41.2	1.4	3.7	1.0
Aged 35 to 44	68.3	67.9	66.3	70.0	0.4	2.0	–1.7
Aged 45 to 54	76.6	76.5	75.2	77.4	0.1	1.4	–0.8
Aged 55 to 59	80.9	80.4	78.8	80.0	0.5	2.1	0.9
Aged 60 to 64	81.9	80.3	79.8	80.1	1.6	2.1	1.8
Aged 65 or older	80.5	80.4	76.3	74.4	0.1	4.2	6.1
Aged 65 to 69	82.5	83.0	80.0	77.9	–0.5	2.5	4.6
Aged 70 to 74	82.0	82.6	78.4	75.2	–0.6	3.6	6.8
Aged 75 or older	78.7	77.7	72.3	71.0	1.0	6.4	7.7

Source: Bureau of the Census, Housing Vacancy Surveys, Internet site http://www.census.gov/hhes/www/housing/hvs/annual03/ann03ind.html; calculations by New Strategist

Homeownership Rises with Age

People aged 65 or older account for nearly one in four homeowners.

The housing industry is booming because the population is aging and older people are more likely to own a home than young adults. A minority of householders under age 35 own a home. The homeownership rate climbs sharply as people age into their thirties and forties, topping 80 percent among those aged 55 or older.

The percentage of householders who rent falls from the 58 percent majority of those under age 35 to less than 20 percent among those aged 55 to 74. Among householders aged 75 or older, a slightly larger 21 percent are renters as elderly widows sell their home and move into smaller apartments, often to be closer to their adult children.

■ The 64 percent majority of the nation's homeowners are aged 45 or older, while the 64 percent majority of renters are under age 45.

Homeowners outnumber renters by far among older householders

(percent distribution of householders aged 65 or older by homeownership status, 2003)

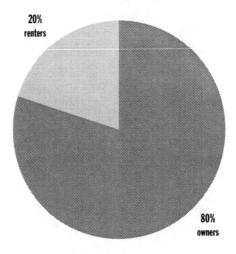

20%
renters

80%
owners

Table 3.2 Owners and Renters by Age of Householder, 2003

(number and percent distribution of householders by age and homeownership status, 2003; numbers in thousands)

	total	owners			renters		
		number	percent	share of total	number	percent	share of total
Total households	**105,560**	**72,054**	**100.0%**	**68.3%**	**33,506**	**100.0%**	**31.7%**
Under age 35	24,738	10,439	14.5	42.2	14,299	42.7	57.8
Aged 35 to 44	22,525	15,394	21.4	68.3	7,131	21.3	31.7
Aged 45 to 54	21,535	16,499	22.9	76.6	5,036	15.0	23.4
Aged 55 to 59	8,550	6,916	9.6	80.9	1,634	4.9	19.1
Aged 60 to 64	6,776	5,552	7.7	81.9	1,224	3.7	18.1
Aged 65 or older	21,436	17,253	23.9	80.5	4,183	12.5	19.5
Aged 65 to 69	5,570	4,597	6.4	82.5	973	2.9	17.5
Aged 70 to 74	5,163	4,236	5.9	82.1	927	2.8	18.0
Aged 75 or older	10,703	8,420	11.7	78.7	2,283	6.8	21.3

Source: Bureau of the Census, Housing Vacancy Survey, Internet site http://www.census.gov/hhes/www/housing/hvs/historic/ histt12.html; calculations by New Strategist

Married Couples Are Most Likely to Be Homeowners

The majority of older householders own their home, however, regardless of household type.

The homeownership rate among all married couples was a lofty 83 percent in 2003, much higher than the 68 percent rate for all households. Among married couples aged 55 or older, the homeownership rate tops 90 percent, peaking at 93 percent among those aged 65 to 74.

Among householders aged 55 or older, homeownership is lowest for those who live alone. Regardless of household type, however, the majority of older householders are homeowners. Among men aged 65 or older who live alone, 68 percent are homeowners. The rate is a slightly higher 70 percent for their female counterparts. For both female- and male-headed family householders in the age group, 82 percent are homeowners.

■ As the large Baby-Boom generation moves into the older age group, its homeownership rate will climb, continuing to fuel the boom in the housing industry.

Most householders aged 65 or older own their home, regardless of household type

(percent of householders aged 65 or older who own their home, by household type, 2003)

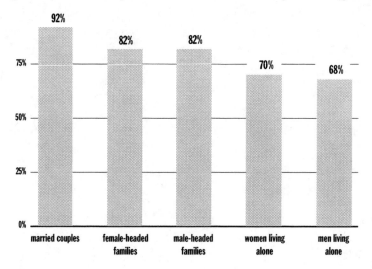

Table 3.3 Homeownership Rate by Age of Householder and Type of Household, 2003

(percent of households owning their home, by age of householder and type of household, 2003)

| | | family households | | | people living alone | |
	total	married couples	female householder, no spouse present	male householder, no spouse present	females	males
Total households	**68.3%**	**83.3%**	**49.6%**	**57.9%**	**59.1%**	**50.0%**
Under age 25	22.8	32.8	23.1	40.4	12.7	16.0
Aged 25 to 29	39.8	57.9	23.0	39.0	23.8	28.2
Aged 30 to 34	56.5	71.6	33.3	49.2	37.3	38.1
Aged 35 to 39	65.1	78.9	43.2	53.5	45.2	44.6
Aged 40 to 44	71.3	84.9	51.6	63.7	49.8	49.6
Aged 45 to 49	75.4	88.3	60.0	69.6	54.2	50.4
Aged 50 to 54	77.9	90.2	61.1	71.5	60.9	55.4
Aged 55 to 59	80.9	91.6	65.8	75.2	65.4	58.7
Aged 60 to 64	81.9	92.2	71.3	75.0	68.6	61.4
Aged 65 or older	80.5	92.1	81.6	81.9	70.0	67.8
Aged 65 to 69	82.5	92.8	76.3	79.4	69.3	64.0
Aged 70 to 74	82.0	92.8	79.8	79.5	71.6	63.7
Aged 75 or older	78.7	91.1	85.0	84.1	69.7	71.3

Source: Bureau of the Census, Housing Vacancy Survey, Internet site http://www.census.gov/hhes/www/housing/hvs/annual03/ann03t15.html

Most Older Blacks and Hispanics Are Homeowners

Non-Hispanic whites have the highest homeownership rate.

Among black and Hispanic householders nationwide, most do not own a home. Among those aged 65 or older, however, the majority are homeowners.

According to the 2000 census, the homeownership rate for householders aged 65 or older ranges from a high of 81 percent for non-Hispanic whites to a low of 62 percent for Asians. The figure is a slightly higher 63 percent for Hispanic, 64 percent for black, and 72 percent for American Indian householders in the age group.

The homeownership rate falls slightly among the oldest householders—aged 85 or older—as many of the frail elderly sell their homes and move into smaller apartments. The majority of householders aged 85 or older are homeowners, however, regardless of race or Hispanic origin.

■ American Indians are more likely to be homeowners than blacks or Hispanics because many live in nonmetropolitan areas where housing prices are lower.

The majority of older Americans are homeowners, regardless of race or Hispanic origin

(percent of householders aged 65 or older who own their home, by race and Hispanic origin, 2000)

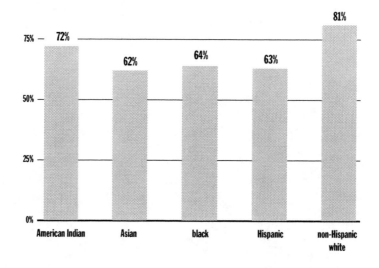

Table 3.4 Homeowners by Age, Race, and Hispanic Origin of Householder, 2000 Census

(percent of households owning their home by age, race, and Hispanic origin of householder, 2000)

	total	American Indian	Asian	black	Hispanic	non-Hispanic white
Total households	**66.2%**	**55.4%**	**52.8%**	**46.0%**	**45.7%**	**72.4%**
Under age 25	17.9	19.2	11.3	10.4	15.3	20.5
Aged 25 to 34	45.6	38.3	32.1	27.2	32.9	53.0
Aged 35 to 44	66.2	54.7	57.8	44.4	48.8	73.2
Aged 45 to 54	74.9	63.7	67.9	55.2	56.8	80.3
Aged 55 to 64	79.8	70.6	71.2	61.6	61.9	84.1
Aged 65 or older	78.1	72.4	62.0	64.3	62.8	80.6
Aged 65 to 74	81.3	73.5	65.2	64.5	64.4	84.7
Aged 75 to 84	77.3	72.0	57.9	64.3	61.5	79.3
Aged 85 or older	66.1	66.3	51.6	62.2	54.8	67.0

Note: Each racial category includes those who identified themselves as being of the race alone and those who identified themselves as being of the race in combination with one or more other races. Hispanics may be of any race. Non-Hispanic whites include only those who identified themselves as white alone and non-Hispanic.
Source: Bureau of the Census, Census 2000, American Factfinder, Internet site http://factfinder.census.gov/home/saff/main.html?_lang=en

Among Older Americans, Homeownership Is Highest in the South

The rate of homeownership is also highest in nonmetropolitan areas.

Nationally, the Midwest has the highest homeownership rate (73 percent in 2001), but among people aged 65 or older homeownership is highest in the South at 85 percent. In every region, older Americans are much more likely to own a home than is the average householder. In the West, the contrast is particularly striking, with 79 percent of householders aged 65 or older owning a home versus a much smaller 63 percent average.

Regardless of their metropolitan status, the majority of older householders are homeowners. The figures range from a high of 86 percent for those living in nonmetropolitan areas to a low of 70 percent for those in central cities.

■ With the population aging, homeownership rates should rise in every region during the next few decades.

Most older Americans own their home, regardless of region

(percent of householders aged 65 or older who own their home, by region, 2001)

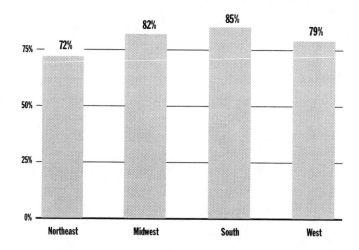

Table 3.5 Households by Region, Age, and Homeownership Status, 2001

(number and percent distribution of total households and households headed by people aged 65 or older by region of residence and homeownership status, 2001; numbers in thousands)

	total			householders aged 65 or older		
	total	owner	renter	total	owner	renter
Total households	**106,261**	**72,265**	**33,996**	**21,812**	**17,513**	**4,299**
Northeast	20,321	12,987	7,334	4,777	3,434	1,344
Midwest	24,758	18,049	6,709	5,163	4,240	923
South	38,068	26,715	11,353	7,805	6,611	1,194
West	23,115	14,514	8,600	4,067	3,229	838
PERCENT DISTRIBUTION BY HOMEOWNERSHIP STATUS						
Total households	**100.0%**	**68.0%**	**32.0%**	**100.0%**	**80.3%**	**19.7%**
Northeast	100.0	63.9	36.1	100.0	71.9	28.1
Midwest	100.0	72.9	27.1	100.0	82.1	17.9
South	100.0	70.2	29.8	100.0	84.7	15.3
West	100.0	62.8	37.2	100.0	79.4	20.6
PERCENT DISTRIBUTION BY REGION						
Total households	**100.0%**	**100.0%**	**100.0%**	**100.0%**	**100.0%**	**100.0%**
Northeast	19.1	18.0	21.6	21.9	19.6	31.3
Midwest	23.3	25.0	19.7	23.7	24.2	21.5
South	35.8	37.0	33.4	35.8	37.7	27.8
West	21.8	20.1	25.3	18.6	18.4	19.5

Source: Bureau of the Census, American Housing Survey for the United States in 2001; *Internet site http://www.census.gov/hhes/ www/housing/ahs/ahs01/ahs01.html; calculations by New Strategist*

Table 3.6 Households by Metropolitan Residence, Age, and Homeownership Status, 2001

(number and percent distribution of total households and households headed by people aged 65 or older by metropolitan residence and homeownership status, 2001; numbers in thousands)

	total			householders aged 65 or older		
	total	owner	renter	total	owner	renter
Total households	**106,261**	**72,265**	**33,996**	**21,812**	**17,513**	**4,299**
In metropolitan areas	85,304	56,290	29,014	16,474	12,921	3,553
In central cities	31,731	16,870	14,861	6,066	4,235	1,832
In suburbs	53,574	39,420	14,153	10,407	8,686	1,722
Outside metropolitan areas	20,957	15,975	4,982	5,338	4,592	746

PERCENT DISTRIBUTION BY HOMEOWNERSHIP STATUS

Total households	**100.0%**	**68.0%**	**32.0%**	**100.0%**	**80.3%**	**19.7%**
In metropolitan areas	100.0	66.0	34.0	100.0	78.4	21.6
In central cities	100.0	53.2	46.8	100.0	69.8	30.2
In suburbs	100.0	73.6	26.4	100.0	83.5	16.5
Outside metropolitan areas	100.0	76.2	23.8	100.0	86.0	14.0

PERCENT DISTRIBUTION BY METROPOLITAN RESIDENCE

Total households	**100.0%**	**100.0%**	**100.0%**	**100.0%**	**100.0%**	**100.0%**
In metropolitan areas	80.3	77.9	85.3	75.5	73.8	82.6
In central cities	29.9	23.3	43.7	27.8	24.2	42.6
In suburbs	50.4	54.5	41.6	47.7	49.6	40.1
Outside metropolitan areas	19.7	22.1	14.7	24.5	26.2	17.4

Source: Bureau of the Census, American Housing Survey for the United States in 2001; *Internet site http://www.census.gov/hhes/www/housing/ahs/ahs01/ahs01.html; calculations by New Strategist*

Most Older Americans Live in Single-Family Homes

The majority of older homeowners have three or more bedrooms.

Sixty-nine percent of householders aged 65 or older live in single-family detached homes. Nineteen percent live in apartment buildings, while 7 percent live in mobile homes. Not surprisingly, older homeowners are much more likely than renters to live in single-family homes (81 versus 19 percent).

Despite their smaller household size, many older householders have large homes. Sixty-seven percent of older homeowners have three or more bedrooms, and 46 percent have two or more bathrooms. Because older householders share their home with fewer people, they have more living space per capita than the average person. Among householders aged 65 or older, the average person has 1,037 square feet of living space. Among all householders, the average person has just 720 square feet of living space.

Older renters have less living space per person, but still more than the average American—923 square feet. Forty-six percent have only one bedroom and 78 percent have only one bathroom.

■ Many householders downsize as they age, but others want extra bedrooms and bathrooms for visiting children and grandchildren.

Older householders have more living space than the average person

(square feet per capita for the average person and people aged 65 or older, by homeownership status, 2001)

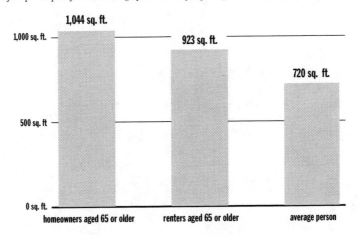

Table 3.7 Number of Units in Structure by Age of Householder, 2001

(number and percent distribution of households by age of householder and number of units in structure of home, 2001; numbers in thousands)

	total	one, detached	one, attached	multi-unit dwellings total	2 to 4	5 to 9	10 to 19	20 to 49	50 or more	mobile homes
Total households	106,261	67,129	7,305	24,609	8,200	4,994	4,620	3,253	3,543	7,219
Under age 55	70,331	42,022	5,189	18,390	6,305	3,998	3,842	2,352	1,895	4,731
Aged 55 or older	35,929	25,106	2,117	6,218	1,895	996	778	902	1,648	2,487
Aged 55 to 64	14,117	10,125	889	2,077	723	423	288	262	381	1,026
Aged 65 or older	21,812	14,981	1,228	4,141	1,172	573	490	640	1,267	1,461
Aged 65 to 74	10,755	7,655	584	1,779	537	281	230	295	436	736
Aged 75 or older	11,057	7,326	644	2,362	635	292	260	345	831	725
Median age	47	49	43	39	39	37	36	41	52	46

PERCENT DISTRIBUTION BY AGE OF HOUSEHOLDER

	total	one, detached	one, attached	multi-unit dwellings total	2 to 4	5 to 9	10 to 19	20 to 49	50 or more	mobile homes
Total households	100.0%	100.0%	100.0%	100.0%	100.0%	100.0%	100.0%	100.0%	100.0%	100.0%
Under age 55	66.2	62.6	71.0	74.7	76.9	80.1	83.2	72.3	53.5	65.5
Aged 55 or older	33.8	37.4	29.0	25.3	23.1	19.9	16.8	27.7	46.5	34.5
Aged 55 to 64	13.3	15.1	12.2	8.4	8.8	8.5	6.2	8.1	10.8	14.2
Aged 65 or older	20.5	22.3	16.8	16.8	14.3	11.5	10.6	19.7	35.8	20.2
Aged 65 to 74	10.1	11.4	8.0	7.2	6.5	5.6	5.0	9.1	12.3	10.2
Aged 75 or older	10.4	10.9	8.8	9.6	7.7	5.8	5.6	10.6	23.5	10.0

PERCENT DISTRIBUTION BY UNITS IN STRUCTURE

	total	one, detached	one, attached	multi-unit dwellings total	2 to 4	5 to 9	10 to 19	20 to 49	50 or more	mobile homes
Total households	100.0%	63.2%	6.9%	23.2%	7.7%	4.7%	4.3%	3.1%	3.3%	6.8%
Under age 55	100.0	59.7	7.4	26.1	9.0	5.7	5.5	3.3	2.7	6.7
Aged 55 or older	100.0	69.9	5.9	17.3	5.3	2.8	2.2	2.5	4.6	6.9
Aged 55 to 64	100.0	71.7	6.3	14.7	5.1	3.0	2.0	1.9	2.7	7.3
Aged 65 or older	100.0	68.7	5.6	19.0	5.4	2.6	2.2	2.9	5.8	6.7
Aged 65 to 74	100.0	71.2	5.4	16.5	5.0	2.6	2.1	2.7	4.1	6.8
Aged 75 or older	100.0	66.3	5.8	21.4	5.7	2.6	2.4	3.1	7.5	6.6

Source: Bureau of the Census, American Housing Survey for the United States in 2001; Internet site http://www.census.gov/hhes/www/housing/ahs/ahs01/ahs01.html; calculations by New Strategist

Table 3.8 Number of Units in Structures Occupied by Householders Aged 65 or Older, 2001

(number and percent distribution of householders aged 65 or older by number of units in structure and homeownership status, 2001; numbers in thousands)

	total	owner	renter
Total householders			
aged 65 or older	**21,812**	**17,513**	**4,299**
1 unit, detached	14,981	14,149	832
1 unit, attached	1,228	914	314
2 to 4 units	1,171	370	802
5 to 9 units	573	130	444
10 to 19 units	491	157	334
20 to 49 units	639	159	480
50 or more units	1,267	261	1,006
Mobile home	1,462	1,375	87

PERCENT DISTRIBUTION BY HOMEOWNERSHIP STATUS

	total	owner	renter
Total householders			
aged 65 or older	**100.0%**	**80.3%**	**19.7%**
1 unit, detached	100.0	94.4	5.6
1 unit, attached	100.0	74.4	25.6
2 to 4 units	100.0	31.6	68.5
5 to 9 units	100.0	22.7	77.5
10 to 19 units	100.0	32.0	68.0
20 to 49 units	100.0	24.9	75.1
50 or more units	100.0	20.6	79.4
Mobile home	100.0	94.1	6.0

PERCENT DISTRIBUTION BY NUMBER OF UNITS IN STRUCTURE

	total	owner	renter
Total householders			
aged 65 or older	**100.0%**	**100.0%**	**100.0%**
1 unit, detached	68.7	80.8	19.4
1 unit, attached	5.6	5.2	7.3
2 to 4 units	5.4	2.1	18.7
5 to 9 units	2.6	0.7	10.3
10 to 19 units	2.3	0.9	7.8
20 to 49 units	2.9	0.9	11.2
50 or more units	5.8	1.5	23.4
Mobile home	6.7	7.9	2.0

Source: Bureau of the Census, American Housing Survey for the United States in 2001; Internet site http://www.census.gov/hhes/ www/housing/ahs/ahs01/ahs01.html; calculations by New Strategist

Table 3.9 Size of Housing Unit Occupied by Householders Aged 65 or Older, 2001

(number and percent distribution of householders aged 65 or older by size of unit and homeownership status, 2001; numbers in thousands)

	number			percent distribution by homeownership status			percent distribution by size of unit		
	total	owner	renter	total	owner	renter	total	owner	renter
Total householders aged 65 or older	**21,812**	**17,513**	**4,299**	**100.0%**	**80.3%**	**19.7%**	**100.0%**	**100.0%**	**100.0%**
Number of rooms									
1 room	64	3	61	100.0	4.7	95.3	0.3	0.0	1.4
2 rooms	193	33	160	100.0	17.1	82.9	0.9	0.2	3.7
3 rooms	1,960	330	1,630	100.0	16.8	83.2	9.0	1.9	37.9
4 rooms	3,634	2,356	1,278	100.0	64.8	35.2	16.7	13.5	29.7
5 rooms	5,578	4,893	685	100.0	87.7	12.3	25.6	27.9	15.9
6 rooms	5,042	4,732	311	100.0	93.9	6.2	23.1	27.0	7.2
7 rooms	2,872	2,778	94	100.0	96.7	3.3	13.2	15.9	2.2
8 rooms	1,372	1,328	45	100.0	96.8	3.3	6.3	7.6	1.1
9 rooms	525	513	11	100.0	97.7	2.1	2.4	2.9	0.3
10 or more rooms	571	547	24	100.0	95.8	4.2	2.6	3.1	0.6
Number of bedrooms									
None	124	7	117	100.0	5.6	94.4	0.6	0.0	2.7
1 bedroom	2,586	599	1,987	100.0	23.2	76.8	11.9	3.4	46.2
2 bedrooms	6,771	5,248	1,523	100.0	77.5	22.5	31.0	30.0	35.4
3 bedrooms	9,173	8,633	541	100.0	94.1	5.9	42.1	49.3	12.6
4 or more bedrooms	3,157	3,027	130	100.0	95.9	4.1	14.5	17.3	3.0
Complete bathrooms									
None	183	111	72	100.0	60.7	39.3	0.8	0.6	1.7
1 bathroom	8,914	5,570	3,344	100.0	62.5	37.5	40.9	31.8	77.8
1 and 1/2 bathrooms	4,104	3,729	376	100.0	90.9	9.2	18.8	21.3	8.7
2 or more bathrooms	8,610	8,104	507	100.0	94.1	5.9	39.5	46.3	11.8
Median square footage of unit	1,668	1,693	1,296	–	–	–	–	–	–
Per capita square footage	1,037	1,044	923	–	–	–	–	–	–

Note: (–) means not applicable.
Source: Bureau of the Census, American Housing Survey for the United States in 2001; Internet site http://www.census.gov/hhes/www/housing/ahs/ahs01/ahs01.html; calculations by New Strategist

Few Older Homeowners Live in New Homes

Householders under age 55 are more likely to live in new homes.

Overall, only 6 percent of homeowners live in a new home—meaning one built in the past four years. Among householders aged 55 or older, a smaller 4 percent live in a new home. The percentage falls from 5 percent among 55-to-64-year-olds to just 2 percent of householders aged 75 or older.

Householders aged 55 or older account for 40 percent of the nation's homeowners but for only 23 percent of the owners of homes built in the past four years. They account for only 17 percent of renters in new rental units.

■ With many older adults living in older homes, they are a large and growing market for home remodeling and repair services.

Older householders account for a small share of the owners of recently built homes

(percent of homeowners living in homes built in the past four years, by age of householder, 2001)

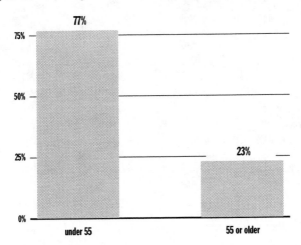

Table 3.10   Owners and Renters of New Homes by Age of Householder, 2001

(number of total occupied housing units, number and percent built in the past four years, and percent distribution of new units by housing tenure and age of householder, 2001; numbers in thousands)

		in new homes		
	total	number	percent of total	percent distribution
Total households	**106,261**	**5,853**	**5.5%**	**100.0%**
Under age 55	70,331	4,579	6.5	78.2
Aged 55 or older	35,929	1,273	3.5	21.7
Aged 55 to 64	14,117	680	4.8	11.6
Aged 65 or older	21,812	593	2.7	10.1
Aged 65 to 74	10,755	359	3.3	6.1
Aged 75 or older	11,057	234	2.1	4.0
Owners	**72,265**	**4,690**	**6.5**	**100.0**
Under age 55	43,296	3,612	8.3	77.0
Aged 55 or older	28,969	1,078	3.7	23.0
Aged 55 to 64	11,456	604	5.3	12.9
Aged 65 or older	17,513	474	2.7	10.1
Aged 65 to 74	8,856	305	3.4	6.5
Aged 75 or older	8,657	169	2.0	3.6
Renters	**33,996**	**1,163**	**3.4**	**100.0**
Under age 55	27,036	967	3.6	83.1
Aged 55 or older	6,960	195	2.8	16.8
Aged 55 to 64	2,661	76	2.9	6.5
Aged 65 or older	4,299	119	2.8	10.2
Aged 65 to 74	1,898	54	2.8	4.6
Aged 75 or older	2,401	65	2.7	5.6

Source: Bureau of the Census, American Housing Survey for the United States in 2001, *Internet site http://www.census.gov/hhes/ www/housing/ahs/ahs01/ahs01.html*

Electricity Is a Less Popular Heating Fuel among Older Americans

They use fuel oil more than average.

Electricity was the main heating fuel for 31 percent of the nation's households in 2001, but it was used by a smaller 27 percent of households headed by people aged 65 or older. In contrast, 9 percent of all households use fuel oil, as do a larger 11 percent of older householders. Regardless of age, piped gas is the most popular heating fuel, used by the majority of households.

The heating fuels used by older Americans differ somewhat from those used by the average household because many older Americans live in older homes. This circumstance accounts for their lesser use of electricity as a heating energy—a popular option in newer homes—and their greater use of fuel oil. Interestingly, despite the labor involved, older Americans are just as likely as the average householder to use wood as their primary heating fuel. About 2 percent of households use wood, regardless of age of householder.

■ As Baby Boomers enter the 55-or-older age groups, the share of older Americans who use electricity as their primary heating fuel will rise.

Piped gas is the most widely used heating fuel among older Americans

(percent distribution of householders aged 65 or older by primary heating fuel used, 2001)

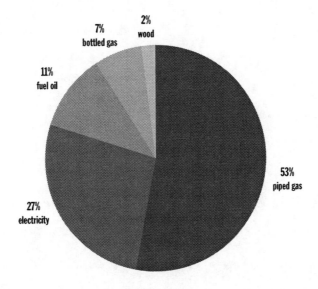

Table 3.11 House Heating Fuel Used by Householders Aged 65 or Older, 2001

(number and percent distribution of total households and householders aged 65 or older by main house heating fuel and homeownership status, 2001; numbers in thousands)

	total	householders aged 65 or older total	owner	renter
Total households using				
heating fuel	**105,860**	**21,757**	**17,481**	**4,276**
Electricity	32,590	5,784	4,077	1,707
Piped gas	54,689	11,457	9,679	1,778
Bottled gas	6,079	1,423	1,300	123
Fuel oil	9,821	2,499	1,926	573
Kerosene or other liquid fuel	652	174	139	34
Coal or coke	128	30	30	–
Wood	1,688	363	317	46
Solar energy	21	4	2	2
Other	193	22	10	12
PERCENT DISTRIBUTION BY TYPE OF HEATING FUEL				
Total households using				
heating fuel	**100.0%**	**100.0%**	**100.0%**	**100.0%**
Electricity	30.8	26.6	23.3	39.9
Piped gas	51.7	52.7	55.4	41.6
Bottled gas	5.7	6.5	7.4	2.9
Fuel oil	9.3	11.5	11.0	13.4
Kerosene or other liquid fuel	0.6	0.8	0.8	0.8
Coal or coke	0.1	0.1	0.2	–
Wood	1.6	1.7	1.8	1.1
Solar energy	–	–	–	0.1
Other	0.2	0.1	0.1	0.3

Note: (–) means fewer than 500 or less than .05 percent.
Source: Bureau of the Census, American Housing Survey for the United States in 2001; Internet site http://www.census.gov/hhes/www/housing/ahs/ahs01/ahs01.html; calculations by New Strategist

Amenities Are Many in the Homes of Older Americans

Most have dishwashers, central air conditioning, and garages or carports.

Older Americans are just as likely as the average household to have a home outfitted with amenities. Fully 84 percent have a porch, deck, balcony, or patio. Washing machines are in 83 percent of the homes of older Americans, while clothes dryers are in 77 percent of their homes. Sixty-six percent have a garage or carport, and 56 percent have central air conditioning. More than half have a dishwasher.

Homeowners are much more likely than renters to have amenities in the home. Fifty-eight percent of older homeowners have a dishwasher, for example, compared with 28 percent of renters. Thirty-six percent of older homeowners have a usable fireplace versus only 7 percent of renters in the age group.

■ Although older Americans were raised with few amenities, they have outfitted their homes with most of the conveniences.

Most older householders have homes with central air conditioning

(percent of households headed by people aged 65 or older with selected amenities, 2001)

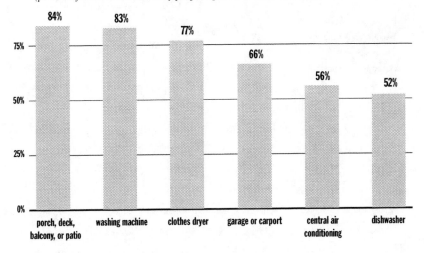

Table 3.12 Amenities of Housing Units Occupied by Householders Aged 65 or Older, 2001

(number and percent distribution of total households and households headed by people aged 65 or older by amenities in unit and homeownership status, 2001; numbers in thousands)

	total	householders aged 65 or older		
		total	owner	renter
Total households	**106,261**	**21,812**	**17,513**	**4,299**
Telephone	102,722	21,252	17,143	4,109
Porch, deck, balcony, patio	88,834	18,236	15,688	2,549
Washing machine	85,562	18,192	16,503	1,689
Clothes dryer	81,591	16,889	15,500	1,389
Gararge or carport	64,547	14,499	13,307	1,191
Dishwasher	62,352	11,355	10,137	1,218
Central air conditioning	60,118	12,156	10,484	1,672
Separate dining room	50,125	10,066	9,153	913
Disposal in kitchen sink	48,604	8,940	7,264	1,676
Usable fireplace	35,097	6,603	6,292	311
With two or more living/ recreation rooms	30,451	6,141	5,907	234
PERCENT WITH AMENITY				
Total households	**100.0%**	**100.0%**	**100.0%**	**100.0%**
Telephone	96.7	97.4	97.9	95.6
Porch, deck, balcony, patio	83.6	83.6	89.6	59.3
Washing machine	80.5	83.4	94.2	39.3
Clothes dryer	76.8	77.4	88.5	32.3
Gararge or carport	60.7	66.5	76.0	27.7
Dishwasher	58.7	52.1	57.9	28.3
Central air conditioning	56.6	55.7	59.9	38.9
Separate dining room	47.2	46.1	52.3	21.2
Disposal in kitchen sink	45.7	41.0	41.5	39.0
Usable fireplace	33.0	30.3	35.9	7.2
With two or more living/ recreation rooms	28.7	28.2	33.7	5.4

Source: Bureau of the Census, American Housing Survey for the United States in 2001, *Internet site http://www.census.gov/hhes/ www/housing/ahs/ahs01/ahs01.html*

Most Older Americans Are Satisfied with Their Home and Neighborhood

Homeowners are happier than renters, but few renters are dissatisfied.

When asked how they would rate their housing unit on a scale of 1 (worst) to 10 (best), 81 percent of householders aged 65 or older rate their home an 8 or higher. Homeowners rate their homes somewhat more highly than renters—82 percent of owners and 75 percent of renters give their home at least an 8. Forty-one percent of homeowners and 36 percent of renters give their home the highest rating of 10.

Opinions are almost as positive when older householders are asked to rate their neighborhood. Seventy-five percent rate their neighborhood an 8 or higher, including 76 percent of homeowners and 70 percent of renters.

■ Older householders rate their home and neighborhood highly because, over the years, those who were unhappy found new places to live.

Most older householders rate their home and neighborhood highly

(percent of householders aged 65 or older who rate their home and neighborhood an 8 or higher on a scale of 1 to 10, with 10 being best, 2001)

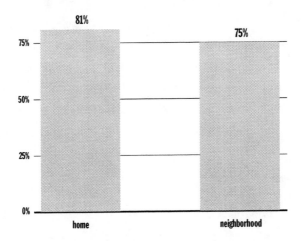

Table 3.13 Opinion of Housing Unit among Householders Aged 65 or Older by Homeownership Status, 2001

(number and percent distribution of householders aged 65 or older by opinion of housing unit and homeownership status, 2001; numbers in thousands)

	total	owner	renter
Total householders aged 65 or older	**21,423**	**17,196**	**4,227**
1 (worst)	97	49	47
2	27	17	10
3	65	35	30
4	131	86	46
5	913	636	277
6	681	518	163
7	1,810	1,412	399
8	5,344	4,239	1,105
9	3,343	2,777	566
10 (best)	8,622	7,108	1,514

PERCENT DISTRIBUTION BY HOMEOWNERSHIP STATUS

	total	owner	renter
Total householders aged 65 or older	**100.0%**	**80.3%**	**19.7%**
1 (worst)	100.0	50.5	48.5
2	100.0	63.0	37.0
3	100.0	53.8	46.2
4	100.0	65.6	35.1
5	100.0	69.7	30.3
6	100.0	76.1	23.9
7	100.0	78.0	22.0
8	100.0	79.3	20.7
9	100.0	83.1	16.9
10 (best)	100.0	82.4	17.6

PERCENT DISTRIBUTION BY OPINION OF HOUSING UNIT

	total	owner	renter
Total householders aged 65 or older	**100.0%**	**100.0%**	**100.0%**
1 (worst)	0.5	0.3	1.1
2	0.1	0.1	0.2
3	0.3	0.2	0.7
4	0.6	0.5	1.1
5	4.3	3.7	6.6
6	3.2	3.0	3.9
7	8.4	8.2	9.4
8	24.9	24.7	26.1
9	15.6	16.1	13.4
10 (best)	40.2	41.3	35.8

Note: Numbers will not add to total because not reported is not shown.
Source: Bureau of the Census, American Housing Survey for the United States in 2001, Internet site http://www.census.gov/hhes/ www/housing/ahs/ahs01/ahs01.html; calculations by New Strategist

Table 3.14 Opinion of Neighborhood among Householders Aged 65 or Older by Homeownership Status, 2001

(number and percent distribution of householders aged 65 or older by homeownership status and opinion of neighborhood, 2001; numbers in thousands)

	total	owner	renter
Total householders aged 65 or older	**21,812**	**17,513**	**4,299**
1 (worst)	122	75	47
2	75	58	17
3	135	108	27
4	208	170	38
5	1,098	807	291
6	849	588	262
7	2,022	1,599	423
8	5,312	4,330	981
9	3,330	2,752	577
10 (best)	7,760	6,300	1,460

PERCENT DISTRIBUTION BY HOMEOWNERSHIP STATUS

Total householders aged 65 or older	**100.0%**	**80.3%**	**19.7%**
1 (worst)	100.0	61.5	38.5
2	100.0	77.3	22.7
3	100.0	80.0	20.0
4	100.0	81.7	18.3
5	100.0	73.5	26.5
6	100.0	69.3	30.9
7	100.0	79.1	20.9
8	100.0	81.5	18.5
9	100.0	82.6	17.3
10 (best)	100.0	81.2	18.8

PERCENT DISTRIBUTION BY OPINION OF NEIGHBORHOOD

Total householders aged 65 or older	**100.0%**	**100.0%**	**100.0%**
1 (worst)	0.6	0.4	1.1
2	0.3	0.3	0.4
3	0.6	0.6	0.6
4	1.0	1.0	0.9
5	5.0	4.6	6.8
6	3.9	3.4	6.1
7	9.3	9.1	9.8
8	24.4	24.7	22.8
9	15.3	15.7	13.4
10 (best)	35.6	36.0	34.0

Note: Numbers will not add to total because not reported is not shown.
Source: Bureau of the Census, American Housing Survey for the United States in 2001, *Internet site http://www.census.gov/hhes/ www/housing/ahs/ahs01/ahs01.html; calculations by New Strategist*

Many Older Americans Live near Open Space, Woodlands

Few are bothered by crime, street noise, or other problems.

Of the 22 million householders aged 65 or older in the United States, 79 percent report having single-family detached houses within 300 feet of their home—83 percent of homeowners and 65 percent of renters. Thirty-three percent of homeowners and 26 percent of renters report having open space, park, woods, farm, or ranchland close by.

Many older householders have commercial or institutional buildings within 300 feet of their home—16 percent of homeowners and 44 percent of renters. Just 3 percent report industries or factories nearby, while a larger 10 percent say a four-lane highway, railroad, or airport is within 300 feet.

Few older householders report bothersome neighborhood problems. The biggest problem is street noise or traffic, reported by 8 percent of homeowners and 9 percent of renters. Crime ranks second but is bothersome to only 5 percent of homeowners and 8 percent of renters. People are the third biggest neighborhood problem, bothering 3 percent of older householders nationwide.

■ Despite media reports of crime problems in many neighborhoods, few older householders say crime is bothersome where they live.

The biggest neighborhood problem among older Americans is street noise

(percent of householders aged 65 or older saying they are bothered by selected neighborhood problems, 2001)

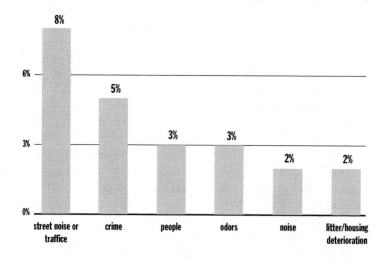

Table 3.15 **Characteristics of the Neighborhood Surrounding Householders Aged 65 or Older by Homeownership Status, 2001**

(number and percent distribution of householders aged 65 or older by description of area within 300 feet of home, by homeownership status, 2001; numbers in thousands)

	total	owner	renter
Total householders aged 65 or older	**21,812**	**17,513**	**4,299**
Single-family detached houses	17,257	14,471	2,785
Single-family attached	2,219	1,495	723
1 to 3 story multiunit	3,633	1,779	1,854
4 to 6 story multiunit	1,103	410	693
7 or more story multiunit	669	202	467
Mobile homes	2,765	2,532	232
Commercial/institutional	4,620	2,727	1,893
Industrial or factories	561	357	204
Open space, park, woods, farm, or ranch	6,866	5,745	1,121
Four or more lane highway, railroad, or airport	2,207	1,503	704
Waterfront property	757	668	89

PERCENT DISTRIBUTION BY HOMEOWNERSHIP STATUS

Total householders aged 65 or older	**100.0%**	**80.3%**	**19.7%**
Single-family detached houses	100.0	83.9	16.1
Single-family attached	100.0	67.4	32.6
1 to 3 story multiunit	100.0	49.0	51.0
4 to 6 story multiunit	100.0	37.2	62.8
7 or more story multiunit	100.0	30.2	69.8
Mobile homes	100.0	91.6	8.4
Commercial/institutional	100.0	59.0	41.0
Industrial or factories	100.0	63.6	36.4
Open space, park, woods, farm, or ranch	100.0	83.7	16.3
Four or more lane highway, railroad, or airport	100.0	68.1	31.9
Waterfront property	100.0	88.2	11.8

PERCENT DISTRIBUTION BY DESCRIPTION OF SURROUNDINGS

Total householders aged 65 or older	**100.0%**	**100.0%**	**100.0%**
Single-family detached houses	79.1	82.6	64.8
Single-family attached	10.2	8.5	16.8
1 to 3 story multiunit	16.7	10.2	43.1
4 to 6 story multiunit	5.1	2.3	16.1
7 or more story multiunit	3.1	1.2	10.9
Mobile homes	12.7	14.5	5.4
Commercial/institutional	21.2	15.6	44.0
Industrial or factories	2.6	2.0	4.7
Open space, park, woods, farm, or ranch	31.5	32.8	26.1
Four or more lane highway, railroad, or airport	10.1	8.6	16.4
Waterfront property	3.5	3.8	2.1

Note: Numbers will not add to total because more than one category may apply to unit.
Source: Bureau of the Census, American Housing Survey for the United States in 2001, Internet site http://www.census.gov/hhes/ www/housing/ahs/ahs01/ahs01.html; calculations by New Strategist

Table 3.16 Neighborhood Problems Reported by Householders Aged 65 or Older by Homeownership Status, 2001

(number and percent of housing units occupied by householders aged 65 or older by neighborhood conditions considered bothersome by householder and percent distribution of bothersome conditions by homeownership status, 2001; numbers in thousands)

	total	owner	renter
Total householders aged 65 or older	**21,812**	**17,513**	**4,299**
Street noise or traffic	1,758	1,353	405
Crime	1,194	866	328
Odors	614	471	143
People	608	463	145
Noise	433	347	87
Litter or housing deterioration	365	307	58
Undesirable commercial/institutional/industrial	133	124	9
Poor city or county services	141	118	23
PERCENT WITH PROBLEM			
Total householders aged 65 or older	**100.0%**	**100.0%**	**100.0%**
Street noise or traffic	8.1	7.7	9.4
Crime	5.5	4.9	7.6
People	2.8	2.7	3.3
Odors	2.8	2.6	3.4
Noise	2.0	2.0	2.0
Litter or housing deterioration	1.7	1.8	1.3
Undesirable commercial/institutional/industrial	0.6	0.7	0.2
Poor city or county services	0.6	0.7	0.5
PERCENT DISTRIBUTION OF PROBLEMS BY HOMEOWNERSHIP STATUS			
Total householders aged 65 or older	**100.0%**	**80.3%**	**19.7%**
Street noise or traffic	100.0	77.0	23.0
Crime	100.0	72.5	27.5
People	100.0	76.7	23.3
Odors	100.0	76.2	23.8
Noise	100.0	80.1	20.1
Litter or housing deterioration	100.0	84.1	15.9
Undesirable commercial/institutional/industrial	100.0	93.2	6.8
Poor city or county services	100.0	83.7	16.3

Note: Numbers will not add to total because not reported is not shown.
Source: Bureau of the Census, American Housing Survey for the United States in 2001, *Internet site http://www.census.gov/hhes/www/housing/ahs/ahs01/ahs01.html; calculations by New Strategist*

Housing Costs Are Lower for Older Americans

Most older homeowners have paid off their mortgage.

Housing costs are lowest for homeowners aged 65 or older regardless of household type. Median monthly housing costs for married homeowners aged 65 or older were just $383 in 2001. For all couples who own a home, median monthly housing costs were a much higher $811.

Among married couples, homeowners have higher monthly housing costs than renters until age 65. Among couples aged 65 or older, renters pay more for housing. The same pattern holds true for elderly men and women who live alone.

Behind the lower housing costs of older homeowners is the fact that most have paid off their mortgage. Only 22 percent of homeowners aged 65 or older have a mortgage. Consequently, older homeowners must devote only 17 percent of their monthly income to housing. Among older renters, the figure is a much higher 35 percent.

■ As Boomers enter the 65-or-older age group, the percentage of elderly homeowners with mortgages is likely to rise because many Boomers have refinanced their homes to pay off other debts.

Housing costs are lowest for older homeowners

(median monthly housing costs for married-couple homeowners, by age of householder, 2001)

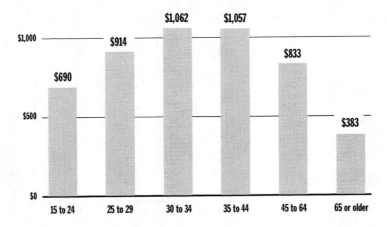

Table 3.17 Median Monthly Housing Costs by Household Type and Age of Householder, 2001

(median monthly housing costs and indexed costs by type of household, age of householder, and housing tenure, 2001)

	median monthly cost			indexed cost		
	total	owners	renters	total	owners	renters
Total households	**$658**	**$685**	**$632**	**100**	**104**	**96**
TWO-OR-MORE-						
PERSON HOUSEHOLDS	**734**	**775**	**682**	**112**	**118**	**104**
Married couples	**783**	**811**	**721**	**119**	**123**	**110**
Aged 15 to 24	638	690	622	97	105	95
Aged 25 to 29	796	914	691	121	139	105
Aged 30 to 34	928	1,062	737	141	161	112
Aged 35 to 44	979	1,057	775	149	161	118
Aged 45 to 64	815	833	740	124	127	113
Aged 65 or older	395	383	651	60	58	99
Other female householder	**639**	**648**	**634**	**97**	**99**	**96**
Aged 15 to 44	661	752	633	101	114	96
Aged 45 to 64	692	724	648	105	110	99
Aged 65 or older	404	365	609	61	56	93
Other male householder	**700**	**708**	**696**	**106**	**108**	**106**
Aged 15 to 44	724	789	703	110	120	107
Aged 45 to 64	690	719	661	105	109	101
Aged 65 or older	463	400	702	70	61	107
SINGLE-PERSON						
HOUSEHOLDS	**488**	**401**	**548**	**74**	**61**	**83**
Female householder	**455**	**374**	**538**	**69**	**57**	**82**
Aged 15 to 44	632	798	586	96	121	89
Aged 45 to 64	527	536	518	80	82	79
Aged 65 or older	318	284	473	48	43	72
Male householder	**531**	**478**	**557**	**81**	**73**	**85**
Aged 15 to 44	611	682	591	93	104	90
Aged 45 to 64	515	501	523	78	76	80
Aged 65 or older	339	298	445	52	45	68

Source: Bureau of the Census, American Housing Survey for the United States in 2001, Internet site http://www.census.gov/hhes/ www/housing/ahs/ahs01/ahs01.html; calculations by New Strategist

Table 3.18 Monthly Housing Costs of Householders Aged 65 or Older by Homeownership Status, 2001

(total and median monthly housing costs, monthly housing costs as a percent of current income, and median monthly amount paid for selected services and utilities, for householders aged 65 or older by homeownership status, 2001; numbers in thousands)

	total	owner	renter
Total householders aged 65 or older	**21,812**	**17,513**	**4,299**
Total monthly housing cost			
Less than $100	559	480	79
$100 to $199	3,326	2,911	415
$200 to $249	2,328	2,071	257
$250 to $299	2,205	1,990	215
$300 to $349	1,861	1,690	171
$350 to $399	1,468	1,297	171
$400 to $449	1,207	951	257
$450 to $499	1,054	782	272
$500 to $599	1,757	1,296	461
$600 to $699	1,235	832	403
$700 to $799	948	639	310
$800 to $999	1,269	889	380
$1,000 to $1,249	751	597	154
$1,250 to $1,499	487	392	95
$1,500 or more	878	697	181
No cash rent	478	–	478
Median (excludes no cash rent)	$363	$338	$515
Monthly housing cost as a percent of current income	19.5%	17.2%	34.8%
Median monthly cost of electricity	$53	$57	$37
Median monthly cost of piped gas	58	61	37
Median monthly cost of fuel oil	73	74	63
Median monthly cost of property insurance	36	37	17
Median monthly cost of water	25	25	20
Median monthly cost of trash removal	16	16	15
Percent with a mortgage	–	21.9%	–
Median monthly payment for principal and interest	–	$467	–
Median monthly amount of real estate taxes	–	77	–

Note: Median costs are for those with the expense; (–) means not applicable.
Source: Bureau of the Census, American Housing Survey for the United States in 2001, Internet site http://www.census.gov/hhes/www/housing/ahs/ahs01/ahs01.html

Value of Homes Owned by Older Americans Is below Average

Home values peak in middle age.

The median value of homes owned by people aged 65 or older stood at $107,398 in 2001, substantially below the $124,624 value of the average owned home. Behind the lesser value is the fact that many older homeowners live in older and smaller-than-average homes. Homes owned by older married couples were valued at a median of $124,713 in 2001—close to the national average. One in four married-couple homeowners aged 65 or older owns a home worth $200,000 or more.

Older homeowners have built substantial equity in their homes because many have paid off their mortgages. The median purchase price of their owned homes was just $29,471. Some will spend this equity on living expenses as they age, while others will leave it to their children.

■ Home values have been rising steadily and are now significantly higher than the 2001 figures shown in the table.

Home values are lower among older couples

(median value of homes owned by married couples, by age of householder, 2001)

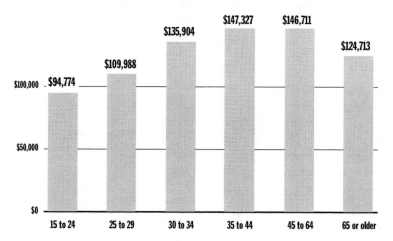

Table 3.19 Value of Owner-Occupied Homes by Type of Household and Age of Householder, 2001

(total number of homeowners and percent distribution by value of home, median value of housing unit, and indexed median value, by type of household and age of householder, 2001)

	total		under $100,000	$100,000 to $149,999	$150,000 to $199,999	$200,000 to $249,999	$250,000 to $299,999	$300,000 or more	median value of home	indexed median value
	number (in 000s)	percent								
Total homeowners	72,265	100.0%	39.3%	21.6%	14.1%	7.9%	5.2%	11.8%	$124,624	100
TWO-OR-MORE-PERSON										
HOUSEHOLDS	56,867	100.0	36.2	21.7	14.8	8.6	5.7	13.0	131,805	106
Married couples	44,618	100.0	32.8	21.9	15.5	9.4	6.3	14.1	139,364	112
Under age 25	490	100.0	53.7	19.2	11.2	6.5	3.1	5.9	94,774	76
Aged 25 to 29	2,039	100.0	44.9	25.7	14.4	6.0	3.4	5.6	109,988	88
Aged 30 to 34	3,744	100.0	31.8	25.3	15.7	9.6	7.0	10.6	135,904	109
Aged 35 to 44	11,182	100.0	29.1	22.0	16.5	10.2	7.1	15.1	147,327	118
Aged 45 to 64	18,681	100.0	30.0	21.4	15.8	10.0	6.4	16.5	146,711	118
Aged 65 or older	8,482	100.0	39.8	20.6	14.1	8.3	5.4	11.8	124,713	100
Other female										
householder	7,829	100.0	50.8	20.8	11.8	5.6	3.4	7.7	98,944	79
Under age 45	3,290	100.0	56.6	19.5	10.7	4.7	2.6	5.9	92,177	74
Aged 45 to 64	2,927	100.0	45.3	21.7	12.4	7.1	4.1	9.4	110,821	89
Aged 65 or older	1,612	100.0	48.8	21.8	12.7	4.7	3.8	8.3	102,977	83
Other male										
householder	4,419	100.0	44.8	21.7	13.3	6.0	3.8	10.4	111,924	90
Under age 45	2,377	100.0	46.2	23.7	12.0	5.8	3.7	8.6	107,989	87
Aged 45 to 64	1,505	100.0	42.6	19.6	13.2	6.8	4.4	13.4	118,762	95
Aged 65 or older	537	100.0	44.5	19.0	18.6	4.8	2.8	10.1	113,887	91
SINGLE-PERSON										
HOUSEHOLDS	15,398	100.0	51.1	21.1	11.4	5.4	3.4	7.6	98,253	79
Female										
householder	9,448	100.0	51.8	21.4	11.8	5.1	3.0	6.9	97,337	78
Under age 45	1,295	100.0	43.9	28.4	11.4	6.0	3.3	7.0	110,798	89
Aged 45 to 64	2,890	100.0	48.7	21.4	12.9	5.1	3.6	8.3	103,018	83
Aged 65 or older	5,262	100.0	55.5	19.8	11.3	4.8	2.6	6.0	92,013	74
Male householder	5,950	100.0	50.1	20.6	10.6	5.9	4.1	8.8	99,898	80
Under age 45	2,228	100.0	48.7	22.8	10.1	5.6	3.6	9.2	102,821	83
Aged 45 to 64	2,103	100.0	50.2	19.3	10.7	6.3	5.2	8.3	99,693	80
Aged 65 or older	1,620	100.0	51.8	19.2	11.2	5.9	3.1	8.8	97,048	78

Source: Bureau of the Census, American Housing Survey for the United States in 2001, Internet site http://www.census.gov/hhes/ www/housing/ahs/ahs01/ahs01.html; calculations by New Strategist

Table 3.20 Housing Value and Purchase Price for Homeowners Aged 65 or Older, 2001

(number and percent distribution of homeowners aged 65 or older by value of home, purchase price, and major source of down payment, 2001: numbers in thousands)

	number	percent
Total homeowners aged 65 or older	**17,513**	**100.0%**
Value of home		
Under $50,000	2,638	15.1
$50,000 to $99,999	5,523	31.5
$100,000 to $149,999	3,553	20.3
$150,000 to $199,999	2,271	13.0
$200,000 to $249,999	1,155	6.6
$250,000 to $299,999	719	4.1
$300,000 or more	1,653	9.4
Median value	$107,398	–
Purchase price		
Home purchased or built	16,529	94.4
Under $50,000	9,929	56.7
$50,000 to $99,999	2,776	15.9
$100,000 to $149,999	1,128	6.4
$150,000 to $199,999	574	3.3
$200,000 to $249,999	237	1.4
$250,000 to $299,999	133	0.8
$300,000 or more	210	1.2
Received as inheritance or gift	799	4.6
Median purchase price	$29,471	–
Major source of down payment		
Sale of previous home	6,083	36.8
Savings or cash on hand	7,292	44.1
Sale of other investment	139	0.8
Borrowing, other than mortgage on this property	617	3.7
Inheritance or gift	258	1.6
Land where built used for financing	114	0.7
Other	515	3.1
No down payment	1,123	6.8

Note: Numbers may not add to total because not reported is not shown; (–) means not applicable.
Source: Bureau of the Census, American Housing Survey for the United States in 2001, Internet site http://www.census.gov/hhes/ www/housing/ahs/ahs01/ahs01.html; calculations by New Strategist

Mobility Rate Is Low in Old Age

Behind the lower mobility of older Americans are high rates of homeownership and strong community ties.

While 14 percent of Americans aged 1 or older moved between March 2002 and March 2003, the proportion was a much smaller 5 percent among people aged 55 or older. Within the 55-or-older age group, mobility is slightly higher among those aged 55 to 64—rising to nearly 7 percent among those aged 55 to 59—because of retirement migration and downsizing as the nest empties. Movers aged 55 or older are more likely than younger movers to head to a different state, however. Twenty-seven percent of movers aged 55 or older went to a different state compared with a much smaller 18 percent of movers under age 55.

Not surprisingly, people aged 65 or older are more likely than younger movers to say they moved because of retirement—although only 2 percent cite this as their primary reason for moving. They are also most likely to say they moved for a change in climate (2 percent). A substantial share say they moved for health reasons, including 23 percent of those aged 75 or older. Regardless of age, however, the largest share of people move for housing-related reasons.

■ Americans are moving less than they once did. Several factors are behind the lower mobility rate, including the aging of the population, the rise in homeownership, and the proliferation of dual-income couples.

Older movers are more likely than younger ones to head to a different state

(percent of movers who moved to a different state between March 2002 and March 2003, by age)

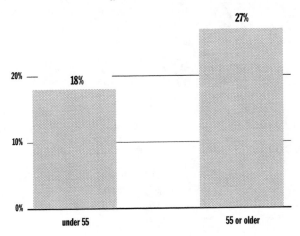

Table 3.21 Geographical Mobility by Age, 2002 to 2003

(total number and percent distribution of people aged 1 or older by mobility status between March 2002 and March 2003, by selected age groups; numbers in thousands)

	total	nonmovers	total movers	same county	different county, same state	different state, same division	different division, same region	different region	abroad
Total, aged 1 or older	282,556	242,463	40,093	23,468	7,728	3,752	1,181	2,695	1,269
Under age 55	220,923	183,956	36,968	21,929	7,060	3,291	1,074	2,420	1,194
Aged 55 or older	61,633	58,507	3,125	1,539	668	461	107	275	75
Aged 55 to 59	15,470	14,417	1,052	551	183	165	50	86	17
Aged 60 to 61	5,093	4,761	332	161	68	68	4	20	11
Aged 62 to 64	6,836	6,466	369	155	96	61	8	32	17
Aged 65 or older	34,234	32,863	1,372	672	321	167	45	137	30
Aged 65 to 69	9,438	9,012	426	226	83	52	11	43	11
Aged 70 to 74	8,673	8,325	348	149	91	45	6	44	13
Aged 75 to 79	7,482	7,205	278	135	65	38	16	21	3
Aged 80 to 84	5,094	4,899	195	79	56	26	7	24	3
Aged 85 or older	3,547	3,422	125	83	26	6	5	5	–

PERCENT DISTRIBUTION BY AGE

	total	nonmovers	total movers	same county	different county, same state	different state, same division	different division, same region	different region	abroad
Total, aged 1 or older	100.0%	100.0%	100.0%	100.0%	100.0%	100.0%	100.0%	100.0%	100.0%
Under age 55	78.2	75.9	92.2	93.4	91.4	87.7	90.9	89.8	94.1
Aged 55 or older	21.8	24.1	7.8	6.6	8.6	12.3	9.1	10.2	5.9
Aged 55 to 59	5.5	5.9	2.6	2.3	2.4	4.4	4.2	3.2	1.3
Aged 60 to 61	1.8	2.0	0.8	0.7	0.9	1.8	0.3	0.7	0.9
Aged 62 to 64	2.4	2.7	0.9	0.7	1.2	1.6	0.7	1.2	1.3
Aged 65 or older	12.1	13.6	3.4	2.9	4.2	4.5	3.8	5.1	2.4
Aged 65 to 69	3.3	3.7	1.1	1.0	1.1	1.4	0.9	1.6	0.9
Aged 70 to 74	3.1	3.4	0.9	0.6	1.2	1.2	0.5	1.6	1.0
Aged 75 to 79	2.6	3.0	0.7	0.6	0.8	1.0	1.4	0.8	0.2
Aged 80 to 84	1.8	2.0	0.5	0.3	0.7	0.7	0.6	0.9	0.2
Aged 85 or older	1.3	1.4	0.3	0.4	0.3	0.2	0.4	0.2	–

PERCENT DISTRIBUTION BY MOBILITY STATUS

	total	nonmovers	total movers	same county	different county, same state	different state, same division	different division, same region	different region	abroad
Total, aged 1 or older	100.0%	85.8%	14.2%	8.3%	2.7%	1.3%	0.4%	1.0%	0.4%
Under age 55	100.0	83.3	16.7	9.9	3.2	1.5	0.5	1.1	0.5
Aged 55 or older	100.0	94.9	5.1	2.5	1.1	0.7	0.2	0.4	0.1
Aged 55 to 59	100.0	93.2	6.8	3.6	1.2	1.1	0.3	0.6	0.1
Aged 60 to 61	100.0	93.5	6.5	3.2	1.3	1.3	0.1	0.4	0.2
Aged 62 to 64	100.0	94.6	5.4	2.3	1.4	0.9	0.1	0.5	0.2
Aged 65 or older	100.0	96.0	4.0	2.0	0.9	0.5	0.1	0.4	0.1
Aged 65 to 69	100.0	95.5	4.5	2.4	0.9	0.6	0.1	0.5	0.1
Aged 70 to 74	100.0	96.0	4.0	1.7	1.1	0.5	0.1	0.5	0.1
Aged 75 to 79	100.0	96.3	3.7	1.8	0.9	0.5	0.2	0.3	0.0
Aged 80 to 84	100.0	96.2	3.8	1.6	1.1	0.5	0.1	0.5	0.1
Aged 85 or older	100.0	96.5	3.5	2.3	0.7	0.2	0.1	0.1	–

	total	nonmovers	total movers	same county	different county, same state	different state, same division	different division, same region	different region	abroad
PERCENT DISTRIBUTION OF MOVERS BY TYPE OF MOVE									
Total, aged 1 or older	–	–	**100.0%**	**58.5%**	**19.3%**	**9.4%**	**2.9%**	**6.7%**	**3.2%**
Under age 55	–	–	100.0	59.3	19.1	8.9	2.9	6.5	3.2
Aged 55 or older	–	–	100.0	49.2	21.4	14.8	3.4	8.8	2.4
Aged 55 to 59	–	–	100.0	52.4	17.4	15.7	4.8	8.2	1.6
Aged 60 to 61	–	–	100.0	48.5	20.5	20.5	1.2	6.0	3.3
Aged 62 to 64	–	–	100.0	42.0	26.0	16.5	2.2	8.7	4.6
Aged 65 or older	–	–	100.0	49.0	23.4	12.2	3.3	10.0	2.2
Aged 65 to 69	–	–	100.0	53.1	19.5	12.2	2.6	10.1	2.6
Aged 70 to 74	–	–	100.0	42.8	26.1	12.9	1.7	12.6	3.7
Aged 75 to 79	–	–	100.0	48.6	23.4	13.7	5.8	7.6	1.1
Aged 80 to 84	–	–	100.0	40.5	28.7	13.3	3.6	12.3	1.5
Aged 85 or older	–	–	100.0	66.4	20.8	4.8	4.0	4.0	–

Note: (–) means not applicable or sample is too small to make a reliable estimate.
Source: Bureau of the Census, Geographical Mobility: March 2002 to March 2003, Detailed Tables for P20-549, *2003 Current Population Survey, Internet site http://www.census.gov/population/www/socdemo/migrate/p20-549.html; calculations by New Strategist*

Table 3.22 Reason for Moving by Age, 2002 to 2003

(number and percent distribution of movers between March 2003 and March 2003 by primary reason for move and age; numbers in thousands)

	total	under 45	45–64	aged 65 or older total	65–74	75+
TOTAL MOVERS	**40,093**	**33,520**	**5,203**	**1,371**	**774**	**597**
Family reasons	**10,548**	**8,997**	**1,151**	**401**	**211**	**190**
Change in marital status	2,679	2,256	358	65	47	18
To establish own household	2,814	2,558	224	33	22	11
Other family reason	5,055	4,183	569	303	142	161
Job reasons	**6,247**	**5,319**	**859**	**69**	**49**	**20**
New job or job transfer	3,546	3,063	460	23	17	6
To look for work or lost job	749	648	102	–	–	–
To be closer to work/easier commute	1,275	1,110	158	5	1	4
Retired	101	25	45	32	24	8
Other job-related reason	576	473	94	9	7	2
Housing reasons	**20,578**	**17,107**	**2,830**	**636**	**419**	**217**
Wanted own home, not rent	4,078	3,495	532	50	36	14
Wanted new or better home/apartment	7,942	6,727	1,034	181	127	54
Wanted better neighborhood/ less crime	1,530	1,291	199	39	26	13
Wanted cheaper housing	2,622	2,147	358	116	68	48
Other housing reason	4,406	3,447	707	250	162	88
Other reasons	**2,722**	**2,096**	**364**	**261**	**93**	**168**
To attend or leave college	1,010	985	21	3	–	3
Change of climate	160	87	46	26	12	14
Health reasons	565	244	124	197	61	136
Other reasons	987	780	173	35	20	15

PERCENT DISTRIBUTION BY REASON	total	under 45	45–64	aged 65 or older		
				total	65–74	75+
TOTAL MOVERS	100.0%	100.0%	100.0%	100.0%	100.0%	100.0%
Family reasons	26.3	26.8	22.1	29.2	27.3	31.8
Change in marital status	6.7	6.7	6.9	4.7	6.1	3.0
To establish own household	7.0	7.6	4.3	2.4	2.8	1.8
Other family reason	12.6	12.5	10.9	22.1	18.3	27.0
Job reasons	15.6	15.9	16.5	5.0	6.3	3.4
New job or job transfer	8.8	9.1	8.8	1.7	2.2	0.1
To look for work or lost job	1.9	1.9	2.0	–	–	–
To be closer to work/easier commute	3.2	3.3	3.0	0.4	0.1	0.7
Retired	0.3	0.1	0.9	2.3	3.1	1.3
Other job-related reason	1.4	1.4	1.8	0.7	0.9	0.3
Housing reasons	51.3	51.0	54.4	46.4	54.1	36.3
Wanted own home, not rent	10.2	10.4	10.2	3.6	4.7	2.3
Wanted new or better home/apartment	19.8	20.1	19.9	13.2	16.4	9.1
Wanted better neighborhood/less crime	3.8	3.9	3.8	2.8	3.4	2.2
Wanted cheaper housing	6.5	6.4	6.9	8.5	8.8	8.0
Other housing reason	11.0	10.3	13.6	18.2	20.9	14.7
Other reasons	6.8	6.3	7.0	19.0	12.0	28.1
To attend or leave college	2.5	2.9	0.4	0.2	–	0.5
Change of climate	0.4	0.3	0.9	1.9	1.6	2.3
Health reasons	1.4	0.7	2.4	14.4	7.9	22.8
Other reasons	2.5	2.3	3.3	2.6	2.6	2.5

| | total | under 45 | 45–64 | aged 65 or older | | |
				total	65–74	75+
PERCENT DISTRIBUTION BY AGE						
TOTAL MOVERS	**100.0%**	**83.6%**	**13.0%**	**3.4%**	**1.9%**	**1.5%**
Family reasons	**100.0**	**85.3**	**10.9**	**3.8**	**2.0**	**1.8**
Change in marital status	100.0	84.2	13.4	2.4	1.8	0.7
To establish own household	100.0	90.9	8.0	1.2	0.8	0.4
Other family reason	100.0	82.7	11.3	6.0	2.8	3.2
Job reasons	**100.0**	**85.1**	**13.8**	**1.1**	**0.8**	**0.3**
New job or job transfer	100.0	86.4	13.0	0.6	0.5	0.2
To look for work or lost job	100.0	86.5	13.6	–	–	–
To be closer to work/easier commute	100.0	87.1	12.4	0.4	0.1	0.3
Retired	100.0	24.8	44.6	31.7	23.8	7.9
Other job-related reason	100.0	82.1	16.3	1.6	1.2	0.3
Housing reasons	**100.0**	**83.1**	**13.8**	**3.1**	**2.0**	**1.1**
Wanted own home, not rent	100.0	85.7	13.1	1.2	0.9	0.3
Wanted new or better home/apartment	100.0	84.7	13.0	2.3	1.6	0.7
Wanted better neighborhood/ less crime	100.0	84.4	13.0	2.5	1.7	0.8
Wanted cheaper housing	100.0	81.9	13.7	4.4	2.6	1.8
Other housing reason	100.0	78.2	16.1	5.7	3.7	2.0
Other reasons	**100.0**	**77.0**	**13.4**	**9.6**	**3.4**	**6.2**
To attend or leave college	100.0	97.5	2.1	0.3	–	0.3
Change of climate	100.0	54.4	28.7	16.2	7.5	8.8
Health reasons	100.0	43.2	21.9	34.9	10.8	24.1
Other reasons	100.0	79.0	17.5	3.5	2.0	1.5

Note: (–) means number is less than 500 or sample is too small to make a reliable estimate.
Source: Bureau of the Census, Geographical Mobility: March 2002 to March 2003, Detailed Tables for P20-549, 2003 Current Population Survey, Internet site http://www.census.gov/population/www/socdemo/migrate/p20-549.html; calculations by New Strategist

4

Income

■ Householders aged 55 to 64 saw their median income climb just 0.8 percent between 2000 and 2002. Although slight, this increase was better than the 4 percent decline in the median income of householders aged 65 or older.

■ Household income falls as people age and retire from the labor force. Median household income in 2002 stood at $28,173 for householders aged 65 to 74 and $19,300 for those aged 75 or older.

■ The most affluent older householders are couples aged 55 to 59 because most are still in the labor force. Their median income was a lofty $71,015 in 2002, and nearly 30 percent had incomes of $100,000 or more.

■ Between 2000 and 2002, the median income of men aged 65 or older fell 4.1 percent, after adjusting for inflation. The median income of women in the age group fell 0.9 percent.

■ Among Americans aged 65 or older, from 88 to 95 percent received Social Security income in 2002, making it the most common source of income for the age group.

■ The poverty rate is below average for older Americans. Ten percent of people aged 55 or older are poor compared with 12 percent of all Americans.

Incomes of Older Householders Have Fallen Since 2000

But the median income of householders aged 65 or older is still above its 1990 level.

Householders aged 55 to 64 saw their median income climb just 0.8 percent between 2000 and 2002. Although slight, this increase was better than the decline in median income for householders aged 65 or older. Between 2000 and 2002, householders aged 65 to 74 saw their median income fall 4 percent, after adjusting for inflation, while those aged 75 or older experienced a 2 percent drop. Despite these declines, the median income of householders aged 65 or older was 4 percent greater in 2002 than in 1990, after adjusting for inflation— $23,152 versus $22,488.

Falling interest rates are one factor behind the recent income decline among older householders. Householders aged 55 to 64 bucked this trend as fewer opted for early retirement, choosing to stay in the labor force as their savings evaporated in the stock market decline.

■ Most Boomers will have to postpone retirement, further boosting the incomes of householders aged 55 to 64 as they fill the age group.

Householders aged 55 to 64 have made gains

(percent change in median income of total households and households headed by people aged 55 or older, by age, 2000–02; in 2002 dollars)

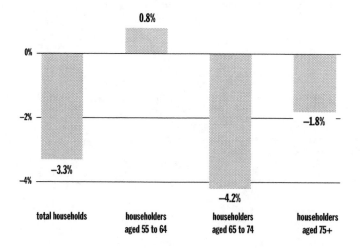

Table 4.1 Median Income of Households Headed by People Aged 55 or Older, 1980 to 2002

(median income of total households and households headed by people aged 55 or older, 1980 to 2002; in 2002 dollars)

	total households	55 to 64	householders aged 65 or older		
			total	65 to 74	75 to 84
2002	$42,409	$47,203	$23,152	$28,173	$19,300
2001	42,899	46,593	23,486	28,620	19,479
2000	43,848	46,838	24,104	29,397	19,647
1999	44,044	48,125	24,616	29,464	20,677
1998	42,844	47,561	23,941	28,770	19,705
1997	41,346	46,208	23,197	28,259	19,083
1996	40,503	45,436	22,193	26,716	18,253
1995	39,931	44,619	22,377	26,988	17,977
1994	38,725	42,288	21,719	25,712	17,681
1993	38,287	41,024	21,755	26,117	17,560
1992	38,482	42,699	21,524	25,589	17,108
1991	38,790	42,882	21,857	25,833	17,940
1990	39,949	43,181	22,488	27,073	17,545
1989	40,484	43,163	22,088	26,553	16,948
1988	39,766	42,218	21,797	25,523	17,245
1987	39,453	41,722	21,865	25,921	17,089
1986	38,975	41,916	21,673	–	–
1985	37,648	40,739	21,128	–	–
1984	36,921	39,687	21,082	–	–
1983	35,774	39,016	20,071	–	–
1982	35,986	39,383	19,697	–	–
1981	36,042	39,759	18,713	–	–
1980	36,608	40,405	18,151	–	–
Percent change					
2000–2002	–3.3%	0.8%	–4.0%	–4.2%	–1.8%
1990–2002	6.2	9.3	3.0	4.1	1.0
1980–2002	15.8	16.8	27.6	–	–

Note: (–) means data are not available.
Source: Bureau of the Census, data from the Current Population Survey Annual Demographic Supplements, Internet site http://www.census.gov/hhes/income/histinc/h10.html; calculations by New Strategist

Many Older Householders Have High Incomes

Nearly 4 million have incomes of $100,000 or more.

Household income falls as people age, retire from the labor force, and live on savings, pensions, and Social Security benefits. While the $47,203 median income of householders aged 55 to 64 exceeds that of the average household, the median income of householders aged 65 or older is below average. Median income stood at $28,173 for householders aged 65 to 74 in 2002, and at $19,300 for those aged 75 or older.

Many older householders are affluent, however. Twenty-one percent of householders aged 55 to 59 have annual incomes of $100,000 or more, as do 5 percent of those aged 65 or older. Among the nation's 12 million householders with incomes of $100,000 or more, 25 percent are aged 55 or older.

■ If Boomers postpone retirement—as seems likely—the household incomes of the 55-to-64 age group should grow substantially as working Boomers fill the age group.

Incomes decline with age

(median income of households by age of householder, 2002)

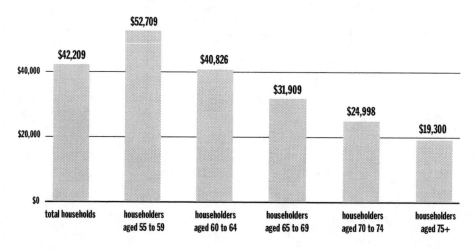

Table 4.2 Income of Households Headed by People Aged 55 or Older, 2002: Total Households

(number and percent distribution of total households and households headed by people aged 55 or older, by income, 2002; households in thousands as of 2003)

		aged 55 or older								
							aged 65 or older			
			aged 55 to 64					aged 65 to 74		
	total	total	total	55–59	60–64	total	total	65–69	70–74	75+
Total households	**111,278**	**38,919**	**16,260**	**9,192**	**7,069**	**22,659**	**11,360**	**5,845**	**5,516**	**11,299**
Under $10,000	10,090	4,855	1,482	736	745	3,373	1,380	626	752	1,993
$10,000–$19,999	15,063	8,352	1,887	909	978	6,465	2,616	1,168	1,449	3,849
$20,000–$29,999	14,362	5,983	1,844	948	895	4,139	2,014	942	1,072	2,127
$30,000–$39,999	12,795	4,457	1,765	908	857	2,692	1,450	800	650	1,244
$40,000–$49,999	10,743	3,227	1,516	864	653	1,711	1,051	608	442	660
$50,000–$59,999	9,226	2,486	1,363	784	579	1,123	705	397	309	418
$60,000–$69,999	7,633	1,964	1,150	670	479	814	564	332	233	250
$70,000–$79,999	6,695	1,562	975	591	384	587	406	216	190	180
$80,000–$89,999	5,039	1,120	778	479	299	342	210	134	77	131
$90,000–$99,999	3,952	921	626	389	238	295	199	134	65	97
$100,000 or more	15,676	3,991	2,875	1,914	961	1,116	766	489	277	349
Median income	$42,409	$33,200	$47,203	$52,709	$40,826	$23,152	$28,173	$31,909	$24,998	$19,300
Total households	**100.0%**	**100.0%**	**100.0%**	**100.0%**	**100.0%**	**100.0%**	**100.0%**	**100.0%**	**100.0%**	**100.0%**
Under $10,000	9.1	12.5	9.1	8.0	10.5	14.9	12.1	10.7	13.6	17.6
$10,000–$19,999	13.5	21.5	11.6	9.9	13.8	28.5	23.0	20.0	26.3	34.1
$20,000–$29,999	12.9	15.4	11.3	10.3	12.7	18.3	17.7	16.1	19.4	18.8
$30,000–$39,999	11.5	11.5	10.9	9.9	12.1	11.9	12.8	13.7	11.8	11.0
$40,000–$49,999	9.7	8.3	9.3	9.4	9.2	7.6	9.3	10.4	8.0	5.8
$50,000–$59,999	8.3	6.4	8.4	8.5	8.2	5.0	6.2	6.8	5.6	3.7
$60,000–$69,999	6.9	5.1	7.1	7.3	6.8	3.6	5.0	5.7	4.2	2.2
$70,000–$79,999	6.0	4.0	6.0	6.4	5.4	2.6	3.6	3.7	3.4	1.6
$80,000–$89,999	4.5	2.9	4.8	5.2	4.2	1.5	1.8	2.3	1.4	1.2
$90,000–$99,999	3.6	2.4	3.8	4.2	3.4	1.3	1.8	2.3	1.2	0.9
$100,000 or more	14.1	10.3	17.7	20.8	13.6	4.9	6.7	8.4	5.0	3.1

Source: Bureau of the Census, data from the 2003 Current Population Survey Annual Social and Economic Supplement, Internet site http://ferret.bls.census.gov/macro/032003/hhinc/new02_000.htm; calculations by New Strategist

Non-Hispanic Whites Have Higher Incomes than Blacks or Hispanics

Among older Americans, Asians have the highest incomes, however.

Non-Hispanic white householders aged 55 to 64 had a median income of $51,088 in 2002, much greater than the $35,020 median for Hispanics and $31,818 median for blacks in the age group. Asian householders aged 55 to 64 had a median income of $60,356, surpassing that of non-Hispanic whites. Twenty-five percent of Asian and 19 percent of non-Hispanic white householders aged 55 to 64 had an income of $100,000 or more in 2002. This compares with only 9 percent of blacks and 10 percent of Hispanics.

Income disparities are not as great for householders aged 65 or older. The median income of Asian householders aged 65 or older was $25,206 in 2002 versus a slightly lower $24,154 for non-Hispanic whites. Among their Hispanic counterparts, median household income was $18,164, while the black median stood at $16,385. Black householders aged 75 or older have the lowest incomes, just $14,094 in 2002.

The incomes of Asian and non-Hispanic white households are higher than those of black households because married couples (many with two incomes) head a much larger share. Asian and non-Hispanic white household incomes exceed those of Hispanics because many Hispanics have little education or earning power.

■ The income disparities among older householders by race and Hispanic origin will persist because the underlying factors—the scarcity of married couples among blacks and the poor education of Hispanics—persist among younger generations of Americans.

Older blacks have the lowest incomes

(median income of households headed by people aged 65 or older, by race and Hispanic origin, 2002)

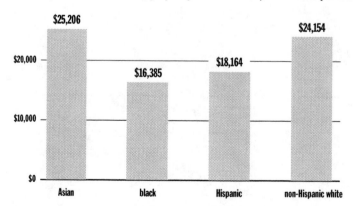

Table 4.3 Income of Households Headed by People Aged 55 or Older, 2002: Asian Households

(number and percent distribution of total Asian households and Asian households headed by people aged 55 or older, by income, 2002; households in thousands as of 2003)

			aged 55 or older							
							aged 65 or older			
			aged 55 to 64					aged 65 to 74		
	total	total	total	55–59	60–64	total	total	65–69	70–74	75+
Total Asian households	**4,079**	**929**	**482**	**284**	**197**	**447**	**279**	**154**	**125**	**168**
Under $10,000	329	103	26	18	9	77	39	16	24	39
$10,000–$19,999	379	154	45	29	17	109	60	32	29	48
$20,000–$29,999	407	101	43	25	20	58	33	15	18	27
$30,000–$39,999	436	90	43	21	22	47	24	14	10	22
$40,000–$49,999	359	54	37	22	15	17	11	7	3	4
$50,000–$59,999	355	61	45	23	21	16	7	4	2	9
$60,000–$69,999	270	73	49	23	25	24	20	10	10	4
$70,000–$79,999	261	63	36	28	9	27	17	14	3	9
$80,000–$89,999	228	25	15	12	3	10	8	8	–	–
$90,000–$99,999	166	29	23	15	7	6	6	5	–	–
$100,000 or more	889	179	120	71	49	59	54	30	23	5
Median income	$52,285	$43,443	$60,356	$63,587	$58,681	$25,206	$31,681	$40,981	$24,085	$19,300
Total Asian households	**100.0%**	**100.0%**	**100.0%**	**100.0%**	**100.0%**	**100.0%**	**100.0%**	**100.0%**	**100.0%**	**100.0%**
Under $10,000	8.1	11.1	5.4	6.3	4.6	17.2	14.0	10.4	19.2	23.2
$10,000–$19,999	9.3	16.6	9.3	10.2	8.6	24.4	21.5	20.8	23.2	28.6
$20,000–$29,999	10.0	10.9	8.9	8.8	10.2	13.0	11.8	9.7	14.4	16.1
$30,000–$39,999	10.7	9.7	8.9	7.4	11.2	10.5	8.6	9.1	8.0	13.1
$40,000–$49,999	8.8	5.8	7.7	7.7	7.6	3.8	3.9	4.5	2.4	2.4
$50,000–$59,999	8.7	6.6	9.3	8.1	10.7	3.6	2.5	2.6	1.6	5.4
$60,000–$69,999	6.6	7.9	10.2	8.1	12.7	5.4	7.2	6.5	8.0	2.4
$70,000–$79,999	6.4	6.8	7.5	9.9	4.6	6.0	6.1	9.1	2.4	5.4
$80,000–$89,999	5.6	2.7	3.1	4.2	1.5	2.2	2.9	5.2	–	–
$90,000–$99,999	4.1	3.1	4.8	5.3	3.6	1.3	2.2	3.2	–	–
$100,000 or more	21.8	19.3	24.9	25.0	24.9	13.2	19.4	19.5	18.4	3.0

Note: Asian householders include those who identified themselves as Asian alone and those who identified themselves as Asian in combination with one or more other races. (–) means number is less than 500 or sample is too small to make a reliable estimate.
Source: Bureau of the Census, data from the 2003 Current Population Survey Annual Social and Economic Supplement, Internet site http://ferret.bls.census.gov/macro/032003/hhinc/new02_000.htm; calculations by New Strategist

Table 4.4 Income of Households Headed by People Aged 55 or Older, 2002: Black Households

(number and percent distribution of total black households and black households headed by people aged 55 or older, by income, 2002; households in thousands as of 2003)

	total	aged 55 or older								
		total	aged 55 to 64			aged 65 or older		aged 65 to 74		
			total	55–59	60–64	total	total	65–69	70–74	75+
Total black households	**13,778**	**3,867**	**1,794**	**1,022**	**772**	**2,073**	**1,187**	**639**	**548**	**886**
Under $10,000	2,432	884	290	158	133	594	307	149	158	287
$10,000–$19,999	2,486	954	336	169	166	618	322	178	144	297
$20,000–$29,999	2,111	547	250	142	106	297	161	77	84	137
$30,000–$39,999	1,809	417	212	117	96	205	135	73	62	69
$40,000–$49,999	1,190	276	166	95	71	110	82	49	31	29
$50,000–$59,999	918	203	116	75	42	87	57	35	22	31
$60,000–$69,999	698	145	96	61	36	49	40	26	15	8
$70,000–$79,999	566	103	72	42	31	31	23	9	14	8
$80,000–$89,999	384	72	50	36	16	22	18	9	9	4
$90,000–$99,999	280	53	39	25	14	14	9	8	1	5
$100,000 or more	904	211	167	105	62	44	33	24	8	12
Median income	$29,177	$23,249	$31,181	$34,091	$26,703	$16,385	$18,616	$19,405	$17,809	$14,094
Total black households	**100.0%**	**100.0%**	**100.0%**	**100.0%**	**100.0%**	**100.0%**	**100.0%**	**100.0%**	**100.0%**	**100.0%**
Under $10,000	17.7	22.9	16.2	15.5	17.2	28.7	25.9	23.3	28.8	32.4
$10,000–$19,999	18.0	24.7	18.7	16.5	21.5	29.8	27.1	27.9	26.3	33.5
$20,000–$29,999	15.3	14.1	13.9	13.9	13.7	14.3	13.6	12.1	15.3	15.5
$30,000–$39,999	13.1	10.8	11.8	11.4	12.4	9.9	11.4	11.4	11.3	7.8
$40,000–$49,999	8.6	7.1	9.3	9.3	9.2	5.3	6.9	7.7	5.7	3.3
$50,000–$59,999	6.7	5.2	6.5	7.3	5.4	4.2	4.8	5.5	4.0	3.5
$60,000–$69,999	5.1	3.7	5.4	6.0	4.7	2.4	3.4	4.1	2.7	0.9
$70,000–$79,999	4.1	2.7	4.0	4.1	4.0	1.5	1.9	1.4	2.6	0.9
$80,000–$89,999	2.8	1.9	2.8	3.5	2.1	1.1	1.5	1.4	1.6	0.5
$90,000–$99,999	2.0	1.4	2.2	2.4	1.8	0.7	0.8	1.3	0.2	0.6
$100,000 or more	6.6	5.5	9.3	10.3	8.0	2.1	2.8	3.8	1.5	1.4

Note: Black householders include those who identified themselves as black alone and those who identified themselves as black in combination with one or more other races.
Source: Bureau of the Census, data from the 2003 Current Population Survey Annual Social and Economic Supplement, Internet site http://ferret.bls.census.gov/macro/032003/hhinc/new02_000.htm; calculations by New Strategist

Table 4.5 Income of Households Headed by People Aged 55 or Older, 2002: Hispanic Households

(number and percent distribution of total Hispanic households and Hispanic households headed by people aged 55 or older, by income, 2002; households in thousands as of 2003)

		aged 55 or older								
						aged 65 or older				
			aged 55 to 64				aged 65 to 74			
	total	total	total	55–59	60–64	total	total	65–69	70–74	75+
Total Hispanic households	11,339	2,269	1,150	654	496	1,119	692	399	294	427
Under $10,000	1,247	433	149	67	80	284	154	86	69	129
$10,000–$19,999	1,879	515	189	98	91	326	188	91	98	137
$20,000–$29,999	1,949	319	155	96	58	164	97	55	42	66
$30,000–$39,999	1,574	277	159	88	70	118	75	50	25	43
$40,000–$49,999	1,109	181	114	61	54	67	58	40	17	9
$50,000–$59,999	945	118	74	37	38	44	34	24	9	11
$60,000–$69,999	693	113	74	48	27	39	30	14	15	8
$70,000–$79,999	505	62	41	29	13	21	15	11	4	4
$80,000–$89,999	372	71	56	32	24	15	10	6	4	6
$90,000–$99,999	249	30	22	19	4	8	6	6	–	2
$100,000 or more	815	153	117	80	37	36	25	18	7	11
Median income	$33,103	$26,707	$35,020	$37,193	$32,535	$18,164	$20,243	$24,393	$18,092	$14,388
Total Hispanic households	100.0%	100.0%	100.0%	100.0%	100.0%	100.0%	100.0%	100.0%	100.0%	100.0%
Under $10,000	11.0	19.1	13.0	10.2	16.1	25.4	22.3	21.6	23.5	30.2
$10,000–$19,999	16.6	22.7	16.4	15.0	18.3	29.1	27.2	22.8	33.3	32.1
$20,000–$29,999	17.2	14.1	13.5	14.7	11.7	14.7	14.0	13.8	14.3	15.5
$30,000–$39,999	13.9	12.2	13.8	13.5	14.1	10.5	10.8	12.5	8.5	10.1
$40,000–$49,999	9.8	8.0	9.9	9.3	10.9	6.0	8.4	10.0	5.8	2.1
$50,000–$59,999	8.3	5.2	6.4	5.7	7.7	3.9	4.9	6.0	3.1	2.6
$60,000–$69,999	6.1	5.0	6.4	7.3	5.4	3.5	4.3	3.5	5.1	1.9
$70,000–$79,999	4.5	2.7	3.6	4.4	2.6	1.9	2.2	2.8	1.4	0.9
$80,000–$89,999	3.3	3.1	4.9	4.9	4.8	1.3	1.4	1.5	1.4	1.4
$90,000–$99,999	2.2	1.3	1.9	2.9	0.8	0.7	0.9	1.5	–	0.5
$100,000 or more	7.2	6.7	10.2	12.2	7.5	3.2	3.6	4.5	2.4	2.6

Note: Hispanics may be of any race. (–) means number is less than 500 or sample is too small to make a reliable estimate.
Source: Bureau of the Census, data from the 2003 Current Population Survey Annual Social and Economic Supplement, Internet site http://ferret.bls.census.gov/macro/032003/hhinc/new02_000.htm; calculations by New Strategist

Table 4.6 Income of Households Headed by People Aged 55 or Older, 2002: Non-Hispanic White Households

(number and percent distribution of total non-Hispanic white households and non-Hispanic white households headed by people aged 55 or older, by income, 2002; households in thousands as of 2003)

		aged 55 or older								
							aged 65 or older			
			aged 55 to 64					aged 65 to 74		
	total	total	total	55–59	60–64	total	total	65–69	70–74	75+
Total non-Hispanic white households	81,166	31,512	12,668	7,130	5,538	18,844	9,097	4,576	4,521	9,747
Under $10,000	5,977	3,382	992	479	513	2,390	870	370	500	1,519
$10,000–$19,999	10,170	6,662	1,302	606	697	5,360	2,017	848	1,168	3,343
$20,000–$29,999	9,797	4,966	1,368	673	695	3,598	1,706	785	923	1,892
$30,000–$39,999	8,829	3,629	1,332	671	662	2,297	1,200	652	548	1,096
$40,000–$49,999	7,982	2,685	1,184	672	511	1,501	887	501	386	613
$50,000–$59,999	6,958	2,084	1,109	632	477	975	605	331	274	370
$60,000–$69,999	5,926	1,614	922	535	387	692	463	272	191	230
$70,000–$79,999	5,301	1,316	817	491	326	499	346	177	167	153
$80,000–$89,999	4,034	945	651	398	253	294	173	110	62	121
$90,000–$99,999	3,235	801	534	324	210	267	177	115	61	88
$100,000 or more	12,958	3,428	2,455	1,649	806	973	652	413	239	321
Median income	$46,900	$34,982	$51,088	$57,431	$43,936	$24,154	$29,701	$33,941	$26,152	$20,046
Total non-Hispanic white households	100.0%	100.0%	100.0%	100.0%	100.0%	100.0%	100.0%	100.0%	100.0%	100.0%
Under $10,000	7.4	10.7	7.8	6.7	9.3	12.7	9.6	8.1	11.1	15.6
$10,000–$19,999	12.5	21.1	10.3	8.5	12.6	28.4	22.2	18.5	25.8	34.3
$20,000–$29,999	12.1	15.8	10.8	9.4	12.5	19.1	18.8	17.2	20.4	19.4
$30,000–$39,999	10.9	11.5	10.5	9.4	12.0	12.2	13.2	14.2	12.1	11.2
$40,000–$49,999	9.8	8.5	9.3	9.4	9.2	8.0	9.8	10.9	8.5	6.3
$50,000–$59,999	8.6	6.6	8.8	8.9	8.6	5.2	6.7	7.2	6.1	3.8
$60,000–$69,999	7.3	5.1	7.3	7.5	7.0	3.7	5.1	5.9	4.2	2.4
$70,000–$79,999	6.5	4.2	6.4	6.9	5.9	2.6	3.8	3.9	3.7	1.6
$80,000–$89,999	5.0	3.0	5.1	5.6	4.6	1.6	1.9	2.4	1.4	1.2
$90,000–$99,999	4.0	2.5	4.2	4.5	3.8	1.4	1.9	2.5	1.3	0.9
$100,000 or more	16.0	10.9	19.4	23.1	14.6	5.2	7.2	9.0	5.3	3.3

Note: Non-Hispanic white householders include only those who identified themselves as white alone and non-Hispanic.
Source: Bureau of the Census, data from the 2003 Current Population Survey Annual Social and Economic Supplement, Internet site http://ferret.bls.census.gov/macro/032003/hhinc/new02_000.htm; calculations by New Strategist

Many Older Couples Are Comfortably Well Off

Older men and women who live alone have much lower incomes.

Among householders aged 55 to 64, the median income of married couples stood at $63,881 in 2002—more than $16,000 greater than the median income of the average household in the age group. For couples aged 65 or older, median household income was $34,159, well above the $23,152 average. The most affluent older householders are couples aged 55 to 59 because most are still in the labor force. Their median income was $71,015 in 2002. Nearly 30 percent had incomes of $100,000 or more.

The median income of male-headed families surpasses that of married couples in the 65-or-older age groups. Behind the higher incomes of male-headed families is the likely presence of an additional earner in the household—such as a grown son or daughter in the labor force.

Women who live alone have the lowest income. Among householders aged 75 or older, women who live alone had a median income of just $13,010 in 2002, well below the $19,300 median for all households in the age group.

■ The household income of older Americans should rise in the years ahead as Boomers enter the age group and postpone retirement.

Women who live alone have the lowest income

(median income of householders aged 65 or older, by household type, 2002)

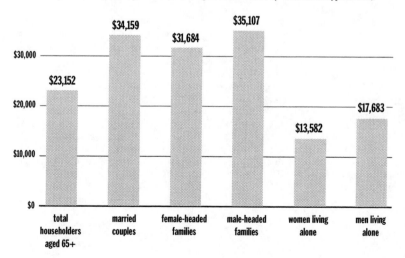

Table 4.7 Income of Households by Household Type, 2002: Aged 55 to 64

(number and percent distribution of households headed by people aged 55 to 64, by income and household type, 2002; households in thousands as of 2003)

| | | family households | | | nonfamily households | | | |
| | | | | | female householder | | male householder | |
	total	married couples	female hh, no spouse present	male hh, no spouse present	total	living alone	total	living alone
Total householders								
aged 55 to 64	**16,260**	**9,543**	**1,305**	**413**	**2,976**	**2,741**	**2,023**	**1,764**
Under $10,000	1,482	335	115	30	630	622	372	358
$10,000 to $19,999	1,887	564	228	44	628	607	423	395
$20,000 to $29,999	1,844	754	195	50	540	510	304	267
$30,000 to $39,999	1,765	936	196	57	361	320	214	182
$40,000 to $49,999	1,516	893	143	48	257	228	174	147
$50,000 to $59,999	1,363	887	137	39	170	154	133	110
$60,000 to $69,999	1,150	887	82	28	85	70	67	54
$70,000 to $79,999	975	745	43	27	89	78	70	55
$80,000 to $89,999	778	600	49	16	48	39	66	57
$90,000 to $99,999	626	514	28	9	22	19	54	40
$100,000 or more	2,875	2,427	92	65	143	91	148	101
Median income	$47,203	$63,881	$35,273	$45,201	$23,423	$21,996	$27,555	$25,182
Total householders								
aged 55 to 64	**100.0%**	**100.0%**	**100.0%**	**100.0%**	**100.0%**	**100.0%**	**100.0%**	**100.0%**
Under $10,000	9.1	3.5	8.8	7.3	21.2	22.7	18.4	20.3
$10,000 to $19,999	11.6	5.9	17.5	10.7	21.1	22.1	20.9	22.4
$20,000 to $29,999	11.3	7.9	14.9	12.1	18.1	18.6	15.0	15.1
$30,000 to $39,999	10.9	9.8	15.0	13.8	12.1	11.7	10.6	10.3
$40,000 to $49,999	9.3	9.4	11.0	11.6	8.6	8.3	8.6	8.3
$50,000 to $59,999	8.4	9.3	10.5	9.4	5.7	5.6	6.6	6.2
$60,000 to $69,999	7.1	9.3	6.3	6.8	2.9	2.6	3.3	3.1
$70,000 to $79,999	6.0	7.8	3.3	6.5	3.0	2.8	3.5	3.1
$80,000 to $89,999	4.8	6.3	3.8	3.9	1.6	1.4	3.3	3.2
$90,000 to $99,999	3.8	5.4	2.1	2.2	0.7	0.7	2.7	2.3
$100,000 or more	17.7	25.4	7.1	15.7	4.8	3.3	7.3	5.7

Source: Bureau of the Census, data from the 2003 Current Population Survey Annual Social and Economic Supplement, Internet site http://ferret.bls.census.gov/macro/032003/hhinc/new02_000.htm; calculations by New Strategist

Table 4.8 Income of Households by Household Type, 2002: Aged 55 to 59

(number and percent distribution of households headed by people aged 55 to 59, by income and household type, 2002; households in thousands as of 2003)

| | | family households | | | nonfamily households | | | |
| | | | | | female householder | | male householder | |
	total	married couples	female hh, no spouse present	male hh, no spouse present	total	living alone	total	living alone
Total householders aged 55 to 59	**9,192**	**5,513**	**753**	**245**	**1,552**	**1,406**	**1,128**	**980**
Under $10,000	736	150	60	18	283	280	223	216
$10,000 to $19,999	909	250	148	27	272	257	211	197
$20,000 to $29,999	948	346	106	21	283	269	189	167
$30,000 to $39,999	908	464	106	31	205	181	102	92
$40,000 to $49,999	864	485	88	38	155	138	99	84
$50,000 to $59,999	784	504	76	31	107	93	67	56
$60,000 to $69,999	670	510	52	16	47	39	45	35
$70,000 to $79,999	591	436	22	19	67	57	47	40
$80,000 to $89,999	479	391	23	11	27	21	29	21
$90,000 to $99,999	389	326	23	5	11	11	24	13
$100,000 or more	1,914	1,649	50	29	97	58	89	60
Median income	$52,709	$71,015	$36,017	$46,386	$26,931	$25,730	$27,557	$24,674
Total householders aged 55 to 59	**100.0%**	**100.0%**	**100.0%**	**100.0%**	**100.0%**	**100.0%**	**100.0%**	**100.0%**
Under $10,000	8.0	2.7	8.0	7.3	18.2	19.9	19.8	22.0
$10,000 to $19,999	9.9	4.5	19.7	11.0	17.5	18.3	18.7	20.1
$20,000 to $29,999	10.3	6.3	14.1	8.6	18.2	19.1	16.8	17.0
$30,000 to $39,999	9.9	8.4	14.1	12.7	13.2	12.9	9.0	9.4
$40,000 to $49,999	9.4	8.8	11.7	15.5	10.0	9.8	8.8	8.6
$50,000 to $59,999	8.5	9.1	10.1	12.7	6.9	6.6	5.9	5.7
$60,000 to $69,999	7.3	9.3	6.9	6.5	3.0	2.8	4.0	3.6
$70,000 to $79,999	6.4	7.9	2.9	7.8	4.3	4.1	4.2	4.1
$80,000 to $89,999	5.2	7.1	3.1	4.5	1.7	1.5	2.6	2.1
$90,000 to $99,999	4.2	5.9	3.1	2.0	0.7	0.8	2.1	1.3
$100,000 or more	20.8	29.9	6.6	11.8	6.2	4.1	7.9	6.1

Source: Bureau of the Census, data from the 2003 Current Population Survey Annual Social and Economic Supplement, Internet site http://ferret.bls.census.gov/macro/032003/hhinc/new02_000.htm; calculations by New Strategist

Table 4.9 Income of Households by Household Type, 2002: Aged 60 to 64

(number and percent distribution of households headed by people aged 60 to 64, by income and household type, 2002; households in thousands as of 2003)

| | | family households | | | nonfamily households | | | |
| | | | | | female householder | | male householder | |
	total	married couples	female hh, no spouse present	male hh, no spouse present	total	living alone	total	living alone
Total householders								
aged 60 to 64	**7,069**	**4,030**	**552**	**168**	**1,423**	**1,334**	**895**	**784**
Under $10,000	745	184	55	12	347	341	147	141
$10,000 to $19,999	978	313	81	17	356	349	212	198
$20,000 to $29,999	895	408	88	29	257	243	115	100
$30,000 to $39,999	857	472	91	26	157	141	111	89
$40,000 to $49,999	653	408	54	10	104	90	75	63
$50,000 to $59,999	579	382	60	7	62	60	66	54
$60,000 to $69,999	479	377	29	12	37	31	23	18
$70,000 to $79,999	384	309	21	8	25	22	22	16
$80,000 to $89,999	299	209	27	6	21	19	37	36
$90,000 to $99,999	238	187	5	4	12	9	29	26
$100,000 or more	961	778	41	36	46	33	59	41
Median income	$40,826	$55,393	$34,471	$43,159	$20,246	$18,993	$27,549	$25,712
Total householders								
aged 60 to 64	**100.0%**	**100.0%**	**100.0%**	**100.0%**	**100.0%**	**100.0%**	**100.0%**	**100.0%**
Under $10,000	10.5	4.6	10.0	7.1	24.4	25.6	16.4	18.0
$10,000 to $19,999	13.8	7.8	14.7	10.1	25.0	26.2	23.7	25.3
$20,000 to $29,999	12.7	10.1	15.9	17.3	18.1	18.2	12.8	12.8
$30,000 to $39,999	12.1	11.7	16.5	15.5	11.0	10.6	12.4	11.4
$40,000 to $49,999	9.2	10.1	9.8	6.0	7.3	6.7	8.4	8.0
$50,000 to $59,999	8.2	9.5	10.9	4.2	4.4	4.5	7.4	6.9
$60,000 to $69,999	6.8	9.4	5.3	7.1	2.6	2.3	2.6	2.3
$70,000 to $79,999	5.4	7.7	3.8	4.8	1.8	1.6	2.5	2.0
$80,000 to $89,999	4.2	5.2	4.9	3.6	1.5	1.4	4.1	4.6
$90,000 to $99,999	3.4	4.6	0.9	2.4	0.8	0.7	3.2	3.3
$100,000 or more	13.6	19.3	7.4	21.4	3.2	2.5	6.6	5.2

Source: Bureau of the Census, data from the 2003 Current Population Survey Annual Social and Economic Supplement, Internet site http://ferret.bls.census.gov/macro/032003/hhinc/new02_000.htm; calculations by New Strategist

Table 4.10 Income of Households by Household Type, 2002: Aged 65 or Older

(number and percent distribution of households headed by people aged 65 or older, by income and household type, 2002; households in thousands as of 2003)

| | | family households | | | nonfamily households | | | |
| | | | | | female householder | | male householder | |
	total	married couples	female hh, no spouse present	male hh, no spouse present	total	living alone	total	living alone
Total householders aged 65 or older	**22,659**	**9,564**	**1,743**	**434**	**8,020**	**7,824**	**2,898**	**2,725**
Under $10,000	3,373	340	152	34	2,278	2,268	567	561
$10,000 to $19,999	6,465	1,602	366	74	3,440	3,410	981	955
$20,000 to $29,999	4,139	2,054	286	85	1,165	1,120	550	518
$30,000 to $39,999	2,692	1,601	295	49	497	459	250	234
$40,000 to $49,999	1,711	1,047	226	59	238	218	140	123
$50,000 to $59,999	1,123	735	139	34	108	94	108	89
$60,000 to $69,999	814	508	93	35	97	89	81	66
$70,000 to $79,999	587	430	44	25	36	25	50	46
$80,000 to $89,999	342	253	25	15	24	22	25	12
$90,000 to $99,999	295	206	32	8	26	26	23	15
$100,000 or more	1,116	787	81	19	108	93	121	107
Median income	$23,152	$34,159	$31,684	$35,107	$13,773	$13,582	$18,597	$17,683
Total householders aged 65 or older	**100.0%**	**100.0%**	**100.0%**	**100.0%**	**100.0%**	**100.0%**	**100.0%**	**100.0%**
Under $10,000	14.9	3.6	8.7	7.8	28.4	29.0	19.6	20.6
$10,000 to $19,999	28.5	16.8	21.0	17.1	42.9	43.6	33.9	35.1
$20,000 to $29,999	18.3	21.5	16.4	19.6	14.5	14.3	19.0	19.0
$30,000 to $39,999	11.9	16.7	16.9	11.3	6.2	5.9	8.6	8.6
$40,000 to $49,999	7.6	10.9	13.0	13.6	3.0	2.8	4.8	4.5
$50,000 to $59,999	5.0	7.7	8.0	7.8	1.3	1.2	3.7	3.3
$60,000 to $69,999	3.6	5.3	5.3	8.1	1.2	1.1	2.8	2.4
$70,000 to $79,999	2.6	4.5	2.5	5.8	0.4	0.3	1.7	1.7
$80,000 to $89,999	1.5	2.6	1.4	3.5	0.3	0.3	0.9	0.4
$90,000 to $99,999	1.3	2.2	1.8	1.8	0.3	0.3	0.8	0.6
$100,000 or more	4.9	8.2	4.6	4.4	1.3	1.2	4.2	3.9

Source: Bureau of the Census, data from the 2003 Current Population Survey Annual Social and Economic Supplement, Internet site http://ferret.bls.census.gov/macro/032003/hhinc/new02_000.htm; calculations by New Strategist

Table 4.11 Income of Households by Household Type, 2002: Aged 65 to 74

(number and percent distribution of households headed by people aged 65 to 74, by income and household type, 2002; households in thousands as of 2003)

| | | family households | | | nonfamily households | | | |
| | | | | | female householder | | male householder | |
	total	married couples	female hh, no spouse present	male hh, no spouse present	total	living alone	total	living alone
Total householders								
aged 65 to 74	**11,360**	**5,865**	**845**	**199**	**3,040**	**2,911**	**1,412**	**1,291**
Under $10,000	1,380	194	78	17	783	775	307	307
$10,000 to $19,999	2,616	861	166	28	1,132	1,115	430	410
$20,000 to $29,999	2,014	1,087	152	41	519	493	215	198
$30,000 to $39,999	1,450	951	123	22	235	209	119	108
$40,000 to $49,999	1,051	688	119	20	143	124	80	66
$50,000 to $59,999	705	484	71	14	69	61	67	52
$60,000 to $69,999	564	380	49	21	62	55	53	43
$70,000 to $79,999	406	311	25	13	25	15	32	26
$80,000 to $89,999	210	166	12	10	8	8	14	6
$90,000 to $99,999	199	148	19	2	14	14	15	6
$100,000 or more	766	594	31	12	50	40	79	70
Median income	$28,173	$38,031	$31,635	$36,895	$15,598	$15,083	$19,039	$17,517
Total householders								
aged 65 to 74	**100.0%**	**100.0%**	**100.0%**	**100.0%**	**100.0%**	**100.0%**	**100.0%**	**100.0%**
Under $10,000	12.1	3.3	9.2	8.5	25.8	26.6	21.7	23.8
$10,000 to $19,999	23.0	14.7	19.6	14.1	37.2	38.3	30.5	31.8
$20,000 to $29,999	17.7	18.5	18.0	20.6	17.1	16.9	15.2	15.3
$30,000 to $39,999	12.8	16.2	14.6	11.1	7.7	7.2	8.4	8.4
$40,000 to $49,999	9.3	11.7	14.1	10.1	4.7	4.3	5.7	5.1
$50,000 to $59,999	6.2	8.3	8.4	7.0	2.3	2.1	4.7	4.0
$60,000 to $69,999	5.0	6.5	5.8	10.6	2.0	1.9	3.8	3.3
$70,000 to $79,999	3.6	5.3	3.0	6.5	0.8	0.5	2.3	2.0
$80,000 to $89,999	1.8	2.8	1.4	5.0	0.3	0.3	1.0	0.5
$90,000 to $99,999	1.8	2.5	2.2	1.0	0.5	0.5	1.1	0.5
$100,000 or more	6.7	10.1	3.7	6.0	1.6	1.4	5.6	5.4

Source: Bureau of the Census, data from the 2003 Current Population Survey Annual Social and Economic Supplement, Internet site http://ferret.bls.census.gov/macro/032003/hhinc/new02_000.htm; calculations by New Strategist

Table 4.12 Income of Households by Household Type, 2002: Aged 65 to 69

(number and percent distribution of households headed by people aged 65 to 69, by income and household type, 2002; households in thousands as of 2003)

| | total | family households | | | nonfamily households | | | |
| | | | | | female householder | | male householder | |
		married couples	female hh, no spouse present	male hh, no spouse present	total	living alone	total	living alone
Total householders aged 65 to 69	**5,845**	**3,205**	**445**	**103**	**1,426**	**1,359**	**666**	**601**
Under $10,000	626	97	43	12	356	349	117	117
$10,000 to $19,999	1,168	421	80	18	464	455	186	176
$20,000 to $29,999	942	489	88	16	240	226	110	101
$30,000 to $39,999	800	536	58	13	128	123	65	62
$40,000 to $49,999	608	389	66	2	98	89	54	47
$50,000 to $59,999	397	263	47	7	47	38	34	25
$60,000 to $69,999	332	241	15	17	32	29	27	20
$70,000 to $79,999	216	168	9	7	13	11	18	13
$80,000 to $89,999	134	112	9	4	5	5	5	3
$90,000 to $99,999	134	103	12	2	7	7	10	5
$100,000 or more	489	390	14	7	37	28	41	33
Median income	$31,909	$41,492	$31,262	$34,762	$16,540	$16,051	$22,661	$20,800
Total householders aged 65 to 69	**100.0%**	**100.0%**	**100.0%**	**100.0%**	**100.0%**	**100.0%**	**100.0%**	**100.0%**
Under $10,000	10.7	3.0	9.7	11.7	25.0	25.7	17.6	19.5
$10,000 to $19,999	20.0	13.1	18.0	17.5	32.5	33.5	27.9	29.3
$20,000 to $29,999	16.1	15.3	19.8	15.5	16.8	16.6	16.5	16.8
$30,000 to $39,999	13.7	16.7	13.0	12.6	9.0	9.1	9.8	10.3
$40,000 to $49,999	10.4	12.1	14.8	1.9	6.9	6.5	8.1	7.8
$50,000 to $59,999	6.8	8.2	10.6	6.8	3.3	2.8	5.1	4.2
$60,000 to $69,999	5.7	7.5	3.4	16.5	2.2	2.1	4.1	3.3
$70,000 to $79,999	3.7	5.2	2.0	6.8	0.9	0.8	2.7	2.2
$80,000 to $89,999	2.3	3.5	2.0	3.9	0.4	0.4	0.8	0.5
$90,000 to $99,999	2.3	3.2	2.7	1.9	0.5	0.5	1.5	0.8
$100,000 or more	8.4	12.2	3.1	6.8	2.6	2.1	6.2	5.5

Source: Bureau of the Census, data from the 2003 Current Population Survey Annual Social and Economic Supplement, Internet site http://ferret.bls.census.gov/macro/032003/hhinc/new02_000.htm; calculations by New Strategist

Table 4.13 Income of Households by Household Type, 2002: Aged 70 to 74

(number and percent distribution of households headed by people aged 70 to 74, by income and household type, 2002; households in thousands as of 2003)

| | | family households | | | nonfamily households | | | |
| | | | | | female householder | | male householder | |
	total	married couples	female hh, no spouse present	male hh, no spouse present	total	living alone	total	living alone
Total householders								
aged 70 to 74	**5,516**	**2,660**	**400**	**95**	**1,614**	**1,551**	**746**	**689**
Under $10,000	752	97	35	6	428	428	190	190
$10,000 to $19,999	1,449	441	86	9	669	661	243	233
$20,000 to $29,999	1,072	597	63	26	280	268	105	96
$30,000 to $39,999	650	415	64	9	106	86	56	47
$40,000 to $49,999	442	299	53	18	45	35	25	19
$50,000 to $59,999	309	221	22	7	23	23	34	27
$60,000 to $69,999	233	139	33	3	29	25	28	22
$70,000 to $79,999	190	143	16	5	12	5	14	14
$80,000 to $89,999	77	56	4	6	2	2	9	3
$90,000 to $99,999	65	46	6	–	7	7	5	1
$100,000 or more	277	205	17	4	13	12	38	37
Median income	$24,998	$34,084	$32,008	$38,854	$14,967	$14,474	$17,112	$16,107
Total householders								
aged 70 to 74	**100.0%**	**100.0%**	**100.0%**	**100.0%**	**100.0%**	**100.0%**	**100.0%**	**100.0%**
Under $10,000	13.6	3.6	8.8	6.3	26.5	27.6	25.5	27.6
$10,000 to $19,999	26.3	16.6	21.5	9.5	41.4	42.6	32.6	33.8
$20,000 to $29,999	19.4	22.4	15.8	27.4	17.3	17.3	14.1	13.9
$30,000 to $39,999	11.8	15.6	16.0	9.5	6.6	5.5	7.5	6.8
$40,000 to $49,999	8.0	11.2	13.2	18.9	2.8	2.3	3.4	2.8
$50,000 to $59,999	5.6	8.3	5.5	7.4	1.4	1.5	4.6	3.9
$60,000 to $69,999	4.2	5.2	8.2	3.2	1.8	1.6	3.8	3.2
$70,000 to $79,999	3.4	5.4	4.0	5.3	0.7	0.3	1.9	2.0
$80,000 to $89,999	1.4	2.1	1.0	6.3	0.1	0.1	1.2	0.4
$90,000 to $99,999	1.2	1.7	1.5	–	0.4	0.5	0.7	0.1
$100,000 or more	5.0	7.7	4.2	4.2	0.8	0.8	5.1	5.4

Note: (–) means number is less than 500 or sample is too small to make a reliable estimate.
Source: Bureau of the Census, data from the 2003 Current Population Survey Annual Social and Economic Supplement, Internet site http://ferret.bls.census.gov/macro/032003/hhinc/new02_000.htm; calculations by New Strategist

Table 4.14 Income of Households by Household Type, 2002: Aged 75 or Older

(number and percent distribution of households headed by people aged 75 or older, by income and household type, 2002; households in thousands as of 2003)

| | total | family households | | | nonfamily households | | | |
| | | | | | female householder | | male householder | |
		married couples	female hh, no spouse present	male hh, no spouse present	total	living alone	total	living alone
Total householders aged 75 or older	**11,299**	**3,700**	**898**	**235**	**4,980**	**4,914**	**1,486**	**1,434**
Under $10,000	1,993	146	76	16	1,497	1,493	261	255
$10,000 to $19,999	3,849	742	201	47	2,308	2,294	552	546
$20,000 to $29,999	2,127	967	134	44	647	626	334	320
$30,000 to $39,999	1,244	651	173	27	262	250	131	126
$40,000 to $49,999	660	359	108	38	95	94	60	56
$50,000 to $59,999	418	252	69	19	39	35	41	37
$60,000 to $69,999	250	128	43	15	36	34	28	24
$70,000 to $79,999	180	118	18	13	12	10	18	18
$80,000 to $89,999	131	88	12	4	16	14	11	6
$90,000 to $99,999	97	59	12	5	12	12	9	9
$100,000 or more	349	192	50	7	57	53	42	37
Median income	$19,300	$29,950	$31,720	$34,548	$13,082	$13,010	$18,229	$17,810
Total householders aged 75 or older	**100.0%**	**100.0%**	**100.0%**	**100.0%**	**100.0%**	**100.0%**	**100.0%**	**100.0%**
Under $10,000	17.6	3.9	8.5	6.8	30.1	30.4	17.6	17.8
$10,000 to $19,999	34.1	20.1	22.4	20.0	46.3	46.7	37.1	38.1
$20,000 to $29,999	18.8	26.1	14.9	18.7	13.0	12.7	22.5	22.3
$30,000 to $39,999	11.0	17.6	19.3	11.5	5.3	5.1	8.8	8.8
$40,000 to $49,999	5.8	9.7	12.0	16.2	1.9	1.9	4.0	3.9
$50,000 to $59,999	3.7	6.8	7.7	8.1	0.8	0.7	2.8	2.6
$60,000 to $69,999	2.2	3.5	4.8	6.4	0.7	0.7	1.9	1.7
$70,000 to $79,999	1.6	3.2	2.0	5.5	0.2	0.2	1.2	1.3
$80,000 to $89,999	1.2	2.4	1.3	1.7	0.3	0.3	0.7	0.4
$90,000 to $99,999	0.9	1.6	1.3	2.1	0.2	0.2	0.6	0.6
$100,000 or more	3.1	5.2	5.6	3.0	1.1	1.1	2.8	2.6

Source: Bureau of the Census, data from the 2003 Current Population Survey Annual Social and Economic Supplement, Internet site http://ferret.bls.census.gov/macro/032003/hhinc/new02_000.htm; calculations by New Strategist

Older Americans Have Lost Ground

Only those aged 55 to 64 have seen their incomes grow since 2000.

Between 2000 and 2002, the median income of men aged 65 or older fell 4.1 percent, after adjusting for inflation. The median income of women in the age group fell 0.9 percent. Behind the decline are falling interest rates, cutting the incomes of older Americans. In contrast to these declines, the incomes of men and women aged 55 to 64 rose between 2000 and 2002—up a strong 8.5 percent for women and 1.6 percent for men. This increase is likely a result of the rising labor force participation rate in the age group.

Despite the 2000–2002 income decline among men and women aged 65 or older, the 2002 median incomes of those in the age group are far higher than they were in 1980—up 28 percent for men and 31 percent for women. The median incomes of men and women in the 55-to-64 age group are also well above their 1980 level. Behind the rising incomes of older Americans over the past two decades are the entry of a more affluent generation into the age group and the increasing labor force participation of women.

■ The median income of men and women aged 55 to 64 should continue to grow as labor force participation rates in the age group climb.

Incomes have grown since 2000 for 55-to-64-year-olds

(percent change in median income of people aged 55 or older, by sex, 2000–02; in 2002 dollars)

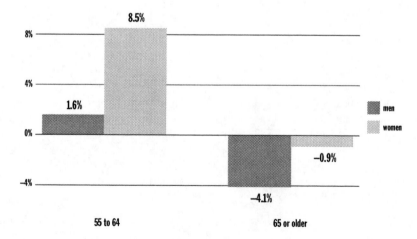

Table 4.15 Median Income of Men Aged 55 or Older, 1980 to 2002

(median income of men aged 15 or older and aged 55 or older, 1980 to 2002; percent change for selected years; in 2002 dollars)

| | total men | 55 to 64 | men aged 65 or older | | |
			total	65 to 74	75 or older
2002	$29,238	$36,277	$19,436	$21,291	$17,508
2001	29,564	36,204	20,001	22,040	17,800
2000	29,597	35,702	20,270	22,416	17,955
1999	29,433	36,309	20,588	22,991	18,106
1998	29,189	36,113	20,015	21,743	18,156
1997	28,170	34,812	19,853	21,957	17,214
1996	27,199	33,694	19,039	21,231	16,540
1995	26,439	33,959	19,316	21,500	16,593
1994	26,070	32,498	18,305	19,923	16,395
1993	25,862	30,809	18,362	19,959	16,450
1992	25,694	32,176	18,335	19,859	16,186
1991	26,357	32,782	18,486	19,745	16,787
1990	27,075	33,093	18,922	21,304	15,585
1989	27,861	34,210	18,356	20,259	15,192
1988	27,618	33,080	18,216	20,364	14,940
1987	26,925	33,128	18,056	20,304	14,682
1986	26,791	32,927	18,072	–	–
1985	26,000	32,290	17,375	–	–
1984	25,696	32,164	17,212	–	–
1983	25,061	32,020	16,687	–	–
1982	24,888	31,806	16,392	–	–
1981	25,459	32,813	15,378	–	–
1980	25,900	32,896	15,170	–	–
Percent change					
2000–2002	–1.2%	1.6%	–4.1%	–5.0%	–2.5%
1990–2002	8.0	9.6	2.7	–0.1	12.3
1980–2002	12.9	10.3	28.1	–	–

Note: (–) means data are not available.
Source: Bureau of the Census, data from the Current Population Survey Annual Demographic Supplements, Internet site http:// www.census.gov/hhes/income/histinc/p08.html; calculations by New Strategist

Table 4.16 Median Income of Women Aged 55 or Older, 1980 to 2002

(median income of women aged 15 or older and aged 55 or older, 1980 to 2002; percent change for selected years; in 2002 dollars)

	total women	55 to 64	women aged 65 or older total	65 to 74	75 or older
2002	$16,812	$19,165	$11,406	$11,279	$11,503
2001	16,878	18,106	11,493	11,379	11,577
2000	16,774	17,669	11,511	11,390	11,602
1999	16,523	17,176	11,809	11,831	11,793
1998	15,899	16,169	11,573	11,517	11,619
1997	15,311	16,062	11,242	11,330	11,169
1996	14,624	15,196	10,985	11,020	10,953
1995	14,215	14,508	10,963	10,871	11,047
1994	13,762	13,043	10,742	10,594	10,877
1993	13,537	13,272	10,416	10,597	10,251
1992	13,458	12,728	10,279	10,319	10,238
1991	13,489	12,750	10,544	10,475	10,611
1990	13,435	12,541	10,732	10,927	10,528
1989	13,479	12,833	10,721	11,131	10,332
1988	12,977	12,237	10,375	10,599	10,143
1987	12,558	11,416	10,439	10,576	10,291
1986	11,914	11,549	10,058	–	–
1985	11,504	11,434	10,064	–	–
1984	11,313	11,261	9,916	–	–
1983	10,823	10,498	9,590	–	–
1982	10,502	10,538	9,572	–	–
1981	10,313	10,157	8,892	–	–
1980	10,170	10,182	8,736	–	–
Percent change					
2000–2002	0.2%	8.5%	–0.9%	–1.0%	–0.8%
1990–2002	25.1	52.8	6.3	3.2	9.3
1980–2002	65.3	88.2	30.6	–	–

Note: (–) means data are not available.
Source: Bureau of the Census, data from the Current Population Survey Annual Demographic Supplements, Internet site http://www.census.gov/hhes/income/histinc/p08.html; calculations by New Strategist

Among Workers, Older Men Command High Salaries

Income peaks among working men aged 55 or older.

Among men who work full-time, those with the highest incomes are aged 55 or older. Men aged 70 to 74 who work full-time had a median income of $54,071 in 2002—the highest among men of any age—but only 9 percent are full-time workers. Among the 64 percent of men aged 55 to 59 who work full-time, median income is a substantial $49,885.

Incomes drop with age not because workers get paid less, but because fewer people work. The proportion of full-time workers drops from the 64 majority of men aged 55 to 59 to a 45 percent minority of men aged 60 to 64. Only 10 percent of men aged 65 or older work full-time.

Among men aged 55 or older, non-Hispanic whites have the highest incomes, a median of $27,946 in 2002. Asian men aged 55 or older have a far lower median, just $20,606. The median income of Asian men is higher than that of blacks or Hispanics, however. The median income of black men aged 55 or older stood at $18,680, while that of Hispanics was just $15,197.

■ Older men with high earnings may be more likely to stay on the job than those who earn less, driving up the median income of older men who work full-time.

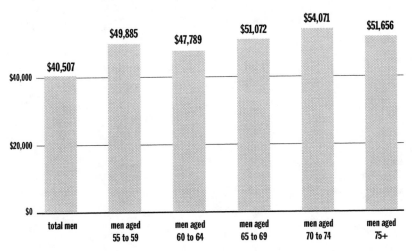

Incomes are high among older men who work full-time

(median income of men who work full-time by age, 2002)

Category	Median Income
total men	$40,507
men aged 55 to 59	$49,885
men aged 60 to 64	$47,789
men aged 65 to 69	$51,072
men aged 70 to 74	$54,071
men aged 75+	$51,656

Table 4.17 Income of Men Aged 55 or Older, 2002: Total Men

(number and percent distribution of men aged 16 or older and aged 55 or older by income, 2002; median income by work status, and percent working year-round, full-time; men in thousands as of 2003)

		aged 55 or older								
							aged 65 or older			
			aged 55 to 64					aged 65 to 74		
	total	total	total	55–59	60–64	total	total	65–69	70–74	75+
TOTAL MEN	108,814	27,694	13,166	7,493	5,673	14,528	8,275	4,317	3,957	6,253
Without income	9,026	671	416	208	208	255	133	87	45	122
With income	99,788	27,023	12,750	7,285	5,465	14,273	8,142	4,230	3,912	6,131
Under $10,000	16,061	3,789	1,412	719	693	2,377	1,257	535	723	1,119
$10,000–$19,999	18,536	7,011	2,036	1,013	1,025	4,975	2,591	1,211	1,379	2,385
$20,000–$29,999	16,206	4,506	1,773	959	814	2,733	1,470	755	715	1,262
$30,000–$39,999	13,528	3,160	1,714	987	728	1,446	919	540	378	528
$40,000–$49,999	9,485	2,131	1,307	786	521	824	548	356	191	277
$50,000–$59,999	7,048	1,664	1,111	658	454	553	399	212	186	156
$60,000–$69,999	4,735	1,080	694	424	270	386	272	155	117	113
$70,000–$79,999	3,769	894	660	461	199	234	152	109	43	82
$80,000–$89,999	2,355	611	464	312	154	147	96	62	34	51
$90,000–$99,999	1,512	376	268	164	104	108	73	51	24	35
$100,000 or more	6,556	1,798	1,308	801	507	490	366	247	120	124
Median income of men with income	$29,238	$25,712	$36,277	$39,538	$32,053	$19,436	$21,291	$24,272	$18,803	$17,508
Median income of full-time workers	40,507	50,985	49,223	49,885	47,789	52,032	52,064	51,072	54,071	51,656
Percent working full-time	54.0%	27.0%	55.8%	64.2%	44.8%	9.9%	14.4%	19.2%	9.2%	3.9%
TOTAL MEN	100.0%	100.0%	100.0%	100.0%	100.0%	100.0%	100.0%	100.0%	100.0%	100.0%
Without income	8.3	2.4	3.2	2.8	3.7	1.8	1.6	2.0	1.1	2.0
With income	91.7	97.6	96.8	97.2	96.3	98.2	98.4	98.0	98.9	98.1
Under $10,000	14.8	13.7	10.7	9.6	12.2	16.4	15.2	12.4	18.3	17.9
$10,000–$19,999	17.0	25.3	15.5	13.5	18.1	34.2	31.3	28.1	34.8	38.1
$20,000–$29,999	14.9	16.3	13.5	12.8	14.3	18.8	17.8	17.5	18.1	20.2
$30,000–$39,999	12.4	11.4	13.0	13.2	12.8	10.0	11.1	12.5	9.6	8.4
$40,000–$49,999	8.7	7.7	9.9	10.5	9.2	5.7	6.6	8.2	4.8	4.4
$50,000–$59,999	6.5	6.0	8.4	8.8	8.0	3.8	4.8	4.9	4.7	2.5
$60,000–$69,999	4.4	3.9	5.3	5.7	4.8	2.7	3.3	3.6	3.0	1.8
$70,000–$79,999	3.5	3.2	5.0	6.2	3.5	1.6	1.8	2.5	1.1	1.3
$80,000–$89,999	2.2	2.2	3.5	4.2	2.7	1.0	1.2	1.4	0.9	0.8
$90,000–$99,999	1.4	1.4	2.0	2.2	1.8	0.7	0.9	1.2	0.6	0.6
$100,000 or more	6.0	6.5	9.9	10.7	8.9	3.4	4.4	5.7	3.0	2.0

Source: Bureau of the Census, data from the 2003 Current Population Survey Annual Social and Economic Supplement, Internet site http://ferret.bls.census.gov/macro/032003/perinc/toc.htm; calculations by New Strategist

Table 4.18 Income of Men Aged 55 or Older, 2002: Asian Men

(number and percent distribution of Asian men aged 16 or older and aged 55 or older by income, 2002; median income by work status, and percent working year-round, full-time; men in thousands as of 2003)

		aged 55 or older								
						aged 65 or older				
			aged 55 to 64				aged 65 to 74			
	total	total	total	55–59	60–64	total	total	65–69	70–74	75+
TOTAL ASIAN MEN	4,688	896	452	253	199	444	290	138	153	153
Without income	549	68	27	11	16	41	21	7	15	19
With income	4,139	828	425	242	183	403	269	131	138	134
Under $10,000	708	187	61	28	33	126	74	23	51	53
$10,000–$19,999	701	192	69	41	27	123	86	35	50	36
$20,000–$29,999	589	122	73	40	33	49	27	15	13	22
$30,000–$39,999	536	86	54	29	26	32	26	20	5	6
$40,000–$49,999	371	60	37	24	14	23	12	11	1	10
$50,000–$59,999	235	24	15	5	10	9	8	5	3	1
$60,000–$69,999	206	26	17	12	5	9	8	5	3	–
$70,000–$79,999	199	35	24	21	4	11	8	6	2	2
$80,000–$89,999	141	13	11	7	4	2	2	–	2	–
$90,000–$99,999	95	15	10	9	1	5	4	2	2	–
$100,000 or more	360	68	52	24	29	16	14	8	6	2
Median income of men with income	$30,839	$20,606	$31,514	$33,386	$29,847	$15,325	$16,432	$24,597	$12,600	$13,132
Median income of full-time workers	42,448	–	41,062	40,476	42,833	–	–	–	–	–
Percent working full-time	56.2%	29.4%	62.2%	67.6%	55.3%	13.5%	19.0%	28.3%	10.5%	3.3%
TOTAL ASIAN MEN	100.0%	100.0%	100.0%	100.0%	100.0%	100.0%	100.0%	100.0%	100.0%	100.0%
Without income	11.7	7.6	6.0	4.3	8.0	9.2	7.2	5.1	9.8	12.4
With income	88.3	92.4	94.0	95.7	92.0	90.8	92.8	94.9	90.2	87.6
Under $10,000	15.1	20.9	13.5	11.1	16.6	28.4	25.5	16.7	33.3	34.6
$10,000–$19,999	15.0	21.4	15.3	16.2	13.6	27.7	29.7	25.4	32.7	23.5
$20,000–$29,999	12.6	13.6	16.2	15.8	16.6	11.0	9.3	10.9	8.5	14.4
$30,000–$39,999	11.4	9.6	11.9	11.5	13.1	7.2	9.0	14.5	3.3	3.9
$40,000–$49,999	7.9	6.7	8.2	9.5	7.0	5.2	4.1	8.0	0.7	6.5
$50,000–$59,999	5.0	2.7	3.3	2.0	5.0	2.0	2.8	3.6	2.0	0.7
$60,000–$69,999	4.4	2.9	3.8	4.7	2.5	2.0	2.8	3.6	2.0	–
$70,000–$79,999	4.2	3.9	5.3	8.3	2.0	2.5	2.8	4.3	1.3	1.3
$80,000–$89,999	0.3	1.5	2.4	2.8	2.0	0.5	0.7	–	1.3	–
$90,000–$99,999	2.0	1.7	2.2	3.6	0.5	1.1	1.4	1.4	1.3	–
$100,000 or more	7.7	7.6	11.5	9.5	14.6	3.6	4.8	5.8	3.9	1.3

Note: Asians include those who identified themselves as Asian alone and those who identified themselves as Asian in combination with one or more other races. (–) means number is less than 500 or sample is too small to make a reliable estimate.
Source: Bureau of the Census, data from the 2003 Current Population Survey Annual Social and Economic Supplement, Internet site http://ferret.bls.census.gov/macro/032003/perinc/toc.htm; calculations by New Strategist

Table 4.19 Income of Men Aged 55 or Older, 2002: Black Men

(number and percent distribution of black men aged 16 or older and aged 55 or older by income, 2002; median income by work status, and percent working year-round, full-time; men in thousands as of 2003)

						aged 55 or older				
							aged 65 or older			
			aged 55 to 64					aged 65 to 74		
	total	total	total	55–59	60–64	total	total	65–69	70–74	75+
TOTAL BLACK MEN	**12,188**	**2,312**	**1,172**	**659**	**513**	**1,140**	**717**	**387**	**330**	**423**
Without income	**2,092**	**140**	**94**	**48**	**46**	**46**	**22**	**15**	**7**	**23**
With income	**10,096**	**2,172**	**1,078**	**611**	**467**	**1,094**	**695**	**372**	**323**	**400**
Under $10,000	2,416	542	214	111	104	328	195	89	106	133
$10,000–$19,999	2,254	645	238	123	116	407	247	138	109	161
$20,000–$29,999	1,813	343	164	104	60	179	114	53	63	66
$30,000–$39,999	1,373	223	148	90	58	75	58	34	22	17
$40,000–$49,999	829	147	108	55	52	39	30	23	7	9
$50,000–$59,999	527	100	74	36	38	26	18	12	7	8
$60,000–$69,999	264	35	22	16	5	13	13	7	6	–
$70,000–$79,999	214	41	35	29	5	6	5	3	2	1
$80,000–$89,999	115	20	17	15	2	3	2	1	1	–
$90,000–$99,999	70	13	12	6	6	1	1	1	–	–
$100,000 or more	221	59	44	26	18	15	11	10	1	4
Median income of men with income	$21,509	$18,680	$25,604	$26,869	$21,901	$14,162	$15,151	$15,346	$14,956	$12,867
Median income of full-time workers	31,966	35,339	38,495	37,370	40,748	33,279	33,207	–	–	–
Percent working full-time	45.2%	23.2%	43.5%	50.5%	34.5%	9.9%	13.1%	16.8%	8.8%	4.5%
TOTAL BLACK MEN	**100.0%**	**100.0%**	**100.0%**	**100.0%**	**100.0%**	**100.0%**	**100.0%**	**100.0%**	**100.0%**	**100.0%**
Without income	**17.2**	**6.1**	**8.0**	**7.3**	**9.0**	**4.0**	**3.1**	**3.9**	**2.1**	**5.4**
With income	**82.8**	**93.9**	**92.0**	**92.7**	**91.0**	**96.0**	**96.9**	**96.1**	**97.9**	**94.6**
Under $10,000	19.8	23.4	18.3	16.8	20.3	28.8	27.2	23.0	32.1	31.4
$10,000–$19,999	18.5	27.9	20.3	18.7	22.6	35.7	34.4	35.7	33.0	38.1
$20,000–$29,999	14.9	14.8	14.0	15.8	11.7	15.7	15.9	13.7	19.1	15.6
$30,000–$39,999	11.3	9.6	12.6	13.7	11.3	6.6	8.1	8.8	6.7	4.0
$40,000–$49,999	6.8	6.4	9.2	8.3	10.1	3.4	4.2	5.9	2.1	2.1
$50,000–$59,999	4.3	4.3	6.3	5.5	7.4	2.3	2.5	3.1	2.1	1.9
$60,000–$69,999	2.2	1.5	1.9	2.4	1.0	1.1	1.8	1.8	1.8	–
$70,000–$79,999	1.8	1.8	3.0	4.4	1.0	0.5	0.7	0.8	0.6	0.2
$80,000–$89,999	0.9	0.9	1.5	2.3	0.4	0.3	0.3	0.3	0.3	–
$90,000–$99,999	0.6	0.6	1.0	0.9	1.2	0.1	0.1	0.3	–	–
$100,000 or more	1.8	2.6	3.8	3.9	3.5	1.3	1.5	2.6	0.3	0.9

Note: Blacks include those who identified themselves as black alone and those who identified themselves as black in combination with one or more other races. (–) means number is less than 500 or sample is too small to make a reliable estimate.
Source: Bureau of the Census, data from the 2003 Current Population Survey Annual Social and Economic Supplement, Internet site http://ferret.bls.census.gov/macro/032003/perinc/toc.htm; calculations by New Strategist

Table 4.20 Income of Men Aged 55 or Older, 2002: Hispanic Men

(number and percent distribution of Hispanic men aged 16 or older and aged 55 or older by income, 2002; median income by work status, and percent working year-round, full-time; men in thousands as of 2003)

		aged 55 or older								
						aged 65 or older				
			aged 55 to 64					aged 65 to 74		
	total	total	total	55–59	60–64	total	total	65–69	70–74	75+
TOTAL HISPANIC MEN	**14,353**	**1,924**	**1,018**	**591**	**427**	**906**	**557**	**321**	**236**	**349**
Without income	**1,729**	**98**	**57**	**22**	**35**	**41**	**25**	**21**	**5**	**15**
With income	**12,624**	**1,826**	**961**	**569**	**392**	**865**	**532**	**300**	**231**	**334**
Under $10,000	2,395	552	183	99	83	369	196	94	102	172
$10,000–$19,999	3,629	515	236	138	97	279	178	97	82	102
$20,000–$29,999	2,715	275	170	98	74	105	69	42	28	35
$30,000–$39,999	1,526	155	117	73	43	38	31	22	10	7
$40,000–$49,999	869	106	75	50	24	31	25	20	6	5
$50,000–$59,999	566	80	63	40	22	17	13	9	4	4
$60,000–$69,999	304	39	32	20	13	7	7	7	1	–
$70,000–$79,999	201	39	36	22	14	3	3	3	–	–
$80,000–$89,999	104	–	15	8	8	–	–	–	–	–
$90,000–$99,999	63	9	4	2	1	5	5	5	–	–
$100,000 or more	251	43	31	19	12	12	5	5	–	7
Median income of men with income	$20,702	$15,197	$22,394	$23,831	$21,459	$11,628	$13,352	$15,737	$11,144	$9,791
Median income of full-time workers	26,137	31,034	30,730	31,119	29,108	31,185	29,653	–	–	–
Percent working full-time	57.0%	25.4%	57.2%	64.1%	47.3%	9.7%	13.6%	18.4%	6.8%	3.4%
TOTAL HISPANIC MEN	**100.0%**	**100.0%**	**100.0%**	**100.0%**	**100.0%**	**100.0%**	**100.0%**	**100.0%**	**100.0%**	**100.0%**
Without income	**12.1**	**5.1**	**5.6**	**3.7**	**8.2**	**4.5**	**4.5**	**6.5**	**2.1**	**4.3**
With income	**88.0**	**94.9**	**94.4**	**96.3**	**91.8**	**95.5**	**95.5**	**93.5**	**97.9**	**95.7**
Under $10,000	16.7	28.7	18.0	16.8	19.4	40.7	35.2	29.3	43.2	49.3
$10,000–$19,999	25.3	26.8	23.2	23.4	22.7	30.8	32.0	30.2	34.7	29.2
$20,000–$29,999	18.9	14.3	16.7	16.6	17.3	11.6	12.4	13.1	11.9	10.0
$30,000–$39,999	10.6	8.1	11.5	12.4	10.1	4.2	5.6	6.9	4.2	0.2
$40,000–$49,999	6.1	5.5	7.4	8.5	5.6	3.4	4.5	6.2	2.5	1.4
$50,000–$59,999	3.9	4.2	6.2	6.8	5.2	1.9	2.3	2.8	1.7	1.1
$60,000–$69,999	2.1	2.0	3.1	3.4	3.0	0.8	1.3	2.2	0.4	–
$70,000–$79,999	1.4	2.0	3.5	3.7	3.3	0.3	0.5	0.9	–	–
$80,000–$89,999	0.7	–	1.5	1.4	1.9	–	–	–	–	–
$90,000–$99,999	0.4	0.5	0.4	0.3	0.2	0.6	0.9	1.6	–	–
$100,000 or more	1.7	2.2	3.1	3.2	2.8	1.3	0.9	1.6	–	0.2

Note: Hispanics may be of any race; (–) means number is less than 500 or sample is too small to make a reliable estimate.
Source: Bureau of the Census, data from the 2003 Current Population Survey Annual Social and Economic Supplement, Internet site http://ferret.bls.census.gov/macro/032003/perinc/toc.htm; calculations by New Strategist

Table 4.21 Income of Men Aged 55 or Older, 2002: Non-Hispanic White Men

(number and percent distribution of non-Hispanic white men aged 16 or older and aged 55 or older by income, 2002; median income by work status, and percent working year-round, full-time; men in thousands as of 2003)

	total	aged 55 or older								
		total	aged 55 to 64			aged 65 or older				
			total	55–59	60–64	total	aged 65 to 74			75+
							total	65–69	70–74	
TOTAL NON-HISPANIC										
WHITE MEN	**76,722**	**22,318**	**10,402**	**5,909**	**4,493**	**11,916**	**6,621**	**3,418**	**3,203**	**5,294**
Without income	4,576	361	234	123	112	127	63	46	18	63
With income	72,146	21,957	10,168	5,786	4,381	11,789	6,558	3,372	3,185	5,231
Under $10,000	10,338	2,471	940	472	468	1,531	777	321	456	754
$10,000–$19,999	11,849	5,596	1,477	696	781	4,119	2,047	918	1,129	2,070
$20,000–$29,999	10,984	3,721	1,341	705	637	2,380	1,245	636	609	1,134
$30,000–$39,999	8,664	1,569	777	591	1,286	792	457	334	494	7
$40,000–$49,999	6,633	1,122	647	426	726	475	299	176	250	5
$50,000–$59,999	5,164	928	570	377	498	358	185	173	140	4
$60,000–$69,999	3,841	838	518	326	222	320	222	127	120	79
$70,000–$79,999	3,139	775	563	387	177	212	133	97	38	79
$80,000–$89,999	1,973	563	421	282	140	142	92	59	32	51
$90,000–$99,999	1,270	333	236	144	92	97	62	41	22	35
$100,000 or more	5,703	1,628	1,181	732	449	447	335	224	111	111
Median income of men with income	$32,034	$27,946	$39,608	$42,889	$34,836	$20,785	$23,064	$26,832	$20,106	$18,657
Median income of full-time workers	45,153	54,339	51,634	52,358	50,664	56,000	56,069	54,540	57,901	55,732
Percent working full-time	54.8%	27.7%	56.9%	65.7%	45.3%	9.8%	14.5%	19.3%	9.4%	3.9%
TOTAL NON-HISPANIC										
WHITE MEN	**100.0%**	**100.0%**	**100.0%**	**100.0%**	**100.0%**	**100.0%**	**100.0%**	**100.0%**	**100.0%**	**100.0%**
Without income	6.0	1.6	2.2	2.1	2.5	1.1	1.0	1.3	0.6	1.2
With income	94.0	98.4	97.8	97.9	97.5	98.9	99.1	98.7	99.4	98.8
Under $10,000	13.5	11.1	9.0	8.0	10.4	12.8	11.7	9.4	14.2	14.2
$10,000–$19,999	15.4	25.1	14.2	11.8	17.4	34.6	30.9	26.9	35.2	39.1
$20,000–$29,999	14.3	16.7	12.9	11.9	14.2	20.0	18.8	18.6	19.0	21.4
$30,000–$39,999	11.3	7.0	7.5	10.0	28.6	6.6	6.9	9.8	15.4	0.1
$40,000–$49,999	8.6	5.0	6.2	7.2	16.2	4.0	4.5	5.1	7.8	0.1
$50,000–$59,999	6.7	4.2	5.5	6.4	11.1	3.0	2.8	5.1	4.4	0.1
$60,000–$69,999	5.0	3.8	5.0	5.5	4.9	2.7	3.4	3.7	3.7	1.5
$70,000–$79,999	4.1	3.5	5.4	6.5	3.9	1.8	2.0	2.8	1.2	1.5
$80,000–$89,999	2.6	2.5	4.1	4.8	3.1	1.2	1.4	1.7	1.0	1.0
$90,000–$99,999	1.7	1.5	2.3	2.4	2.1	0.8	0.9	1.2	0.7	0.7
$100,000 or more	7.4	7.3	11.4	12.4	10.0	3.8	5.1	6.6	3.5	2.1

Note: Non-Hispanic whites include only those who identified themselves as white alone and non-Hispanic.
Source: Bureau of the Census, data from the 2003 Current Population Survey Annual Social and Economic Supplement, Internet site http://ferret.bls.census.gov/macro/032003/perinc/toc.htm; calculations by New Strategist

Older Women Have Low Incomes

Those who work are much better off than those who are not in the labor force.

The median income of women aged 55 or older who work full-time stood at $34,030 in 2002, more than double the $13,934 median for all women in the age group. Few older women work full-time, however. The proportion ranges from a high of 46 percent among women aged 55 to 59 to just 4 percent of women aged 65 or older.

Because most women aged 65 or older do not work, and because most did not spend much time in the labor force, their incomes are extremely low—with much of their financial support coming from Social Security. The median income of all women aged 65 or older was just $11,406 in 2002. Non-Hispanic white women in the age group have the highest incomes, a median of $11,976. Their Hispanic counterparts have the lowest income—a median of just $7,642. For black women the figure is $9,479, and for Asians $9,242.

■ The incomes of older women will rise substantially in the years ahead as the working women of the Baby-Boom generation enter the 55-or-older age group.

Among older women, the incomes of workers are more than double the average

(median income of women aged 55 or older by work status, 2002)

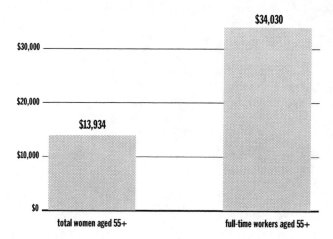

Table 4.22 Income of Women Aged 55 or Older, 2002: Total Women

(number and percent distribution of women aged 16 or older and aged 55 or older by income, 2002; median income by work status, and percent working year-round, full-time; women in thousands as of 2003)

	total	aged 55 or older								
		total	aged 55 to 64			total	aged 65 or older			
							total	aged 65 to 74		
	total	total	total	55–59	60–64	total	total	65–69	70–74	75+
TOTAL WOMEN	116,436	33,939	14,233	7,977	6,257	19,706	9,836	5,121	4,715	9,870
Without income	13,949	1,952	1,307	758	551	645	351	186	165	295
With income	102,487	31,987	12,926	7,219	5,706	19,061	9,485	4,935	4,550	9,575
Under $10,000	33,026	12,033	3,921	1,872	2,050	8,112	4,183	2,128	2,056	3,929
$10,000–$19,999	24,289	9,458	2,719	1,413	1,307	6,739	2,923	1,430	1,494	3,815
$20,000–$29,999	16,626	4,203	2,090	1,271	820	2,113	1,113	580	534	999
$30,000–$39,999	11,180	2,400	1,483	897	586	917	509	319	192	406
$40,000–$49,999	6,784	1,413	939	614	326	474	302	193	109	172
$50,000–$59,999	3,886	841	614	391	223	227	161	103	60	65
$60,000–$69,999	2,264	574	392	241	152	182	123	76	47	59
$70,000–$79,999	1,428	294	234	175	60	60	33	19	14	27
$80,000–$89,999	787	157	122	82	40	35	18	14	4	17
$90,000–$99,999	558	125	75	54	21	50	30	19	11	20
$100,000 or more	1,658	488	333	211	122	155	87	54	32	68
Median income of women w/ income	$16,812	$13,934	$19,165	$22,171	$15,395	$11,406	$11,279	$11,600	$10,975	$11,503
Median income of full-time workers	30,970	34,030	32,701	33,377	32,030	34,672	34,153	35,161	31,909	36,129
Percent working full-time	36.0%	15.3%	38.0%	45.7%	28.2%	4.3%	7.4%	10.4%	4.1%	1.3%
TOTAL WOMEN	100.0%	100.0%	100.0%	100.0%	100.0%	100.0%	100.0%	100.0%	100.0%	100.0%
Without income	12.0	5.8	9.2	9.5	8.8	3.3	3.6	3.6	3.5	3.0
With income	88.0	94.2	90.8	90.5	91.2	96.7	96.4	96.4	96.5	97.0
Under $10,000	28.4	35.5	27.5	23.5	32.8	41.2	42.5	41.6	43.6	39.8
$10,000–$19,999	20.9	27.9	19.1	17.7	20.9	34.2	29.7	27.9	31.7	38.7
$20,000–$29,999	14.3	12.4	14.7	15.9	13.1	10.7	11.3	11.3	11.3	10.1
$30,000–$39,999	9.6	7.1	10.4	11.2	9.4	4.7	5.2	6.2	4.1	4.1
$40,000–$49,999	5.8	4.2	6.6	7.7	5.2	2.4	3.1	3.8	2.3	1.7
$50,000–$59,999	3.3	2.5	4.3	4.9	3.6	1.2	1.6	2.0	1.3	0.7
$60,000–$69,999	1.9	1.7	2.8	3.0	2.4	0.9	1.3	1.5	1.0	0.6
$70,000–$79,999	1.2	0.9	1.6	2.2	1.0	0.3	0.3	0.4	0.3	0.3
$80,000–$89,999	0.7	0.5	0.9	1.0	0.6	0.2	0.2	0.3	0.1	0.2
$90,000–$99,999	0.5	0.4	0.5	0.7	0.3	0.3	0.3	0.4	0.2	0.2
$100,000 or more	1.4	1.4	2.3	2.6	1.9	0.8	0.9	1.1	0.7	0.7

Source: Bureau of the Census, data from the 2003 Current Population Survey Annual Social and Economic Supplement, Internet site http://ferret.bls.census.gov/macro/032003/perinc/toc.htm; calculations by New Strategist

Table 4.23 Income of Women Aged 55 or Older, 2002: Asian Women

(number and percent distribution of Asian women aged 16 or older and aged 55 or older by income, 2002; median income by work status, and percent working year-round, full-time; women in thousands as of 2003)

	total	aged 55 or older total	aged 55 to 64 total	55–59	60–64	aged 65 or older total	aged 65 to 74 total	65–69	70–74	75+
TOTAL ASIAN WOMEN	5,131	1,073	522	289	232	551	340	185	155	211
Without income	994	154	81	41	39	73	45	28	17	27
With income	4,137	919	441	248	193	478	295	157	138	184
Under $10,000	1,373	407	135	54	81	272	154	72	82	119
$10,000–$19,999	804	193	77	40	37	116	74	47	29	42
$20,000–$29,999	642	106	79	56	23	27	18	9	10	8
$30,000–$39,999	396	47	37	23	16	10	9	8	1	1
$40,000–$49,999	291	48	28	18	10	20	17	12	6	2
$50,000–$59,999	214	37	28	18	10	9	7	5	2	3
$60,000–$69,999	118	32	19	15	4	13	6	–	6	8
$70,000–$79,999	92	–	9	6	4	–	–	–	–	–
$80,000–$89,999	45	–	8	5	3	–	–	–	–	–
$90,000–$99,999	40	4	1	1	–	3	–	–	–	3
$100,000 or more	125	26	18	13	5	8	8	5	2	–
Median income of women w/ income	$17,898	$13,004	$20,584	$24,453	$13,079	$9,242	$9,732	$11,542	$9,208	$8,503
Median income of full-time workers	32,031	–	35,757	32,365	–	–	–	–	–	–
Percent working full-time	37.0%	16.7%	40.0%	53.3%	23.7%	5.1%	7.9%	10.8%	4.5%	0.5%
TOTAL ASIAN WOMEN	100.0%	100.0%	100.0%	100.0%	100.0%	100.0%	100.0%	100.0%	100.0%	100.0%
Without income	19.4	14.4	15.5	14.2	16.8	13.2	13.2	15.1	11.0	12.8
With income	80.6	85.6	84.5	85.8	83.2	86.8	86.8	84.9	89.0	87.2
Under $10,000	26.8	37.9	25.9	18.7	34.9	49.4	45.3	38.9	52.9	56.4
$10,000–$19,999	15.7	18.0	14.8	13.8	15.9	21.1	21.8	25.4	18.7	19.9
$20,000–$29,999	12.5	9.9	15.1	19.4	9.9	4.9	5.3	4.9	6.5	3.8
$30,000–$39,999	7.7	4.4	7.1	8.0	6.9	1.8	2.6	4.3	0.6	0.5
$40,000–$49,999	5.7	4.5	5.4	6.2	4.3	3.6	5.0	6.5	3.9	0.9
$50,000–$59,999	4.2	3.4	5.4	6.2	4.3	1.6	2.1	2.7	1.3	1.4
$60,000–$69,999	2.3	3.0	3.6	5.2	1.7	2.4	1.8	–	3.9	3.8
$70,000–$79,999	1.8	–	1.7	2.1	1.7	–	–	–	–	–
$80,000–$89,999	0.9	–	1.5	1.7	1.3	–	–	–	–	–
$90,000–$99,999	0.8	0.4	0.2	0.3	–	0.5	–	–	–	1.4
$100,000 or more	2.4	2.4	3.4	4.5	2.2	1.5	2.4	2.7	1.3	–

Note: Asians include those who identified themselves as Asian alone and those who identified themselves as Asian in combination with one or more other races. (–) means less than 500 or sample is too small to make a reliable estimate.
Source: Bureau of the Census, data from the 2003 Current Population Survey Annual Social and Economic Supplement, Internet site http://ferret.bls.census.gov/macro/032003/perinc/toc.htm; calculations by New Strategist

Table 4.24 Income of Women Aged 55 or Older, 2002: Black Women

(number and percent distribution of black women aged 16 or older and aged 55 or older by income, 2002; median income by work status, and percent working year-round, full-time; women in thousands as of 2003)

		aged 55 or older				aged 65 or older				
							aged 65 to 74			
			aged 55 to 64							
	total	total	total	55–59	60–64	total	total	65–69	70–74	75+
TOTAL BLACK WOMEN	**14,887**	**3,304**	**1,522**	**860**	**661**	**1,782**	**972**	**509**	**463**	**810**
Without income	2,222	236	119	77	41	117	68	29	39	48
With income	12,665	3,068	1,403	783	620	1,665	904	480	424	762
Under $10,000	4,069	1,307	402	174	229	905	464	228	234	442
$10,000–$19,999	3,156	849	341	188	153	508	282	155	128	226
$20,000–$29,999	2,196	354	239	153	86	115	74	43	31	41
$30,000–$39,999	1,434	220	152	95	57	68	39	26	12	28
$40,000–$49,999	774	141	108	77	28	33	23	12	12	9
$50,000–$59,999	411	72	60	36	24	12	5	3	2	7
$60,000–$69,999	260	50	41	20	21	9	6	6	–	4
$70,000–$79,999	143	23	16	11	5	7	5	3	2	2
$80,000–$89,999	71	14	13	11	2	1	1	1	–	–
$90,000–$99,999	50	4	3	2	1	1	–	–	–	1
$100,000 or more	100	32	25	14	11	7	6	4	2	1
Median income of women w/ income	$16,671	$12,144	$18,144	$21,383	$13,581	$9,479	$9,806	$10,370	$9,330	$9,221
Median income of full-time workers	27,703	31,514	31,158	30,923	31,464	31,672	–	–	–	–
Percent working full-time	40.7%	15.5%	39.8%	47.3%	30.1%	4.8%	6.6%	8.3%	4.8%	2.7%
TOTAL BLACK WOMEN	**100.0%**	**100.0%**	**100.0%**	**100.0%**	**100.0%**	**100.0%**	**100.0%**	**100.0%**	**100.0%**	**100.0%**
Without income	14.9	7.1	7.8	9.0	6.2	6.6	7.0	5.7	8.4	5.9
With income	85.1	92.9	92.2	91.1	93.8	93.4	9.3	94.3	91.6	94.1
Under $10,000	27.3	39.6	26.4	20.2	34.6	50.8	47.7	44.8	50.5	54.6
$10,000–$19,999	21.2	25.7	22.4	21.9	23.1	28.5	29.0	30.5	27.6	27.9
$20,000–$29,999	14.8	10.7	15.7	17.8	13.0	6.5	7.6	8.4	6.7	5.1
$30,000–$39,999	9.6	6.7	10.0	11.1	8.6	3.8	4.0	5.1	2.6	3.5
$40,000–$49,999	5.2	4.3	7.1	9.0	4.2	1.9	2.4	2.4	2.6	1.1
$50,000–$59,999	2.8	2.2	3.9	4.2	3.6	0.7	0.5	0.6	0.4	0.9
$60,000–$69,999	1.7	1.5	2.7	2.3	3.2	0.5	0.6	1.2	–	0.5
$70,000–$79,999	1.0	0.7	1.1	1.3	0.8	0.4	0.5	0.6	0.4	0.2
$80,000–$89,999	0.5	0.4	0.9	1.3	0.3	0.1	0.1	0.2	–	–
$90,000–$99,999	0.3	0.1	0.2	0.2	0.2	0.1	–	–	–	0.1
$100,000 or more	0.7	1.0	1.6	1.6	1.7	0.4	0.6	0.8	0.4	0.1

Note: Blacks include those who identified themselves as black alone and those who identified themselves as black in combination with one or more other races. (–) means number is less than 500 or sample is too small to make a reliable estimate.
Source: Bureau of the Census, data from the 2003 Current Population Survey Annual Social and Economic Supplement, Internet site http://ferret.bls.census.gov/macro/032003/perinc/toc.htm; calculations by New Strategist

Table 4.25 Income of Women Aged 55 or Older, 2002: Hispanic Women

(number and percent distribution of Hispanic women aged 16 or older and aged 55 or older by income, 2002; median income by work status, and percent working year-round, full-time; women in thousands as of 2003)

		aged 55 or older								
							aged 65 or older			
			aged 55 to 64					aged 65 to 74		
	total	total	total	55–59	60–64	total	total	65–69	70–74	75+
TOTAL HISPANIC WOMEN	13,607	2,231	1,084	602	482	1,147	666	372	294	480
Without income	3,589	379	244	143	101	135	82	37	44	53
With income	10,018	1,852	840	459	381	1,012	584	335	250	427
Under $10,000	3,822	1,045	358	176	182	687	389	221	167	298
$10,000–$19,999	2,821	442	219	124	94	223	126	67	59	97
$20,000–$29,999	1,602	169	112	69	43	57	36	19	18	22
$30,000–$39,999	839	72	55	36	20	17	14	14	–	3
$40,000–$49,999	444	51	37	22	17	14	12	9	3	2
$50,000–$59,999	215	25	23	9	15	2	–	–	–	2
$60,000–$69,999	110	18	12	7	6	6	4	2	2	2
$70,000–$79,999	64	11	9	7	3	2	1	1	–	1
$80,000–$89,999	30	–	5	5	–	–	–	–	–	–
$90,000–$99,999	10	–	1	1	–	–	–	–	–	–
$100,000 or more	63	11	8	5	4	3	2	1	2	1
Median income of women w/ income	$13,364	$9,094	$11,880	$13,147	$10,537	$7,642	$7,645	$7,454	$7,875	$7,639
Median income of full-time workers	22,355	–	24,030	23,803	24,295	–	–	–	–	–
Percent working full-time	33.7%	13.1%	30.8%	36.4%	24.1%	3.9%	5.9%	8.9%	2.0%	1.0%
TOTAL HISPANIC WOMEN	100.0%	100.0%	100.0%	100.0%	100.0%	100.0%	100.0%	100.0%	100.0%	100.0%
Without income	26.4	17.0	22.5	23.8	21.0	11.8	12.3	9.9	15.0	11.0
With income	73.6	83.0	77.5	76.2	79.1	88.2	87.7	90.1	85.0	89.0
Under $10,000	28.1	46.8	33.0	29.2	37.8	59.9	58.4	59.4	56.8	62.1
$10,000–$19,999	20.7	19.8	20.2	20.6	19.5	19.4	18.9	18.0	20.1	20.2
$20,000–$29,999	11.8	7.6	10.3	11.5	8.9	5.0	5.4	5.1	6.1	4.6
$30,000–$39,999	6.2	3.2	5.1	6.0	4.1	1.5	2.1	3.8	–	0.6
$40,000–$49,999	3.3	2.3	3.4	3.7	3.5	1.2	1.8	2.4	1.0	0.4
$50,000–$59,999	1.6	1.1	2.1	1.5	3.1	0.2	–	–	–	0.4
$60,000–$69,999	0.8	0.8	1.1	1.2	1.2	0.5	0.6	0.5	0.7	0.4
$70,000–$79,999	0.5	0.5	0.8	1.2	0.6	0.2	0.2	0.3	–	0.2
$80,000–$89,999	0.2	–	0.5	0.8	–	–	–	–	–	–
$90,000–$99,999	0.1	–	0.1	0.2	–	–	–	–	–	–
$100,000 or more	0.5	0.5	0.7	0.8	0.8	0.3	0.3	0.3	0.7	0.2

Note: Hispanics may be of any race. (–) means number is less than 500 or sample is too small to make a reliable estimate.
Source: Bureau of the Census, data from the 2003 Current Population Survey Annual Social and Economic Supplement, Internet site http://ferret.bls.census.gov/macro/032003/perinc/toc.htm; calculations by New Strategist

Table 4.26 Income of Women Aged 55 or Older, 2002: Non-Hispanic White Women

(number and percent distribution of non-Hispanic white women aged 16 or older and aged 55 or older by income, 2002; median income by work status, and percent working year-round, full-time; women in thousands as of 2003)

		aged 55 or older								
							aged 65 or older			
			aged 55 to 64					aged 65 to 74		
	total	total	total	55–59	60–64	total	total	65–69	70–74	75+
TOTAL NON-HISPANIC WHITE WOMEN	81,851	27,073	10,970	6,148	4,822	16,103	7,782	3,996	3,786	8,320
Without income	7,037	1,161	842	482	360	319	153	90	63	165
With income	74,814	25,912	10,128	5,666	4,462	15,784	7,629	3,906	3,723	8,155
Under $10,000	23,423	9,192	2,988	1,454	1,535	6,204	3,155	1,590	1,565	3,050
$10,000–$19,999	17,326	7,913	2,074	1,060	1,012	5,839	2,408	1,132	1,276	3,431
$20,000–$29,999	12,052	3,544	1,636	972	664	1,908	980	508	472	928
$30,000–$39,999	8,440	2,037	1,223	736	488	814	445	267	178	369
$40,000–$49,999	5,230	1,160	757	488	268	403	247	160	87	157
$50,000–$59,999	3,018	693	492	321	172	201	149	95	54	53
$60,000–$69,999	1,760	465	315	196	119	150	105	67	39	46
$70,000–$79,999	1,120	244	196	150	45	48	26	12	13	23
$80,000–$89,999	631	128	94	59	34	34	17	13	4	17
$90,000–$99,999	452	113	68	48	20	45	30	19	11	16
$100,000 or more	1,360	419	282	181	102	137	71	44	26	67
Median income of women w/ income	$17,389	$14,588	$20,010	$23,202	$16,313	$11,976	$11,889	$12,228	$11,591	$12,036
Median income of full-time workers	32,347	34,800	33,797	34,788	32,219	35,283	35,294	36,231	32,523	35,252
Percent working full-time	35.6%	15.4%	38.4%	46.1%	28.7%	4.3%	7.6%	10.8%	4.1%	1.2%
TOTAL NON-HISPANIC WHITE WOMEN	100.0%	100.0%	100.0%	100.0%	100.0%	100.0%	100.0%	100.0%	100.0%	100.0%
Without income	8.6	4.3	7.7	7.8	7.5	2.0	2.0	2.3	1.7	2.0
With income	91.4	95.7	92.3	92.2	92.5	98.0	98.0	97.7	98.3	98.0
Under $10,000	28.6	34.0	27.2	23.6	31.8	38.5	40.5	39.8	41.3	36.7
$10,000–$19,999	21.2	29.2	18.9	17.2	21.0	36.3	30.9	28.3	33.7	41.2
$20,000–$29,999	14.7	13.1	14.9	15.8	13.8	11.8	12.6	12.7	12.5	11.2
$30,000–$39,999	10.3	7.5	11.1	12.0	10.1	5.1	5.7	6.7	4.7	4.4
$40,000–$49,999	6.4	4.3	6.9	7.9	5.6	2.5	3.2	4.0	2.3	1.9
$50,000–$59,999	3.7	2.6	4.5	5.2	3.6	1.2	1.9	2.4	1.4	0.6
$60,000–$69,999	2.2	1.7	2.9	3.2	2.5	0.9	1.3	1.7	1.0	0.6
$70,000–$79,999	1.4	0.9	1.8	2.4	0.9	0.3	0.3	0.3	0.3	0.3
$80,000–$89,999	0.8	0.5	0.9	1.0	0.7	0.2	0.2	0.3	0.1	0.2
$90,000–$99,999	0.6	0.4	0.6	0.8	0.4	0.3	0.4	0.5	0.3	0.2
$100,000 or more	1.7	1.5	2.6	2.9	2.1	0.9	0.9	1.1	0.7	0.8

Note: Non-Hispanic whites include only those who identified themselves as white alone and non-Hispanic.
Source: Bureau of the Census, data from the 2003 Current Population Survey Annual Social and Economic Supplement, Internet site http://ferret.bls.census.gov/macro/032003/perinc/toc.htm; calculations by New Strategist

Education Boosts Earnings of Older Americans

Men and women with college degrees earn the most.

College-educated men aged 55 to 64 who work full-time earned a median of $70,353 in 2002, 53 percent more than the $45,995 earned by the average full-time worker in the age group. For women aged 55 to 64 who work full-time, those with a college degree earned a median of $47,413, or 52 percent more than the $31,294 average.

Getting an education boosts earnings not only because the college-educated command higher salaries, but because they are more likely to work full-time. Among men aged 55 to 64, 65 percent of those with a college degree work full-time versus a smaller 52 percent of those with only a high school diploma. Among women aged 55 to 64, 46 percent of the college educated work full-time compared with 36 percent of women with no more than a high school diploma.

Education plays an important role in earnings even among people aged 65 or older. Sixteen percent of men aged 65 or older with a college diploma work full-time, with median earnings of $59,615 in 2002. In contrast, only 8 percent of their high-school educated counterparts work full-time, with median earnings of $30,505. Among women aged 65 or older who work full-time, those with a college degree earn nearly twice as much as those with only a high school diploma.

■ Education has long guaranteed higher earnings, but the warranty may be running out as the Internet allows educated workers in other countries to compete with Americans for the same jobs.

Among older Americans, college graduates earn more

(median earnings of full-time workers aged 55 to 64, by sex and educational attainment, 2002)

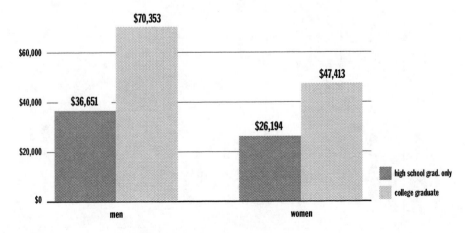

$70,353

$60,000

$47,413

$40,000 — $36,651

$26,194

$20,000

high school grad. only

college graduate

$0

men   women

Table 4.27 Earnings of Men by Education, 2002: Aged 55 to 64

(number and percent distribution of men aged 55 to 64 by earnings and education, 2002; men in thousands as of 2003)

							bachelor's degree or more				
	total	less than 9th grade	9th to 12th grade, no degree	high school graduate, including GED	some college, no degree	associate's degree	total	bachelor's degree	master's degree	professional degree	doctoral degree
TOTAL MEN AGED 55 TO 64	13,166	866	1,120	3,872	2,182	932	4,193	2,287	1,194	331	381
Without earnings	3,478	407	443	1,150	516	212	749	456	204	41	48
With earnings	9,688	459	677	2,722	1,666	720	3,444	1,831	990	290	333
Under $10,000	973	93	86	325	153	97	218	107	71	14	27
$10,000 to $19,999	1,225	117	161	420	179	78	268	159	76	15	19
$20,000 to $29,999	1,301	122	159	467	205	116	232	163	45	15	11
$30,000 to $39,999	1,340	59	120	474	264	93	333	222	80	13	18
$40,000 to $49,999	1,094	34	61	362	238	110	290	169	91	7	23
$50,000 to $59,999	919	12	29	279	199	65	336	165	137	4	28
$60,000 to $69,999	603	5	9	127	146	60	254	140	65	16	33
$70,000 to $79,999	639	3	23	105	121	37	351	193	112	26	19
$80,000 to $89,999	319	4	14	60	50	12	178	92	45	21	19
$90,000 to $99,999	202	2	4	22	19	19	137	78	21	8	28
$100,000 or more	1,074	6	10	83	94	35	846	343	245	152	107
Median earnings of men with earnings	$40,017	$20,805	$25,832	$31,917	$40,989	$36,517	$60,832	$52,306	$58,725	$100,000	$76,019
Median earnings of full-time workers	45,995	25,029	29,061	36,651	46,121	44,020	70,353	61,312	70,536	100,000	82,644
Percent working full-time	55.8%	36.8%	42.9%	51.9%	58.2%	56.5%	65.4%	64.7%	64.6%	71.0%	67.5%

TOTAL MEN AGED 55 TO 64	total	less than 9th grade	9th to 12th grade, no degree	high school graduate, including GED	some college, no degree	associate's degree	bachelor's degree or more				
							total	bachelor's degree	master's degree	professional degree	doctoral degree
	100.0%	100.0%	100.0%	100.0%	100.0%	100.0%	100.0%	100.0%	100.0%	100.0%	100.0%
Without earnings	26.4	47.0	39.6	29.7	23.6	22.7	17.9	19.9	17.1	12.4	12.6
With earnings	73.6	53.0	60.4	70.3	76.4	77.3	82.1	80.1	82.9	87.6	87.4
Under $10,000	7.4	10.7	7.7	8.4	7.0	10.4	5.2	4.7	5.9	4.2	7.1
$10,000 to $19,999	9.3	13.5	14.4	10.8	8.2	8.4	6.4	7.0	6.4	4.5	5.0
$20,000 to $29,999	9.9	14.1	14.2	12.1	9.4	12.4	5.5	7.1	3.8	4.5	2.9
$30,000 to $39,999	10.2	6.8	10.7	12.2	12.1	10.0	7.9	9.7	6.7	3.9	4.7
$40,000 to $49,999	8.3	3.9	5.4	9.3	10.9	11.8	6.9	7.4	7.6	2.1	6.0
$50,000 to $59,999	7.0	1.4	2.6	7.2	9.1	7.0	8.0	7.2	11.5	1.2	7.3
$60,000 to $69,999	4.6	0.6	0.8	3.3	6.7	6.4	6.1	6.1	5.4	4.8	8.7
$70,000 to $79,999	4.9	0.3	2.1	2.7	5.5	4.0	8.4	8.4	9.4	7.9	5.0
$80,000 to $89,999	2.4	0.5	1.2	1.5	2.3	1.3	4.2	4.0	3.8	6.3	5.0
$90,000 to $99,999	1.5	0.2	0.4	0.6	0.9	2.0	3.3	3.4	1.8	2.4	7.3
$100,000 or more	8.2	0.7	0.9	2.1	4.3	3.8	20.2	15.0	20.5	45.9	28.1

Source: Bureau of the Census, data from the 2003 Current Population Survey Annual Social and Economic Supplement, Internet site http://ferret.bls.census.gov/macro/032003/perinc/new03_000.htm; calculations by New Strategist

Table 4.28 Earnings of Men by Education, 2002: Aged 65 or Older

(number and percent distribution of men aged 65 or older by earnings and education, 2002; men in thousands as of 2003)

							bachelor's degree or more				
	total	less than 9th grade	9th to 12th grade, no degree	high school graduate, including GED	some college, no degree	associate's degree	total	bachelor's degree	master's degree	professional degree	doctoral degree
TOTAL MEN AGED 65+	14,528	2,286	1,792	4,553	1,981	599	3,317	1,854	801	368	295
Without earnings	11,343	2,002	1,507	3,586	1,517	454	2,278	1,319	546	240	174
With earnings	3,184	284	285	967	464	145	1,039	535	255	128	121
Under $10,000	968	124	106	328	133	43	233	133	58	23	19
$10,000 to $19,999	638	81	56	212	102	27	160	104	35	4	17
$20,000 to $29,999	409	37	41	150	57	29	92	48	31	7	9
$30,000 to $39,999	279	15	33	85	47	13	87	60	15	6	5
$40,000 to $49,999	185	12	19	38	27	14	73	46	11	7	10
$50,000 to $59,999	165	6	12	54	34	3	55	28	21	4	1
$60,000 to $69,999	114	3	1	30	14	4	62	28	8	10	15
$70,000 to $79,999	122	–	10	17	18	–	78	30	25	16	8
$80,000 to $89,999	51	–	3	8	3	4	33	18	5	5	4
$90,000 to $99,999	42	–	1	13	9	1	19	4	6	1	7
$100,000 or more	213	4	3	30	19	6	149	35	39	48	28
Median earnings of men with earnings	$19,677	$11,259	$14,296	$16,002	$19,404	$20,581	$32,409	$26,767	$31,384	$70,938	$60,772
Median earnings of full-time workers	36,963	20,261	30,679	30,505	36,581	–	59,615	40,974	57,452	–	–
Percent working full-time	9.9%	4.3%	6.5%	8.4%	12.4%	11.4%	15.8%	14.7%	14.1%	19.0%	23.4%

	total	less than 9th grade	9th to 12th grade, no degree	high school graduate, including GED	some college, no degree	associate's degree	bachelor's degree or more				
							total	bachelor's degree	master's degree	professional degree	doctoral degree
TOTAL MEN AGED 65+	100.0%	100.0%	100.0%	100.0%	100.0%	100.0%	100.0%	100.0%	100.0%	100.0%	100.0%
Without earnings	78.1	87.6	84.1	78.8	76.6	75.8	68.7	71.1	68.2	65.2	59.0
With earnings	21.9	12.4	15.9	21.2	23.4	24.2	31.3	28.9	31.8	34.8	41.0
Under $10,000	6.7	5.4	5.9	7.2	6.7	7.2	7.0	7.2	7.2	6.2	6.4
$10,000 to $19,999	4.4	3.5	3.1	4.7	5.1	4.5	4.8	5.6	4.4	1.1	5.8
$20,000 to $29,999	2.8	1.6	2.3	3.3	2.9	4.8	2.8	2.6	3.9	1.9	3.1
$30,000 to $39,999	1.9	0.7	1.8	1.9	2.4	2.2	2.6	3.2	1.9	1.6	1.7
$40,000 to $49,999	1.3	0.5	1.1	0.8	1.4	2.3	2.2	2.5	1.4	1.9	3.4
$50,000 to $59,999	1.1	0.3	0.7	1.2	1.7	0.5	1.7	1.5	2.6	1.1	0.3
$60,000 to $69,999	0.8	0.1	0.1	0.7	0.7	0.7	1.9	1.5	1.0	2.7	5.1
$70,000 to $79,999	0.8	–	0.6	0.4	0.9	–	2.4	1.6	3.1	4.3	2.7
$80,000 to $89,999	0.4	–	0.2	0.2	0.2	0.7	1.0	1.0	0.6	1.4	1.4
$90,000 to $99,999	0.3	–	0.1	0.3	0.5	0.2	0.6	0.2	0.7	0.3	2.4
$100,000 or more	1.5	0.2	0.2	0.7	1.0	1.0	4.5	1.9	4.9	13.0	9.5

Note: (–) means number is less than 500 or sample is too small to make a reliable estimate.
Source: Bureau of the Census, data from the 2003 Current Population Survey Annual Social and Economic Supplement, Internet site http://ferret.bls.census.gov/macro/032003/perinc/new03_000.htm; calculations by New Strategist

Table 4.29 Earnings of Women by Education, 2002: Aged 55 to 64

(number and percent distribution of women aged 55 to 64 by earnings and education, 2002; women in thousands as of 2003)

	total	less than 9th grade	9th to 12th grade, no degree	high school graduate, including GED	some college, no degree	associate's degree	bachelor's degree or more				
							total	bachelor's degree	master's degree	professional degree	doctoral degree
TOTAL WOMEN AGED 55 TO 64	**14,233**	**835**	**1,239**	**5,295**	**2,470**	**1,173**	**3,222**	**1,966**	**1,036**	**104**	**115**
Without earnings	**5,613**	**558**	**723**	**2,228**	**883**	**385**	**838**	**592**	**203**	**17**	**25**
With earnings	**8,620**	**277**	**516**	**3,067**	**1,587**	**788**	**2,384**	**1,374**	**833**	**87**	**90**
Under $10,000	1,610	94	149	639	282	125	318	229	83	3	2
$10,000 to $19,999	1,832	112	178	817	335	129	262	159	81	9	12
$20,000 to $29,999	1,728	46	100	771	338	181	291	206	74	7	3
$30,000 to $39,999	1,244	16	40	447	220	169	353	212	117	13	12
$40,000 to $49,999	857	5	29	234	169	85	336	181	148	2	4
$50,000 to $59,999	494	–	10	50	125	63	245	127	95	13	10
$60,000 to $69,999	323	3	3	47	37	15	218	93	106	9	10
$70,000 to $79,999	201	2	5	27	31	10	128	59	47	11	10
$80,000 to $89,999	66	–	–	7	7	–	52	24	21	4	2
$90,000 to $99,999	44	–	1	–	15	–	27	10	10	3	2
$100,000 or more	219	–	–	28	26	12	154	73	48	13	20
Median earnings of women with earnings	$24,801	$12,786	$15,453	$20,828	$25,227	$27,266	$38,615	$33,250	$42,472	$54,394	$56,121
Median earnings of full-time workers	31,294	16,844	20,742	26,194	31,294	32,991	47,413	42,181	49,166	–	–
Percent working full-time	38.0%	18.3%	24.5%	35.9%	43.6%	42.1%	46.0%	41.4%	51.4%	63.5%	60.0%

	total	less than 9th grade	9th to 12th grade, no degree	high school graduate, including GED	some college, no degree	associate's degree	bachelor's degree or more				
							total	bachelor's degree	master's degree	professional degree	doctoral degree
TOTAL WOMEN AGED 55 TO 64	100.0%	100.0%	100.0%	100.0%	100.0%	100.0%	100.0%	100.0%	100.0%	100.0%	100.0%
Without earnings	**39.4**	**66.8**	**58.4**	**42.1**	**35.7**	**32.8**	**26.0**	**30.1**	**19.6**	**16.3**	**21.7**
With earnings	**60.6**	**33.2**	**41.6**	**57.9**	**64.3**	**67.2**	**74.0**	**69.9**	**80.4**	**83.7**	**78.3**
Under $10,000	11.3	11.3	12.0	12.1	11.4	10.7	9.9	11.6	8.0	2.9	1.7
$10,000 to $19,999	12.9	13.4	14.4	15.4	13.6	11.0	8.1	8.1	7.8	8.7	10.4
$20,000 to $29,999	12.1	5.5	8.1	14.6	13.7	15.4	9.0	10.5	7.1	6.7	2.6
$30,000 to $39,999	8.7	1.9	3.2	8.4	8.9	14.4	11.0	10.8	11.3	12.5	10.4
$40,000 to $49,999	6.0	0.6	2.3	4.4	6.8	7.2	10.4	9.2	14.3	1.9	3.5
$50,000 to $59,999	3.5	–	0.8	0.9	5.1	5.4	7.6	6.5	9.2	12.5	8.7
$60,000 to $69,999	2.3	0.4	0.2	0.9	1.5	1.3	6.8	4.7	10.2	8.7	8.7
$70,000 to $79,999	1.4	0.2	0.4	0.5	1.3	0.9	4.0	3.0	4.5	10.6	8.7
$80,000 to $89,999	0.5	–	–	0.1	0.3	–	1.6	1.2	2.0	3.8	1.7
$90,000 to $99,999	0.3	–	0.1	–	0.6	–	0.8	0.5	1.0	2.9	1.7
$100,000 or more	1.5	–	–	0.5	1.1	1.0	4.8	3.7	4.6	12.5	17.4

Note: (–) means number is less than 500 or sample is too small to make a reliable estimate.

Source: Bureau of the Census, data from the 2003 Current Population Survey Annual Social and Economic Supplement, Internet site http://ferret.bls.census.gov/macro/032003/perinc/new03_000.htm; calculations by New Strategist

Table 4.30 Earnings of Women by Education, 2002: Aged 65 or Older

(number and percent distribution of women aged 65 or older by earnings and education, 2002; women in thousands as of 2003)

	total	less than 9th grade	9th to 12th grade, no degree	high school graduate, including GED	some college, no degree	associate's degree	bachelor's degree or more				
							total	bachelor's degree	master's degree	professional degree	doctoral degree
TOTAL WOMEN AGED 65+	19,706	2,974	2,724	7,833	2,558	990	2,626	1,766	673	109	78
Without earnings	17,210	2,818	2,531	6,774	2,121	833	2,132	1,485	515	79	53
With earnings	2,496	156	193	1,059	437	157	494	281	158	30	25
Under $10,000	1,137	88	102	502	187	51	207	120	72	11	3
$10,000 to $19,999	520	32	49	262	78	37	62	49	13	1	–
$20,000 to $29,999	345	18	21	149	75	15	66	48	17	1	–
$30,000 to $39,999	196	16	12	66	40	21	39	21	18	–	–
$40,000 to $49,999	120	1	4	47	26	12	30	12	10	2	6
$50,000 to $59,999	79	–	–	10	18	13	38	16	9	7	5
$60,000 to $69,999	37	–	2	16	4	2	13	2	5	4	2
$70,000 to $79,999	18	1	–	–	5	2	9	2	5	–	2
$80,000 to $89,999	7	–	–	–	–	–	7	1	4	2	–
$90,000 to $99,999	7	–	–	–	–	–	7	3	3	–	1
$100,000 or more	31	–	1	6	6	4	14	6	2	3	4
Median earnings of women with earnings	$11,282	$8,217	$9,081	$10,703	$11,805	$17,983	$15,939	$12,458	$15,744	–	–
Median earnings of full-time workers	27,194	–	–	22,708	30,097	–	40,606	31,564	–	–	–
Percent working full-time	4.3%	1.9%	2.2%	4.4%	6.1%	5.4%	7.0%	5.4%	8.5%	17.4%	16.7%

| | total | less than 9th grade | 9th to 12th grade, no degree | high school graduate, including GED | some college, no degree | associate's degree | bachelor's degree or more | | | | |
							total	bachelor's degree	master's degree	professional degree	doctoral degree
TOTAL WOMEN AGED 65+	100.0%	100.0%	100.0%	100.0%	100.0%	100.0%	100.0%	100.0%	100.0%	100.0%	100.0%
Without earnings	87.3	94.8	92.9	86.5	82.9	84.1	81.2	84.1	76.5	72.5	67.9
With earnings	12.7	5.2	7.1	13.5	17.1	15.9	18.8	15.9	23.5	27.5	32.1
Under $10,000	5.8	3.0	3.7	6.4	7.3	5.2	7.9	6.8	10.7	10.1	3.8
$10,000 to $19,999	2.6	1.1	1.8	3.3	3.1	3.7	2.4	2.8	1.9	0.9	–
$20,000 to $29,999	1.8	0.6	0.8	1.9	2.9	1.5	2.5	2.7	2.5	0.9	–
$30,000 to $39,999	1.0	0.5	0.4	0.8	1.6	2.1	1.5	1.2	2.7	–	–
$40,000 to $49,999	0.6	0.0	0.1	0.6	1.0	1.2	1.1	0.7	1.5	1.8	7.7
$50,000 to $59,999	0.4	–	–	0.1	0.7	1.3	1.4	0.9	1.3	6.4	6.4
$60,000 to $69,999	0.2	–	0.1	0.2	0.2	0.2	0.5	0.1	0.7	3.7	2.6
$70,000 to $79,999	0.1	0.0	–	–	0.2	0.2	0.3	0.1	0.7	–	2.6
$80,000 to $89,999	0.0	–	–	–	–	–	0.3	0.1	0.6	1.8	–
$90,000 to $99,999	0.0	–	–	–	–	–	0.3	0.2	0.4	–	1.3
$100,000 or more	0.2	–	0.0	0.1	0.2	0.4	0.5	0.3	0.3	2.8	5.1

Note: (–) means number is less than 500 or sample is too small to make a reliable estimate.
Source: Bureau of the Census, data from the 2003 Current Population Survey Annual Social and Economic Supplement, Internet site http://ferret.bls.census.gov/macro/032003/perinc/new03_000.htm; calculations by New Strategist

Most Older Americans Receive Social Security Benefits

The Social Security income of older Americans exceeds their pension and interest income.

Among Americans aged 65 or older, from 88 to 95 percent received income from Social Security in 2002, making it the most common source of income for the age group. The amount of Social Security income received by people aged 65 or older is modest, however, ranging from $11,498 to $11,935 annually for men and from $7,797 to $9,002 for women. Among men and women aged 55 to 64, only 17 to 21 percent receive Social Security benefits, most of them because they opted to retire at age 62.

Besides Social Security, the only other type of income received by the majority of people aged 65 or older is interest. But the median amount of interest income received by older Americans is small, ranging from just $1,649 to $1,787.

Among men aged 65 to 74, a substantial 31 percent had earnings in 2002, as did 21 percent of their female counterparts. More than 40 percent of men aged 65 or older received pension income in 2002, with the median amount received ranging from $9,463 to $11,645. A smaller 22 percent of women in the age group received pension income, with the annual amount ranging from $4,848 to $6,753.

■ As Boomers enter the 65-or-older age group, expect the percentage of older Americans with earnings to increase.

Social Security income is modest

(median annual Social Security income received by people aged 65 or older, by age and sex, 2002)

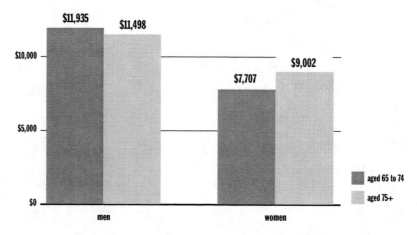

Table 4.31 Sources of Income for Men Aged 55 to 64, 2002

(number and percent distribution of men aged 55 to 64 with income and median income for those with income, by selected sources of income, 2002; men in thousands as of 2003)

	number	percent with income	median income
Total men aged 55 to 64 with income	**12,750**	**100.0%**	**$36,277**
Earnings	9,688	76.0	40,017
Wages and salary	8,591	67.4	40,846
Nonfarm self-employment	1,420	11.1	20,366
Farm self-employment	259	2.0	2,237
Social Security	2,178	17.1	11,521
SSI (Supplemental Security Income)	350	2.7	6,388
Public assistance	43	0.3	–
Veterans' benefits	504	4.0	6,254
Survivor benefits	64	0.5	–
Disability benefits	288	2.3	9,960
Unemployment compensation	694	5.4	4,199
Workers' compensation	227	1.8	3,985
Property income	7,835	61.5	1,730
Interest	7,387	57.9	1,519
Dividends	2,975	23.3	1,555
Rents, royalties, estates or trusts	1,236	9.7	2,271
Retirement income	2,560	20.1	19,116
Pension income	2,296	1.8	19,927
Alimony	3	0.0	–
Child support	10	0.1	–
Educational assistance	43	0.3	–
Financial assistance from other household	54	0.4	–
Other income	78	0.6	1,500

Note: (–) means sample is too small to make a reliable estimate.
Source: Bureau of the Census, data from the 2003 Current Population Survey Annual Social and Economic Supplement, Internet site http://ferret.bls.census.gov/macro/032003/perinc/new08_000.htm; calculations by New Strategist

Table 4.32 Sources of Income for Men Aged 65 to 74, 2002

(number and percent distribution of men aged 65 to 74 with income and median income for those with income, by selected sources of income, 2002; men in thousands as of 2003)

	number	percent with income	median income
Total men aged 65 to 74 with income	**8,142**	**100.0%**	**$21,291**
Earnings	2,563	31.5	20,681
Wages and salary	2,135	26.2	21,225
Nonfarm self-employment	392	4.8	15,493
Farm self-employment	148	1.8	5,249
Social Security	7,191	88.3	11,935
SSI (Supplemental Security Income)	188	2.3	3,822
Public assistance	13	0.2	–
Veterans' benefits	376	4.6	7,234
Survivor benefits	112	1.4	5,810
Disability benefits	85	1.0	6,555
Unemployment compensation	93	1.1	3,355
Workers' compensation	46	0.6	–
Property income	4,838	59.4	1,966
Interest	4,564	56.1	1,694
Dividends	1,636	20.1	1,679
Rents, royalties, estates or trusts	807	9.9	2,451
Retirement income	3,542	43.5	11,539
Pension income	3,394	41.7	11,645
Alimony	2	0.0	–
Child support	7	0.1	–
Educational assistance	7	0.1	–
Financial assistance from other household	19	0.2	–
Other income	53	0.7	–

Note: (–) means sample is too small to make a reliable estimate.
Source: Bureau of the Census, data from the 2003 Current Population Survey Annual Social and Economic Supplement, Internet site http://ferret.bls.census.gov/macro/032003/perinc/new08_000.htm; calculations by New Strategist

Table 4.33 Sources of Income for Men Aged 75 or Older, 2002

(number and percent distribution of men aged 75 or older with income and median income for those with income, by selected sources of income, 2002; men in thousands as of 2003)

	number	percent with income	median income
Total men aged 75 or older with income	**6,131**	**100.0%**	**$17,508**
Earnings	622	10.1	15,355
Wages and salary	481	7.8	16,029
Nonfarm self-employment	104	1.7	7,632
Farm self-employment	52	0.8	–
Social Security	5,683	92.7	11,498
SSI (Supplemental Security Income)	181	3.0	4,792
Public assistance	10	0.2	–
Veterans' benefits	454	7.4	3,438
Survivor benefits	104	1.7	5,205
Disability benefits	43	0.7	–
Unemployment compensation	31	0.5	–
Workers' compensation	21	0.3	–
Property income	3,699	60.3	2,102
Interest	3,529	57.6	1,787
Dividends	1,252	20.4	1,839
Rents, royalties, estates or trusts	478	7.8	3,404
Retirement income	2,958	48.2	9,434
Pension income	2,838	46.3	9,463
Alimony	0	0.0	–
Child support	0	0.0	–
Educational assistance	1	0.0	–
Financial assistance from other household	15	0.2	–
Other income	50	0.8	–

Note: (–) means sample is too small to make a reliable estimate.
Source: Bureau of the Census, data from the 2003 Current Population Survey Annual Social and Economic Supplement, Internet site http://ferret.bls.census.gov/macro/032003/perinc/new08_000.htm; calculations by New Strategist

Table 4.34 Sources of Income for Women Aged 55 to 64, 2002

(number and percent distribution of women aged 55 to 64 with income and median income for those with income, by selected sources of income, 2002; women in thousands as of 2003)

	number	percent with income	median income
Total women aged 55 to 64 with income	**12,926**	**100.0%**	**$19,165**
Earnings	8,620	66.7	24,801
Wages and salary	8,005	61.9	25,556
Nonfarm self-employment	795	6.2	7,965
Farm self-employment	118	0.9	1,709
Social Security	2,724	21.1	7,061
SSI (Supplemental Security Income)	542	4.2	5,282
Public assistance	84	0.6	2,007
Veterans' benefits	59	0.5	–
Survivor benefits	364	2.8	6,911
Disability benefits	208	1.6	6,115
Unemployment compensation	371	2.9	3,656
Workers' compensation	114	0.9	2,400
Property income	8,094	62.6	1,657
Interest	7,645	59.1	1,487
Dividends	2,855	22.1	1,534
Rents, royalties, estates or trusts	1,266	9.8	2,085
Retirement income	1,722	13.3	8,988
Pension income	1,240	9.6	10,504
Alimony	99	0.8	5,565
Child support	86	0.7	3,062
Educational assistance	50	0.4	–
Financial assistance from other household	97	0.8	4,325
Other income	94	0.7	2,111

Note: (–) means sample is too small to make a reliable estimate.
Source: Bureau of the Census, data from the 2003 Current Population Survey Annual Social and Economic Supplement, Internet site http://ferret.bls.census.gov/macro/032003/perinc/new08_000.htm; calculations by New Strategist

Table 4.35 Sources of Income for Women Aged 65 to 74, 2002

(number and percent distribution of women aged 65 to 74 with income and median income for those with income, by selected sources of income, 2002; women in thousands as of 2003)

	number	percent with income	median income
Total women aged 65 to 74 with income	**9,485**	**100.0%**	**$11,279**
Earnings	2,030	21.4	11,706
Wages and salary	1,823	19.2	12,119
Nonfarm self-employment	224	2.4	6,796
Farm self-employment	37	0.4	–
Social Security	8,469	89.3	7,797
SSI (Supplemental Security Income)	406	4.3	3,617
Public assistance	51	0.5	–
Veterans' benefits	95	0.1	5,966
Survivor benefits	573	6.0	4,735
Disability benefits	36	0.4	–
Unemployment compensation	54	0.6	–
Workers' compensation	47	0.5	–
Property income	5,385	56.8	1,834
Interest	5,071	53.5	1,649
Dividends	1,733	18.3	1,727
Rents, royalties, estates or trusts	770	8.1	1,827
Retirement income	2,522	26.6	6,553
Pension income	2,054	21.7	6,753
Alimony	35	0.4	–
Child support	14	0.1	–
Educational assistance	9	0.1	–
Financial assistance from other household	30	0.3	–
Other income	62	0.7	–

Note: (–) means sample is too small to make a reliable estimate.
Source: Bureau of the Census, data from the 2003 Current Population Survey Annual Social and Economic Supplement, Internet site http://ferret.bls.census.gov/macro/032003/perinc/new08_000.htm; calculations by New Strategist

Table 4.36 Sources of Income for Women Aged 75 or Older, 2002

(number and percent distribution of women aged 75 or older with income and median income for those with income, by selected sources of income, 2002; women in thousands as of 2003)

	number	percent with income	median income
Total women aged 75 or older with income	**9,575**	**100.0%**	**$11,503**
Earnings	466	4.9	8,494
Wages and salary	396	4.1	7,403
Nonfarm self-employment	69	0.7	–
Farm self-employment	10	0.1	–
Social Security	9,050	94.5	9,002
SSI (Supplemental Security Income)	418	4.4	2,793
Public assistance	26	0.3	–
Veterans' benefits	201	2.1	4,693
Survivor benefits	877	9.2	5,903
Disability benefits	27	0.3	–
Unemployment compensation	20	0.2	–
Workers' compensation	29	0.3	–
Property income	5,210	54.4	1,959
Interest	4,974	51.9	1,711
Dividends	1,562	16.3	1,801
Rents, royalties, estates or trusts	693	7.2	2,197
Retirement income	2,863	29.9	5,396
Pension income	2,109	22.0	4,848
Alimony	18	0.2	–
Child support	3	0.0	–
Educational assistance	–	–	–
Financial assistance from other household	65	0.7	–
Other income	61	0.6	–

Note: (–) means sample is too small to make a reliable estimate.
Source: Bureau of the Census, data from the 2003 Current Population Survey Annual Social and Economic Supplement, Internet site http://ferret.bls.census.gov/macro/032003/perinc/new08_000.htm; calculations by New Strategist

Poverty Rates Are below Average for Older Americans

Ten percent of people aged 55 or older are poor compared with 12 percent of all Americans.

Of the nation's 35 million poor in 2002, only 18 percent were aged 55 or older. Older blacks and Hispanics are more than twice as likely to be poor as Asians and non-Hispanic whites, however. Among people aged 55 or older, only 8 percent of Asians and non-Hispanic whites are poor versus 20 percent of blacks and 19 percent of Hispanics.

Non-Hispanic whites account for a 45 percent minority of the nation's poor, while blacks and Hispanics each account for about one in four of the poor. Among older Americans, however, non-Hispanic whites account for the 65 percent majority of the poor. Blacks account for 19 percent and Hispanics for 13 percent. Asians account for only 2.5 percent of poor people aged 55 or older.

■ The black and Hispanic share of poor people aged 55 or older will rise as more diverse younger generations enter the 55-or-older age groups.

Among older Americans, blacks are most likely to be poor

(percent of people aged 55 or older living below poverty level, by race and Hispanic origin, 2002)

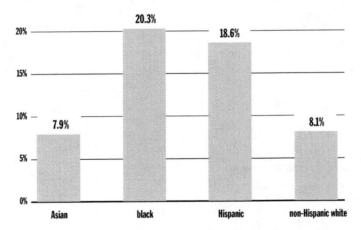

Table 4.37 People below Poverty Level by Age, Race, and Hispanic Origin, 2002

(number, percent, and percent distribution of people below poverty level, by age, race and Hispanic origin, 2002; people in thousands as of 2003)

	total	Asian	black	Hispanic	non-Hispanic white
NUMBER IN POVERTY					
TOTAL PEOPLE	**34,570**	**1,243**	**8,884**	**8,555**	**15,567**
Under age 55	**28,429**	**1,087**	**7,744**	**7,782**	**11,573**
Aged 55 or older	**6,141**	**156**	**1,140**	**773**	**3,994**
Aged 55 to 59	1,302	41	239	169	829
Aged 60 to 64	1,263	29	210	165	844
Aged 65 or older	3,576	86	691	439	2,321
Aged 65 to 74	1,696	45	393	247	990
Aged 75 or older	1,880	41	298	192	1,331
PERCENT IN POVERTY					
TOTAL PEOPLE	**12.1%**	**10.0%**	**23.9%**	**21.8%**	**8.0%**
Under age 55	**12.7**	**10.3**	**24.5**	**22.2**	**8.0**
Aged 55 or older	**10.0**	**7.9**	**20.3**	**18.6**	**8.1**
Aged 55 to 59	8.4	7.6	15.7	14.2	6.9
Aged 60 to 64	10.6	6.7	17.8	18.1	9.1
Aged 65 or older	10.4	8.7	23.6	21.4	8.3
Aged 65 to 74	9.4	7.1	23.2	20.2	6.9
Aged 75 or older	11.7	11.3	24.2	23.1	9.8
PERCENT DISTRIBUTION OF POOR BY AGE					
TOTAL PEOPLE	**100.0%**	**100.0%**	**100.0%**	**100.0%**	**100.0%**
Under age 55	**82.2**	**87.4**	**87.2**	**91.0**	**74.3**
Aged 55 or older	**17.8**	**12.6**	**12.8**	**9.0**	**25.7**
Aged 55 to 59	3.8	3.3	2.7	2.0	5.3
Aged 60 to 64	3.7	2.3	2.4	1.9	5.4
Aged 65 or older	10.3	6.9	7.8	5.1	14.9
Aged 65 to 74	4.9	3.6	4.4	2.9	6.4
Aged 75 or older	5.4	3.3	3.4	2.2	8.6
PERCENT DISTRIBUTION OF POOR BY RACE AND HISPANIC ORIGIN					
TOTAL PEOPLE	**100.0%**	**3.6%**	**25.7%**	**24.7%**	**45.0%**
Under age 55	**100.0**	**3.8**	**27.2**	**27.4**	**40.7**
Aged 55 or older	**100.0**	**2.5**	**18.6**	**12.6**	**65.0**
Aged 55 to 59	100.0	3.1	18.4	13.0	63.7
Aged 60 to 64	100.0	2.3	16.6	13.1	66.8
Aged 65 or older	100.0	2.4	19.3	12.3	64.9
Aged 65 to 74	100.0	2.7	23.2	14.6	58.4
Aged 75 or older	100.0	2.2	15.9	10.2	70.8

Note: Numbers will not add to total because each racial category includes those who identified themselves as being of the race alone and those who identified themselves as being of the race in combination with one or more other races, because Hispanics may be of any race, and because not all races are shown. Non-Hispanic whites include only those who identified themselves as "white alone" and non-Hispanic.
Source: Bureau of the Census, data from the 2003 Current Population Survey Annual Social and Economic Supplement, Internet sites http://ferret.bls.census.gov/macro/032003/pov/new34_100.htm and http://ferret.bls.census.gov/macro/032003/pov/new01_000.htm; calculations by New Strategist

5

Labor Force

■ The end of early retirement can be seen in labor force participation trends among older Americans. Since 2000—despite massive job losses nationwide—the percentage of men aged 55 or older in the labor force has grown.

■ The sixties is a time of transition for most Americans, when their roles change from worker to retiree. The labor force participation rate drops sharply for men and women in their sixties.

■ The proportion of couples in which neither husband nor wife works becomes the majority in the 65-to-74 age group.

■ While only 11 percent of all men in the labor force work part-time, the proportion is 17 percent among men aged 55 or older.

■ Men and women aged 55 or older account for 27 percent of the self-employed, a much greater proportion than their share of all workers.

■ Job tenure is down for men aged 55 to 64. In 1991, men in the age group had been with their current employer a median of 13.4 years. By 2002, the figure had fallen to 10.2 years.

■ Among men aged 55 or older, labor force participation should rise 2.8 percentage points between 2003 and 2012 compared with a decline of 0.3 percentage points among men under age 55.

Older Men Are More Likely to Work

The increase in participation has been especially sharp for men aged 62 to 69.

The end of early retirement can be seen clearly in labor force participation trends among older Americans. Since 2000—and despite massive job losses nationwide—the percentage of men aged 55 or older in the labor force has grown, in some cases substantially. The labor force participation rate of men aged 62 to 64, the typical age of retirement, grew 2.6 percentage points between 2000 and 2003—to 50 percent. The figure had been as low as 45 percent in the mid-1990s. Among men aged 65 to 69, labor force participation increased 2.5 percentage points between 2000 and 2003—to 33 percent, the highest rate in more than two decades.

Among older women, labor force participation rates rose substantially as well. Much of the increase stems from the entry of a more career-oriented generation into the age group. Nevertheless, some of the rise is a result of declining stock market values and lower interest rates, which drive older Americans back to work to supplement their dwindling retirement income.

■ As the Baby-Boom generation enters the 55-or-older age group, the labor force participation rates of older Americans will continue to rise as early retirement becomes less common.

A growing share of men in their sixties are in the labor force

(percent of men aged 60 to 69 in the labor force, 2000 and 2003)

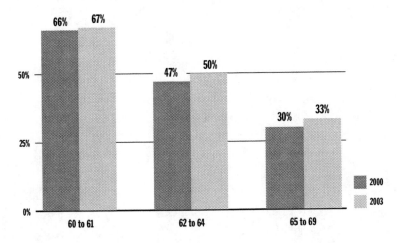

Table 5.1 Labor Force Participation Rate of People Aged 55 or Older by Sex, 1990 to 2003

(labor force participation rate of people aged 16 or older and aged 55 or older, by sex, 1990 to 2003; percentage point change, 2000–2003 and 1990–2003)

				percentage point change	
	2003	2000	1990	2000–03	1990–03
Men aged 16 or older	**73.5%**	**74.8%**	**76.4%**	**–1.3**	**–2.9**
Aged 55 to 64	68.7	67.3	67.8	1.4	0.9
Aged 55 to 59	77.6	77.0	79.9	0.6	–2.3
Aged 60 to 64	57.2	54.9	55.5	2.3	1.7
Aged 60 to 61	67.0	66.0	68.8	1.0	–1.8
Aged 62 to 64	49.6	47.0	46.5	2.6	3.1
Aged 65 or older	18.6	17.7	16.3	0.9	2.3
Aged 65 to 69	32.8	30.3	26.0	2.5	6.8
Aged 70 to 74	18.8	18.0	15.4	0.8	3.4
Aged 75 or older	8.3	8.1	7.1	0.2	1.2
Women aged 16 or older	**59.5**	**59.9**	**57.5**	**–0.4**	**2.0**
Aged 55 to 64	56.6	51.9	45.2	4.7	11.4
Aged 55 to 59	65.5	61.4	55.3	4.1	10.2
Aged 60 to 64	45.3	40.2	35.5	5.1	9.8
Aged 60 to 61	53.9	49.0	42.9	4.9	11.0
Aged 62 to 64	38.6	34.1	30.7	4.5	7.9
Aged 65 or older	10.6	9.4	8.6	1.2	2.0
Aged 65 to 69	22.7	19.5	17.0	3.2	5.7
Aged 70 to 74	11.2	10.0	8.2	1.2	3.0
Aged 75 or older	4.1	3.6	2.7	0.5	1.4

Source: Bureau of Labor Statistics, Public Query Data Tool, Internet site http://www.bls.gov/data; calculations by New Strategist

Labor Force Participation Rate Drops Sharply after Age 55

The majority of men drop out of the labor force in their sixties.

The sixties is a time of transition for most Americans, when their roles change from worker to retiree. The labor force participation rate drops sharply with age. Among men aged 55 to 59, 78 percent are in the labor force. The figure falls to 57 percent among men aged 60 to 64, then drops to 33 percent among those aged 65 to 69. Only 8 percent of men aged 75 or older are in the labor force.

The 66 percent majority of women aged 55 to 59 are in the labor force, a figure that falls to a 45 percent minority among women aged 60 to 64. Only 23 percent of women aged 65 to 69 and 4 percent of those aged 75 or older are in the labor force.

■ The labor force participation rate of older Americans will rise in the coming decades as Baby Boomers postpone retirement.

Labor force participation falls with age

(percent of people aged 55 or older in the labor force, by sex, 2003)

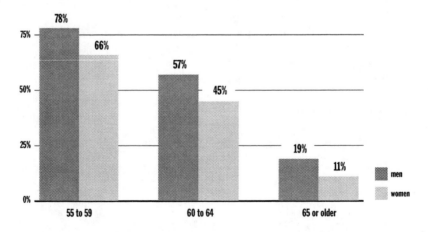

Table 5.2 Employment Status by Sex and Age, 2003

(number and percent of people aged 16 or older in the civilian labor force by sex, age, and employment status, 2003; numbers in thousands)

	civilian noninstitutional population	civilian labor force			unemployed	
		total	percent of population	employed	number	percent of labor force
Total, aged 16 or older	**221,168**	**146,510**	**66.2%**	**137,736**	**8,774**	**6.0%**
Under age 55	159,187	124,406	78.2	116,530	7,877	6.3
Aged 55 or older	61,981	22,104	35.7	21,206	897	4.1
Aged 55 to 59	15,625	11,142	71.3	10,685	457	4.1
Aged 60 to 64	12,103	6,170	51.0	5,913	257	4.2
Aged 65 or older	34,253	4,792	14.0	4,608	183	3.8
Aged 65 to 69	9,591	2,627	27.4	2,515	112	4.2
Aged 70 to 74	8,456	1,231	14.6	1,189	43	3.5
Aged 75 or older	16,207	934	5.8	904	29	3.1
Men, aged 16 or older	**106,435**	**78,238**	**73.5**	**73,332**	**4,906**	**6.3**
Under age 55	78,634	66,402	84.4	62,014	4,387	6.6
Aged 55 or older	27,801	11,836	42.6	11,318	519	4.4
Aged 55 to 59	7,528	5,842	77.6	5,584	258	4.4
Aged 60 to 64	5,777	3,302	57.2	3,149	154	4.7
Aged 65 or older	14,496	2,692	18.6	2,585	107	4.0
Aged 65 to 69	4,449	1,461	32.8	1,397	64	4.4
Aged 70 to 74	3,769	708	18.8	680	28	3.9
Aged 75 or older	6,279	524	8.3	508	16	3.0
Women, aged 16 or older	**114,733**	**68,272**	**59.5**	**64,404**	**3,868**	**5.7**
Under age 55	80,552	58,005	72.0	54,515	3,490	6.0
Aged 55 or older	34,181	10,267	30.0	9,889	378	3.7
Aged 55 to 59	8,097	5,300	65.5	5,101	199	3.8
Aged 60 to 64	6,326	2,868	45.3	2,765	103	3.6
Aged 65 or older	19,758	2,099	10.6	2,023	76	3.6
Aged 65 to 69	5,142	1,166	22.7	1,119	47	4.1
Aged 70 to 74	4,687	524	11.2	509	15	2.9
Aged 75 or older	9,928	410	4.1	396	13	3.3

Source: Bureau of Labor Statistics, 2003 Current Population Survey, Internet site http://www.bls.gov/cps/home.htm; calculations by New Strategist

Labor Force Rate Differs by Race and Hispanic Origin

Asian men are most likely to work in old age.

Older Asian men are more likely to work than older blacks, Hispanics, or whites. Among men aged 55 or older, only 38 percent of blacks, 43 percent of whites, and 45 percent of Hispanics are in the labor force. Among Asian men in the age group, 51 percent are working. In the 65-or-older age group, the labor force participation rate ranges from a low of 17 percent among black men to a high of 20 percent among Asian men.

Among women aged 55 or older, the labor force participation rate varies little by race and Hispanic origin. From 28 to 31 percent of women aged 55 or older are in the labor force. Among those aged 65 or older, the labor force participation rate ranges from 9 to 11 percent.

■ Regardless of race or Hispanic origin, labor force participation of older workers will rise as Baby-Boomers enter the age group in the years ahead.

Older Asian men are more likely to work

(percent of men aged 55 or older in the labor force by race and Hispanic origin, 2003)

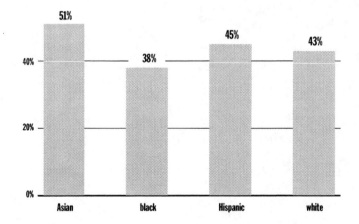

Table 5.3 Employment Status of Men by Race, Hispanic Origin, and Age, 2003

(number and percent of men aged 16 or older in the civilian labor force by race, Hispanic origin, age, and employment status, 2003; numbers in thousands)

	civilian noninstitutional population	total	percent of population	employed	number	percent of labor force
			civilian labor force		**unemployed**	
ASIAN MEN						
Total, aged 16 or older	**4,338**	**3,277**	**75.6%**	**3,073**	**204**	**6.2%**
Under age 55	3,472	2,838	81.7	2,660	179	6.3
Aged 55 or older	866	439	50.7	413	25	5.7
Aged 55 to 59	260	217	83.2	204	12	5.6
Aged 60 to 64	197	139	70.4	130	9	6.3
Aged 65 or older	409	83	20.3	79	4	4.5
Aged 65 to 69	147	55	37.6	54	2	3.2
Aged 70 to 74	107	14	13.1	12	–	–
Aged 75 or older	154	14	8.8	14	–	–
BLACK MEN						
Total, aged 16 or older	**11,454**	**7,711**	**67.3**	**6,820**	**891**	**11.6**
Under age 55	9,172	6,840	74.6	6,006	834	12.2
Aged 55 or older	2,282	871	38.2	814	57	6.5
Aged 55 to 59	625	421	67.5	390	31	7.4
Aged 60 to 64	564	264	46.7	248	16	5.9
Aged 65 or older	1,093	186	17.0	176	10	5.6
Aged 65 to 69	381	107	28.1	102	4	4.1
Aged 70 to 74	298	48	16.2	45	4	7.5
Aged 75 or older	414	31	7.4	28	2	–
HISPANIC MEN						
Total, aged 16 or older	**14,098**	**11,288**	**80.1**	**10,479**	**809**	**7.2**
Under age 55	12,247	10,458	85.4	9,695	763	7.3
Aged 55 or older	1,851	830	44.8	784	46	5.5
Aged 55 to 59	573	441	77.1	417	25	5.6
Aged 60 to 64	416	239	57.5	223	16	6.8
Aged 65 or older	862	150	17.4	144	5	3.6
Aged 65 to 69	305	85	27.7	81	3	4.0
Aged 70 to 74	230	35	15.4	34	1	3.9
Aged 75 or older	327	30	9.1	29	1	–
WHITE MEN						
Total, aged 16 or older	**88,249**	**65,509**	**74.2**	**61,866**	**3,643**	**5.6**
Under age 55	63,989	55,150	86.2	51,931	3,219	5.8
Aged 55 or older	24,260	10,359	42.7	9,935	424	4.1
Aged 55 to 59	6,513	5,117	78.6	4,911	206	4.0
Aged 60 to 64	4,929	2,856	57.9	2,729	127	4.4
Aged 65 or older	12,818	2,386	18.6	2,295	91	3.8
Aged 65 to 69	3,855	1,274	33.1	1,218	56	4.4
Aged 70 to 74	3,309	636	19.2	615	21	3.3
Aged 75 or older	5,654	475	8.4	462	13	2.8

Note: Race is shown only for those selecting that race group only. People who selected more than one race are not included. Hispanics may be of any race. (–) means number is less than 500 or sample is too small to make a reliable estimate.
Source: Bureau of Labor Statistics, 2003 Current Population Survey, Internet site http://www.bls.gov/cps/home.htm; calculations by New Strategist

Table 5.4 Employment Status of Women by Race, Hispanic Origin, and Age, 2003

(number and percent of women aged 16 or older in the civilian labor force by race, Hispanic origin, age, and employment status, 2003; numbers in thousands)

	civilian noninstitutional population	civilian labor force total	percent of population	employed	unemployed number	percent of labor force
ASIAN WOMEN						
Total, aged 16 or older	4,882	2,845	58.3%	2,683	162	5.7%
Under age 55	3,799	2,508	66.0	2,362	146	5.8
Aged 55 or older	1,083	337	31.1	321	16	4.7
Aged 55 to 59	309	198	64.0	187	11	5.3
Aged 60 to 64	219	91	41.5	87	4	4.6
Aged 65 or older	555	48	8.7	47	1	3.1
Aged 65 to 69	175	33	19.0	32	1	–
Aged 70 to 74	161	9	5.3	8	–	–
Aged 75 or older	219	7	3.0	7	–	–
BLACK WOMEN						
Total, aged 16 or older	14,232	8,815	61.9	7,919	895	10.2
Under age 55	10,975	7,854	71.6	7,013	839	10.7
Aged 55 or older	3,257	961	29.5	906	56	5.8
Aged 55 to 59	845	505	59.8	475	30	5.9
Aged 60 to 64	659	276	41.8	260	16	5.8
Aged 65 or older	1,753	180	10.3	171	10	5.3
Aged 65 to 69	518	110	21.2	103	7	6.5
Aged 70 to 74	438	36	8.3	35	1	3.1
Aged 75 or older	797	34	4.3	33	1	–
HISPANIC WOMEN						
Total, aged 16 or older	13,452	7,525	55.9	6,894	631	8.4
Under age 55	11,181	6,896	61.7	6,297	599	8.7
Aged 55 or older	2,271	629	27.7	597	32	5.1
Aged 55 to 59	630	351	55.8	333	18	5.1
Aged 60 to 64	475	169	35.6	159	10	5.7
Aged 65 or older	1,166	109	9.4	105	4	4.4
Aged 65 to 69	386	70	18.1	68	2	3.1
Aged 70 to 74	297	26	8.8	24	2	–
Aged 75 or older	483	14	2.8	13	1	–
WHITE WOMEN						
Total, aged 16 or older	93,043	55,037	59.2	52,369	2,668	4.8
Under age 55	63,679	46,215	72.6	43,846	2,369	5.1
Aged 55 or older	29,364	8,822	30.0	8,523	299	3.4
Aged 55 to 59	6,807	4,516	66.3	4,362	154	3.4
Aged 60 to 64	5,341	2,454	46.0	2,373	81	3.3
Aged 65 or older	17,216	1,852	10.8	1,788	64	3.5
Aged 65 to 69	4,374	1,012	23.1	974	38	3.8
Aged 70 to 74	4,034	474	11.7	460	14	2.9
Aged 75 or older	8,808	366	4.2	354	12	3.3

Note: Race is shown only for those selecting that race group only. People who selected more than one race are not included. Hispanics may be of any race. (–) means number is less than 500 or sample is too small to make a reliable estimate.
Source: Bureau of Labor Statistics, 2003 Current Population Survey, Internet site http://www.bls.gov/cps/home.htm; calculations by New Strategist

Few Older Couples Are Dual Earners

Many couples aged 55 to 64 are dual earners, however.

Dual incomes are the norm among married couples. Both husband and wife are in the labor force in 56 percent of the nation's couples. In another 22 percent, the husband is the only worker. Not far behind are the 17 percent of couples in which neither spouse is in the labor force. The wife is the sole worker among 6 percent of couples.

The 69 percent majority of couples under age 55 are dual earners. Among those aged 55 or older, however, both spouses are in the labor force in only 27 percent. The figure is a much higher 46 percent among couples aged 55 to 64. The wife is the only one employed in a substantial 12 percent of couples in the 55-to-64 age group. In these homes, typically, the older husband is retired while the younger wife is still at work. In 72 percent of couples aged 65 or older, neither husband nor wife is working.

■ As Boomers fill the 55-to-64 age group, the dual-income couple share will rise because fewer Boomers will have the opportunity to retire before age 65.

Dual earners account for nearly half of couples aged 55 to 64

(percent of married couples in which both husband and wife are in the labor force, by age, 2002)

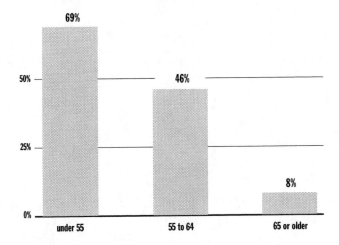

Table 5.5 Labor Force Status of Married-Couple Family Groups by Age of Reference Person, 2002

(number and percent distribution of married-couple family groups by age of reference person and labor force status of husband and wife, 2002; numbers in thousands)

| | total | husband and/or wife in labor force | | | neither husband nor wife in labor force |
		husband and wife	husband only	wife only	
Total married-couple family groups	**57,919**	**32,194**	**12,672**	**3,470**	**9,583**
Under age 55	39,156	27,188	9,625	1,438	903
Aged 55 or older	18,764	5,003	3,048	2,032	8,679
Aged 55 to 64	9,062	4,206	2,003	1,127	1,726
Aged 65 or older	9,702	797	1,045	905	6,953
Aged 65 to 74	6,006	684	822	746	3,753
Aged 75 or older	3,696	113	223	159	3,200
PERCENT DISTRIBUTION					
Total married-couple family groups	**100.0%**	**55.6%**	**21.9%**	**6.0%**	**16.5%**
Under age 55	100.0	69.4	24.6	3.7	2.3
Aged 55 or older	100.0	26.7	16.2	10.8	46.3
Aged 55 to 64	100.0	46.4	22.1	12.4	19.1
Aged 65 or older	100.0	8.2	10.8	9.3	71.7
Aged 65 to 74	100.0	11.4	13.7	12.4	62.5
Aged 75 or older	100.0	3.1	6.0	4.3	86.6

Note: Number of married-couple family groups exceeds number of married-couple householders because some households contain more than one married couple.
Source: Bureau of the Census, 2002 Current Population Survey Annual Demographic Supplement, Internet site http://www.census.gov/population/www/socdemo/hh-fam/cps2002.html; calculations by New Strategist

Few Working Americans Are Aged 55 or Older

Only 15 percent of the nation's 138 million employed are aged 55 or older.

The share of workers aged 55 or older varies by occupation. Only 7 percent of computer software engineers are aged 55 or older, for example, because of the rapid technological change that has occurred since older Americans began their career. Only 5 percent of firefighters or police are aged 55 or older, in part because of the physical requirements of the job and also because of early retirement options in those careers.

Workers aged 55 or older account for a disproportionate share of some occupations, however. They are half of all legislators, for example. They are 49 percent of farmers and ranchers and at least one-third of clergy and real estate agents. They account for 31 percent of psychologists.

■ As Boomers age into their late fifties and early sixties, expect to see a growing share of older workers in technical jobs.

People aged 55 or older account for few workers in technical occupations

(percent of workers aged 55 or older, by occupation, 2003)

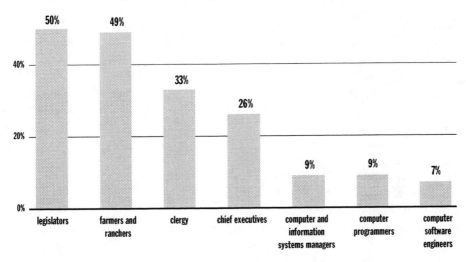

Table 5.6 Occupations of Workers Aged 55 or Older, 2003

(number of employed workers aged 16 or older, median age of workers, and number of workers aged 55 or older, by occupation, 2003; numbers in thousands)

	total	median age	aged 55 or older total	aged 55 or older 55 to 64	aged 55 or older 65 or older
TOTAL WORKERS	**137,736**	**40.4**	**21,206**	**16,598**	**4,608**
Management and professional occupations	**47,929**	**42.6**	**8,234**	**6,561**	**1,673**
Management, business and financial operations	19,934	44.0	3,947	3,055	892
Management	14,468	44.7	3,022	2,307	715
Business and financial operations	5,465	42.1	926	749	177
Professional and related occupations	27,995	41.5	4,286	3,506	780
Computer and mathematical	3,122	38.6	264	239	25
Architecture and engineering	2,727	41.5	389	322	67
Life, physical, and social sciences	1,375	41.2	213	170	43
Community and social services	2,184	43.1	419	321	98
Legal	1,508	43.1	292	232	60
Education, training, and library	7,768	42.6	1,393	1,177	216
Arts, design, entertainment, sports, and media	2,663	40.0	376	278	98
Health care practitioner and technician	6,648	41.9	939	766	173
Service occupations	**22,086**	**36.3**	**2,872**	**2,122**	**750**
Health care support	2,926	38.1	355	294	61
Protective service	2,727	39.9	375	272	103
Food preparation and serving	7,254	28.6	613	440	173
Building and grounds cleaning and maintenance	4,947	40.8	878	651	227
Personal care and service	4,232	37.9	651	465	186
Sales and office occupations	**35,496**	**39.7**	**5,770**	**4,421**	**1,349**
Sales and related occupations	15,960	38.8	2,659	1,940	719
Office and administrative support	19,536	40.5	3,112	2,482	630
Natural resources, construction, and maintenance occupations	**14,205**	**38.9**	**1,625**	**1,342**	**283**
Farming, fishing, and forestry	1,050	36.7	141	103	38
Construction and extraction	8,114	38.2	824	683	141
Installation, maintenance, and repair	5,041	40.4	660	556	104
Production, transportation, and material moving occupations	**18,020**	**40.7**	**2,706**	**2,152**	**554**
Production	9,700	41.1	1,413	1,176	237
Transportation and material moving	8,320	40.1	1,292	976	316

Source: Bureau of Labor Statistics, unpublished data from the 2003 Current Population Survey; calculations by New Strategist

Table 5.7 Distribution of Workers Aged 55 or Older by Occupation, 2003

(percent distribution of employed people aged 16 or older and aged 55 or older by occupation, 2003)

	total	aged 55 or older		
		total	55 to 64	65 or older
TOTAL WORKERS	**100.0%**	**100.0%**	**100.0%**	**100.0%**
Management and professional occupations	**34.8**	**38.8**	**39.5**	**36.3**
Management, business and financial operations	14.5	18.6	18.4	19.4
Management	10.5	14.3	13.9	15.5
Business and financial operations	4.0	4.4	4.5	3.8
Professional and related occupations	20.3	20.2	21.1	16.9
Computer and mathematical	2.3	1.2	1.4	0.5
Architecture and engineering	2.0	1.8	1.9	1.5
Life, physical, and social sciences	1.0	1.0	1.0	0.9
Community and social services	1.6	2.0	1.9	2.1
Legal	1.1	1.4	1.4	1.3
Education, training, and library	5.6	6.6	7.1	4.7
Arts, design, entertainment, sports, and media	1.9	1.8	1.7	2.1
Health care practitioner and technician	4.8	4.4	4.6	3.8
Service occupations	**16.0**	**13.5**	**12.8**	**16.3**
Health care support	2.1	1.7	1.8	1.3
Protective service	2.0	1.8	1.6	2.2
Food preparation and serving	5.3	2.9	2.7	3.8
Building and grounds cleaning and maintenance	3.6	4.1	3.9	4.9
Personal care and service	3.1	3.1	2.8	4.0
Sales and office occupations	**25.8**	**27.2**	**26.6**	**29.3**
Sales and related occupations	11.6	12.5	11.7	15.6
Office and administrative support	14.2	14.7	15.0	13.7
Natural resources, construction, and maintenance occupations	**10.3**	**7.7**	**8.1**	**6.1**
Farming, fishing, and forestry	0.8	0.7	0.6	0.8
Construction and extraction	5.9	3.9	4.1	3.1
Installation, maintenance, and repair	3.7	3.1	3.3	2.3
Production, transportation, and material moving occupations	**13.1**	**12.8**	**13.0**	**12.0**
Production	7.0	6.7	7.1	5.1
Transportation and material moving	6.0	6.1	5.9	6.9

Source: Calculations by New Strategist based on Bureau of Labor Statistics' unpublished 2003 Current Population Survey data

Table 5.8 Share of Workers Aged 55 or Older by Occupation, 2003

(employed persons aged 55 or older as a percent of total employed people aged 16 or older by occupation, 2003)

	total	aged 55 or older total	55 to 64	65 or older
TOTAL WORKERS	**100.0%**	**15.4%**	**12.1%**	**3.3%**
Management and professional occupations	**100.0**	**17.2**	**13.7**	**3.5**
Management, business and financial operations	100.0	19.8	15.3	4.5
Management	100.0	20.9	15.9	4.9
Business and financial operations	100.0	16.9	13.7	3.2
Professional and related occupations	100.0	15.3	12.5	2.8
Computer and mathematical	100.0	8.5	7.7	0.8
Architecture and engineering	100.0	14.3	11.8	2.5
Life, physical, and social sciences	100.0	15.5	12.4	3.1
Community and social services	100.0	19.2	14.7	4.5
Legal	100.0	19.4	15.4	4.0
Education, training, and library	100.0	17.9	15.2	2.8
Arts, design, entertainment, sports, and media	100.0	14.1	10.4	3.7
Health care practitioner and technician	100.0	14.1	11.5	2.6
Service occupations	**100.0**	**13.0**	**9.6**	**3.4**
Health care support	100.0	12.1	10.1	2.1
Protective service	100.0	13.8	10.0	3.8
Food preparation and serving	100.0	8.5	6.1	2.4
Building and grounds cleaning and maintenance	100.0	17.7	13.2	4.6
Personal care and service	100.0	15.4	11.0	4.4
Sales and office occupations	**100.0**	**16.3**	**12.5**	**3.8**
Sales and related occupations	100.0	16.7	12.2	4.5
Office and administrative support	100.0	15.9	12.7	3.2
Natural resources, construction, and maintenance occupations	**100.0**	**11.4**	**9.4**	**2.0**
Farming, fishing, and forestry	100.0	13.4	9.8	3.6
Construction and extraction	100.0	10.2	8.4	1.7
Installation, maintenance, and repair	100.0	13.1	11.0	2.1
Production, transportation, and material moving occupations	**100.0**	**15.0**	**11.9**	**3.1**
Production	100.0	14.6	12.1	2.4
Transportation and material moving	100.0	15.5	11.7	3.8

Source: Calculations by New Strategist based on Bureau of Labor Statistics' unpublished 2003 Current Population Survey data

Table 5.9 Workers Aged 55 or Older by Detailed Occupation, 2003

(number of employed workers aged 16 or older, median age, and number and percent aged 55 or older, by selected detailed occupation, 2003; numbers in thousands)

	total workers	median age	total aged 55 or older		aged 55 to 64		aged 65 or older	
			number	percent of total	number	percent of total	number	percent of total
Total workers	**137,736**	**40.4**	**21,206**	**15.4%**	**16,598**	**12.1%**	**4,608**	**3.3%**
Chief executives	1,617	48.2	413	25.5	328	20.3	85	5.3
Legislators	14	53.2	7	50.0	4	28.6	3	21.4
Marketing and sales managers	888	41.6	119	13.4	103	11.6	16	1.8
Computer, info. systems mgrs.	347	41.7	30	8.6	29	8.4	1	0.3
Financial managers	1,041	42.1	159	15.3	140	13.4	19	1.8
Human resources managers	263	45.1	48	18.3	46	17.5	2	0.8
Farmers and ranchers	825	54.0	402	48.7	201	24.4	201	24.4
Education administrators	748	48.9	194	25.9	170	22.7	24	3.2
Food service managers	875	39.5	111	12.7	88	10.1	23	2.6
Medical, health services managers	480	46.1	83	17.3	71	14.8	12	2.5
Accountants and auditors	1,639	41.1	242	14.8	195	11.9	47	2.9
Computer scientists and systems analysts	722	40.4	80	11.1	72	10.0	8	1.1
Computer programmers	563	38.7	50	8.9	46	8.2	4	0.7
Computer software engineers	758	38.3	55	7.3	49	6.5	6	0.8
Architects	180	42.0	30	16.7	23	12.8	7	3.9
Civil engineers	278	42.9	50	18.0	38	13.7	12	4.3
Electrical engineers	363	42.7	46	12.7	42	11.6	4	1.1
Mechanical engineers	285	41.0	41	14.4	33	11.6	8	2.8
Medical scientists	101	39.9	12	11.9	10	9.9	2	2.0
Psychologists	185	50.2	58	31.4	44	23.8	14	7.6
Social workers	673	41.4	100	14.9	87	12.9	13	1.9
Clergy	410	49.9	134	32.7	84	20.5	50	12.2
Lawyers	952	44.4	208	21.8	160	16.8	48	5.0
Postsecondary teachers	1,121	43.8	275	24.5	213	19.0	62	5.5
Preschool, kindergarten teachers	665	38.9	84	12.6	73	11.0	11	1.7
Elementary and middle school teachers	2,557	42.7	422	16.5	371	14.5	51	2.0
Secondary school teachers	1,124	43.7	198	17.6	176	15.7	22	2.0
Librarians	194	49.6	56	28.9	49	25.3	7	3.6
Teacher assistants	932	41.8	134	14.4	116	12.4	18	1.9
Artists	212	43.8	48	22.6	36	17.0	12	5.7
Actors	30	36.6	4	13.3	3	10.0	1	3.3
Athletes	215	30.1	19	8.8	12	5.6	7	3.3
Editors	163	40.8	25	15.3	21	12.9	4	2.5
Writers and authors	190	44.8	45	23.7	31	16.3	14	7.4
Dentists	188	46.0	49	26.1	37	19.7	12	6.4
Pharmacists	232	42.1	52	22.4	37	15.9	15	6.5
Physicians and surgeons	819	44.2	154	18.8	110	13.4	44	5.4
Registered nurses	2,449	43.1	356	14.5	305	12.5	51	2.1
Physical therapists	182	37.6	13	7.1	12	6.6	1	0.5

	total workers	median age	total aged 55 or older		aged 55 to 64		aged 65 or older	
			number	percent of total	number	percent of total	number	percent of total
Licensed practical nurses	531	43.3	83	15.6%	70	13.2%	13	2.4%
Nursing, psychiatric, and home health aides	1,811	39.2	260	14.4	211	11.7	49	2.7
Firefighters	258	38.3	12	4.7	11	4.3	1	0.4
Police and sheriff's patrol officers	612	38.7	32	5.2	30	4.9	2	0.3
Security guards and gaming surveillance officers	781	40.7	190	24.3	124	15.9	66	8.5
Chefs and head cooks	281	37.8	28	10.0	21	7.5	7	2.5
Cooks	1,814	32.1	175	9.6	130	7.2	45	2.5
Food preparation workers	612	29.4	64	10.5	43	7.0	21	3.4
Waiters and waitresses	1,842	24.6	89	4.8	59	3.2	30	1.6
Janitors and building cleaners	1,973	43.2	440	22.3	320	16.2	120	6.1
Maids, housekeeping cleaners	1,370	42.2	256	18.7	193	14.1	63	4.6
Grounds maintenance workers	1,135	34.1	112	9.9	82	7.2	30	2.6
Hairdressers, hair stylists, and cosmetologists	718	39.0	101	14.1	84	11.7	17	2.4
Child care workers	1,284	35.4	170	13.2	123	9.6	47	3.7
Cashiers	2,903	26.1	282	9.7	186	6.4	96	3.3
Retail salespersons	3,113	35.9	531	17.1	360	11.6	171	5.5
Insurance sales agents	552	44.1	118	21.4	88	15.9	30	5.4
Securities, commodities, and financial services sales agents	389	39.8	57	14.7	41	10.5	16	4.1
Sales representatives, wholesale and manufacturing	1,399	41.7	226	16.2	186	13.3	40	2.9
Real estate brokers, sales agents	850	48.6	284	33.4	200	23.5	84	9.9
Bookkeeping, accounting, and auditing clerks	1,545	44.5	359	23.2	257	16.6	102	6.6
Customer service representatives	1,747	36.0	194	11.1	163	9.3	31	1.8
Receptionists, information clerks	1,376	36.9	245	17.8	168	12.2	77	5.6
Stock clerks and order fillers	1,360	33.6	150	11.0	114	8.4	36	2.6
Secretaries and admin. assistants	3,632	43.7	709	19.5	592	16.3	117	3.2
Misc. agricultural workers	741	33.8	82	11.1	54	7.3	28	3.8
Carpenters	1,595	37.4	148	9.3	119	7.5	29	1.8
Construction laborers	1,151	34.8	101	8.8	84	7.3	17	1.5
Automotive service technicians and mechanics	884	37.6	89	10.1	76	8.6	13	1.5
Miscellaneous assemblers and fabricators	1,080	39.9	142	13.1	115	10.6	27	2.5
Machinists	454	42.3	74	16.3	67	14.8	7	1.5
Aircraft pilots, flight engineers	116	44.2	21	18.1	18	15.5	3	2.6
Driver/sales workers and truck drivers	3,214	42.1	560	17.4	437	13.6	123	3.8
Freight, stock and material movers, hand laborers	1,748	33.4	148	8.5	112	6.4	36	2.1

Source: Bureau of Labor Statistics, unpublished tables from the 2003 Current Population Survey; calculations by New Strategist

Part-time Work Appeals to Many

Workers aged 65 or older are much more likely than average to work part-time.

While only 11 percent of all men in the labor force work part-time, the proportion is 17 percent among men aged 55 or older. Part-time work rises with age among older men, from 10 percent of those aged 55 to 64 to 40 percent of those aged 65 or older. Among working women aged 55 or older, 30 percent work part-time. The proportion rises to 55 percent among those aged 65 or older.

Because so many older Americans work part-time, they account for a disproportionate share of part-time workers. Men aged 55 or older account for 25 percent of all men with part-time jobs.

■ More older Americans will work part-time as Boomers enter their sixties and look for ways to supplement their retirement income.

Many older workers choose part-time jobs

(percent of workers aged 55 or older who work part-time, by sex and age, 2003)

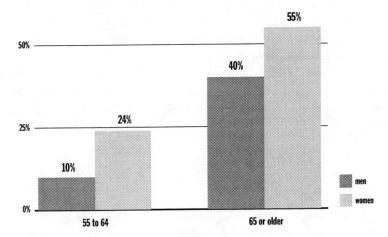

Table 5.10 Full- and Part-time Workers by Age and Sex, 2003

(number and percent distribution of employed people aged 16 or older in the civilian labor force by full- and part-time employment status, by age and sex, 2003; numbers in thousands)

	men			women		
	total	full-time	part-time	total	full-time	part-time
Total employed	**73,332**	**65,379**	**7,953**	**64,405**	**47,946**	**16,459**
Under age 55	62,014	56,011	6,003	54,515	41,041	13,474
Aged 55 or older	11,318	9,368	1,950	9,890	6,905	2,985
Aged 55 to 64	8,733	7,824	909	7,866	5,984	1,882
Aged 65 or older	2,585	1,544	1,041	2,023	920	1,103
Aged 65 to 69	1,397	911	486	1,119	567	552
Aged 70 to 74	680	370	310	508	187	321
Aged 75 or older	508	263	245	396	166	230
PERCENT DISTRIBUTION BY AGE						
Total employed	**100.0%**	**100.0%**	**100.0%**	**100.0%**	**100.0%**	**100.0%**
Under age 55	84.6	85.7	75.5	84.6	85.6	81.9
Aged 55 or older	15.4	14.3	24.5	15.4	14.4	18.1
Aged 55 to 64	11.9	12.0	11.4	12.2	12.5	11.4
Aged 65 or older	3.5	2.4	13.1	3.1	1.9	6.7
Aged 65 to 69	1.9	1.4	6.1	1.7	1.2	3.4
Aged 70 to 74	0.9	0.6	3.9	0.8	0.4	2.0
Aged 75 or older	0.7	0.4	3.1	0.6	0.3	1.4
PERCENT DISTRIBUTION BY EMPLOYMENT STATUS						
Total employed	**100.0%**	**89.2%**	**10.8%**	**100.0%**	**74.4%**	**25.6%**
Under age 55	100.0	90.3	9.7	100.0	75.3	24.7
Aged 55 or older	100.0	82.8	17.2	100.0	69.8	30.2
Aged 55 to 64	100.0	89.6	10.4	100.0	76.1	23.9
Aged 65 or older	100.0	59.7	40.3	100.0	45.5	54.5
Aged 65 to 69	100.0	65.2	34.8	100.0	50.7	49.3
Aged 70 to 74	100.0	54.4	45.6	100.0	36.8	63.2
Aged 75 or older	100.0	51.8	48.2	100.0	41.9	58.1

Source: Unpublished data from the Bureau of Labor Statistics; calculations by New Strategist

Many Older Americans Are Self-Employed

Men and women aged 65 or older are more likely than average to work for themselves.

While only 7 percent of all employed workers aged 16 or older are self-employed, 19 percent of workers aged 65 or older work for themselves. Self-employment usually requires specialized skills, and those most likely to have such skills are older workers with decades of experience. Men and women aged 55 or older account for 27 percent of the self-employed, a much greater proportion than their share of all workers.

Older men are more likely to be self-employed than older women. While 10 percent of employed women aged 55 or older work for themselves, the proportion is 16 percent among men. Twenty-three percent of men aged 65 or older are self-employed versus 14 percent of their female counterparts.

■ As Boomers enter the 55-or-older age group, the number of self-employed Americans will rise.

Self-employment is common among older men

(percent of employed men aged 16 or older and aged 55 or older who are self-employed, 2003)

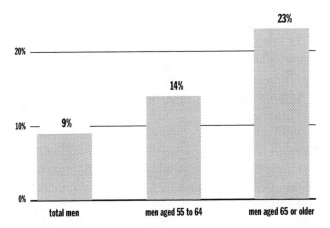

Table 5.11 Self-Employed Workers by Sex and Age, 2003

(number of employed workers aged 16 or older, number and percent who are self-employed, and percent distribution of self-employed, by sex and age, 2003; numbers in thousands)

	total	self-employed number	self-employed percent	percent distribution of self-employed by age
Total workers	**137,736**	**10,295**	**7.5%**	**100.0%**
Under age 55	116,530	7,477	6.4	72.6
Aged 55 or older	21,206	2,818	13.3	27.4
Aged 55 to 64	16,598	1,938	11.7	18.8
Aged 65 or older	4,608	880	19.1	8.5
Total men	**73,331**	**6,430**	**8.8**	**100.0**
Under age 55	62,013	4,609	7.4	71.7
Aged 55 or older	11,318	1,821	16.1	28.3
Aged 55 to 64	8,733	1,231	14.1	19.1
Aged 65 or older	2,585	590	22.8	9.2
Total women	**64,404**	**3,866**	**6.0**	**100.0**
Under age 55	54,516	2,868	5.3	74.2
Aged 55 or older	9,888	998	10.1	25.8
Aged 55 to 64	7,865	707	9.0	18.3
Aged 65 or older	2,023	291	14.4	7.5

Source: Bureau of Labor Statistics, 2003 Current Population Survey, Internet site http://www.bls.gov/cps/home.htm; calculations by New Strategist

Among Older Men, Job Tenure Is Down

Women's job tenure has been more stable.

Job tenure is down for men in most age groups, but the biggest drop occurred among men aged 55 to 64. In 1991, men aged 55 to 64 had been with their current employer a median of 13.4 years. By 2002, the figure had fallen by more than three years, to 10.2 years. Job tenure also fell slightly among women aged 55 to 64.

Statistics on long-term employment also reveal erosion in employer-employee relationships. The proportion of men aged 60 to 64 who have worked for their current employer for at least ten years has fallen 10 percentage points, from 58 to 48 percent between 1991 and 2002. Among women in the age group, long-term employment rose between 1991 and 2000, but fell between 2000 and 2002.

■ Unless job losses continue, long-term employment may rise if fewer older men opt for early retirement.

Fewer men aged 55 to 64 have long-term jobs

(percent of men aged 55 to 64 who have worked for their current employer for ten or more years, 1991 and 2002)

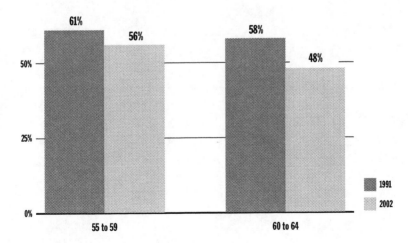

Table 5.12 Job Tenure by Sex and Age, 1991 to 2002

(median number of years that employed wage and salary workers aged 25 or older have been with their current employer, by sex and age, 1991 to 2002; change in years, 2000–2002 and 1991–2002)

	2002	2000	1991	change in years 2000–02	change in years 1991–02
Total workers aged 25 or older	**4.7**	**4.7**	**4.8**	**0.0**	**−0.1**
Aged 25 to 34	2.7	2.6	2.9	0.1	−0.2
Aged 35 to 44	4.6	4.8	5.4	−0.2	−0.8
Aged 45 to 54	7.6	8.2	8.9	−0.6	−1.3
Aged 55 to 64	9.9	10.0	11.1	−0.1	−1.2
Aged 65 or older	8.7	9.5	8.1	−0.8	0.6
Total men aged 25 or older	**4.9**	**5.0**	**5.4**	**−0.1**	**−0.5**
Aged 25 to 34	2.9	2.7	3.1	0.2	−0.2
Aged 35 to 44	5.1	5.4	6.5	−0.3	−1.4
Aged 45 to 54	9.1	9.5	11.2	−0.4	−2.1
Aged 55 to 64	10.2	10.2	13.4	0.0	−3.2
Aged 65 or older	8.1	9.1	7.0	−1.0	1.1
Total women aged 25 or older	**4.4**	**4.4**	**4.3**	**0.0**	**0.1**
Aged 25 to 34	2.5	2.5	2.7	0.0	−0.2
Aged 35 to 44	4.3	4.3	4.5	0.0	−0.2
Aged 45 to 54	6.5	7.3	6.7	−0.8	−0.2
Aged 55 to 64	9.6	9.9	9.9	−0.3	−0.3
Aged 65 or older	9.5	9.7	9.5	−0.2	0.0

Source: Bureau of Labor Statistics, Internet site http://www.bls.gov/news.release/tenure.t01.htm; calculations by New Strategist

Table 5.13 Long-Term Employment of People Aged 55 or Older by Sex, 1991 to 2002

(percent of employed wage and salary workers aged 25 or older and aged 55 or older who have been with their current employer for ten or more years, by sex, 1991 to 2002; percentage point change in share, 2000–2002 and 1991–2002)

	2002	2000	1991	percentage point change 2000–02	percentage point change 1991–02
Total workers aged 25 or older	**31.0%**	**31.7%**	**32.2%**	**–0.7**	**–1.2**
Aged 55 to 59	53.2	53.1	56.7	0.1	–3.5
Aged 60 to 64	50.3	53.2	55.4	–2.9	–5.1
Aged 65 or older	48.1	50.0	46.3	–1.9	1.8
Men aged 25 or older	**33.0**	**33.6**	**35.9**	**–0.6**	**–2.9**
Aged 55 to 59	56.4	53.7	61.0	2.7	–4.6
Aged 60 to 64	48.3	52.5	57.5	–4.2	–9.2
Aged 65 or older	46.4	48.9	42.6	–2.5	3.8
Women aged 25 or older	**28.8**	**29.5**	**28.2**	**–0.7**	**1.3**
Aged 55 to 59	49.9	52.5	51.4	–2.6	1.1
Aged 60 to 64	52.3	54.0	53.1	–1.7	0.9
Aged 65 or older	50.0	51.2	49.9	–1.2	1.3

Source: Bureau of Labor Statistics, Internet site http://www.bls.gov/news.release/tenure.t02.htm; calculations by New Strategist

Independent Contracting Appeals to Older Workers

More than one in five workers aged 65 or older has an alternative work arrangement.

Older workers are most likely to have alternative work arrangements. The Bureau of Labor Statistics defines alternative workers as independent contractors, on-call workers (such as substitute teachers), temporary-help agency workers, and people who work for contract firms (such as lawn or janitorial service companies).

The most popular alternative work arrangement is independent contracting—which includes most of the self-employed. Among the 12.5 million alternative workers, 8.6 million, or 69 percent, are independent contractors. Among alternative workers aged 65 or older, fully 80 percent are independent contractors, accounting for 17 percent of all workers in the 65-or-older age group. This age group is also more likely than average to do on-call work.

■ Many older workers opt for self-employment because it gives them more control over their work schedule, and their government-provided health insurance coverage allows them the freedom to strike out on their own.

Older workers are most likely to be independent contractors

(percent of employed workers who are independent contractors, by age, 2001)

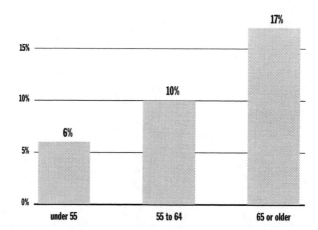

Table 5.14 Alternative Work Arrangements by Age, 2001

(number and percent distribution of employed people aged 16 or older with alternative work arrangements by age and type of alternative work, 2001; numbers in thousands)

	employed	with traditional work arrangements	with alternative work arrangements				
			total	independent contractors	on-call workers	temporary help agency workers	workers provided by contract firms
Total people	**134,605**	**121,917**	**12,476**	**8,585**	**2,089**	**1,169**	**633**
Under age 55	116,621	106,496	9,912	6,549	1,778	1,027	558
Aged 55 to 64	13,955	12,227	1,720	1,357	191	124	48
Aged 65 or older	4,029	3,193	844	679	119	18	28
PERCENT DISTRIBUTION BY ALTERNATIVE WORK STATUS							
Total people	**100.0%**	**90.6%**	**9.3%**	**6.4%**	**1.6%**	**0.9%**	**0.5%**
Under age 55	100.0	91.3	8.5	5.6	1.5	0.9	0.5
Aged 55 to 64	100.0	87.6	12.3	9.7	1.4	0.9	0.3
Aged 65 or older	100.0	79.3	20.9	16.9	3.0	0.4	0.7
PERCENT DISTRIBUTION BY AGE							
Total people	**100.0%**	**100.0%**	**100.0%**	**100.0%**	**100.0%**	**100.0%**	**100.0%**
Under age 55	86.6	87.4	79.4	76.3	85.1	87.9	88.2
Aged 55 to 64	10.4	10.0	13.8	15.8	9.1	10.6	7.6
Aged 65 or older	3.0	2.6	6.8	7.9	5.7	1.5	4.4

Note: Numbers may not add to total because the total employed includes day laborers, an alternative arrangement not shown separately, and a small number of workers who were both on call and provided by contract firms. Independent contractors are self-employed (except incorporated) or wage and salary workers who obtain customers on their own to provide a product or service. On-call workers are in a pool of workers who are called to work only as needed, such as substitute teachers and construction workers supplied by a union hiring hall. Temporary help agency workers are those who said they are paid by a temporary help agency. Workers provided by contract firms are those employed by a company that provides employees or their services to others under contract, such as security, landscaping, and computer programming.
Source: Bureau of Labor Statistics, Contingent and Alternative Employment Arrangements, February 2001, USDL 01-153, Internet site http://www.bls.gov/news.release/conemp.toc.htm; calculations by New Strategist

Many Workers Have Flexible Schedules

Men are more likely than women to have flexible schedules.

Twenty-nine percent of the nation's wage and salary workers have flexible schedules—meaning they may vary the time they begin or end work, according to the Bureau of Labor Statistics. Men are more likely than women to have flexible schedules—30 versus 27 percent in 2001.

The percentage of workers with flexible schedules varies little by age. Among men, those aged 65 or older are most likely to have flexible schedules (37 percent). Among women, those aged 65 or older are least likely to have flexible schedules (22 percent).

Fifteen percent of wage and salary workers do not work a regular daytime schedule. The youngest workers are most likely to work shifts—23 percent of those aged 16 to 24 work the evening, night, or other shift. The figure bottoms out at 13 percent among 55-to-64-year-olds, then rises to 15 percent among workers aged 65 or older.

■ Older workers are less likely to work a regular daytime shift because many are part-timers supplementing their retirement income with evening work.

Older workers are more likely than the middle aged to be shift workers

(percent of wage and salary workers who do not work a regular daytime schedule, by age, 2001)

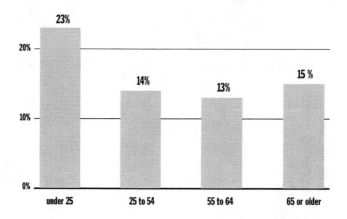

Table 5.15 Workers with Flexible Work Schedules by Age, 2001

(number and percent distribution of full-time wage and salary workers aged 16 or older with flexible work sched-ules, by sex and age, 2001; numbers in thousands)

| | total | with flexible schedules | |
		number	percent
Full-time wage and salary workers	**99,631**	**28,724**	**28.8%**
Under age 55	88,304	25,668	29.1
Aged 55 to 64	9,971	2,633	26.4
Aged 65 or older	1,357	423	31.2
Men	**56,066**	**16,792**	**30.0**
Under age 55	49,689	14,892	30.0
Aged 55 to 64	5,531	1,590	28.7
Aged 65 or older	847	311	36.7
Women	**43,566**	**11,931**	**27.4**
Under age 55	38,615	10,775	27.9
Aged 55 to 64	4,440	1,043	23.5
Aged 65 or older	510	112	22.0

Note: Flexible schedules are those that allow workers to vary the time they begin or end work.
Source: Bureau of Labor Statistics, Workers on Flexible and Shift Schedules in 2001, *USDL 02-225, 2002, Internet site http://www.bls.gov/news.release/flex.toc.htm*

Table 5.16 Workers by Shift Usually Worked and Age, 2001

(number of full-time wage and salary workers aged 16 or older and percent distribution by age and shift ususally worked, 2001; numbers in thousands)

	total	under 25	25 to 54	55 to 64	65 or older
Total full-time wage and salary workers, number	**99,631**	**11,104**	**77,200**	**9,971**	**1,357**
Total full-time wage and salary workers, percent	**100.0%**	**100.0%**	**100.0%**	**100.0%**	**100.0%**
Regular daytime schedule	84.8	76.6	85.8	86.3	84.9
Shift workers	14.5	22.5	13.5	13.2	15.0
Evening shift	4.8	9.4	4.2	4.5	3.9
Night shift	3.3	4.8	3.2	3.1	2.1
Rotating shift	2.3	3.3	2.3	1.7	1.7
Split shift	0.4	0.3	0.4	0.4	1.3
Employer-arranged irregular schedule	2.8	3.8	2.6	2.8	5.5
Other	0.7	0.8	0.7	0.6	0.5

Source: Bureau of Labor Statistics. Workers on Flexible and Shift Schedules in 2001, *USDL 02-225, 2002, Internet site http:// www.bls.gov/news.release/flex.toc.htm*

Most Minimum-Wage Workers Are Young Adults

The percentage of workers earning minimum wage or less rises in old age, however.

Among the nation's 73 million workers who are paid hourly rates, only 2 million (3 percent) make minimum wage or less, according to the Bureau of Labor Statistics. Fully 91 percent of minimum-wage workers are under age 55. Only 9 percent are aged 55 or older, and just 5 percent are aged 65 or older.

While 3 percent of all workers paid hourly rates make minimum wage or less, the figure falls to about 1 percent among the middle-aged. Among workers aged 60 or older, however, the proportion rises. Five percent of workers aged 65 or older are paid minimum wage or less.

■ Older workers are more likely to earn minimum wage than the middle aged because many are part-timers supplementing their retirement income.

Older workers are more likely than average to earn minimum wage or less

(percent of workers making minimum wage or less by age, 2002)

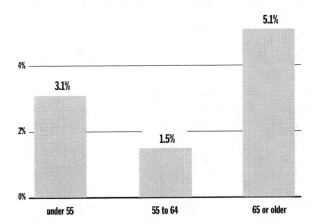

Table 5.17 Workers Earning Minimum Wage by Age, 2002

(number and percent distribution of workers paid hourly rates and workers paid at or below minimum wage, by age, 2002; numbers in thousands)

	total paid hourly rates	at or below minimum wage		
		total	at $5.15/hour	below $5.15/hour
Total aged 16 or older	**72,720**	**2,168**	**570**	**1,598**
Under age 55	63,890	1,963	511	1,452
Aged 55 or older	8,831	205	59	146
Aged 55 to 64	6,883	106	25	81
Aged 55 to 59	4,413	57	12	45
Aged 60 to 64	2,471	49	13	36
Aged 65 or older	1,948	99	34	65
Aged 65 to 69	1,107	52	14	38
Aged 70 or older	841	47	20	27
PERCENT DISTRIBUTION BY AGE				
Total aged 16 or older	**100.0%**	**100.0%**	**100.0%**	**100.0%**
Under age 55	87.9	90.5	89.6	90.9
Aged 55 or older	12.1	9.5	10.4	9.1
Aged 55 to 64	9.5	4.9	4.4	5.1
Aged 55 to 59	6.1	2.6	2.1	2.8
Aged 60 to 64	3.4	2.3	2.3	2.3
Aged 65 or older	2.7	4.6	6.0	4.1
Aged 65 to 69	1.5	2.4	2.5	2.4
Aged 70 or older	1.2	2.2	3.5	1.7
PERCENT DISTRIBUTION BY WAGE STATUS				
Total aged 16 or older	**100.0%**	**3.0%**	**0.8%**	**2.2%**
Under age 55	100.0	3.1	0.8	2.3
Aged 55 or older	100.0	2.3	0.7	1.7
Aged 55 to 64	100.0	1.5	0.4	1.2
Aged 55 to 59	100.0	1.3	0.3	1.0
Aged 60 to 64	100.0	2.0	0.5	1.5
Aged 65 or older	100.0	5.1	1.7	3.3
Aged 65 to 69	100.0	4.7	1.3	3.4
Aged 70 or older	100.0	5.6	2.4	3.2

Source: Bureau of Labor Statistics, Characteristics of Minimum Wage Workers, *2002, Internet site http://www.bls.gov/cps/ minwage2002.htm; calculations by New Strategist*

Union Membership Peaks among Workers Aged 45 to 54

Men are more likely than women to be union members.

Union membership has fallen sharply over the past few decades. In 1970, 30 percent of nonagricultural workers were members of labor unions. In 2003, only 13 percent were union members. A slightly larger 14 percent of workers are represented by unions.

The percentage of workers who belong to a union peaks in the 45-to-54 age group at 20 percent of men and 16 percent of women. A larger percentage of men are union members because they are more likely to work in jobs that are traditional strongholds of labor unions. In fact, the decline of labor unions is partly the result of the shift in jobs from manufacturing to services.

■ Union membership will continue to decline because the increasingly cut-throat economy rewards companies with more flexible workforces.

Few workers belong to unions

(percent of employed wage and salary workers who are members of unions, by age, 2003)

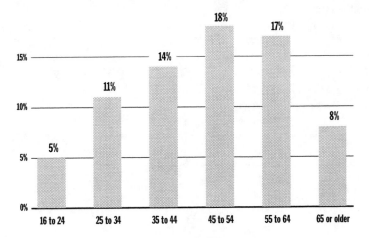

Table 5.18 Union Membership by Sex and Age, 2003

(number and percent of employed wage and salary workers aged 16 or older by union affiliation, sex, and age, 2003; numbers in thousands)

	total employed	represented by unions		members of unions	
		number	percent	number	percent
Total aged 16+	**122,358**	**17,448**	**14.3%**	**15,776**	**12.9%**
Aged 16 to 24	18,904	1,124	5.9	966	5.1
Aged 25 to 34	28,179	3,455	12.3	3,097	11.0
Aged 35 to 44	30,714	4,717	15.4	4,308	14.0
Aged 45 to 54	27,567	5,307	19.3	4,848	17.6
Aged 55 to 64	13,633	2,547	18.7	2,300	16.9
Aged 65 or older	3,361	297	8.8	258	7.7
Men aged 16+	**63,236**	**9,848**	**15.6**	**9,044**	**14.3**
Aged 16 to 24	9,683	685	7.1	595	6.1
Aged 25 to 34	15,263	2,005	13.1	1,826	12.0
Aged 35 to 44	16,080	2,735	17.0	2,535	15.8
Aged 45 to 54	13,723	2,891	21.1	2,684	19.6
Aged 55 to 64	6,776	1,377	20.3	1,271	18.8
Aged 65 or older	1,710	155	9.0	133	7.8
Women aged 16+	**59,122**	**7,601**	**12.9**	**6,732**	**11.4**
Aged 16 to 24	9,221	439	4.8	371	4.0
Aged 25 to 34	12,916	1,451	11.2	1,270	9.8
Aged 35 to 44	14,634	1,982	13.5	1,773	12.1
Aged 45 to 54	13,844	2,416	17.5	2,163	15.6
Aged 55 to 64	6,857	1,170	17.1	1,029	15.0
Aged 65 or older	1,651	142	8.6	125	7.6

Source: Bureau of Labor Statistics, 2003 Current Population Survey, Internet site http://www.bls.gov/cps/home.htm

More Older Americans Will Work

Changes in Social Security, fewer defined-benefit pension plans, and meager savings will keep people at work.

The labor force participation rate of older Americans will rise between 2003 and 2012, according to projections by the Bureau of Labor Statistics. Among men aged 55 or older, labor force participation should rise 2.8 percentage points during those years compared with a decline of 0.3 percentage points among men under age 55. For women, the participation rate of those aged 55 or older should rise 4.4 percentage points versus a smaller 2.7 percentage point gain for those under age 55.

Behind the rising participation rates of older workers is the end of early retirement as the Baby-Boom generation reaches its sixties. The increase in the age at which workers become eligible for full Social Security benefits, the disappearance of defined-benefit pension plans, meager savings, and stock market volatility will keep millions more older workers on the job.

According to a survey by AARP, most older workers see retirement as a chance to spend more time with family and friends, an opportunity to relax, and a time to have more fun. With fully 68 percent planning to work for pay in "retirement," however, many older Americans may be disappointed in their so-called leisure years.

■ Between 2003 and 2012, the number of workers aged 55 or older will increase by fully 9 million, a 42 percent increase.

Look for big gains in the number of workers aged 55 or older

(percent change in number of workers by age and sex, 2003–12)

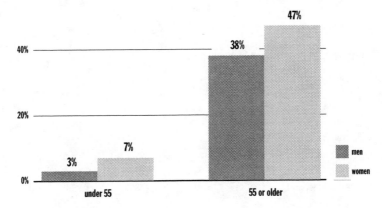

Table 5.19 Projections of the Labor Force by Sex and Age, 2003 to 2012

(number and percent of people aged 16 or older in the civilian labor force by sex and age, 2003 and 2012; percent change in number and percentage point change in participation rate, 2003–12; numbers in thousands)

	number			participation rate		
	2003	2012	percent change 2003–12	2003	2012	percentage point change 2003–12
Total labor force	**147,003**	**162,269**	**10.4%**	**67.1%**	**67.2%**	**0.1**
Total men in labor force	**78,560**	**85,252**	**8.5**	**74.4**	**73.1**	**–1.3**
Under age 55	66,730	68,896	3.2	85.4	85.1	–0.3
Aged 55 or older	11,830	16,356	38.3	43.0	45.8	2.8
Aged 55 to 64	9,232	12,714	37.7	69.3	69.9	0.6
Aged 55 to 59	5,907	7,684	30.1	77.8	77.9	0.1
Aged 60 to 64	3,325	5,031	51.3	58.0	60.4	2.4
Aged 60 to 61	1,708	2,374	39.0	67.2	68.7	1.5
Aged 62 to 64	1,617	2,656	64.3	50.7	54.6	3.9
Aged 65 or older	2,598	3,641	40.1	18.3	20.8	2.5
Aged 65 to 74	2,127	3,077	44.7	25.8	29.1	3.3
Aged 65 to 69	1,461	2,269	55.3	32.6	36.3	3.7
Aged 70 to 74	666	808	21.3	17.7	18.7	1.0
Aged 75 or older	471	564	19.7	7.9	8.2	0.3
Aged 75 to 79	307	330	7.5	10.4	10.9	0.5
Aged 80 or older	163	234	43.6	5.5	6.1	0.6
Total women in labor force	**68,443**	**77,017**	**12.5**	**60.4**	**61.6**	**1.2**
Under age 55	58,466	62,346	6.6	72.9	75.6	2.7
Aged 55 or older	9,977	14,671	47.1	30.1	34.5	4.4
Aged 55 to 64	8,043	11,902	48.0	55.8	60.6	4.8
Aged 55 to 59	5,211	7,355	41.1	64.5	70.0	5.5
Aged 60 to 64	2,831	4,547	60.6	44.7	49.7	5.0
Aged 60 to 61	1,487	2,303	54.9	53.4	61.1	7.7
Aged 62 to 64	1,345	2,244	66.8	37.8	41.8	4.0
Aged 65 or older	1,934	2,769	43.2	10.3	12.1	1.8
Aged 65 to 74	1,608	2,333	45.1	16.4	18.9	2.5
Aged 65 to 69	1,080	1,619	49.9	20.9	22.8	1.9
Aged 70 to 74	528	714	35.2	11.4	13.7	2.3
Aged 75 or older	326	436	33.7	3.6	4.1	0.5
Aged 75 to 79	226	278	23.0	5.6	7.0	1.4
Aged 80 or older	100	158	58.0	2.0	2.4	0.4

Source: Bureau of Labor Statistics, Internet site http://www.bls.gov/emp/emplab1.htm; calculations by New Strategist

Table 5.20 Retirement Definitions and Plans, 2003

(percent of working people aged 50 to 70 who "very much" or "somewhat" agree that the statement fits their personal definition of retirement, and percent distribution by plans for retirement, 2003)

	percent who agree very much or somewhat
RETIREMENT MEANS	
Spending more time with family and friends	78%
A chance to relax	73
A chance to have more fun	73
Receiving retirement benefits from Social Security or pension payments	72
A chance to do things you never had time for	72
A chance to travel	67
Doing volunteer or charity work	57
Slowing down and working fewer hours/part-time	56
Working for enjoyment, no money	53
A chance to stop working for pay completely	48
Having to do some kind of work to help pay the bills	42
A chance to leave your main career to try a different type of work	28
Feeling less useful or less productive	20

	percent distribution
PLANS FOR RETIREMENT	
Total	**100%**
Not work for pay at all	29
Work for pay	68
Work part-time, doing the same type of work you do now	24
Work part-time, doing something different	22
Start your own business/work for yourself, doing the same type of work you do now	5
Start your own business/work for yourself, doing something different	5
Work full-time, doing the same type of work you do now	5
Work full-time, doing something different	2
Never expect to retire	5
Don't know	3

Source: © 2003, AARP, Staying Ahead of the Curve 2003: The AARP Working in Retirement Study

6

Living Arrangements

■ Among the 23 million households headed by people aged 65 or older, a 42 percent minority are married couples.

■ Among older Americans, married couples are a much larger share of Asian, Hispanic, and non-Hispanic white households than of black households.

■ Average household size is just over two people in the 60-to-64 age group. It falls below two in the 65-to-74 age group.

■ Among householders aged 55 to 64, a substantial 24 percent have children living with them. The figure falls to 12 percent among householders aged 65 or older.

■ Fifty-nine percent of women aged 85 or older live alone versus only 31 percent of their male counterparts.

■ Among people aged 85 or older, fully 79 percent of women but only 34 percent of men are currently widowed.

Married Couples Lose Ground with Age

Only 42 percent of householders aged 65 or older are married couples.

Married couples headed the 52 percent majority of the nation's 111 million households in 2003. But among the 23 million households headed by people aged 65 or older, a 42 percent minority are couples. Older people are less likely than the average American to live with their spouse because an important transition in living arrangements occurs among people in their seventies. While married couples account for the majority of households headed by 60-to-69-year-olds, the proportion falls to 48 percent among householders aged 70 to 74, and drops to 33 percent among those aged 75 or older.

The married-couple share of older households falls as older women become widowed and begin to live alone. Women who live alone account for 27 percent of all households headed by people aged 55 or older, ranging from 15 percent of households headed by 55-to-59-year-olds to 43 percent of those headed by people aged 75 or older. In the oldest age group, the most common household type is women who live alone.

■ American women must prepare themselves emotionally and financially for living alone in old age.

Married-couple share of households falls in older age groups

(percent of households headed by married couples, by age, 2003)

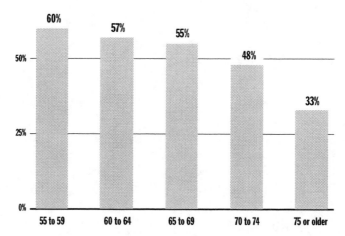

Table 6.1 Households Headed by People Aged 55 or Older by Household Type, 2003: Total Households

(number and percent distribution of total households and households headed by people aged 55 or older, by household type, 2003; numbers in thousands)

| | | aged 55 or older | | | | | |
| | | | | aged 65 or older | | | |
	total	total	55 to 59	60 to 64	total	65 to 69	70 to 74	75 or older
Total households	**111,278**	**38,920**	**9,192**	**7,069**	**22,659**	**5,845**	**5,516**	**11,299**
Family households	75,596	23,002	6,511	4,750	11,741	3,753	3,156	4,833
Married couples	57,320	19,107	5,513	4,030	9,564	3,205	2,660	3,700
Female householder,								
no spouse present	13,620	3,048	753	552	1,743	445	400	898
Male householder,								
no spouse present	4,656	847	245	168	434	103	95	235
Nonfamily households	35,682	15,917	2,680	2,319	10,918	2,092	2,360	6,466
Female householder	19,662	10,995	1,552	1,423	8,020	1,426	1,614	4,980
Living alone	16,919	10,564	1,406	1,334	7,824	1,359	1,551	4,914
Male householder	16,020	4,921	1,128	895	2,898	666	746	1,486
Living alone	12,511	4,489	980	784	2,725	601	689	1,434
PERCENT DISTRIBUTION BY TYPE								
Total households	**100.0%**	**100.0%**	**100.0%**	**100.0%**	**100.0%**	**100.0%**	**100.0%**	**100.0%**
Family households	67.9	59.1	70.8	67.2	51.8	64.2	57.2	42.8
Married couples	51.5	49.1	60.0	57.0	42.2	54.8	48.2	32.7
Female householder,								
no spouse present	12.2	7.8	8.2	7.8	7.7	7.6	7.3	7.9
Male householder,								
no spouse present	4.2	2.2	2.7	2.4	1.9	1.8	1.7	2.1
Nonfamily households	32.1	40.9	29.2	32.8	48.2	35.8	42.8	57.2
Female householder	17.7	28.3	16.9	20.1	35.4	24.4	29.3	44.1
Living alone	15.2	27.1	15.3	18.9	34.5	23.3	28.1	43.5
Male householder	14.4	12.6	12.3	12.7	12.8	11.4	13.5	13.2
Living alone	11.2	11.5	10.7	11.1	12.0	10.3	12.5	12.7
PERCENT DISTRIBUTION BY AGE								
Total households	**100.0%**	**35.0%**	**8.3%**	**6.4%**	**20.4%**	**5.3%**	**5.0%**	**10.2%**
Family households	100.0	30.4	8.6	6.3	15.5	5.0	4.2	6.4
Married couples	100.0	33.3	9.6	7.0	16.7	5.6	4.6	6.5
Female householder,								
no spouse present	100.0	22.4	5.5	4.1	12.8	3.3	2.9	6.6
Male householder,								
no spouse present	100.0	18.2	5.3	3.6	9.3	2.2	2.0	5.1
Nonfamily households	100.0	44.6	7.5	6.5	30.6	5.9	6.6	18.1
Female householder	100.0	55.9	7.9	7.2	40.8	7.3	8.2	25.3
Living alone	100.0	62.4	8.3	7.9	46.2	8.0	9.2	29.0
Male householder	100.0	30.7	7.0	5.6	18.1	4.2	4.7	9.3
Living alone	100.0	35.9	7.8	6.3	21.8	4.8	5.5	11.5

Source: Bureau of the Census, 2003 Current Population Survey, Annual Social and Economic Supplement, Internet site http:// ferret.bls.census.gov/macro/032003/hhinc/new02_000.htm; calculations by New Strategist

Households of Older Americans Differ by Race and Hispanic Origin

Among older households, married couples are a much larger share of Asian, Hispanic, and non-Hispanic white households than of black households.

There are sharp differences in household composition among older people by race and Hispanic origin. Among householders aged 65 or older, 55 percent of Asian, 48 percent of Hispanic, and 43 percent of non-Hispanic whites are married couples. In contrast, married couples head only 28 percent of black households in the age group. Female-headed families are common among older blacks, accounting for nearly one in six households headed by blacks aged 65 or older. The corresponding figure for non-Hispanic whites is just 6 percent.

Asian and Hispanic women are less likely to live alone in old age than black or non-Hispanic white women. Only 30 percent of Asian or Hispanic householders aged 75 or older are women who live alone. The figures are a higher 43 percent among blacks and 44 percent among non-Hispanic whites.

■ Many Asians and Hispanics are immigrants, bringing with them a traditional family structure that persists into old age.

The married-couple share of households varies by race and ethnicity

(married-couple share of households headed by people aged 65 or older, by race and Hispanic origin, 2003)

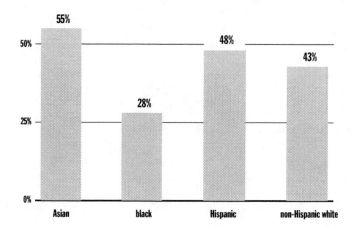

Table 6.2 Households Headed by People Aged 55 or Older by Household Type, 2003: Asian Households

(number and percent distribution of total households headed by Asians and households headed by Asians aged 55 or older, by household type, 2003; numbers in thousands)

| | total | aged 55 or older | | | aged 65 or older | | | |
		total	55 to 59	60 to 64	total	65 to 69	70 to 74	75 or older
Total Asian households	**4,079**	**928**	**284**	**197**	**447**	**154**	**125**	**168**
Family households	2,939	683	225	166	292	114	87	91
Married couples	2,344	564	182	138	244	105	72	68
Female householder, no spouse present	354	93	36	17	40	9	14	16
Male householder, no spouse present	241	27	7	11	9	–	2	7
Nonfamily households	1,140	244	59	31	154	40	38	77
Female householder	567	174	34	23	117	35	26	57
Living alone	435	158	30	23	105	29	25	51
Male householder	573	70	25	8	37	5	12	20
Living alone	411	65	23	5	37	5	12	20
PERCENT DISTRIBUTION BY TYPE								
Total Asian households	**100.0%**	**100.0%**	**100.0%**	**100.0%**	**100.0%**	**100.0%**	**100.0%**	**100.0%**
Family households	72.1	73.6	79.2	84.3	65.3	74.0	69.6	54.2
Married couples	57.5	60.8	64.1	70.1	54.6	68.2	57.6	40.5
Female householder, no spouse present	8.7	10.0	12.7	8.6	8.9	5.8	11.2	9.5
Male householder, no spouse present	5.9	2.9	2.5	5.6	2.0	–	1.6	4.2
Nonfamily households	27.9	26.3	20.8	15.7	34.5	26.0	30.4	45.8
Female householder	13.9	18.8	12.0	11.7	26.2	22.7	20.8	33.9
Living alone	10.7	17.0	10.6	11.7	23.5	18.8	20.0	30.4
Male householder	14.1	7.5	8.8	4.1	8.3	3.2	9.6	11.9
Living alone	10.1	7.0	8.1	2.5	8.3	3.2	9.6	11.9
PERCENT DISTRIBUTION BY AGE								
Total Asian households	**100.0%**	**22.8%**	**7.0%**	**4.8%**	**11.0%**	**3.8%**	**3.1%**	**4.1%**
Family households	100.0	23.2	7.7	5.6	9.9	3.9	3.0	3.1
Married couples	100.0	24.1	7.8	5.9	10.4	4.5	3.1	2.9
Female householder, no spouse present	100.0	26.3	10.2	4.8	11.3	2.5	4.0	4.5
Male householder, no spouse present	100.0	11.2	2.9	4.6	3.7	–	0.8	2.9
Nonfamily households	100.0	21.4	5.2	2.7	13.5	3.5	3.3	6.8
Female householder	100.0	30.7	6.0	4.1	20.6	6.2	4.6	10.1
Living alone	100.0	36.3	6.9	5.3	24.1	6.7	5.7	11.7
Male householder	100.0	12.2	4.4	1.4	6.5	0.9	2.1	3.5
Living alone	100.0	15.8	5.6	1.2	0.9	1.2	2.9	4.9

Note: Number of Asian households includes both those identifying themselves as Asian alone and those identifying themselves as Asian in combination with other races. (–) means number is less than 500 or sample is too small to make a reliable estimate.
Source: Bureau of the Census, 2003 Current Population Survey, Annual Social and Economic Supplement, Internet site http://ferret.bls.census.gov/macro/032003/hhinc/new02_000.htm; calculations by New Strategist

Table 6.3 Households Headed by People Aged 55 or Older by Household Type, 2003: Black Households

(number and percent distribution of total black households and black households headed by people aged 55 or older, by household type, 2003; numbers in thousands)

	total	aged 55 or older						
		total	55 to 59	60 to 64	aged 65 or older			
					total	65 to 69	70 to 74	75 or older
Total black households	**13,778**	**3,867**	**1,022**	**772**	**2,073**	**639**	**548**	**886**
Family households	9,128	2,046	612	433	1,001	350	289	363
Married couples	4,268	1,213	372	264	577	218	182	177
Female householder, no spouse present	4,069	708	203	138	367	113	96	158
Male householder, no spouse present	791	127	37	32	58	19	11	28
Nonfamily households	4,650	1,820	410	339	1,071	289	259	523
Female householder	2,550	1,182	251	223	708	169	155	384
Living alone	2,318	1,145	239	215	691	163	148	380
Male householder	2,100	638	159	116	363	119	104	140
Living alone	1,753	577	144	97	336	107	95	133
PERCENT DISTRIBUTION BY TYPE								
Total black households	**100.0%**	**100.0%**	**100.0%**	**100.0%**	**100.0%**	**100.0%**	**100.0%**	**100.0%**
Family households	66.3	52.9	59.9	56.1	48.3	54.8	52.7	41.0
Married couples	31.0	31.4	36.4	34.2	27.8	34.1	33.2	20.0
Female householder, no spouse present	29.5	18.3	19.9	17.9	17.7	17.7	17.5	17.8
Male householder, no spouse present	5.7	3.3	3.6	4.1	2.8	3.0	2.0	3.2
Nonfamily households	33.7	47.1	40.1	43.9	51.7	45.2	47.3	59.0
Female householder	18.5	30.6	24.6	28.9	34.2	26.4	28.3	43.3
Living alone	16.8	29.6	23.4	27.8	33.3	25.5	27.0	42.9
Male householder	15.2	16.5	15.6	15.0	17.5	18.6	19.0	15.8
Living alone	12.7	14.9	14.1	12.6	16.2	16.7	17.3	15.0
PERCENT DISTRIBUTION BY AGE								
Total black households	**100.0%**	**28.1%**	**7.4%**	**5.6%**	**15.1%**	**4.6%**	**4.0%**	**6.4%**
Family households	100.0	22.4	6.7	4.7	11.0	3.8	3.2	4.0
Married couples	100.0	28.4	8.7	6.2	13.5	5.1	4.3	4.1
Female householder, no spouse present	100.0	17.4	5.0	3.4	9.0	2.8	2.4	3.9
Male householder, no spouse present	100.0	16.1	4.7	4.1	7.3	2.4	1.4	3.5
Nonfamily households	100.0	39.1	8.8	7.3	23.0	6.2	5.6	11.2
Female householder	100.0	46.4	9.8	8.7	27.8	6.6	6.1	15.1
Living alone	100.0	49.4	10.3	9.3	29.8	7.0	6.4	16.4
Male householder	100.0	30.4	7.6	5.5	17.3	5.7	5.0	6.7
Living alone	100.0	32.9	8.2	5.5	19.2	6.1	5.4	7.6

Note: Number of black households includes both those identifying themselves as black alone and those identifying themselves as black in combination with other races.
Source: Bureau of the Census, 2003 Current Population Survey, Annual Social and Economic Supplement, Internet site http://ferret.bls.census.gov/macro/032003/hhinc/new02_000.htm; calculations by New Strategist

Table 6.4   Households Headed by People Aged 55 or Older by Household Type, 2003: Hispanic Households

(number and percent distribution of total Hispanic households and Hispanic households headed by people aged 55 or older, by household type, 2003; numbers in thousands)

		aged 55 or older						
					aged 65 or older			
	total	total	55 to 59	60 to 64	total	65 to 69	70 to 74	75 or older
Total Hispanic households	**11,339**	**2,269**	**654**	**496**	**1,119**	**399**	**294**	**427**
Family households	9,090	1,622	504	379	739	294	189	248
Married couples	6,189	1,221	405	284	532	227	142	163
Female householder, no spouse present	2,029	307	76	70	161	57	40	64
Male householder, no spouse present	872	85	22	25	38	10	7	21
Nonfamily households	2,249	655	150	117	388	104	105	179
Female householder	1,021	426	86	77	263	65	67	131
Living alone	791	393	74	69	250	60	63	127
Male householder	1,228	229	64	40	125	39	37	48
Living alone	809	199	58	32	109	28	35	46
PERCENT DISTRIBUTION BY TYPE								
Total Hispanic households	**100.0%**	**100.0%**	**100.0%**	**100.0%**	**100.0%**	**100.0%**	**100.0%**	**100.0%**
Family households	80.2	71.5	77.1	76.4	66.0	73.7	64.3	58.1
Married couples	54.6	53.8	61.9	57.3	47.5	56.9	48.3	38.2
Female householder, no spouse present	17.9	13.5	11.6	14.1	14.4	14.3	13.6	15.0
Male householder, no spouse present	7.7	3.7	3.4	5.0	3.4	2.5	2.4	4.9
Nonfamily households	19.8	28.9	22.9	23.6	34.7	26.1	35.7	41.9
Female householder	9.0	18.8	13.1	15.5	23.5	16.3	22.8	30.7
Living alone	7.0	17.3	11.3	13.9	22.3	15.0	21.4	29.7
Male householder	10.8	10.1	9.8	8.1	11.2	9.8	12.6	11.2
Living alone	7.1	8.8	8.9	6.5	9.7	7.0	11.9	10.8
PERCENT DISTRIBUTION BY AGE								
Total Hispanic households	**100.0%**	**20.0%**	**5.8%**	**4.4%**	**9.9%**	**3.5%**	**2.6%**	**3.8%**
Family households	100.0	17.8	5.5	4.2	8.1	3.2	2.1	2.7
Married couples	100.0	19.7	6.5	4.6	8.6	3.7	2.3	2.6
Female householder, no spouse present	100.0	15.1	3.7	3.4	7.9	2.8	2.0	3.2
Male householder, no spouse present	100.0	9.7	2.5	2.9	4.4	1.1	0.8	2.4
Nonfamily households	100.0	29.1	6.7	5.2	17.3	4.6	4.7	8.0
Female householder	100.0	41.7	8.4	7.5	25.8	6.4	6.6	12.8
Living alone	100.0	49.7	9.4	8.7	31.6	7.6	8.0	16.1
Male householder	100.0	18.6	5.2	3.3	10.2	3.2	3.0	3.9
Living alone	100.0	24.6	7.2	4.0	13.5	3.5	4.3	5.7

Source: Bureau of the Census, 2003 Current Population Survey, Annual Social and Economic Supplement, Internet site http:// ferret.bls.census.gov/macro/032003/hhinc/new02_000.htm; calculations by New Strategist

Table 6.5 Households Headed by People Aged 55 or Older by Household Type, 2003: Non-Hispanic White Households

(number and percent distribution of total non-Hispanic white households and non-Hispanic white households headed by people aged 55 or older, by household type, 2003; numbers in thousands)

		aged 55 or older				aged 65 or older		
	total	total	55 to 59	60 to 64	total	65 to 69	70 to 74	75 or older
Total non-Hispanic white households	**81,166**	**31,512**	**7,130**	**5,538**	**18,844**	**4,576**	**4,521**	**9,747**
Family households	53,845	18,466	5,111	3,738	9,617	2,947	2,568	4,101
Married couples	44,101	15,968	4,509	3,316	8,143	2,620	2,247	3,277
Female householder, no spouse present	7,070	1,907	431	328	1,148	254	246	648
Male householder, no spouse present	2,674	591	171	94	326	73	76	177
Nonfamily households	27,321	13,046	2,018	1,800	9,228	1,629	1,952	5,646
Female householder	15,353	9,117	1,159	1,081	6,877	1,138	1,362	4,376
Living alone	13,233	8,779	1,042	1,015	6,722	1,088	1,311	4,322
Male householder	11,968	3,930	860	719	2,351	491	590	1,270
Living alone	9,421	3,600	736	638	2,226	453	545	1,227
PERCENT DISTRIBUTION BY TYPE								
Total non-Hispanic white households	**100.0%**	**100.0%**	**100.0%**	**100.0%**	**100.0%**	**100.0%**	**100.0%**	**100.0%**
Family households	66.3	58.6	71.7	67.5	51.0	64.4	56.8	42.1
Married couples	54.3	50.7	63.2	59.9	43.2	57.3	49.7	33.6
Female householder, no spouse present	8.7	6.1	6.0	5.9	6.1	5.6	5.4	6.6
Male householder, no spouse present	3.3	1.9	2.4	1.7	1.7	1.6	1.7	1.8
Nonfamily households	33.7	41.4	28.3	32.5	49.0	35.6	43.2	57.9
Female householder	18.9	28.9	16.3	19.5	36.5	24.9	30.1	44.9
Living alone	16.3	27.9	14.6	18.3	35.7	23.8	29.0	44.3
Male householder	14.7	12.5	12.1	13.0	12.5	10.7	13.1	13.0
Living alone	11.6	11.4	10.3	11.5	11.8	9.9	12.1	12.6
PERCENT DISTRIBUTION BY AGE								
Total non-Hispanic white households	**100.0%**	**38.8%**	**8.8%**	**6.8%**	**23.2%**	**5.6%**	**5.6%**	**1.2%**
Family households	100.0	34.3	9.5	6.9	17.9	5.5	4.8	7.6
Married couples	100.0	36.2	10.2	7.5	18.5	5.9	5.1	7.4
Female householder, no spouse present	100.0	27.0	6.1	4.6	16.2	3.6	3.5	9.2
Male householder, no spouse present	100.0	22.1	6.4	3.5	12.2	2.7	2.8	6.6
Nonfamily households	100.0	47.8	7.4	6.6	33.8	6.0	7.1	20.7
Female householder	100.0	59.4	7.5	7.0	44.8	7.4	8.9	28.5
Living alone	100.0	66.3	7.9	7.7	50.8	8.2	9.9	32.7
Male householder	100.0	32.8	7.2	6.0	19.6	4.1	4.9	10.6
Living alone	100.0	38.2	7.8	6.8	23.6	4.8	5.8	13.0

Note: Number of non-Hispanic white households includes only those identifying themselves as white alone and non-Hispanic.
Source: Bureau of the Census, 2003 Current Population Survey, Annual Social and Economic Supplement, Internet site http:// ferret.bls.census.gov/macro/032003/hhinc/new02_000.htm; calculations by New Strategist

Household Size Shrinks in the Older Age Groups

Average household size falls below two in the 65-to-74 age group.

The average American household was home to 2.58 people in 2002. Household size peaks among householders aged 35 to 39, who are most likely to have at least one child at home. As householders age through their forties, the nest empties. The average number of children per household falls below one in the 45-to-49 age group.

Average household size is just over two people in the 60-to-64 age group. It falls to 1.89 in the 65-to-74 age group as (usually) women become widows. Households headed by people aged 75 or older average just 1.56 people.

■ Most older householders are either empty-nesters or people living alone. Few have children at home.

Household size is smallest among the oldest householders

(average household size by age of householder, 2002)

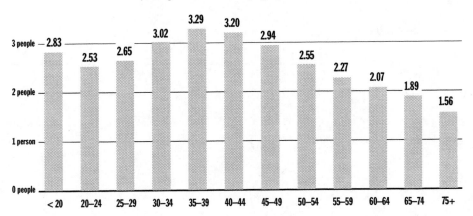

Table 6.6 Average Size of Household by Age of Householder, 2002

(number of households, average number of people per household, and average number of people under age 18 per household, by age of householder, 2002; numbers in thousands)

	number	average number of people	average number of people under age 18
Total households	**109,297**	**2.58**	**0.66**
Under age 20	907	2.83	0.80
Aged 20 to 24	5,484	2.53	0.58
Aged 25 to 29	8,412	2.65	0.86
Aged 30 to 34	10,576	3.02	1.22
Aged 35 to 39	11,599	3.29	1.42
Aged 40 to 44	12,432	3.20	1.20
Aged 45 to 49	11,754	2.94	0.78
Aged 50 to 54	10,455	2.55	0.39
Aged 55 to 59	8,611	2.27	0.20
Aged 60 to 64	6,592	2.07	0.14
Aged 65 to 74	11,472	1.89	0.09
Aged 75 or older	11,004	1.56	0.03

Source: Bureau of the Census, 2002 Current Population Survey Annual Demographic Supplement, http://www.census.gov/population/www/socdemo/hh-fam/cps2002.html

Few Older Americans Have Children under Age 18 at Home

Many householders aged 55 to 64 have adult children in their home, however.

Among householders aged 55 to 64, a substantial 24 percent have children living with them. Eighteen percent have children aged 18 or older, while only 6 percent have children under age 18 at home. Some of these children are in college dormitories, however, since the Census Bureau regards children in dorms as living at home. Among householders aged 65 or older, 12 percent have children in their home, almost all of them adults.

The percentage of older householders with children at home varies sharply by race and Hispanic origin. Among Asian householders aged 55 to 64, fully 46 percent have children at home, and 10 percent have children under age 18. The figures are similar for Hispanic households in the age group. Among black householders aged 55 to 64, a smaller 30 percent have children living with them, and among non-Hispanic whites the figure is just 20 percent.

■ The presence of children in the home creates lifestyle differences among older Americans by race and Hispanic origin.

The nest is slow to empty for Asians and Hispanics

(percent of householders aged 55 to 64 with children at home, by race and Hispanic origin, 2002)

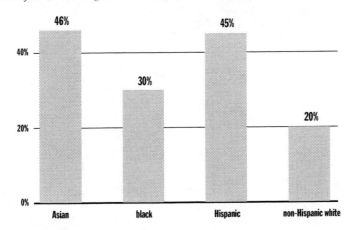

Table 6.7 Householders Aged 55 or Older by Presence and Age of Children at Home, 2002: Total Households

(number and percent distribution of total households and households headed by people aged 55 or older, by presence and age of own children at home, 2002; numbers in thousands)

| | | aged 55 or older | | | aged 65 or older | |
	total	total	55 to 64	total	65 to 74	75 or older
Total households	**109,297**	**37,679**	**15,203**	**22,476**	**11,472**	**11,004**
With children of any age	45,812	6,387	3,630	2,757	1,604	1,153
Under age 25	40,967	2,401	2,076	325	275	50
Under age 18	35,705	1,103	923	180	149	31
Under age 12	26,376	380	290	90	73	17
Under age 6	15,376	134	101	33	27	6
PERCENT DISTRIBUTION						
Total households	**100.0%**	**100.0%**	**100.0%**	**100.0%**	**100.0%**	**100.0%**
With children of any age	41.9	17.0	23.9	12.3	14.0	10.5
Under age 25	37.5	6.4	13.7	1.4	2.4	0.5
Under age 18	32.7	2.9	6.1	0.8	1.3	0.3
Under age 12	24.1	1.0	1.9	0.4	0.6	0.2
Under age 6	14.1	0.4	0.7	0.1	0.2	0.1

Source: Bureau of the Census, Children's Living Arrangements and Characteristics: March 2002, Detailed Tables, *Internet site http://www.census.gov/population/www/socdemo/hh-fam/cps2002.html; calculations by New Strategist*

Table 6.8 Householders Aged 55 or Older by Presence and Age of Children at Home, 2002: Asian Households

(number and percent distribution of total households headed by Asians and households headed by Asians aged 55 or older, by presence and age of own children at home, 2002; numbers in thousands)

		aged 55 or older			aged 65 or older	
	total	total	55 to 64	total	65 to 74	75 or older
Total Asian households	**4,071**	**855**	**436**	**419**	**251**	**168**
With children of any age	2,015	311	200	111	74	37
Under age 25	1,813	133	113	20	19	1
Under age 18	1,582	59	45	14	13	1
Under age 12	1,188	22	15	7	6	1
Under age 6	731	5	2	3	3	–
PERCENT DISTRIBUTION						
Total Asian households	**100.0%**	**100.0%**	**100.0%**	**100.0%**	**100.0%**	**100.0%**
With children of any age	49.5	36.4	45.9	26.5	29.5	22.0
Under age 25	44.5	15.6	25.9	4.8	7.6	0.6
Under age 18	38.9	6.9	10.3	3.3	5.2	0.6
Under age 12	29.2	2.6	3.4	1.7	2.4	0.6
Under age 6	18.0	0.6	0.5	0.7	1.2	–

Note: (–) means number is less than 500 or sample is too small to make a reliable estimate.
Source: Bureau of the Census, Children's Living Arrangements and Characteristics: March 2002, Detailed Tables, *Internet site http://www.census.gov/population/www/socdemo/hh-fam/cps2002.html; calculations by New Strategist*

Table 6.9   Householders Aged 55 or Older by Presence and Age of Children at Home, 2002: Black Households

(number and percent distribution of total households headed by blacks and households headed by blacks aged 55 or older, by presence and age of own children at home, 2002; numbers in thousands)

		aged 55 or older				
				aged 65 or older		
	total	total	55 to 64	total	65 to 74	75 or older
Total black households	**13,315**	**3,624**	**1,648**	**1,976**	**1,214**	**762**
With children of any age	6,515	898	499	399	253	146
Under age 25	5,742	293	242	51	39	12
Under age 18	5,065	146	113	33	24	9
Under age 12	3,821	73	57	16	11	5
Under age 6	2,131	24	19	5	5	–
PERCENT DISTRIBUTION						
Total black households	**100.0%**	**100.0%**	**100.0%**	**100.0%**	**100.0%**	**100.0%**
With children of any age	48.9	24.8	30.3	20.2	20.8	19.2
Under age 25	43.1	8.1	14.7	2.6	3.2	1.6
Under age 18	38.0	4.0	6.9	1.7	2.0	1.2
Under age 12	28.7	2.0	3.5	0.8	0.9	0.7
Under age 6	16.0	0.7	1.2	0.3	0.4	–

Note: (–) means number is less than 500 or sample is too small to make a reliable estimate.
Source: Bureau of the Census, Children's Living Arrangements and Characteristics: March 2002, Detailed Tables, *Internet site http://www.census.gov/population/www/socdemo/hh-fam/cps2002.html; calculations by New Strategist*

Table 6.10   **Householders Aged 55 or Older by Presence and Age of Children at Home, 2002: Hispanic Households**

(number and percent distribution of total households headed by Hispanics and households headed by Hispanics aged 55 or older, by presence and age of own children at home, 2002: numbers in thousands)

| | total | aged 55 or older | | | | |
| | | total | 55 to 64 | aged 65 or older | | |
				total	65 to 74	75 or older
Total Hispanic households	**10,499**	**2,082**	**1,020**	**1,062**	**654**	**408**
With children of any age	6,468	731	455	276	186	90
Under age 25	5,931	318	268	50	44	6
Under age 18	5,343	140	108	32	29	3
Under age 12	4,358	46	36	10	8	2
Under age 6	2,821	22	19	3	3	–
PERCENT DISTRIBUTION						
Total Hispanic households	**100.0%**	**100.0%**	**100.0%**	**100.0%**	**100.0%**	**100.0%**
With children of any age	61.6	35.1	44.6	26.0	28.4	22.1
Under age 25	56.5	15.3	26.3	4.7	6.7	1.5
Under age 18	50.9	6.7	10.6	3.0	4.4	0.7
Under age 12	41.5	2.2	3.5	0.9	1.2	0.5
Under age 6	26.9	1.1	1.9	0.3	0.5	–

Note: (–) means number is less than 500 or sample is too small to make a reliable estimate.
Source: Bureau of the Census, Children's Living Arrangements and Characteristics: March 2002, Detailed Tables, Internet site http://www.census.gov/population/www/socdemo/hh-fam/cps2002.html; calculations by New Strategist

Table 6.11 Householders Aged 55 or Older by Presence and Age of Children at Home, 2002: Non-Hispanic White Households

(number and percent distribution of total households headed by non-Hispanic whites and households headed by non-Hispanic whites aged 55 or older, by presence and age of own children at home, 2002; numbers in thousands)

| | | aged 55 or older | | | | |
| | | | | aged 65 or older | | |
	total	total	55 to 64	total	65 to 74	75 or older
Total non-Hispanic white households	**80,818**	**30,935**	**12,010**	**18,925**	**9,298**	**9,627**
With children of any age	30,572	4,403	2,447	1,956	1,086	870
Under age 25	27,277	1,644	1,441	203	172	31
Under age 18	23,532	751	652	99	82	17
Under age 12	16,897	237	181	56	47	9
Under age 6	9,634	86	65	21	15	6
PERCENT DISTRIBUTION						
Total non-Hispanic white households	**100.0%**	**100.0%**	**100.0%**	**100.0%**	**100.0%**	**100.0%**
With children of any age	37.8	14.2	20.4	10.3	11.7	9.0
Under age 25	33.8	5.3	12.0	1.1	1.8	0.3
Under age 18	29.1	2.4	5.4	0.5	0.9	0.2
Under age 12	20.9	0.8	1.5	0.3	0.5	0.1
Under age 6	11.9	0.3	0.5	0.1	0.2	0.1

Source: Bureau of the Census, Children's Living Arrangements and Characteristics: March 2002, Detailed Tables, *Internet site http://www.census.gov/population/www/socdemo/hh-fam/cps2002.html; calculations by New Strategist*

Lifestyles of Men and Women Diverge in Old Age

Most older men live with a wife, while most older women live alone.

The lifestyles of men and women become increasingly different with age. Because men die at a younger age than women and because women tend to marry men who are slightly older, most women spend the end of their lives alone, whereas most men die while still married.

In the 55-to-64 age group, 62 percent of women and 74 percent of men live with their spouse. This 12 percentage point gap in living arrangements grows to a 45 percentage point chasm in the 85-or-older age group—when a substantial 57 percent of men, but only 12 percent of women, still live with their spouse. Fifty-nine percent of women aged 85 or older lived alone in 2002 versus only 31 percent of their male counterparts.

■ The wants and needs of men and women in old age differ because of their contrasting living arrangements.

Many older women live alone

(percent of people aged 65 or older who live alone, by age and sex, 2002)

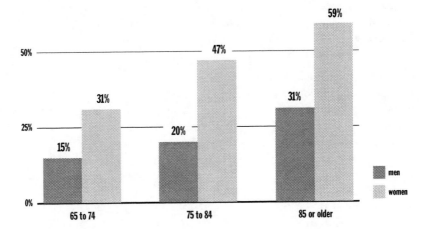

Table 6.12 Living Arrangements of Men aged 55 or older, 2002

(number and percent distribution of total men and men aged 55 or older by living arrangement, 2002; numbers in thousands)

	total	aged 55 or older		aged 65 or older			
		total	55 to 64	total	65 to 74	75 to 84	85 or older
Total men	**106,819**	**26,590**	**12,363**	**14,227**	**8,243**	**4,896**	**1,088**
In family household	84,724	21,432	10,162	11,270	6,756	3,785	729
Living with spouse	56,747	19,354	9,111	10,243	6,223	3,404	616
Other family householder	4,439	821	389	432	217	170	45
Living with parents	18,077	227	203	24	24	–	–
Other family member	5,461	1,030	459	571	292	211	68
In nonfamily household	22,096	5,159	2,200	2,959	1,488	1,112	359
Living alone	12,004	4,113	1,549	2,564	1,225	1,001	338
Living with nonrelatives	10,092	1,046	651	395	263	111	21
PERCENT DISTRIBUTION BY LIVING ARRANGEMENT							
Total men	**100.0%**	**100.0%**	**100.0%**	**100.0%**	**100.0%**	**100.0%**	**100.0%**
In family household	79.3	80.6	82.2	79.2	82.0	77.3	67.0
Living with spouse	53.1	72.8	73.7	72.0	75.5	69.5	56.6
Other family householder	4.2	3.1	3.1	3.0	2.6	3.5	4.1
Living with parents	16.9	0.9	1.6	0.2	0.3	–	–
Other family member	5.1	3.9	3.7	4.0	3.5	4.3	6.2
In nonfamily household	20.7	19.4	17.8	20.8	18.1	22.7	33.0
Living alone	11.2	15.5	12.5	18.0	14.9	20.4	31.1
Living with nonrelatives	9.4	3.9	5.3	2.8	3.2	2.3	1.9
PERCENT DISTRIBUTION BY AGE							
Total men	**100.0%**	**24.9%**	**11.6%**	**13.3%**	**7.7%**	**4.6%**	**1.0%**
In family household	100.0	25.3	12.0	13.3	8.0	4.5	0.9
Living with spouse	100.0	34.1	16.1	18.1	11.0	6.0	1.1
Other family householder	100.0	18.5	8.8	9.7	4.9	3.8	1.0
Living with parents	100.0	1.3	1.1	0.1	0.1	–	–
Other family member	100.0	18.9	8.4	10.5	5.3	3.9	1.2
In nonfamily household	100.0	23.3	10.0	13.4	6.7	5.0	1.6
Living alone	100.0	34.3	12.9	21.4	10.2	8.3	2.8
Living with nonrelatives	100.0	10.4	6.5	3.9	2.6	1.1	0.2

Note: (–) means number is less than 500.
Source: Bureau of the Census, 2002 Current Population Survey Annual Demographic Supplement, Internet site http://www.census.gov/population/www/socdemo/hh-fam/cps2002.html; calculations by New Strategist

Table 6.13 Living Arrangements of Women Aged 55 or Older, 2002

(number and percent distribution of total women and women aged 55 or older by living arrangement, 2002; numbers in thousands)

		aged 55 or older					
				aged 65 or older			
	total	total	55 to 64	total	65 to 74	75 to 84	85 or older
Total women	**114,639**	**33,020**	**13,497**	**19,523**	**9,876**	**7,291**	**2,356**
In family household	90,451	21,576	10,330	11,246	6,595	3,736	915
Living with spouse	56,747	16,238	8,397	7,841	5,124	2,446	271
Other family householder	13,143	2,805	1,188	1,617	807	597	213
Living with parents	14,475	158	131	27	25	2	–
Other family member	6,086	2,375	614	1,761	639	691	431
In nonfamily household	24,188	11,445	3,167	8,278	3,282	3,556	1,440
Living alone	16,771	10,601	2,699	7,902	3,054	3,447	1,401
Living with nonrelatives	7,417	844	468	376	228	109	39
PERCENT DISTRIBUTION BY LIVING ARRANGEMENT							
Total women	**100.0%**	**100.0%**	**100.0%**	**100.0%**	**100.0%**	**100.0%**	**100.0%**
In family household	78.9	65.3	76.5	57.6	66.8	51.2	38.8
Living with spouse	49.5	49.2	62.2	40.2	51.9	33.5	11.5
Other family householder	11.5	8.5	8.8	8.3	8.2	8.2	9.0
Living with parents	12.6	0.5	1.0	0.1	0.3	0.0	–
Other family member	5.3	7.2	4.5	9.0	6.5	9.5	18.3
In nonfamily household	21.1	34.7	23.5	42.4	33.2	48.8	61.1
Living alone	14.6	32.1	20.0	40.5	30.9	47.3	59.5
Living with nonrelatives	6.5	2.6	3.5	1.9	2.3	1.5	1.7
PERCENT DISTRIBUTION BY AGE							
Total women	**100.0%**	**28.8%**	**11.8%**	**17.0%**	**8.6%**	**6.4%**	**2.1%**
In family household	100.0	23.9	11.4	12.4	7.3	4.1	1.0
Living with spouse	100.0	28.6	14.8	13.8	9.0	4.3	0.5
Other family householder	100.0	21.3	9.0	12.3	6.1	4.5	1.6
Living with parents	100.0	1.1	0.9	0.2	0.2	0.0	–
Other family member	100.0	39.0	10.1	28.9	10.5	11.4	7.1
In nonfamily household	100.0	47.3	13.1	34.2	13.6	14.7	6.0
Living alone	100.0	63.2	16.1	47.1	18.2	20.6	8.4
Living with nonrelatives	100.0	11.4	6.3	5.1	3.1	1.5	0.5

Note: (–) means number is less than 500.
Source: Bureau of the Census, 2002 Current Population Survey Annual Demographic Supplement, Internet site http:// www.census.gov/population/www/socdemo/hh-fam/cps2002.html; calculations by New Strategist

Table 6.14 People Who Live Alone by Sex and Age, 2003

(number of people aged 15 or older and number and percent who live alone by sex and age, 2003; numbers in thousands)

		living alone	
	total	number	percent
Total people	**225,250**	**127,468**	**56.6%**
Under age 55	163,616	14,378	8.8
Aged 55 or older	61,634	15,052	24.4
Aged 55 to 64	27,400	4,504	16.4
Aged 55 to 59	15,470	2,386	15.4
Aged 60 to 64	11,930	2,118	17.8
Aged 65 or older	34,234	10,548	30.8
Aged 65 to 74	18,111	4,200	23.2
Aged 65 to 69	9,438	1,960	20.8
Aged 70 to 74	8,673	2,240	25.8
Aged 75 or older	16,123	6,348	39.4
Total men	**108,814**	**63,734**	**58.6**
Under age 55	81,119	8,023	9.9
Aged 55 or older	27,693	4,488	16.2
Aged 55 to 64	13,166	1,764	13.4
Aged 55 to 59	7,493	980	13.1
Aged 60 to 64	5,673	784	13.8
Aged 65 or older	14,527	2,724	18.8
Aged 65 to 74	8,274	1,290	15.6
Aged 65 to 69	4,317	601	13.9
Aged 70 to 74	3,957	689	17.4
Aged 75 or older	6,253	1,434	22.9
Total women	**116,436**	**40,957**	**35.2**
Under age 55	82,498	6,355	7.7
Aged 55 or older	33,940	10,564	31.1
Aged 55 to 64	14,234	2,740	19.2
Aged 55 to 59	7,977	1,406	17.6
Aged 60 to 64	6,257	1,334	21.3
Aged 65 or older	19,706	7,824	39.7
Aged 65 to 74	9,836	2,910	29.6
Aged 65 to 69	5,121	1,359	26.5
Aged 70 to 74	4,715	1,551	32.9
Aged 75 or older	9,870	4,914	49.8

Source: Bureau of the Census, 2003 Current Population Survey, Annual Social and Economic Supplement, Internet sites http:// ferret.bls.census.gov/macro/032003/perinc/new01_019.htm and http://ferret.bls.census.gov/macro/032003/hhinc/new02_000.html; calculations by New Strategist

The Widowed Population Rises Sharply in Old Age

Fewer than half of people aged 75 or older are currently married.

Among all Americans aged 15 or older, only 6 percent are currently widowed. The figure stands at 32 percent among people aged 65 or older. The proportion rises from a 21 percent minority among those aged 65 to 74 to the 65 percent majority of people aged 85 or older. Women are far more likely to be currently widowed than men, since they tend to marry slightly older men and because widowed men are more likely to remarry. Among people aged 85 or older, fully 79 percent of women but only 34 percent of men are currently widowed.

Overall, 52 percent of Americans aged 15 or older are currently married. Among those aged 65 or older, the figure stands at an above-average 54 percent. It falls below the 50 percent mark in the 75-to-84 age group. Among people aged 85 or older, only 26 percent are currently married. Again, the figures differ sharply by gender. Fifty-eight percent of men aged 85 or older are currently married versus just 12 percent of their female counterparts.

Marital status patterns are similar among older Americans by race and Hispanic origin. The only exception is that older black women are far less likely to be married than Asian, Hispanic, or non-Hispanic white women.

■ The lifestyles of men and women diverge with age as a growing proportion of women become widows and live alone.

Older women are likely to be widows

(percent of people aged 65 or older who are currently widowed, by age and sex, 2002)

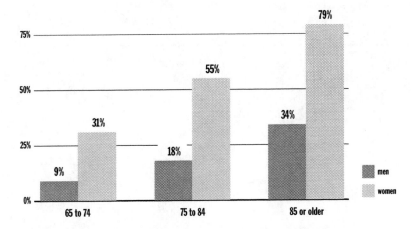

Table 6.15 Marital Status of People by Sex and Age, 2002: Total People

(number and percent distribution of people aged 15 or older by sex, age, and current marital status, 2002; numbers in thousands)

	total	never married	married, spouse present	married, spouse absent	separated	divorced	widowed
Total people	**221,459**	**63,090**	**115,838**	**2,926**	**4,606**	**20,955**	**14,044**
Under age 55	161,850	60,333	79,674	2,109	3,753	14,528	1,452
Aged 55 or older	59,609	2,757	36,164	817	853	6,427	12,592
Aged 55 to 64	25,859	1,533	17,796	343	542	3,921	1,725
Aged 65 or older	33,750	1,224	18,368	474	311	2,506	10,867
Aged 65 to 74	18,118	649	11,536	259	225	1,725	3,724
Aged 75 to 84	12,188	425	5,929	166	72	683	4,913
Aged 85 or older	3,444	150	903	49	14	98	2,230
Total women	**114,639**	**28,861**	**57,919**	**1,376**	**2,808**	**12,268**	**11,408**
Under age 55	81,619	27,453	41,425	969	2,336	8,325	1,111
Aged 55 or older	33,020	1,408	16,494	407	472	3,943	10,297
Aged 55 to 64	13,497	715	8,530	157	305	2,384	1,407
Aged 65 or older	19,523	693	7,964	250	167	1,559	8,890
Aged 65 to 74	9,876	346	5,214	131	114	1,053	3,018
Aged 75 to 84	7,291	230	2,474	92	44	441	4,010
Aged 85 or older	2,356	117	276	27	9	65	1,862
Total men	**106,819**	**34,229**	**57,919**	**1,551**	**1,798**	**8,686**	**2,636**
Under age 55	80,229	32,879	38,250	1,142	1,417	6,201	341
Aged 55 or older	26,590	1,350	19,669	409	381	2,485	2,295
Aged 55 to 64	12,363	818	9,265	186	237	1,538	318
Aged 65 or older	14,227	532	10,404	223	144	947	1,977
Aged 65 to 74	8,243	304	6,322	128	111	672	706
Aged 75 to 84	4,896	195	3,455	73	28	242	903
Aged 85 or older	1,088	33	627	22	5	33	368

PERCENT DISTRIBUTION	total	never married	married, spouse present	married, spouse absent	separated	divorced	widowed
Total people	**100.0%**	**28.5%**	**52.3%**	**1.3%**	**2.1%**	**9.5%**	**6.3%**
Under age 55	100.0	37.3	49.2	1.3	2.3	9.0	0.9
Aged 55 or older	100.0	4.6	60.7	1.4	1.4	10.8	21.1
Aged 55 to 64	100.0	5.9	68.8	1.3	2.1	15.2	6.7
Aged 65 or older	100.0	3.6	54.4	1.4	0.9	7.4	32.2
Aged 65 to 74	100.0	3.6	63.7	1.4	1.2	9.5	20.6
Aged 75 to 84	100.0	3.5	48.6	1.4	0.6	5.6	40.3
Aged 85 or older	100.0	4.4	26.2	1.4	0.4	2.8	64.8
Total women	**100.0**	**25.2**	**50.5**	**1.2**	**2.4**	**10.7**	**10.0**
Under age 55	100.0	33.6	50.8	1.2	2.9	10.2	1.4
Aged 55 or older	100.0	4.3	50.0	1.2	1.4	11.9	31.2
Aged 55 to 64	100.0	5.3	63.2	1.2	2.3	17.7	10.4
Aged 65 or older	100.0	3.5	40.8	1.3	0.9	8.0	45.5
Aged 65 to 74	100.0	3.5	52.8	1.3	1.2	10.7	30.6
Aged 75 to 84	100.0	3.2	33.9	1.3	0.6	6.1	55.0
Aged 85 or older	100.0	5.0	11.7	1.1	0.4	2.8	79.0
Total men	**100.0**	**32.0**	**54.2**	**1.5**	**1.7**	**8.1**	**2.5**
Under age 55	100.0	41.0	47.7	1.4	1.8	7.7	0.4
Aged 55 or older	100.0	5.1	74.0	1.5	1.4	9.3	8.6
Aged 55 to 64	100.0	6.6	74.9	1.5	1.9	12.4	2.6
Aged 65 or older	100.0	3.7	73.1	1.6	1.0	6.7	13.9
Aged 65 to 74	100.0	3.7	76.7	1.6	1.3	8.2	8.6
Aged 75 to 84	100.0	4.0	70.6	1.5	0.6	4.9	18.4
Aged 85 or older	100.0	3.0	57.6	2.0	0.5	3.0	33.8

Source: Bureau of the Census, 2002 Current Population Survey Annual Demographic Supplement, Internet site http:// www.census.gov/population/www/socdemo/hh-fam/cps2002.html

Table 6.16 Marital Status by Sex and Age, 2002: Asians

(number and percent distribution of total Asians aged 15 or older by sex, age, and current marital status, 2002; numbers in thousands)

	total	never married	married, spouse present	married, spouse absent	separated	divorced	widowed
Total Asians	**9,837**	**3,229**	**5,246**	**318**	**137**	**488**	**418**
Under age 55	8,000	3,149	4,102	233	107	353	56
Aged 55 or older	1,837	80	1,144	85	30	135	362
Aged 55 to 64	938	53	664	41	18	77	85
Aged 65 or older	899	27	480	44	12	58	277
Aged 65 to 74	551	18	308	39	8	45	132
Aged 75 to 84	295	7	155	5	3	12	113
Aged 85 or older	53	2	17	–	1	1	32
Asian women	**5,079**	**1,363**	**2,822**	**139**	**93**	**316**	**346**
Under age 55	4,062	1,316	2,292	100	72	234	47
Aged 55 or older	1,017	47	530	39	21	82	299
Aged 55 to 64	510	27	324	22	13	52	73
Aged 65 or older	507	20	206	17	8	30	226
Aged 65 to 74	298	14	134	15	6	24	105
Aged 75 to 84	174	4	67	2	2	6	94
Aged 85 or older	35	2	5	–	–	–	27
Asian men	**4,758**	**1,866**	**2,423**	**180**	**44**	**172**	**72**
Under age 55	3,938	1,830	1,809	134	34	121	9
Aged 55 or older	820	36	614	46	10	51	63
Aged 55 to 64	428	27	340	19	5	25	12
Aged 65 or older	392	9	274	27	5	26	51
Aged 65 to 74	253	5	174	24	3	20	27
Aged 75 to 84	121	4	88	3	1	6	19
Aged 85 or older	18	–	12	–	1	–	5

	total	never married	married, spouse present	married, spouse absent	separated	divorced	widowed
PERCENT DISTRIBUTION							
Total Asians	**100.0%**	**32.8%**	**53.3%**	**3.2%**	**1.4%**	**5.0%**	**4.2%**
Under age 55	100.0	39.4	51.3	2.9	1.3	4.4	0.7
Aged 55 or older	100.0	4.4	62.3	4.6	1.6	7.3	19.7
Aged 55 to 64	100.0	5.7	70.8	4.4	1.9	8.2	9.1
Aged 65 or older	100.0	3.0	53.4	4.9	1.3	6.5	30.8
Aged 65 to 74	100.0	3.3	55.9	7.1	1.5	8.2	24.0
Aged 75 to 84	100.0	2.4	52.5	1.7	1.0	4.1	38.3
Aged 85 or older	100.0	3.8	32.1	–	1.9	1.9	60.4
Asian women	**100.0**	**26.8**	**55.6**	**2.7**	**1.8**	**6.2**	**6.8**
Under age 55	100.0	32.4	56.4	2.5	1.8	5.8	1.2
Aged 55 or older	100.0	4.6	52.1	3.8	2.1	8.1	29.4
Aged 55 to 64	100.0	5.3	63.5	4.3	2.5	10.2	14.3
Aged 65 or older	100.0	3.9	40.6	3.4	1.6	5.9	44.6
Aged 65 to 74	100.0	4.7	45.0	5.0	2.0	8.1	35.2
Aged 75 to 84	100.0	2.3	38.5	1.1	1.1	3.4	54.0
Aged 85 or older	100.0	5.7	14.3	–	–	–	77.1
Asian men	**100.0**	**39.2**	**50.9**	**3.8**	**0.9**	**3.6**	**1.5**
Under age 55	100.0	46.5	45.9	3.4	0.9	3.1	0.2
Aged 55 or older	100.0	4.4	74.9	5.6	1.2	6.2	7.7
Aged 55 to 64	100.0	6.3	79.4	4.4	1.2	5.8	2.8
Aged 65 or older	100.0	2.3	69.9	6.9	1.3	6.6	13.0
Aged 65 to 74	100.0	2.0	68.8	9.5	1.2	7.9	10.7
Aged 75 to 84	100.0	3.3	72.7	2.5	0.8	5.0	15.7
Aged 85 or older	100.0	–	66.7	–	5.6	–	27.8

Note: (–) means number is less than 500 or sample is too small to make a reliable estimate.
Source: Bureau of the Census, 2002 Current Population Survey Annual Demographic Supplement, Internet site http://www.census.gov/population/www/socdemo/hh-fam/cps2002.html

Table 6.17 Marital Status by Sex and Age, 2002: Blacks

(number and percent distribution of blacks aged 15 or older by sex, age, and current marital status, 2002; numbers in thousands)

	total	never married	married, spouse present	married, spouse absent	separated	divorced	widowed
Total blacks	**26,137**	**11,334**	**8,640**	**522**	**1,241**	**2,727**	**1,673**
Under age 55	20,790	10,868	6,351	424	956	1,904	288
Aged 55 or older	5,347	466	2,289	98	285	823	1,385
Aged 55 to 64	2,495	305	1,137	59	182	504	308
Aged 65 or older	2,852	161	1,152	39	103	319	1,077
Aged 65 to 74	1,761	113	835	24	76	236	477
Aged 75 to 84	863	38	279	13	21	76	436
Aged 85 or older	228	10	38	2	6	7	164
Black women	**14,442**	**6,068**	**4,216**	**272**	**772**	**1,758**	**1,354**
Under age 55	11,291	5,783	3,223	221	613	1,227	222
Aged 55 or older	3,151	285	993	51	159	531	1,132
Aged 55 to 64	1,421	188	536	26	99	324	248
Aged 65 or older	1,730	97	457	25	60	207	884
Aged 65 to 74	1,009	67	344	18	41	153	387
Aged 75 to 84	560	24	105	7	13	50	361
Aged 85 or older	161	6	8	–	6	4	136
Black men	**11,695**	**5,266**	**4,423**	**249**	**469**	**968**	**319**
Under age 55	9,501	5,085	3,129	203	342	676	67
Aged 55 or older	2,194	181	1,294	46	127	292	252
Aged 55 to 64	1,074	118	600	33	83	180	59
Aged 65 or older	1,120	63	694	13	44	112	193
Aged 65 to 74	751	46	490	6	36	83	90
Aged 75 to 84	303	14	174	6	8	26	75
Aged 85 or older	66	3	30	1	–	3	28

	total	never married	married, spouse present	married, spouse absent	separated	divorced	widowed
PERCENT DISTRIBUTION							
Total blacks	**100.0%**	**43.4%**	**33.1%**	**2.0%**	**4.7%**	**10.4%**	**6.4%**
Under age 55	100.0	52.3	30.5	2.0	4.6	9.2	1.4
Aged 55 or older	100.0	8.7	42.8	1.8	5.3	15.4	25.9
Aged 55 to 64	100.0	12.2	45.6	2.4	7.3	20.2	12.3
Aged 65 or older	100.0	5.6	40.4	1.4	3.6	11.2	37.8
Aged 65 to 74	100.0	6.4	47.4	1.4	4.3	13.4	27.1
Aged 75 to 84	100.0	4.4	32.3	1.5	2.4	8.8	50.5
Aged 85 or older	100.0	4.4	16.7	0.9	2.6	3.1	71.9
Black women	**100.0**	**42.0**	**29.2**	**1.9**	**5.3**	**12.2**	**9.4**
Under age 55	100.0	51.2	28.5	2.0	5.4	10.9	2.0
Aged 55 or older	100.0	9.0	31.5	1.6	5.1	16.9	35.9
Aged 55 to 64	100.0	13.2	37.7	1.8	7.0	22.8	17.5
Aged 65 or older	100.0	5.6	26.4	1.4	3.5	12.0	51.1
Aged 65 to 74	100.0	6.6	34.1	1.8	4.1	15.2	38.4
Aged 75 to 84	100.0	4.3	18.8	1.2	2.3	8.9	64.5
Aged 85 or older	100.0	3.7	5.0	–	3.7	2.5	84.5
Black men	**100.0**	**45.0**	**37.8**	**2.1**	**4.0**	**8.3**	**2.7**
Under age 55	100.0	53.5	32.9	2.1	3.6	7.1	0.7
Aged 55 or older	100.0	8.2	59.0	2.1	5.8	13.3	11.5
Aged 55 to 64	100.0	11.0	55.9	3.1	7.7	16.8	5.5
Aged 65 or older	100.0	5.6	62.0	1.2	3.9	10.0	17.2
Aged 65 to 74	100.0	6.1	65.2	0.8	4.8	11.1	12.0
Aged 75 to 84	100.0	4.6	57.4	2.0	2.6	8.6	24.8
Aged 85 or older	100.0	4.5	45.5	1.5	–	4.5	42.4

Note: (–) means number is less than 500 or sample is too small to make a reliable estimate.
Source: Bureau of the Census, 2002 Current Population Survey Annual Demographic Supplement, Internet site http:// www.census.gov/population/www/socdemo/hh-fam/cps2002.html

Table 6.18 Marital Status by Sex and Age, 2002: Hispanics

(number and percent distribution of Hispanics aged 15 or older by sex, age, and current marital status, 2002; numbers in thousands)

	total	never married	married, spouse present	married, spouse absent	separated	divorced	widowed
Total Hispanics	**26,332**	**9,557**	**12,432**	**846**	**889**	**1,734**	**875**
Under age 55	22,496	9,285	10,207	725	734	1,364	182
Aged 55 or older	3,836	272	2,225	121	155	370	693
Aged 55 to 64	1,939	176	1,245	73	89	228	128
Aged 65 or older	1,897	96	980	48	66	142	565
Aged 65 to 74	1,175	65	670	32	55	103	250
Aged 75 to 84	565	25	250	12	9	38	232
Aged 85 or older	157	6	60	4	2	1	83
Hispanic women	**12,900**	**3,936**	**6,316**	**289**	**604**	**1,026**	**727**
Under age 55	10,788	3,802	5,308	236	505	789	147
Aged 55 or older	2,112	134	1,008	53	99	237	580
Aged 55 to 64	1,024	80	606	29	56	143	111
Aged 65 or older	1,088	54	402	24	43	94	469
Aged 65 to 74	653	40	289	18	37	72	197
Aged 75 to 84	326	10	89	5	4	22	195
Aged 85 or older	109	4	24	1	2	–	77
Hispanic men	**13,432**	**5,621**	**6,116**	**556**	**284**	**707**	**147**
Under age 55	11,708	5,483	4,899	490	228	575	33
Aged 55 or older	1,724	138	1,217	66	56	132	114
Aged 55 to 64	915	96	639	44	34	85	17
Aged 65 or older	809	42	578	22	22	47	97
Aged 65 to 74	522	26	381	13	18	30	54
Aged 75 to 84	239	14	161	7	4	16	37
Aged 85 or older	48	2	36	2	–	1	6

	total	never married	married, spouse present	married, spouse absent	separated	divorced	widowed
PERCENT DISTRIBUTION							
Total Hispanics	**100.0%**	**36.3%**	**47.2%**	**3.2%**	**3.4%**	**6.6%**	**3.3%**
Under age 55	100.0	41.3	45.4	3.2	3.3	6.1	0.8
Aged 55 or older	100.0	7.1	58.0	3.2	4.0	9.6	18.1
Aged 55 to 64	100.0	9.1	64.2	3.8	4.6	11.8	6.6
Aged 65 or older	100.0	5.1	51.7	2.5	3.5	7.5	29.8
Aged 65 to 74	100.0	5.5	57.0	2.7	4.7	8.8	21.3
Aged 75 to 84	100.0	4.4	44.2	2.1	1.6	6.7	41.1
Aged 85 or older	100.0	3.8	38.2	2.5	1.3	0.6	52.9
Hispanic women	**100.0**	**30.5**	**49.0**	**2.2**	**4.7**	**8.0**	**5.6**
Under age 55	100.0	35.2	49.2	2.2	4.7	7.3	1.4
Aged 55 or older	100.0	6.3	47.7	2.5	4.7	11.2	27.5
Aged 55 to 64	100.0	7.8	59.2	2.8	5.5	14.0	10.8
Aged 65 or older	100.0	5.0	36.9	2.2	4.0	8.6	43.1
Aged 65 to 74	100.0	6.1	44.3	2.8	5.7	11.0	30.2
Aged 75 to 84	100.0	3.1	27.3	1.5	1.2	6.7	59.8
Aged 85 or older	100.0	3.7	22.0	0.9	1.8	–	70.6
Hispanic men	**100.0**	**41.8**	**45.5**	**4.1**	**2.1**	**5.3**	**1.1**
Under age 55	100.0	46.8	41.8	4.2	1.9	4.9	0.3
Aged 55 or older	100.0	8.0	70.6	3.8	3.2	7.7	6.6
Aged 55 to 64	100.0	10.5	69.8	4.8	3.7	9.3	1.9
Aged 65 or older	100.0	5.2	71.4	2.7	2.7	5.8	12.0
Aged 65 to 74	100.0	5.0	73.0	2.5	3.4	5.7	10.3
Aged 75 to 84	100.0	5.9	67.4	2.9	1.7	6.7	15.5
Aged 85 or older	100.0	4.2	75.0	4.2	–	2.1	12.5

Note: (–) means number is less than 500 or sample is too small to make a reliable estimate.
Source: Bureau of the Census, 2002 Current Population Survey Annual Demographic Supplement, Internet site http://www.census.gov/population/www/socdemo/hh-fam/cps2002.html

Table 6.19 Marital Status by Sex and Age, 2002: Non-Hispanic Whites

(number and percent distribution of non-Hispanic whites aged 15 or older by sex, age, and current marital status, 2002; numbers in thousands)

	total	never married	married, spouse present	married, spouse absent	separated	divorced	widowed
Total non-Hispanic whites	**158,188**	**38,770**	**89,082**	**1,250**	**2,327**	**15,778**	**10,981**
Under age 55	109,879	36,838	58,716	735	1,939	10,746	903
Aged 55 or older	48,309	1,932	30,366	515	388	5,032	10,078
Aged 55 to 64	20,353	994	14,676	171	259	3,070	1,184
Aged 65 or older	27,956	938	15,690	344	129	1,962	8,894
Aged 65 to 74	14,548	452	9,678	165	87	1,322	2,844
Aged 75 to 84	10,415	353	5,229	136	38	551	4,108
Aged 85 or older	2,993	133	783	43	4	89	1,942
Non-Hispanic white women	**81,625**	**17,373**	**44,303**	**667**	**1,332**	**9,045**	**8,904**
Under age 55	55,064	16,433	30,424	403	1,137	5,988	680
Aged 55 or older	26,561	940	13,879	264	195	3,057	8,224
Aged 55 to 64	10,465	420	7,025	79	140	1,842	959
Aged 65 or older	16,096	520	6,854	185	55	1,215	7,265
Aged 65 to 74	7,859	224	4,417	81	32	793	2,311
Aged 75 to 84	6,196	191	2,200	79	23	362	3,340
Aged 85 or older	2,041	105	237	25	–	60	1,614
Non-Hispanic white men	**76,564**	**21,397**	**44,779**	**583**	**995**	**6,733**	**2,077**
Under age 55	54,816	20,406	28,294	332	804	4,759	223
Aged 55 or older	21,748	991	16,485	251	191	1,974	1,854
Aged 55 to 64	9,888	573	7,651	92	119	1,228	225
Aged 65 or older	11,860	418	8,834	159	72	746	1,629
Aged 65 to 74	6,689	228	5,260	84	54	529	533
Aged 75 to 84	4,219	162	3,029	57	14	189	768
Aged 85 or older	952	28	545	18	4	28	328

	total	never married	married, spouse present	married, spouse absent	separated	divorced	widowed
PERCENT DISTRIBUTION							
Total non-Hispanic whites	**100.0%**	**24.5%**	**56.3%**	**0.8%**	**1.5%**	**10.0%**	**6.9%**
Under age 55	100.0	33.5	53.4	0.7	1.8	9.8	0.8
Aged 55 or older	100.0	4.0	62.9	1.1	0.8	10.4	20.9
Aged 55 to 64	100.0	4.9	72.1	0.8	1.3	15.1	5.8
Aged 65 or older	100.0	3.4	56.1	1.2	0.5	7.0	31.8
Aged 65 to 74	100.0	3.1	66.5	1.1	0.6	9.1	19.5
Aged 75 to 84	100.0	3.4	50.2	1.3	0.4	5.3	39.4
Aged 85 or older	100.0	4.4	26.2	1.4	0.1	3.0	64.9
Non-Hispanic white women	**100.0**	**21.3**	**54.3**	**0.8**	**1.6**	**11.1**	**10.9**
Under age 55	100.0	29.8	55.3	0.7	2.1	10.9	1.2
Aged 55 or older	100.0	3.5	52.3	1.0	0.7	11.5	31.0
Aged 55 to 64	100.0	4.0	67.1	0.8	1.3	17.6	9.2
Aged 65 or older	100.0	3.2	42.6	1.1	0.3	7.5	45.1
Aged 65 to 74	100.0	2.9	56.2	1.0	0.4	10.1	29.4
Aged 75 to 84	100.0	3.1	35.5	1.3	0.4	5.8	53.9
Aged 85 or older	100.0	5.1	11.6	1.2	–	2.9	79.1
Non-Hispanic white men	**100.0**	**27.9**	**58.5**	**0.8**	**1.3**	**8.8**	**2.7**
Under age 55	100.0	37.2	51.6	0.6	1.5	8.7	0.4
Aged 55 or older	100.0	4.6	75.8	1.2	0.9	9.1	8.5
Aged 55 to 64	100.0	5.8	77.4	0.9	1.2	12.4	2.3
Aged 65 or older	100.0	3.5	74.5	1.3	0.6	6.3	13.7
Aged 65 to 74	100.0	3.4	78.6	1.3	0.8	7.9	8.0
Aged 75 to 84	100.0	3.8	71.8	1.4	0.3	4.5	18.2
Aged 85 or older	100.0	2.9	57.2	1.9	0.4	2.9	34.5

Note: (–) means number is less than 500 or sample is too small to make a reliable estimate.
Source: Bureau of the Census, 2002 Current Population Survey Annual Demographic Supplement, Internet site http:// www.census.gov/population/www/socdemo/hh-fam/cps2002.html

7

Population

■ The 2000 census counted 59 million Americans aged 55 or older, accounting for 21 percent of the total population.

■ The number of people aged 65 or older will rise from 35 million in 2000 to nearly 55 million by 2020, a 56 percent gain—much faster than the growth projected for the U.S. population as a whole.

■ Eighty-one percent of people aged 55 or older are non-Hispanic white, according to the 2000 census. This figure is much higher than the 69 percent for the population as a whole.

■ The 55-or-older age group accounts for only 20 percent of the nation's foreign-born population, but it represents a much larger 35 percent of the naturalized foreign born.

■ The number of legal immigrants admitted to the United States numbered over 1 million in 2002. Only about 112,000 were aged 55 or older, accounting for 11 percent of the total.

■ The diversity of older Americans varies by state, but not nearly as dramatically as it does among middle-aged and younger Americans. Only in Hawaii are non-Hispanic whites a minority among the 55-or-older population.

Rapid Growth Is in Store for Older Age Groups

The 65-or-older age group is projected to expand by nearly 20 million in the next two decades.

The 2000 census counted 59 million Americans aged 55 or older, accounting for 21 percent of the total population. Because mortality rates are higher for males than for females, most older Americans are women. The sex ratio falls from 94 men per 100 women in the 55-to-59 age group to just 41 men per 100 women among people aged 85 or older.

The number of people aged 65 or older will rise from 35 million in 2000 to nearly 55 million by 2020, a 56 percent gain—much faster than the growth projected for the U.S. population as a whole, according to the Census Bureau's new population projections. Behind the expansion is the entry of the Baby-Boom generation into the older age groups.

The number of 45-to-64-year-olds will climb fully 30 percent between 2000 and 2010 as the older half of the Baby-Boom generation entirely fills the age group. In the decade that follows, the number of 65-to-84-year-olds will increase by 39 percent thanks to the aging of Boomers.

■ The rapid growth in the number of Americans in their fifties, sixties, and seventies will focus the nation's attention on the wants and needs of the older population.

The number of people aged 45 to 64 will grow 30 percent during this decade

(percent change in number of people by age, 2000–10)

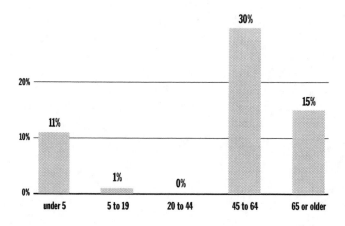

Table 7.1 Population by Age and Generation, 2000 Census

(number and percent distribution of people by age and generation, 2000; numbers in thousands)

	number	percent distribution
TOTAL PEOPLE	**281,422**	**100.0%**
Under age 5	19,176	6.8
Aged 5 to 9	20,550	7.3
Aged 10 to 14	20,528	7.3
Aged 15 to 19	20,220	7.2
Aged 20 to 24	18,964	6.7
Aged 25 to 29	19,381	6.9
Aged 30 to 34	20,510	7.3
Aged 35 to 39	22,707	8.1
Aged 40 to 44	22,442	8.0
Aged 45 to 49	20,092	7.1
Aged 50 to 54	17,586	6.2
Aged 55 or older	**59,266**	**21.1**
Aged 55 to 59	13,469	4.8
Aged 60 to 64	10,805	3.8
Aged 65 or older	34,992	12.4
Aged 65 to 69	9,534	3.4
Aged 70 to 74	8,857	3.1
Aged 75 to 79	7,416	2.6
Aged 80 to 84	4,945	1.8
Aged 85 or older	4,240	1.5
TOTAL PEOPLE	**281,422**	**100.0**
Post-Millennial (under age 6)	23,141	8.2
Millennial (aged 6 to 23)	72,655	25.8
Generation X (aged 24 to 35)	48,049	17.1
Baby Boom (aged 36 to 54)	78,310	27.8
Swing (aged 55 to 67)	**30,061**	**10.7**
World War II (aged 68 or older)	**29,205**	**10.4**

Source: Bureau of the Census, Census 2000 Summary File 1, Internet site http://factfinder.census.gov/servlet/BasicFactsServlet; calculations by New Strategist

Table 7.2 Population by Age and Sex, 2000 Census

(number of people by age and sex, and sex ratio by age, 2000; numbers in thousands)

	total	female	male	sex ratio
TOTAL PEOPLE	**281,422**	**143,368**	**138,054**	**96**
Under age 5	19,176	9,365	9,811	105
Aged 5 to 9	20,550	10,026	10,523	105
Aged 10 to 14	20,528	10,008	10,520	105
Aged 15 to 19	20,220	9,829	10,391	106
Aged 20 to 24	18,964	9,276	9,688	104
Aged 25 to 29	19,381	9,583	9,799	102
Aged 30 to 34	20,510	10,189	10,322	101
Aged 35 to 39	22,707	11,388	11,319	99
Aged 40 to 44	22,442	11,313	11,129	98
Aged 45 to 49	20,092	10,203	9,890	97
Aged 50 to 54	17,586	8,978	8,608	96
Aged 55 to 59	13,469	6,961	6,509	94
Aged 60 to 64	10,805	5,669	5,137	91
Aged 65 to 69	9,534	5,133	4,400	86
Aged 70 to 74	8,857	4,955	3,903	79
Aged 75 to 79	7,416	4,371	3,044	70
Aged 80 to 84	4,945	3,110	1,835	59
Aged 85 or older	4,240	3,013	1,227	41
Aged 55 or older	**59,266**	**33,212**	**26,055**	**79**
Aged 65 or older	34,992	20,582	14,410	70
Aged 75 or older	16,601	10,494	6,106	58
Aged 85 or older	4,240	3,013	1,227	41

Note: The sex ratio is the number of men per 100 women.
Source: Bureau of the Census, Census 2000 Summary File 1, Internet site http://factfinder.census.gov/servlet/BasicFactsServlet; calculations by New Strategist

Table 7.3 Population by Age, 2000 and 2002

(number of people by age, April 1, 2000, and July 1, 2002; percent change 2000–02; numbers in thousands)

	2000	2002	percent change 2000–02
Total people	**281,422**	**288,369**	**2.5%**
Under age 5	19,176	19,609	2.3
Aged 5 to 9	20,550	19,901	–3.2
Aged 10 to 14	20,528	21,136	3.0
Aged 15 to 19	20,220	20,376	0.8
Aged 20 to 24	18,964	20,214	6.6
Aged 25 to 29	19,381	18,972	–2.1
Aged 30 to 34	20,510	20,956	2.2
Aged 35 to 39	22,707	21,915	–3.5
Aged 40 to 44	22,442	23,002	2.5
Aged 45 to 49	20,092	21,302	6.0
Aged 50 to 54	17,586	18,782	6.8
Aged 55 or older	**59,266**	**62,204**	**5.0**
Aged 55 to 64	24,275	26,602	9.6
Aged 55 to 59	13,469	14,991	11.3
Aged 60 to 64	10,805	11,611	7.5
Aged 65 or older	34,992	35,602	1.7
Aged 65 to 74	18,391	18,274	–0.6
Aged 65 to 69	9,534	9,581	0.5
Aged 70 to 74	8,857	8,693	–1.9
Aged 75 to 84	12,361	12,735	3.0
Aged 75 to 79	7,416	7,420	0.1
Aged 80 to 84	4,945	5,314	7.5
Aged 85 or older	4,240	4,593	8.3
Aged 85 to 89	2,790	2,943	5.5
Aged 90 to 94	1,113	1,250	12.4
Aged 95 to 99	287	342	19.2
Aged 100 or older	50	59	16.3

Source: Bureau of the Census, National Population Estimates, Internet site http://eire.census.gov/popest/data/national/tables/asro/NA-EST2002-ASRO-01.php; calculations by New Strategist

Table 7.4 Population by Age, 2000 to 2020

(number and percent distribution of people by age, 2000 to 2020; percent and percentage point change, 2000–2010 and 2010–2020; numbers in thousands)

	2000	2010	2020	percent change 2000–10	percent change 2010–20
Total people	**282,125**	**308,936**	**335,805**	**9.5%**	**8.7%**
Under age 5	19,218	21,426	22,932	11.5	7.0
Aged 5 to 19	61,331	61,810	65,955	0.8	6.7
Aged 20 to 44	104,075	104,444	108,632	0.4	4.0
Aged 45 to 64	62,440	81,012	83,653	29.7	3.3
Aged 65 or older	35,061	40,243	54,632	14.8	35.8
Aged 65 to 84	30,794	34,120	47,363	10.8	38.8
Aged 85 or older	4,267	6,123	7,269	43.5	18.7

	2000	2010	2020	percentage point change 2000–10	percentage point change 2010–20
Percent distribution by age					
Total people	**100.0%**	**100.0%**	**100.0%**	**–**	**–**
Under age 5	6.8	6.9	6.8	0.1	–0.1
Aged 5 to 19	21.7	20.0	19.6	–1.7	–0.4
Aged 20 to 44	36.9	33.8	32.3	–3.1	–1.5
Aged 45 to 64	22.1	26.2	24.9	4.1	–1.3
Aged 65 or older	12.4	13.0	16.3	0.6	3.2
Aged 65 to 84	10.9	11.0	14.1	0.1	3.1
Aged 85 or older	1.5	2.0	2.2	0.5	0.2

Note: (–) means not applicable.
Source: Bureau of the Census, U.S. Interim Projections by Age, Sex, Race, and Hispanic Origin, 2004, Internet site http://www.census.gov/ipc/www/usinterimproj/; calculations by New Strategist

Older Americans Are Less Diverse than Younger Generations

The World War II generation is the least diverse of all.

Eighty-one percent of people aged 55 or older (born before 1946, and including the Swing and World War II generations) are non-Hispanic white, according to the 2000 census. This figure is much higher than the 69 percent for the population as a whole, and dwarfs the share among the youngest Americans—only 58 percent of children under age 5 are non-Hispanic white.

Just 6 percent of people aged 55 or older are Hispanic versus fully 19 percent of children under age 5. Only 9 percent of older Americans are black, versus 17 percent of children under age 5. Within the older age groups, blacks outnumber Hispanics by nearly 2 million. In contrast, Hispanics outnumber blacks among children and young adults.

Only 10 percent of the 7 million multiracial Americans are aged 55 or older. Fully 36 percent of the nation's multiracial are members of the Millennial generation (under age 25 in 2000). Only 1 percent of people aged 55 or older claimed to be multiracial on the 2000 census.

■ The contrast in the racial and ethnic makeup of older versus younger generations of Americans will create political tension in the years ahead.

More than 80 percent of the oldest Americans are non-Hispanic white

(non-Hispanic white share of the population by generation, 2000)

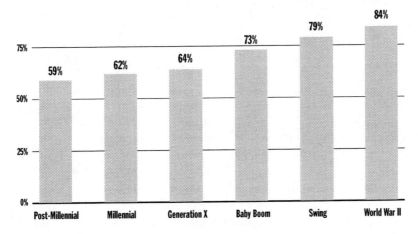

Table 7.5 Population by Age, Race, and Hispanic Origin, 2000 Census

(number and percent distribution of people by age, race, and Hispanic origin, 2000; numbers in thousands)

	total	American Indian	Asian	black	Native Hawaiian	white total	white non-Hispanic	other race	multiracial	Hispanic
TOTAL PEOPLE	281,422	4,119	11,899	36,419	874	216,931	194,553	18,521	6,826	35,306
Under age 5	19,176	359	919	3,167	88	13,656	11,194	2,017	948	3,718
Aged 5 to 14	41,078	791	1,771	6,823	175	29,533	25,186	3,648	1,533	6,787
Aged 15 to 24	39,184	697	1,878	5,853	168	28,164	24,355	3,690	1,174	6,581
Aged 25 to 34	39,892	588	2,179	5,374	140	29,096	25,356	3,578	997	6,510
Aged 35 to 44	45,149	644	1,953	5,699	126	34,984	31,801	2,693	891	5,129
Aged 45 to 54	37,678	501	1,499	4,194	86	30,494	28,387	1,553	607	3,136
Aged 55 or older	**59,266**	**541**	**1,700**	**5,309**	**91**	**51,004**	**48,273**	**1,343**	**676**	**3,444**
Aged 55 to 64	24,275	281	839	2,429	47	20,316	19,028	718	332	1,710
Aged 65 or older	34,992	260	862	2,881	44	30,688	29,245	625	344	1,734
Aged 65 to 74	18,391	157	532	1,647	27	15,853	14,978	392	203	1,077
Aged 75 to 84	12,361	79	262	914	13	11,028	10,592	180	108	506
Aged 85 or older	4,240	24	68	319	4	3,807	3,674	54	34	151
PERCENT DISTRIBUTION BY RACE AND HISPANIC ORIGIN										
TOTAL PEOPLE	100.0%	1.5%	4.2%	12.9%	0.3%	77.1%	69.1%	6.6%	2.4%	12.5%
Under age 5	100.0	1.9	4.8	16.5	0.5	71.2	58.4	10.5	4.9	19.4
Aged 5 to 14	100.0	1.9	4.3	16.6	0.4	71.9	61.3	8.9	3.7	16.5
Aged 15 to 24	100.0	1.8	4.8	14.9	0.4	71.9	62.2	9.4	3.0	16.8
Aged 25 to 34	100.0	1.5	5.5	13.5	0.4	72.9	63.6	9.0	2.5	16.3
Aged 35 to 44	100.0	1.4	4.3	12.6	0.3	77.5	70.4	6.0	2.0	11.4
Aged 45 to 54	100.0	1.3	4.0	11.1	0.2	80.9	75.3	4.1	1.6	8.3
Aged 55 or older	**100.0**	**0.9**	**2.9**	**9.0**	**0.2**	**86.1**	**81.5**	**2.3**	**1.1**	**5.8**
Aged 55 to 64	100.0	1.2	3.5	10.0	0.2	83.7	78.4	3.0	1.4	7.1
Aged 65 or older	100.0	0.7	2.5	8.2	0.1	87.7	83.6	1.8	1.0	5.0
Aged 65 to 74	100.0	0.9	2.9	9.0	0.1	86.2	81.4	2.1	1.1	5.9
Aged 75 to 84	100.0	0.6	2.1	7.4	0.1	89.2	85.7	1.5	0.9	4.1
Aged 85 or older	100.0	0.6	1.6	7.5	0.1	89.8	86.7	1.3	0.8	3.6

Note: Numbers will not add to total because each racial category includes those who identified themselves as being of the race alone and those who identified themselves as being of the race in combination with one or more other races, because the multiracial are shown, and because Hispanics may be of any race. Non-Hispanic whites include only those who identified themselves as "white alone" and non-Hispanic.

Source: Bureau of the Census, Census 2000 Summary File 1; Internet site http://factfinder.census.gov/servlet/BasicFactsServlet; calculations by New Strategist

Table 7.6 Population by Generation, Race, and Hispanic Origin, 2000 Census

(number and percent distribution of people by generation, race, and Hispanic origin, 2000; numbers in thousands)

	total	American Indian	Asian	black	Native Hawaiian	white total	white non-Hispanic	other race	Hispanic
TOTAL PEOPLE	**281,422**	**4,119**	**11,899**	**36,419**	**874**	**216,931**	**194,553**	**18,521**	**35,306**
Post-Millennial (under age 6)	23,141	432	1,100	3,833	106	16,475	13,539	2,414	4,451
Millennial (aged 6 to 23)	72,655	1,356	3,266	11,498	311	52,303	45,002	6,551	11,948
Generation X (aged 24 to 35)	48,049	711	2,592	6,486	169	35,076	30,585	4,295	7,812
Baby Boom (aged 36 to 54)	78,310	1,080	3,240	9,293	198	62,074	57,154	3,919	7,652
Swing (aged 55 to 67)	**30,061**	**337**	**1,024**	**2,999**	**57**	**25,214**	**23,629**	**859**	**2,085**
World War II (aged 68+)	**29,205**	**203**	**676**	**2,310**	**34**	**25,790**	**24,644**	**484**	**1,360**

PERCENT DISTRIBUTION BY RACE AND HISPANIC ORIGIN

	total	American Indian	Asian	black	Native Hawaiian	white total	white non-Hispanic	other race	Hispanic
TOTAL PEOPLE	**100.0%**	**100.0%**	**100.0%**	**100.0%**	**100.0%**	**100.0%**	**100.0%**	**100.0%**	**100.0%**
Post-Millennial (under age 6)	8.2	10.5	9.2	10.5	12.2	7.6	7.0	13.0	12.6
Millennial (aged 6 to 23)	25.8	32.9	27.5	31.6	35.5	24.1	23.1	35.4	33.8
Generation X (aged 24 to 35)	17.1	17.3	21.8	17.8	19.3	16.2	15.7	23.2	22.1
Baby Boom (aged 36 to 54)	27.8	26.2	27.2	25.5	22.6	28.6	29.4	21.2	21.7
Swing (aged 55 to 67)	**10.7**	**8.2**	**8.6**	**8.2**	**6.5**	**11.6**	**12.1**	**4.6**	**5.9**
World War II (aged 68+)	**10.4**	**4.9**	**5.7**	**6.3**	**3.9**	**11.9**	**12.7**	**2.6**	**3.9**

PERCENT DISTRIBUTION BY GENERATION

	total	American Indian	Asian	black	Native Hawaiian	white total	white non-Hispanic	other race	Hispanic
TOTAL PEOPLE	**100.0%**	**1.5%**	**4.2%**	**12.9%**	**0.3%**	**77.1%**	**69.1%**	**6.6%**	**12.5%**
Post-Millennial (under age 6)	100.0	1.9	4.8	16.6	0.5	71.2	58.5	10.4	19.2
Millennial (aged 6 to 23)	100.0	1.9	4.5	15.8	0.4	72.0	61.9	9.0	16.4
Generation X (aged 24 to 35)	100.0	1.5	5.4	13.5	0.4	73.0	63.7	8.9	16.3
Baby Boom (aged 36 to 54)	100.0	1.4	4.1	11.9	0.3	79.3	73.0	5.0	9.8
Swing (aged 55 to 67)	**100.0**	**1.1**	**3.4**	**10.0**	**0.2**	**83.9**	**78.6**	**2.9**	**6.9**
World War II (aged 68+)	**100.0**	**0.7**	**2.3**	**7.9**	**0.1**	**88.3**	**84.4**	**1.7**	**4.7**

Note: Numbers will not add to total because each racial category includes those who identified themselves as being of the race alone and those who identified themselves as being of the race in combination with one or more other races, and because Hispanics may be of any race. Non-Hispanic whites include only those who identified themselves as "white alone" and non-Hispanic. Source: Bureau of the Census, Census 2000 Summary File 2, Internet site http://factfinder.census.gov/servlet/BasicFactsServlet; calculations by New Strategist

Table 7.7 Multiracial Population by Age and Generation, 2000 Census

(number of total people and number and percent distribution of the multiracial population, by age and generation, 2000; numbers in thousands)

	total	multiracial		
		number	percent distribution	share of total
TOTAL PEOPLE	**281,422**	**6,826**	**100.0%**	**2.4%**
Under age 5	19,176	948	13.9	4.9
Aged 5 to 9	20,550	830	12.2	4.0
Aged 10 to 14	20,528	703	10.3	3.4
Aged 15 to 19	20,220	622	9.1	3.1
Aged 20 to 24	18,964	552	8.1	2.9
Aged 25 to 29	19,381	512	7.5	2.6
Aged 30 to 34	20,510	484	7.1	2.4
Aged 35 to 39	22,707	471	6.9	2.1
Aged 40 to 44	22,442	421	6.2	1.9
Aged 45 to 49	20,092	338	5.0	1.7
Aged 50 to 54	17,586	269	3.9	1.5
Aged 55 to 59	13,469	189	2.8	1.4
Aged 60 to 64	10,805	143	2.1	1.3
Aged 65 to 69	9,534	112	1.6	1.2
Aged 70 to 74	8,857	91	1.3	1.0
Aged 75 to 79	7,416	67	1.0	0.9
Aged 80 to 84	4,945	41	0.6	0.8
Aged 85 or older	4,240	34	0.5	0.8
TOTAL PEOPLE	**281,422**	**6,826**	**100.0**	**2.4**
Post-Millennial (under 6)	23,141	1,122	16.4	4.8
Millennial (aged 6 to 23)	72,655	2,429	35.6	3.3
Generation X (aged 24 to 35)	48,049	1,200	17.6	2.5
Baby Boom (aged 36 to 54)	78,310	1,399	20.5	1.8
Swing (aged 55 to 67)	**30,061**	**402**	**5.9**	**1.3**
World War II (68+)	**29,205**	**274**	**4.0**	**0.9**

Source: Bureau of the Census, Census 2000 Summary File 2, Internet site http://factfinder.census.gov/servlet/BasicFactsServlet; calculations by New Strategist

About One in Ten Older Americans Is Foreign Born

Many of the older foreign born are from Europe.

A substantial 12 percent of all Americans in 2002 were foreign born, but the proportion is a smaller 11 percent among people aged 55 or older. Among the 6.4 million people aged 55 or older who were born in a foreign country, the 66 percent majority are naturalized citizens. The 55-or-older age group accounts for only 20 percent of the total foreign-born population, but it represents a much larger 35 percent of the naturalized foreign born.

Among the foreign born aged 55-or-older, 29 percent are from Europe. This share is much larger than the 18 percent who were born in Central America (a region that includes Mexico in these statistics)—and stands in contrast to the origins of the younger foreign-born population. A substantial 26 percent of the older foreign born are from Asia.

■ As older Americans are replaced by younger generations, the European foreign-born population has been surpassed by the foreign born from Central America—primarily Mexico.

The largest share of foreign-born people aged 55 or older are from Europe

(percent distribution of foreign-born people aged 55 or older by region of birth, 2002)

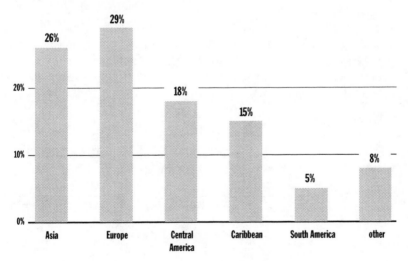

Table 7.8 Population Aged 55 or Older by Citizenship Status, 2002

(number and percent distribution of total people and people age 55 or older by citizenship status, 2002; numbers in thousands)

| | | | foreign born | | |
	total	native born	total	naturalized citizen	not a citizen
TOTAL PEOPLE	**282,082**	**249,629**	**32,453**	**11,962**	**20,491**
Total aged 55 or older	**59,644**	**53,280**	**6,363**	**4,196**	**2,167**
Aged 55 to 64	25,874	22,820	3,054	1,863	1,191
Aged 65 or older	33,770	30,460	3,309	2,333	976
Aged 65 to 74	18,123	16,200	1,922	1,251	671
Aged 75 to 84	12,191	11,115	1,077	828	249
Aged 85 or older	3,456	3,145	310	254	56
PERCENT DISTRIBUTION BY CITIZENSHIP STATUS					
TOTAL PEOPLE	**100.0%**	**88.5%**	**11.5%**	**4.2%**	**7.3%**
Total aged 55 or older	**100.0**	**89.3**	**10.7**	**7.0**	**3.6**
Aged 55 to 64	100.0	88.2	11.8	7.2	4.6
Aged 65 or older	100.0	90.2	9.8	6.9	2.9
Aged 65 to 74	100.0	89.4	10.6	6.9	3.7
Aged 75 to 84	100.0	91.2	8.8	6.8	2.0
Aged 85 or older	100.0	91.0	9.0	7.3	1.6
PERCENT DISTRIBUTION BY AGE					
TOTAL PEOPLE	**100.0%**	**100.0%**	**100.0%**	**100.0%**	**100.0%**
Total aged 55 or older	**21.1**	**21.3**	**19.6**	**35.1**	**10.6**
Aged 55 to 64	9.2	9.1	9.4	15.6	5.8
Aged 65 or older	12.0	12.2	10.2	19.5	4.8
Aged 65 to 74	6.4	6.5	5.9	10.5	3.3
Aged 75 to 84	4.3	4.5	3.3	6.9	1.2
Aged 85 or older	1.2	1.3	1.0	2.1	0.3

Source: Bureau of the Census, Foreign-Born Population of the United States, Current Population Survey, March 2002, *Internet site http://www.census.gov/population/www/socdemo/foreign/ppl-162.html; calculations by New Strategist*

Table 7.9 Foreign-Born Population Aged 55 or Older, 2002

(number and percent distribution of total people and people aged 55 or older by foreign-born status and region of birth, 2002; numbers in thousands)

| | | foreign born | | | | | | | |
| | | | | | Latin America | | | | |
	total	total	Asia	Europe	total	Caribbean	Central America	South America	other
TOTAL PEOPLE	**282,082**	**32,453**	**8,281**	**4,548**	**16,943**	**3,102**	**11,819**	**2,022**	**2,680**
Total aged 55 or older	**59,644**	**6,363**	**1,643**	**1,820**	**2,388**	**923**	**1,146**	**318**	**510**
Aged 55 to 64	25,874	3,054	875	673	1,248	426	640	181	258
Aged 65 or older	33,770	3,309	768	1,147	1,140	497	506	137	252
Aged 65 to 74	18,123	1,922	517	579	711	300	318	94	114
Aged 75 to 84	12,191	1,077	217	414	337	144	154	38	108
Aged 85 or older	3,456	310	34	154	92	53	34	5	30
PERCENT DISTRIBUTION OF FOREIGN-BORN BY REGION OF BIRTH									
TOTAL PEOPLE	–	**100.0%**	**25.5%**	**14.0%**	**52.2%**	**9.6%**	**36.4%**	**6.2%**	**8.3%**
Total aged 55 or older	–	**100.0**	**25.8**	**28.6**	**37.5**	**14.5**	**18.0**	**5.0**	**8.0**
Aged 55 to 64	–	100.0	28.7	22.0	40.9	13.9	21.0	5.9	8.4
Aged 65 or older	–	100.0	23.2	34.7	34.5	15.0	15.3	4.1	7.6
Aged 65 to 74	–	100.0	26.9	30.1	37.0	15.6	16.5	4.9	5.9
Aged 75 to 84	–	100.0	20.1	38.4	31.3	13.4	14.3	3.5	10.0
Aged 85 or older	–	100.0	11.0	49.7	29.7	17.1	11.0	1.6	9.7
PERCENT DISTRIBUTION BY AGE									
TOTAL PEOPLE	**100.0%**	**100.0%**	**100.0%**	**100.0%**	**100.0%**	**100.0%**	**100.0%**	**100.0%**	**100.0%**
Total aged 55 or older	**21.1**	**19.6**	**19.8**	**40.0**	**14.1**	**29.8**	**9.7**	**15.7**	**19.0**
Aged 55 to 64	9.2	9.4	10.6	14.8	7.4	13.7	5.4	9.0	9.6
Aged 65 or older	12.0	10.2	9.3	25.2	6.7	16.0	4.3	6.8	9.4
Aged 65 to 74	6.4	5.9	6.2	12.7	4.2	9.7	2.7	4.6	4.3
Aged 75 to 84	4.3	3.3	2.6	9.1	2.0	4.6	1.3	1.9	4.0
Aged 85 or older	1.2	1.0	0.4	3.4	0.5	1.7	0.3	0.2	1.1

Note: Central America includes Mexico in these statistics; (–) means not applicable.
Source: Bureau of the Census, Foreign-Born Population of the United States, Current Population Survey, March 2002, Internet site http://www.census.gov/population/www/socdemo/foreign/ppl-162.html; calculations by New Strategist

Few Immigrants Are in the Older Age Groups

Only about one in ten immigrants is aged 55 or older.

Over 1 million legal immigrants were admitted to the United States in 2002. Only about 112,000 were aged 55 or older, accounting for 11 percent of the total. Most immigrants are young adults seeking economic opportunity for themselves and their families.

Within the 55-or-older age group, the immigrant share declines steadily with age. Three percent of immigrants admitted to the United States in 2002 were aged 55 to 59, and the figure declines to just 1 percent in the 75-or-older age group.

■ Because most immigrants are children and young adults, immigration has a much greater impact on the diversity of younger Americans than on the older population.

Immigrants aged 55 or older account for just 11 percent of the total

(percent distribution of immigrants by age, 2002)

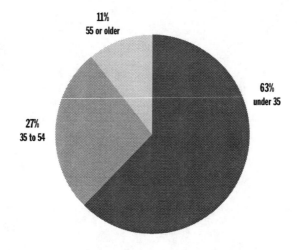

Table 7.10 Immigrants by Age, 2002

(number and percent distribution of immigrants by age, 2002)

	number	percent distribution
Total immigrants	**1,063,732**	**100.0%**
Under age 1	11,673	1.1
Aged 1 to 4	31,791	3.0
Aged 5 to 9	54,493	5.1
Aged 10 to 14	70,860	6.7
Aged 15 to 19	92,566	8.7
Aged 20 to 24	93,132	8.8
Aged 25 to 29	152,476	14.3
Aged 30 to 34	160,962	15.1
Aged 35 to 39	112,247	10.6
Aged 40 to 44	75,743	7.1
Aged 45 to 49	54,811	5.2
Aged 50 to 54	40,319	3.8
Aged 55 or older	**112,450**	**10.6**
Aged 55 to 64	60,895	5.7
Aged 55 to 59	31,694	3.0
Aged 60 to 64	29,201	2.7
Aged 65 or older	51,555	4.8
Aged 65 to 74	39,014	3.7
Aged 75 or older	12,541	1.2

Source: U.S. Citizenship and Immigration Services, 2002 Yearbook of Immigration Statistics, Internet site http://uscis.gov/ graphics/shared/aboutus/statistics/IMM02yrbk/IMM2002list.htm

The Largest Share of Older Americans Lives in the South

People aged 55 or older account for 27 percent of the population of Florida.

The South is home to the largest share of the population, and consequently to the largest share of older Americans. The 2000 census found 36 percent of people aged 55 or older living in the South, where they accounted for 21 percent of the population.

By state, the smallest proportion of older Americans is found in Alaska—just 13 percent of Alaska's residents were aged 55 or older in 2000. Alaska's cold climate drives many aging state residents away. In contrast, Florida's warm climate attracts retirees, which is why the percentage of older Americans in Florida is twice as high as in Alaska.

The diversity of older Americans varies by state, but not nearly as dramatically as it does among middle-aged and younger Americans. Only in Hawaii are non-Hispanic whites a minority among the 55-or-older population. In the nation's most populous state, California, the 66 percent majority of people aged 55 or older are non-Hispanic white versus only 47 percent of the state's total population. In most states, the oldest residents are much less diverse than those in their fifties. In California, sixty-two percent of people aged 55 to 59 are non-Hispanic white versus a much larger 78 percent of those aged 85 or older.

■ The diversity of the older population will surge as Generation X enters the age group beginning in 2020.

The smallest share of older Americans lives in the West

(percent distribution of people aged 55 or older by region, 2000)

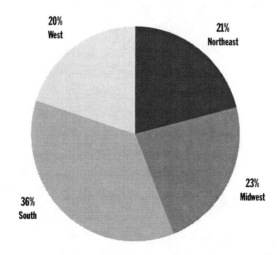

Table 7.11 Population Aged 55 or Older by Region, 2000 Census

(number and percent distribution of people aged 55 or older by age and region, 2000; numbers in thousands)

	total	Northeast	Midwest	South	West
TOTAL PEOPLE	**281,422**	**53,594**	**64,393**	**100,237**	**63,198**
Total aged 55 or older	**59,266**	**12,179**	**13,806**	**21,281**	**11,999**
Aged 55 to 59	13,469	2,676	3,070	4,871	2,852
Aged 60 to 64	10,805	2,131	2,477	3,972	2,226
Aged 65 or older	34,992	7,371	8,259	12,438	6,922
Aged 65 to 69	9,534	1,914	2,181	3,522	1,917
Aged 70 to 74	8,857	1,854	2,067	3,189	1,746
Aged 75 to 79	7,416	1,581	1,745	2,605	1,485
Aged 80 to 84	4,945	1,084	1,202	1,691	968
Aged 85 or older	4,240	938	1,064	1,431	806
PERCENT DISTRIBUTION BY AGE					
TOTAL PEOPLE	**100.0%**	**100.0%**	**100.0%**	**100.0%**	**100.0%**
Total aged 55 or older	**21.1**	**22.7**	**21.4**	**21.2**	**19.0**
Aged 55 to 59	4.8	5.0	4.8	4.9	4.5
Aged 60 to 64	3.8	4.0	3.8	4.0	3.5
Aged 65 or older	12.4	13.8	12.8	12.4	11.0
Aged 65 to 69	3.4	3.6	3.4	3.5	3.0
Aged 70 to 74	3.1	3.5	3.2	3.2	2.8
Aged 75 to 79	2.6	3.0	2.7	2.6	2.3
Aged 80 to 84	1.8	2.0	1.9	1.7	1.5
Aged 85 or older	1.5	1.8	1.7	1.4	1.3
PERCENT DISTRIBUTION BY REGION					
TOTAL PEOPLE	**100.0%**	**19.0%**	**22.9%**	**35.6%**	**22.5%**
Total aged 55 or older	**100.0**	**20.6**	**23.3**	**35.9**	**20.2**
Aged 55 to 59	100.0	19.9	22.8	36.2	21.2
Aged 60 to 64	100.0	19.7	22.9	36.8	20.6
Aged 65 or older	100.0	21.1	23.6	35.5	19.8
Aged 65 to 69	100.0	20.1	22.9	36.9	20.1
Aged 70 to 74	100.0	20.9	23.3	36.0	19.7
Aged 75 to 79	100.0	21.3	23.5	35.1	20.0
Aged 80 to 84	100.0	21.9	24.3	34.2	19.6
Aged 85 or older	100.0	22.1	25.1	33.7	19.0

Source: Bureau of the Census, Census 2000 Summary File 2, Internet site http://factfinder.census.gov/servlet/BasicFactsServlet; calculations by New Strategist

Table 7.12 Regional Populations by Generation, 2000 Census

(number and percent distribution of people by generation and region, 2000; numbers in thousands)

	total	Northeast	Midwest	South	West
TOTAL PEOPLE	**281,422**	**53,594**	**64,393**	**100,237**	**63,198**
Post-Millennial (under age 6)	23,141	4,115	5,255	8,238	5,532
Millennial (aged 6 to 23)	72,655	13,059	16,826	25,834	16,936
Generation X (aged 24 to 35)	48,049	8,938	10,547	17,248	11,315
Baby Boom (aged 36 to 54)	78,310	15,303	17,958	27,635	17,415
Swing (aged 55 to 67)	**30,061**	**5,957**	**6,863**	**10,995**	**6,246**
World War II (aged 68 or older)	**29,205**	**6,222**	**6,944**	**10,286**	**5,753**
PERCENT DISTRIBUTION BY GENERATION					
TOTAL PEOPLE	**100.0%**	**100.0%**	**100.0%**	**100.0%**	**100.0%**
Post-Millennial (under age 6)	8.2	7.7	8.2	8.2	8.8
Millennial (aged 6 to 23)	25.8	24.4	26.1	25.8	26.8
Generation X (aged 24 to 35)	17.1	16.7	16.4	17.2	17.9
Baby Boom (aged 36 to 54)	27.8	28.6	27.9	27.6	27.6
Swing (aged 55 to 67)	**10.7**	**11.1**	**10.7**	**11.0**	**9.9**
World War II (aged 68 or older)	**10.4**	**11.6**	**10.8**	**10.3**	**9.1**
PERCENT DISTRIBUTION BY REGION					
TOTAL PEOPLE	**100.0%**	**19.0%**	**22.9%**	**35.6%**	**22.5%**
Post-Millennial (under age 6)	100.0	17.8	22.7	35.6	23.9
Millennial (aged 6 to 23)	100.0	18.0	23.2	35.6	23.3
Generation X (aged 24 to 35)	100.0	18.6	22.0	35.9	23.5
Baby Boom (aged 36 to 54)	100.0	19.5	22.9	35.3	22.2
Swing (aged 55 to 67)	**100.0**	**19.8**	**22.8**	**36.6**	**20.8**
World War II (aged 68 or older)	**100.0**	**21.3**	**23.8**	**35.2**	**19.7**

Source: Bureau of the Census, Census 2000 Summary File 2, Internet site http://factfinder.census.gov/servlet/BasicFactsServlet; calculations by New Strategist

Table 7.13 Population Aged 55 or Older by State, 2000 Census

(number and percent distribution of total people and people aged 55 or older by state, 2000; numbers in thousands)

| | number | | | | | | | percent distribution | | | | | | |
| | | aged 55 or older | | aged 65 or older | | | | | aged 55 or older | | aged 65 or older | | | |
	total	total	55–64	total	65–74	75–84	85+	total	total	55–64	total	65–74	75–84	85+
United States	281,422	59,266	24,275	34,992	18,391	12,361	4,240	100.0%	21.1%	8.6%	12.4%	6.5%	4.4%	1.5%
Alabama	4,447	995	416	580	317	196	67	100.0	22.4	9.3	13.0	7.1	4.4	1.5
Alaska	627	80	45	36	23	11	3	100.0	12.8	7.1	5.7	3.6	1.7	0.4
Arizona	5,131	1,110	442	668	364	236	69	100.0	21.6	8.6	13.0	7.1	4.6	1.3
Arkansas	2,673	631	257	374	198	129	47	100.0	23.6	9.6	14.0	7.4	4.8	1.7
California	33,872	6,210	2,614	3,596	1,888	1,282	426	100.0	18.3	7.7	10.6	5.6	3.8	1.3
Colorado	4,301	755	339	416	226	142	48	100.0	17.6	7.9	9.7	5.3	3.3	1.1
Connecticut	3,406	779	309	470	232	174	64	100.0	22.9	9.1	13.8	6.8	5.1	1.9
Delaware	784	173	72	102	56	35	11	100.0	22.1	9.1	13.0	7.2	4.4	1.3
District of Columbia	572	120	50	70	36	25	9	100.0	20.9	8.7	12.2	6.3	4.4	1.6
Florida	15,982	4,367	1,559	2,808	1,452	1,024	331	100.0	27.3	9.8	17.6	9.1	6.4	2.1
Georgia	8,186	1,447	662	785	436	262	88	100.0	17.7	8.1	9.6	5.3	3.2	1.1
Hawaii	1,212	268	107	161	85	58	18	100.0	22.1	8.8	13.3	7.0	4.8	1.4
Idaho	1,294	253	108	146	76	52	18	100.0	19.6	8.3	11.3	5.9	4.0	1.4
Illinois	12,419	2,541	1,041	1,500	772	536	192	100.0	20.5	8.4	12.1	6.2	4.3	1.5
Indiana	6,080	1,283	530	753	395	266	92	100.0	21.1	8.7	12.4	6.5	4.4	1.5
Iowa	2,926	694	257	436	212	159	65	100.0	23.7	8.8	14.9	7.2	5.4	2.2
Kansas	2,688	577	220	356	176	129	52	100.0	21.4	8.2	13.3	6.5	4.8	1.9
Kentucky	4,042	877	373	505	274	173	58	100.0	21.7	9.2	12.5	6.8	4.3	1.4
Louisiana	4,469	896	379	517	283	175	59	100.0	20.1	8.5	11.6	6.3	3.9	1.3
Maine	1,275	307	123	183	96	64	23	100.0	24.1	9.7	14.4	7.5	5.0	1.8
Maryland	5,296	1,070	470	599	321	211	67	100.0	20.2	8.9	11.3	6.1	4.0	1.3
Massachusetts	6,349	1,407	546	860	428	316	117	100.0	22.2	8.6	13.5	6.7	5.0	1.8
Michigan	9,938	2,082	863	1,219	643	434	143	100.0	20.9	8.7	12.3	6.5	4.4	1.4

	number							percent distribution						
		aged 55 or older							aged 55 or older					
				aged 65 or older							aged 65 or older			
	total	total	55–64	total	65–74	75–84	85+	total	total	55–64	total	65–74	75–84	85+
Minnesota	4,919	999	405	594	296	213	86	100.0%	20.3%	8.2%	12.1%	6.0%	4.3%	1.7%
Mississippi	2,845	589	246	344	186	115	43	100.0	20.7	8.6	12.1	6.5	4.0	1.5
Missouri	5,595	1,263	507	755	393	264	99	100.0	22.6	9.1	13.5	7.0	4.7	1.8
Montana	902	206	85	121	63	43	15	100.0	22.8	9.4	13.4	6.9	4.8	1.7
Nebraska	1,711	374	142	232	116	83	34	100.0	21.8	8.3	13.6	6.8	4.8	2.0
Nevada	1,998	409	190	219	132	70	17	100.0	20.5	9.5	11.0	6.6	3.5	0.9
New Hampshire	1,236	258	110	148	78	51	18	100.0	20.8	8.9	12.0	6.3	4.2	1.5
New Jersey	8,414	1,867	754	1,113	575	403	136	100.0	22.2	9.0	13.2	6.8	4.8	1.6
New Mexico	1,819	371	159	212	118	71	23	100.0	20.4	8.7	11.7	6.5	3.9	1.3
New York	18,976	4,136	1,688	2,448	1,276	861	312	100.0	21.8	8.9	12.9	6.7	4.5	1.6
North Carolina	8,049	1,693	724	969	534	330	106	100.0	21.0	9.0	12.0	6.6	4.1	1.3
North Dakota	642	148	53	95	46	34	15	100.0	23.0	8.3	14.7	7.1	5.3	2.3
Ohio	11,353	2,517	1,009	1,508	790	541	177	100.0	22.2	8.9	13.3	7.0	4.8	1.6
Oklahoma	3,451	772	316	456	243	156	57	100.0	22.4	9.2	13.2	7.0	4.5	1.7
Oregon	3,421	743	304	438	219	161	57	100.0	21.7	8.9	12.8	6.4	4.7	1.7
Pennsylvania	12,281	3,051	1,132	1,919	969	712	238	100.0	24.8	9.2	15.6	7.9	5.8	1.9
Rhode Island	1,048	241	89	152	74	58	21	100.0	23.0	8.5	14.5	7.0	5.5	2.0
South Carolina	4,012	858	373	485	270	165	50	100.0	21.4	9.3	12.1	6.7	4.1	1.3
South Dakota	755	171	62	108	53	39	16	100.0	22.6	8.3	14.3	7.0	5.2	2.1
Tennessee	5,689	1,237	533	703	383	239	82	100.0	21.7	9.4	12.4	6.7	4.2	1.4
Texas	20,852	3,671	1,598	2,073	1,143	692	238	100.0	17.6	7.7	9.9	5.5	3.3	1.1
Utah	2,233	333	143	190	102	67	22	100.0	14.9	6.4	8.5	4.5	3.0	1.0
Vermont	609	134	57	78	41	27	10	100.0	22.1	9.3	12.7	6.7	4.4	1.6
Virginia	7,079	1,424	632	792	433	273	87	100.0	20.1	8.9	11.2	6.1	3.9	1.2
Washington	5,894	1,159	497	662	337	241	84	100.0	19.7	8.4	11.2	5.7	4.1	1.4
West Virginia	1,808	462	185	277	149	97	32	100.0	25.5	10.2	15.3	8.2	5.3	1.8
Wisconsin	5,364	1,160	458	703	355	252	96	100.0	21.6	8.5	13.1	6.6	4.7	1.8
Wyoming	494	102	45	58	31	20	7	100.0	20.7	9.0	11.7	6.3	4.0	1.4

Source: Bureau of the Census, Census 2000 Summary File 2, Internet site http://factfinder.census.gov/servlet/BasicFactsServlet

Table 7.14 Population Aged 55 or Older by State, Race, and Hispanic Origin, 2000 Census

(total number of people, number aged 55 or older, and percent distribution by race and Hispanic origin, by state, 2000)

	total number	total percent	American Indian	Asian	black	Native Hawaiian	white total	white non-Hispanic	other	Hispanic
ALABAMA										
State total	4,447,100	100.0%	1.0%	0.9%	26.3%	0.1%	72.0%	70.3%	0.9%	1.7%
Total 55+	995,330	100.0	0.7	0.4	18.8	0.0	80.4	79.5	0.2	0.6
Aged 55 to 59	225,450	100.0	1.1	0.6	18.6	0.0	80.2	79.1	0.3	0.8
Aged 60 to 64	190,082	100.0	0.8	0.5	18.8	0.1	80.3	79.3	0.2	0.7
Total 65+	579,798	100.0	0.6	0.3	19.0	0.0	80.5	79.7	0.2	0.5
Aged 65 to 69	167,968	100.0	0.7	0.5	18.7	0.1	80.6	79.6	0.2	0.6
Aged 70 to 74	148,780	100.0	0.6	0.3	18.6	0.0	80.9	80.0	0.2	0.5
Aged 75 to 79	118,108	100.0	0.6	0.2	18.2	0.0	81.4	80.6	0.1	0.5
Aged 80 to 84	77,641	100.0	0.5	0.2	18.6	0.1	81.1	80.3	0.2	0.5
Aged 85 or older	67,301	100.0	0.4	0.2	22.3	0.1	77.5	76.8	0.2	0.5
ALASKA										
State total	626,932	100.0	19.0	5.2	4.3	0.9	74.0	67.6	2.4	4.1
Total 55+	80,449	100.0	16.1	4.9	2.2	0.3	77.8	74.6	1.3	1.9
Aged 55 to 59	27,423	100.0	14.0	4.5	2.2	0.4	80.3	76.9	1.4	2.1
Aged 60 to 64	17,327	100.0	16.0	5.1	2.6	0.3	77.4	73.9	1.4	2.3
Total 65+	35,699	100.0	17.8	5.2	2.1	0.3	76.1	73.1	1.1	1.5
Aged 65 to 69	12,626	100.0	18.8	5.2	2.3	0.5	75.1	71.8	1.1	1.8
Aged 70 to 74	9,881	100.0	17.7	5.6	2.1	0.4	76.1	72.9	1.0	1.5
Aged 75 to 79	6,863	100.0	16.6	5.5	1.9	0.2	77.2	74.5	1.1	1.2
Aged 80 to 84	3,695	100.0	16.1	5.0	2.3	0.3	77.5	75.1	1.2	1.2
Aged 85 or older	2,634	100.0	19.2	3.8	2.0	0.1	75.9	73.7	1.0	1.2
ARIZONA										
State total	5,130,632	100.0	5.7	2.3	3.6	0.3	77.9	63.8	13.2	25.3
Total 55+	1,110,211	100.0	2.9	1.3	1.8	0.1	91.1	84.0	3.9	10.1
Aged 55 to 59	238,675	100.0	3.8	1.7	2.3	0.2	87.9	79.0	5.6	13.3
Aged 60 to 64	203,697	100.0	3.6	1.6	2.2	0.1	89.1	80.7	4.8	12.0
Total 65+	667,839	100.0	2.4	1.0	1.5	0.1	92.9	86.7	3.0	8.3
Aged 65 to 69	189,007	100.0	3.0	1.4	1.9	0.1	90.9	83.4	3.8	10.3
Aged 70 to 74	174,834	100.0	2.4	1.1	1.5	0.1	92.8	86.1	3.2	8.9
Aged 75 to 79	144,201	100.0	2.1	0.8	1.3	0.1	94.2	88.7	2.5	7.2
Aged 80 to 84	91,272	100.0	1.8	0.6	1.2	0.1	94.7	89.9	2.3	6.4
Aged 85 or older	68,525	100.0	2.3	0.6	1.5	0.1	93.9	89.2	2.3	6.2
ARKANSAS										
State total	2,673,400	100.0	1.4	1.0	16.0	0.1	81.2	78.6	1.8	3.2
Total 55+	630,802	100.0	1.1	0.4	9.9	0.1	89.1	87.8	0.4	0.8
Aged 55 to 59	139,393	100.0	1.4	0.6	9.9	0.1	88.6	87.0	0.6	1.2
Aged 60 to 64	117,390	100.0	1.2	0.5	9.8	0.0	89.0	87.5	0.4	1.0
Total 65+	374,019	100.0	0.9	0.3	10.0	0.1	89.3	88.3	0.3	0.6
Aged 65 to 69	105,175	100.0	1.0	0.5	9.5	0.1	89.5	88.3	0.3	0.8
Aged 70 to 74	93,159	100.0	0.9	0.4	9.6	0.1	89.6	88.5	0.3	0.6
Aged 75 to 79	76,517	100.0	0.8	0.3	9.4	0.0	90.1	89.1	0.2	0.5
Aged 80 to 84	52,676	100.0	0.8	0.2	10.1	0.0	89.4	88.4	0.2	0.5
Aged 85 or older	46,492	100.0	0.7	0.2	12.7	0.1	86.9	86.1	0.2	0.4

	total		American Indian	Asian	black	Native Hawaiian	white total	non-Hispanic	other	Hispanic
	number	percent								
CALIFORNIA										
State total	33,871,648	100.0%	1.9%	12.3%	7.4%	0.7%	63.4%	46.7%	19.4%	32.4%
Total 55+	6,209,751	100.0	1.3	11.0	5.8	0.4	76.7	66.5	7.4	15.2
Aged 55 to 59	1,467,252	100.0	1.7	11.6	6.4	0.5	73.2	62.0	9.7	18.3
Aged 60 to 64	1,146,841	100.0	1.6	12.3	6.8	0.4	73.0	61.4	8.9	17.8
Total 65+	3,595,658	100.0	1.0	10.3	5.3	0.3	79.4	70.0	5.9	13.1
Aged 65 to 69	984,535	100.0	1.3	12.3	6.2	0.4	74.8	63.4	7.7	16.6
Aged 70 to 74	903,288	100.0	1.1	11.4	5.3	0.3	77.9	67.3	6.5	14.7
Aged 75 to 79	779,347	100.0	0.9	9.7	4.8	0.2	81.3	72.8	5.1	11.6
Aged 80 to 84	502,831	100.0	0.8	8.5	4.6	0.2	83.5	76.4	4.3	9.5
Aged 85 or older	425,657	100.0	0.7	7.0	4.6	0.2	84.9	78.2	4.3	9.1
COLORADO										
State total	4,301,261	100.0	1.9	2.8	4.4	0.2	85.2	74.5	8.5	17.1
Total 55+	755,380	100.0	1.1	1.8	2.8	0.1	92.3	85.2	3.2	9.2
Aged 55 to 59	194,722	100.0	1.5	1.9	3.1	0.1	90.9	83.5	4.0	10.2
Aged 60 to 64	144,585	100.0	1.3	2.0	3.3	0.1	91.1	83.1	3.7	10.6
Total 65+	416,073	100.0	0.9	1.6	2.5	0.1	93.4	86.8	2.7	8.3
Aged 65 to 69	121,222	100.0	1.1	2.0	3.3	0.1	91.6	83.9	3.3	10.0
Aged 70 to 74	105,088	100.0	1.0	1.8	2.6	0.1	92.9	85.8	2.8	9.0
Aged 75 to 79	85,922	100.0	0.7	1.6	2.1	0.1	94.1	88.0	2.4	7.6
Aged 80 to 84	55,625	100.0	0.7	1.2	1.9	0.1	95.0	89.8	2.0	6.4
Aged 85 or older	48,216	100.0	0.6	0.7	1.9	0.1	95.7	90.8	1.9	6.1
CONNECTICUT										
State total	3,405,565	100.0	0.7	2.8	10.0	0.1	83.3	77.5	5.5	9.4
Total 55+	778,796	100.0	0.4	1.3	5.9	0.1	91.6	88.9	1.8	3.4
Aged 55 to 59	176,961	100.0	0.5	1.9	7.3	0.1	88.9	85.3	2.6	5.0
Aged 60 to 64	131,652	100.0	0.5	1.8	7.9	0.1	88.5	84.9	2.5	4.8
Total 65+	470,183	100.0	0.4	0.9	4.9	0.0	93.4	91.3	1.3	2.5
Aged 65 to 69	117,556	100.0	0.4	1.4	6.6	0.1	90.7	87.7	1.9	3.8
Aged 70 to 74	114,009	100.0	0.4	1.0	5.3	0.0	92.8	90.7	1.3	2.6
Aged 75 to 79	101,096	100.0	0.3	0.7	4.4	0.0	94.2	92.5	1.1	2.0
Aged 80 to 84	73,249	100.0	0.3	0.5	3.3	0.0	95.6	94.0	1.0	1.7
Aged 85 or older	64,273	100.0	0.3	0.4	3.4	0.0	95.8	94.2	0.8	1.6
DELAWARE										
State total	783,600	100.0	0.8	2.4	20.1	0.1	75.9	72.5	2.6	4.8
Total 55+	173,245	100.0	0.5	1.3	12.5	0.1	85.5	84.3	0.6	1.4
Aged 55 to 59	39,320	100.0	0.6	1.9	14.7	0.1	82.5	80.9	1.0	2.0
Aged 60 to 64	32,199	100.0	0.6	2.0	14.2	0.1	83.0	81.6	0.8	1.7
Total 65+	101,726	100.0	0.5	0.9	11.2	0.0	87.5	86.4	0.4	1.1
Aged 65 to 69	29,952	100.0	0.6	1.3	12.7	0.0	85.4	84.1	0.6	1.4
Aged 70 to 74	26,463	100.0	0.5	0.9	10.7	0.0	88.0	86.9	0.5	1.2
Aged 75 to 79	21,248	100.0	0.4	0.7	10.7	0.0	88.2	87.4	0.3	0.9
Aged 80 to 84	13,514	100.0	0.5	0.5	9.7	0.1	89.4	88.7	0.4	0.7
Aged 85 or older	10,549	100.0	0.5	0.5	10.9	0.1	88.3	87.2	0.4	1.0

	total		American			Native	white			
	number	percent	Indian	Asian	black	Hawaiian	total	non-Hispanic	other	Hispanic
DISTRICT OF COLUMBIA										
District total	572,059	100.0%	0.8%	3.1%	61.3%	0.1%	32.2%	27.8%	0.5%	7.9%
Total 55+	119,681	100.0	0.8	1.9	66.7	0.1	30.4	28.0	1.7	3.4
Aged 55 to 59	27,803	100.0	0.9	2.2	59.6	0.1	36.6	33.7	2.5	4.5
Aged 60 to 64	21,980	100.0	0.8	2.2	66.5	0.1	30.0	27.1	2.1	4.2
Total 65+	69,898	100.0	0.8	1.7	69.6	0.1	28.0	26.0	1.3	2.7
Aged 65 to 69	18,525	100.0	0.7	2.1	71.4	0.1	25.7	23.2	1.5	3.4
Aged 70 to 74	17,394	100.0	0.8	1.7	72.3	0.1	25.2	23.2	1.5	2.8
Aged 75 to 79	14,976	100.0	0.8	1.5	70.2	0.0	27.6	25.7	1.3	2.5
Aged 80 to 84	10,028	100.0	0.8	1.4	67.5	0.0	30.6	28.8	1.1	2.2
Aged 85 or older	8,975	100.0	0.9	1.4	62.1	0.1	36.1	34.4	1.0	1.9
FLORIDA										
State total	15,982,378	100.0	0.7	2.1	15.5	0.2	79.7	65.4	4.4	16.8
Total 55+	4,366,610	100.0	0.5	1.0	7.7	0.1	90.4	79.8	1.5	11.2
Aged 55 to 59	821,517	100.0	0.7	1.7	10.5	0.1	86.4	74.0	2.3	13.4
Aged 60 to 64	737,496	100.0	0.6	1.5	9.9	0.1	87.5	74.9	1.9	13.6
Total 65+	2,807,597	100.0	0.4	0.7	6.3	0.1	92.4	82.8	1.1	9.9
Aged 65 to 69	727,495	100.0	0.4	1.1	8.2	0.1	89.9	78.5	1.5	12.1
Aged 70 to 74	724,681	100.0	0.4	0.8	6.5	0.1	92.1	82.2	1.1	10.4
Aged 75 to 79	616,693	100.0	0.3	0.5	5.3	0.0	93.7	85.3	0.9	8.7
Aged 80 to 84	407,441	100.0	0.3	0.4	5.1	0.0	94.1	86.2	0.8	8.1
Aged 85 or older	331,287	100.0	0.3	0.4	5.5	0.1	93.7	85.1	0.8	8.8
GEORGIA										
State total	8,186,453	100.0	0.6	2.4	29.2	0.1	66.1	62.6	2.9	5.3
Total 55+	1,446,731	100.0	0.5	1.4	20.3	0.1	77.8	76.5	0.6	1.4
Aged 55 to 59	375,651	100.0	0.6	1.9	21.2	0.1	76.2	74.6	0.8	1.8
Aged 60 to 64	285,805	100.0	0.6	1.8	21.1	0.1	76.5	75.0	0.7	1.7
Total 65+	785,275	100.0	0.4	1.0	19.6	0.1	79.1	77.9	0.4	1.1
Aged 65 to 69	236,634	100.0	0.5	1.5	20.3	0.1	77.9	76.5	0.5	1.3
Aged 70 to 74	199,061	100.0	0.5	1.1	19.2	0.1	79.4	78.2	0.4	1.1
Aged 75 to 79	157,569	100.0	0.4	0.8	18.3	0.1	80.7	79.7	0.4	0.9
Aged 80 to 84	104,154	100.0	0.4	0.6	19.2	0.1	80.1	79.1	0.3	0.8
Aged 85 or older	87,857	100.0	0.4	0.5	21.8	0.1	77.6	76.7	0.3	0.9
HAWAII										
State total	1,211,537	100.0	2.1	58.0	2.8	23.3	39.3	22.9	3.9	7.2
Total 55+	267,562	100.0	0.8	64.6	0.6	12.5	31.1	24.1	2.0	2.8
Aged 55 to 59	60,561	100.0	1.2	57.0	0.9	16.5	38.1	28.8	2.4	3.5
Aged 60 to 64	46,400	100.0	1.0	60.7	0.8	15.6	33.6	25.5	2.4	3.3
Total 65+	160,601	100.0	0.6	68.6	0.5	10.1	27.7	21.9	1.8	2.4
Aged 65 to 69	42,847	100.0	0.8	65.5	0.6	13.5	29.5	22.2	2.1	3.2
Aged 70 to 74	42,415	100.0	0.6	69.1	0.5	10.6	27.0	21.0	1.9	2.5
Aged 75 to 79	35,386	100.0	0.5	69.5	0.5	8.4	27.6	22.4	1.6	2.1
Aged 80 to 84	22,389	100.0	0.5	69.9	0.4	7.7	27.2	22.7	1.4	1.8
Aged 85 or older	17,564	100.0	0.4	71.4	0.4	6.8	25.8	21.6	1.6	1.9

	total		American Indian	Asian	black	Native Hawaiian	white		other	Hispanic
	number	percent					total	non-Hispanic		
IDAHO										
State total	1,293,953	100.0%	2.1%	1.3%	0.6%	0.2%	92.8%	88.1%	5.0%	7.9%
Total 55+	253,445	100.0	1.3	0.7	0.2	0.1	97.3	95.3	1.3	2.3
Aged 55 to 59	60,024	100.0	1.8	0.9	0.2	0.1	96.3	93.7	2.1	3.3
Aged 60 to 64	47,505	100.0	1.6	0.7	0.2	0.1	96.9	94.5	1.6	2.8
Total 65+	145,916	100.0	1.0	0.7	0.1	0.1	97.8	96.3	1.0	1.7
Aged 65 to 69	40,169	100.0	1.4	0.8	0.2	0.1	97.1	95.1	1.4	2.4
Aged 70 to 74	35,801	100.0	1.1	0.8	0.1	0.1	97.6	96.0	1.1	1.8
Aged 75 to 79	30,443	100.0	0.8	0.8	0.1	0.0	98.1	96.8	0.8	1.4
Aged 80 to 84	21,446	100.0	0.7	0.6	0.1	0.1	98.4	97.3	0.6	1.1
Aged 85 or older	18,057	100.0	0.6	0.4	0.2	0.1	98.7	97.5	0.6	1.1
ILLINOIS										
State total	12,419,293	100.0	0.6	3.8	15.6	0.1	75.1	67.8	6.8	12.3
Total 55+	2,540,658	100.0	0.4	2.5	11.7	0.1	84.1	81.0	2.2	4.3
Aged 55 to 59	577,747	100.0	0.5	3.6	12.9	0.1	80.8	76.8	3.2	6.1
Aged 60 to 64	462,886	100.0	0.4	3.3	13.6	0.1	80.8	76.9	2.9	5.6
Total 65+	1,500,025	100.0	0.3	1.9	10.6	0.0	86.4	83.8	1.6	3.3
Aged 65 to 69	397,443	100.0	0.4	2.6	13.0	0.1	82.6	79.0	2.3	4.9
Aged 70 to 74	374,804	100.0	0.3	2.1	11.4	0.0	85.3	82.5	1.7	3.7
Aged 75 to 79	316,948	100.0	0.3	1.7	9.7	0.0	87.7	85.5	1.3	2.7
Aged 80 to 84	218,799	100.0	0.2	1.4	8.3	0.0	89.6	88.0	1.0	1.8
Aged 85 or older	192,031	100.0	0.2	1.0	8.1	0.1	90.3	88.9	0.9	1.7
INDIANA										
State total	6,080,485	100.0	0.6	1.2	8.8	0.1	88.6	85.8	2.0	3.5
Total 55+	1,282,675	100.0	0.5	0.5	6.1	0.0	92.9	91.7	0.5	1.2
Aged 55 to 59	294,169	100.0	0.6	0.8	6.5	0.0	92.1	90.5	0.7	1.5
Aged 60 to 64	235,675	100.0	0.5	0.7	6.6	0.0	92.1	90.7	0.6	1.4
Total 65+	752,831	100.0	0.4	0.4	5.8	0.0	93.5	92.4	0.4	1.0
Aged 65 to 69	203,737	100.0	0.4	0.6	6.7	0.0	92.3	91.0	0.5	1.3
Aged 70 to 74	191,656	100.0	0.4	0.4	6.1	0.0	93.1	91.9	0.5	1.2
Aged 75 to 79	159,833	100.0	0.3	0.3	5.4	0.0	94.1	93.1	0.4	0.9
Aged 80 to 84	106,047	100.0	0.3	0.2	4.9	0.0	94.7	93.9	0.3	0.7
Aged 85 or older	91,558	100.0	0.3	0.2	5.0	0.0	94.6	93.8	0.3	0.6
IOWA										
State total	2,926,324	100.0	0.6	1.5	2.5	0.1	94.9	92.6	1.6	2.8
Total 55+	693,625	100.0	0.3	0.5	1.0	0.0	98.2	97.4	0.3	0.7
Aged 55 to 59	139,052	100.0	0.4	0.9	1.3	0.0	97.2	96.3	0.5	1.1
Aged 60 to 64	118,360	100.0	0.4	0.8	1.2	0.0	97.6	96.7	0.4	0.9
Total 65+	436,213	100.0	0.2	0.3	0.9	0.0	98.6	98.0	0.2	0.5
Aged 65 to 69	107,373	100.0	0.3	0.6	1.1	0.0	98.0	97.2	0.3	0.7
Aged 70 to 74	104,562	100.0	0.2	0.4	1.0	0.0	98.4	97.7	0.2	0.6
Aged 75 to 79	91,505	100.0	0.2	0.2	0.8	0.0	98.8	98.2	0.2	0.5
Aged 80 to 84	67,655	100.0	0.2	0.2	0.6	0.0	99.1	98.6	0.2	0.4
Aged 85 or older	65,118	100.0	0.2	0.2	0.6	0.0	99.2	98.7	0.2	0.3

	total		American			Native	white			
	number	percent	Indian	Asian	black	Hawaiian	total	non-Hispanic	other	Hispanic
KANSAS										
State total	2,688,418	100.0%	1.8%	2.1%	6.3%	0.1%	87.9%	83.1%	4.0%	7.0%
Total 55+	576,482	100.0	1.0	0.9	3.8	0.1	94.0	92.0	1.0	2.2
Aged 55 to 59	121,645	100.0	1.5	1.5	4.3	0.1	92.3	89.7	1.5	3.0
Aged 60 to 64	98,608	100.0	1.4	1.3	4.4	0.1	92.7	90.2	1.3	2.7
Total 65+	356,229	100.0	0.8	0.6	3.4	0.0	95.0	93.3	0.8	1.8
Aged 65 to 69	90,085	100.0	1.1	1.0	4.2	0.0	93.5	91.3	1.1	2.4
Aged 70 to 74	85,831	100.0	0.9	0.7	3.6	0.0	94.7	92.8	0.9	2.1
Aged 75 to 79	75,125	100.0	0.7	0.5	3.1	0.0	95.5	93.8	0.8	1.8
Aged 80 to 84	53,418	100.0	0.6	0.4	2.9	0.0	96.1	94.9	0.5	1.2
Aged 85 or older	51,770	100.0	0.5	0.3	2.8	0.0	96.3	95.4	0.5	1.0
KENTUCKY										
State total	4,041,769	100.0	0.6	0.9	7.7	0.1	91.0	89.3	0.8	1.5
Total 55+	877,388	100.0	0.6	0.4	5.2	0.0	94.2	93.3	0.2	0.5
Aged 55 to 59	204,483	100.0	0.6	0.6	5.1	0.0	94.0	93.0	0.2	0.6
Aged 60 to 64	168,112	100.0	0.6	0.6	5.2	0.0	94.1	93.1	0.2	0.6
Total 65+	504,793	100.0	0.5	0.3	5.2	0.0	94.4	93.5	0.2	0.4
Aged 65 to 69	144,671	100.0	0.6	0.5	5.3	0.0	94.1	93.1	0.2	0.5
Aged 70 to 74	129,272	100.0	0.6	0.3	5.1	0.0	94.4	93.5	0.2	0.5
Aged 75 to 79	104,760	100.0	0.5	0.2	5.0	0.0	94.7	93.8	0.1	0.4
Aged 80 to 84	67,829	100.0	0.6	0.2	4.9	0.0	94.9	94.0	0.1	0.4
Aged 85 or older	58,261	100.0	0.5	0.2	5.8	0.0	94.0	93.2	0.1	0.4
LOUISIANA										
State total	4,468,976	100.0	1.0	1.4	32.9	0.1	64.8	62.5	1.1	2.4
Total 55+	895,977	100.0	0.7	0.8	24.0	0.1	74.6	72.7	0.6	1.8
Aged 55 to 59	208,761	100.0	0.9	1.1	25.5	0.1	72.6	70.6	0.7	2.0
Aged 60 to 64	170,287	100.0	0.8	1.0	25.5	0.1	72.8	70.7	0.7	2.0
Total 65+	516,929	100.0	0.6	0.6	22.9	0.1	76.1	74.3	0.5	1.6
Aged 65 to 69	148,004	100.0	0.7	0.9	24.1	0.1	74.5	72.5	0.6	1.9
Aged 70 to 74	134,921	100.0	0.7	0.7	22.7	0.1	76.1	74.3	0.5	1.7
Aged 75 to 79	106,823	100.0	0.5	0.5	21.4	0.0	77.8	76.1	0.5	1.5
Aged 80 to 84	68,505	100.0	0.6	0.4	21.7	0.0	77.6	76.0	0.5	1.3
Aged 85 or older	58,676	100.0	0.5	0.4	24.5	0.1	74.9	73.3	0.5	1.3
MAINE										
State total	1,274,923	100.0	1.0	0.9	0.7	0.1	97.9	96.5	0.4	0.7
Total 55+	306,589	100.0	0.6	0.4	0.2	0.0	99.2	98.5	0.2	0.3
Aged 55 to 59	68,490	100.0	0.8	0.5	0.3	0.1	98.9	98.1	0.2	0.3
Aged 60 to 64	54,697	100.0	0.7	0.5	0.2	0.0	98.9	98.1	0.2	0.3
Total 65+	183,402	100.0	0.4	0.3	0.2	0.0	99.4	98.8	0.1	0.2
Aged 65 to 69	50,100	100.0	0.6	0.4	0.2	0.0	99.1	98.4	0.2	0.3
Aged 70 to 74	46,096	100.0	0.4	0.3	0.2	0.0	99.4	98.8	0.1	0.2
Aged 75 to 79	38,098	100.0	0.4	0.2	0.2	0.0	99.5	98.9	0.1	0.3
Aged 80 to 84	25,792	100.0	0.3	0.2	0.2	0.0	99.6	99.0	0.2	0.2
Aged 85 or older	23,316	100.0	0.4	0.1	0.1	0.0	99.7	99.1	0.2	0.2

	total		American			Native	white			
	number	percent	Indian	Asian	black	Hawaiian	total	non-Hispanic	other	Hispanic
MARYLAND										
State total	5,296,486	100.0%	0.7%	4.5%	28.8%	0.1%	65.4%	62.1%	2.5%	4.3%
Total 55+	1,069,683	100.0	0.5	3.2	20.7	0.1	75.6	73.9	0.8	1.7
Aged 55 to 59	268,647	100.0	0.7	4.1	23.5	0.1	71.7	69.7	1.1	2.2
Aged 60 to 64	201,729	100.0	0.6	4.3	23.7	0.1	71.4	69.5	1.0	2.1
Total 65+	599,307	100.0	0.4	2.5	18.4	0.1	78.7	77.3	0.7	1.4
Aged 65 to 69	168,242	100.0	0.5	3.5	22.1	0.1	73.9	72.2	0.8	1.8
Aged 70 to 74	153,043	100.0	0.4	2.7	18.9	0.1	78.1	76.5	0.7	1.6
Aged 75 to 79	128,491	100.0	0.4	2.1	16.4	0.1	81.3	80.0	0.6	1.2
Aged 80 to 84	82,629	100.0	0.3	1.7	15.3	0.1	82.8	81.6	0.5	1.1
Aged 85 or older	66,902	100.0	0.4	1.4	15.8	0.1	82.5	81.3	0.5	1.1
MASSACHUSETTS										
State total	6,349,097	100.0	0.6	4.2	6.3	0.1	86.2	81.9	5.1	6.8
Total 55+	1,406,569	100.0	0.4	2.0	3.6	0.1	93.3	91.5	1.8	2.2
Aged 55 to 59	310,002	100.0	0.5	2.6	4.5	0.1	91.3	88.8	2.4	3.3
Aged 60 to 64	236,405	100.0	0.4	2.6	4.5	0.1	91.2	88.9	2.4	3.1
Total 65+	860,162	100.0	0.3	1.6	3.0	0.1	94.6	93.1	1.4	1.6
Aged 65 to 69	216,498	100.0	0.4	2.3	3.8	0.1	92.6	90.7	1.9	2.4
Aged 70 to 74	211,332	100.0	0.3	1.8	3.2	0.1	94.2	92.6	1.5	1.7
Aged 75 to 79	184,941	100.0	0.3	1.4	2.6	0.1	95.3	93.9	1.2	1.3
Aged 80 to 84	130,699	100.0	0.3	0.1	2.3	0.1	96.1	94.8	1.1	1.1
Aged 85 or older	116,692	100.0	0.3	0.9	2.1	0.1	96.5	95.3	1.0	1.0
MICHIGAN										
State total	9,938,444	100.0	1.3	2.1	14.8	0.1	81.8	78.6	2.0	3.3
Total 55+	2,082,057	100.0	0.7	1.0	10.5	0.0	87.9	86.4	0.7	1.3
Aged 55 to 59	485,895	100.0	1.0	1.5	11.4	0.0	86.3	84.5	0.9	1.6
Aged 60 to 64	377,144	100.0	0.9	1.4	10.9	0.0	87.0	85.2	0.8	1.5
Total 65+	1,219,018	100.0	0.6	0.7	10.0	0.0	88.9	87.5	0.6	1.1
Aged 65 to 69	328,835	100.0	0.8	1.0	11.2	0.0	87.2	85.5	0.7	1.4
Aged 70 to 74	314,045	100.0	0.6	0.7	10.3	0.0	88.4	87.0	0.6	1.2
Aged 75 to 79	260,144	100.0	0.5	0.6	9.6	0.0	89.4	88.2	0.6	1.0
Aged 80 to 84	173,534	100.0	0.5	0.4	8.7	0.0	90.6	89.6	0.5	0.7
Aged 85 or older	142,460	100.0	0.4	0.4	8.7	0.0	90.7	89.8	0.4	0.7
MINNESOTA										
State total	4,919,479	100.0	1.6	3.3	4.1	0.1	90.8	88.2	1.8	2.9
Total 55+	999,135	100.0	0.8	1.2	1.3	0.1	96.8	9.6	0.4	0.7
Aged 55 to 59	226,857	100.0	1.1	1.7	1.7	0.1	95.5	94.5	0.6	1.0
Aged 60 to 64	178,012	100.0	1.0	1.6	1.6	0.1	95.9	94.9	0.5	0.9
Total 65+	594,266	100.0	0.6	0.9	1.0	0.0	97.6	96.9	0.3	0.5
Aged 65 to 69	153,169	100.0	0.8	1.4	1.4	0.0	96.5	95.7	0.4	0.7
Aged 70 to 74	142,656	100.0	0.6	1.0	1.1	0.0	97.3	96.7	0.3	0.5
Aged 75 to 79	122,677	100.0	0.5	0.9	0.9	0.0	97.9	97.3	0.3	0.5
Aged 80 to 84	90,163	100.0	0.4	0.6	0.7	0.0	98.4	97.9	0.2	0.4
Aged 85 or older	85,601	100.0	0.3	0.5	0.6	0.0	98.6	98.1	0.2	0.4

	total		American			Native	white			
	number	percent	Indian	Asian	black	Hawaiian	total	non-Hispanic	other	Hispanic
MISSISSIPPI										
State total	2,844,658	100.0%	0.7%	0.8%	36.6%	0.1%	61.9%	60.7%	0.7%	1.4%
Total 55+	589,346	100.0	0.5	0.5	25.3	0.1	74.0	73.2	0.2	0.6
Aged 55 to 59	132,202	100.0	0.6	0.6	25.7	0.1	73.3	72.4	0.3	0.8
Aged 60 to 64	113,621	100.0	0.6	0.5	25.5	0.1	73.6	72.7	0.2	0.7
Total 65+	343,523	100.0	0.5	0.4	25.1	0.1	74.4	73.7	0.2	0.6
Aged 65 to 69	98,179	100.0	0.5	0.5	24.6	0.0	74.8	74.0	0.2	0.7
Aged 70 to 74	87,531	100.0	0.5	0.4	24.2	0.1	75.3	74.6	0.2	0.5
Aged 75 to 79	68,558	100.0	0.4	0.3	24.1	0.0	75.5	74.8	0.2	0.5
Aged 80 to 84	46,364	100.0	0.4	0.3	25.2	0.1	74.5	73.9	0.1	0.5
Aged 85 or older	42,891	100.0	0.5	0.2	29.7	0.1	70.0	69.3	0.1	0.5
MISSOURI										
State total	5,595,211	100.0	1.1	1.4	11.7	0.1	86.1	83.8	1.2	2.1
Total 55+	1,262,777	100.0	0.8	0.7	7.7	0.0	91.2	90.0	0.3	0.8
Aged 55 to 59	279,073	100.0	1.1	1.0	8.5	0.1	89.9	88.4	0.4	1.0
Aged 60 to 64	228,325	100.0	1.0	0.9	8.5	0.0	90.1	88.7	0.4	1.0
Total 65+	755,379	100.0	0.6	0.5	7.2	0.0	92.1	91.0	0.3	0.7
Aged 65 to 69	205,372	100.0	0.8	0.7	8.2	0.1	90.8	89.5	0.3	0.8
Aged 70 to 74	187,854	100.0	0.7	0.6	7.5	0.0	91.6	90.4	0.3	0.8
Aged 75 to 79	157,207	100.0	0.6	0.4	6.7	0.0	92.7	91.6	0.3	0.6
Aged 80 to 84	106,375	100.0	0.5	0.3	6.2	0.1	93.3	92.4	0.3	0.5
Aged 85 or older	98,571	100.0	0.5	0.2	6.4	0.0	93.3	92.4	0.2	0.5
MONTANA										
State total	902,195	100.0	7.4	0.8	0.5	0.1	92.2	89.5	0.9	2.0
Total 55+	206,068	100.0	3.5	0.4	0.2	0.1	96.4	95.0	0.4	0.8
Aged 55 to 59	47,174	100.0	4.8	0.5	0.2	0.1	95.2	93.5	0.5	1.0
Aged 60 to 64	37,945	100.0	4.7	0.4	0.2	0.1	95.2	93.6	0.4	1.0
Total 65+	120,949	100.0	2.7	0.3	0.1	0.1	97.2	96.0	0.3	0.7
Aged 65 to 69	32,541	100.0	3.9	0.5	0.2	0.1	95.9	94.5	0.4	0.9
Aged 70 to 74	29,978	100.0	2.9	0.3	0.1	0.0	97.0	95.8	0.4	0.8
Aged 75 to 79	24,703	100.0	2.2	0.2	0.1	0.1	97.7	96.6	0.3	0.7
Aged 80 to 84	18,390	100.0	1.7	0.2	0.1	0.0	98.2	97.2	0.3	0.5
Aged 85 or older	15,337	100.0	1.8	0.1	0.1	0.1	98.2	97.3	0.3	0.4
NEBRASKA										
State total	1,711,263	100.0	1.3	1.6	4.4	0.1	90.8	87.3	3.3	5.5
Total 55+	373,735	100.0	0.6	0.6	2.3	0.0	96.2	95.0	0.7	1.5
Aged 55 to 59	77,584	100.0	0.8	0.1	2.9	0.1	94.6	93.1	1.2	2.2
Aged 60 to 64	63,956	100.0	0.8	0.9	2.9	0.0	95.0	93.5	0.9	1.9
Total 65+	232,195	100.0	0.4	0.4	1.9	0.0	97.0	96.0	0.5	1.1
Aged 65 to 69	59,391	100.0	0.6	0.6	2.5	0.0	95.9	94.6	0.7	1.6
Aged 70 to 74	56,308	100.0	0.4	0.5	2.2	0.0	96.7	95.6	0.6	1.3
Aged 75 to 79	47,991	100.0	0.4	0.4	1.6	0.0	97.4	96.5	0.5	1.1
Aged 80 to 84	34,552	100.0	0.3	0.3	1.4	0.0	97.9	97.3	0.3	0.7
Aged 85 or older	33,953	100.0	0.3	0.2	1.5	0.0	98.1	97.4	0.3	0.6

	total		American			Native	white			
NEVADA	number	percent	Indian	Asian	black	Hawaiian	total	non-Hispanic	other	Hispanic
State total	1,998,257	100.0%	2.1%	5.6%	7.5%	0.8%	78.4%	65.2%	9.7%	19.7%
Total 55+	409,128	100.0	1.4	4.3	5.0	0.4	88.0	82.1	2.8	6.9
Aged 55 to 59	105,057	100.0	1.8	4.9	5.4	0.5	85.8	78.9	3.8	8.7
Aged 60 to 64	85,142	100.0	1.6	5.0	5.8	0.5	86.0	79.4	3.2	7.9
Total 65+	218,929	100.0	1.2	3.8	4.5	0.3	89.8	84.7	2.1	5.6
Aged 65 to 69	71,387	100.0	1.4	5.0	5.3	0.4	87.2	81.2	2.6	6.8
Aged 70 to 74	60,388	100.0	1.1	4.0	4.5	0.3	89.5	84.3	2.1	5.8
Aged 75 to 79	44,851	100.0	1.1	2.8	3.8	0.2	91.7	87.3	1.7	4.6
Aged 80 to 84	25,314	100.0	1.0	2.5	3.6	0.2	92.4	88.4	1.7	4.1
Aged 85 or older	16,989	100.0	1.1	2.1	4.1	0.2	92.2	88.0	1.7	4.5
NEW HAMPSHIRE										
State total	1,235,786	100.0	0.6	1.6	1.0	0.1	97.0	95.1	0.9	1.7
Total 55+	257,629	100.0	0.4	0.7	0.4	0.0	98.7	97.9	0.3	0.5
Aged 55 to 59	62,664	100.0	0.6	0.9	0.5	0.0	98.2	97.1	0.4	0.7
Aged 60 to 64	46,995	100.0	0.4	0.8	0.5	0.0	98.4	97.4	0.4	0.8
Total 65+	147,970	100.0	0.3	0.5	0.3	0.0	99.1	98.3	0.2	0.4
Aged 65 to 69	41,143	100.0	0.4	0.8	0.4	0.0	98.6	97.7	0.3	0.5
Aged 70 to 74	37,184	100.0	0.4	0.5	0.3	0.0	99.0	98.3	0.2	0.4
Aged 75 to 79	30,593	100.0	0.3	0.4	0.2	0.0	99.3	98.6	0.2	0.3
Aged 80 to 84	20,819	100.0	0.3	0.4	0.1	0.0	99.5	98.8	0.2	0.3
Aged 85 or older	18,231	100.0	0.3	0.2	0.2	0.0	99.5	98.9	0.1	0.3
NEW JERSEY										
State total	8,414,350	100.0	0.6	6.2	14.4	0.1	74.4	66.0	6.9	13.3
Total 55+	1,867,120	100.0	0.4	3.5	10.2	0.1	84.4	79.3	2.7	6.6
Aged 55 to 59	423,338	100.0	0.5	5.2	12.1	0.1	79.9	73.6	3.9	8.8
Aged 60 to 64	330,646	100.0	0.4	4.9	12.8	0.1	79.7	73.2	3.7	8.9
Total 65+	1,113,136	100.0	0.3	2.5	8.8	0.1	87.5	83.3	2.0	5.1
Aged 65 to 69	293,196	100.0	0.4	3.7	11.3	0.1	83.1	77.3	2.8	7.4
Aged 70 to 74	281,473	100.0	0.3	2.6	9.2	0.1	86.8	82.4	2.1	5.5
Aged 75 to 79	240,131	100.0	0.3	2.0	7.7	0.1	89.3	85.9	1.6	4.1
Aged 80 to 84	162,337	100.0	0.3	1.6	6.7	0.0	90.9	87.9	1.3	3.4
Aged 85 or older	135,999	100.0	0.3	1.2	7.0	0.1	91.1	88.1	1.3	3.3
NEW MEXICO										
State total	1,819,046	100.0	10.5	1.5	2.3	0.2	69.9	44.7	19.4	42.1
Total 55+	370,977	100.0	6.2	0.9	1.4	0.1	83.7	61.7	10.0	30.1
Aged 55 to 59	87,140	100.0	7.3	1.1	1.5	0.1	80.6	58.7	11.9	31.6
Aged 60 to 64	71,612	100.0	7.2	1.0	1.5	0.1	81.5	58.0	11.2	32.7
Total 65+	212,225	100.0	5.3	0.7	1.4	0.1	85.7	64.1	8.8	28.6
Aged 65 to 69	63,227	100.0	6.1	0.9	1.7	0.1	83.5	60.1	9.9	31.5
Aged 70 to 74	54,518	100.0	5.2	0.8	1.4	0.1	85.5	62.9	9.2	29.9
Aged 75 to 79	43,729	100.0	4.6	0.6	1.3	0.1	87.4	66.6	8.0	27.1
Aged 80 to 84	27,445	100.0	4.7	0.4	1.2	0.1	87.9	69.4	7.5	24.5
Aged 85 or older	23,306	100.0	5.5	0.4	1.4	0.1	86.7	67.3	7.6	25.5

	total		American Indian	Asian	black	Native Hawaiian	white		other	Hispanic
	number	percent					total	non-Hispanic		
NEW YORK										
State total	18,976,457	100.0%	0.9%	6.2%	17.0%	0.2%	70.0%	62.0%	9.1%	15.1%
Total 55+	4,136,339	100.0	0.6	4.0	12.8	0.1	80.2	74.7	4.3	8.5
Aged 55 to 59	932,008	100.0	0.7	5.1	15.1	0.1	75.5	69.0	5.8	10.9
Aged 60 to 64	755,979	100.0	0.7	5.2	15.3	0.1	75.5	68.8	5.6	10.8
Total 65+	2,448,352	100.0	0.5	3.2	11.1	0.1	83.4	78.7	3.3	6.8
Aged 65 to 69	657,600	100.0	0.6	4.4	13.5	0.1	78.9	72.9	4.5	9.3
Aged 70 to 74	618,446	100.0	0.5	3.4	11.6	0.1	82.6	77.7	3.5	7.3
Aged 75 to 79	514,132	100.0	0.4	2.8	10.3	0.1	85.0	80.9	2.8	5.8
Aged 80 to 84	346,686	100.0	0.4	2.3	9.2	0.1	86.9	83.3	2.4	5.0
Aged 85 or older	311,488	100.0	0.4	1.9	8.8	0.1	87.9	84.4	2.2	4.5
NORTH CAROLINA										
State total	8,049,313	100.0	1.6	1.7	22.1	0.1	73.1	70.2	2.8	4.7
Total 55+	1,692,760	100.0	1.1	0.7	16.3	0.0	82.0	81.2	0.4	0.8
Aged 55 to 59	400,207	100.0	1.4	1.1	16.7	0.1	80.8	79.7	0.6	1.2
Aged 60 to 64	323,505	100.0	1.3	0.9	16.7	0.1	81.2	80.2	0.5	1.0
Total 65+	969,048	100.0	0.9	0.5	15.9	0.0	82.8	82.1	0.3	0.6
Aged 65 to 69	282,836	100.0	1.0	0.8	16.2	0.0	82.1	81.3	0.4	0.8
Aged 70 to 74	250,941	100.0	0.9	0.5	15.9	0.0	82.8	82.1	0.3	0.6
Aged 75 to 79	201,444	100.0	0.9	0.4	15.3	0.0	83.6	82.9	0.2	0.5
Aged 80 to 84	128,366	100.0	0.9	0.3	15.6	0.0	83.4	82.8	0.2	0.5
Aged 85 or older	105,461	100.0	0.8	0.3	17.1	0.0	82.1	81.5	0.2	0.5
NORTH DAKOTA										
State total	642,200	100.0	5.5	0.8	0.8	0.1	93.4	91.7	0.6	1.2
Total 55+	147,911	100.0	2.2	0.3	0.1	0.0	97.6	97.0	0.2	0.3
Aged 55 to 59	28,926	100.0	3.3	0.5	0.2	0.0	96.1	95.3	0.3	0.5
Aged 60 to 64	24,507	100.0	3.0	0.4	0.2	0.0	96.6	95.8	0.2	0.5
Total 65+	94,478	100.0	1.6	0.2	0.1	0.0	98.3	97.8	0.2	0.3
Aged 65 to 69	23,142	100.0	2.3	0.3	0.1	0.0	97.5	96.8	0.2	0.4
Aged 70 to 74	22,759	100.0	1.8	0.3	0.1	0.0	98.1	97.5	0.2	0.3
Aged 75 to 79	19,085	100.0	1.4	0.1	0.1	0.0	98.6	98.1	0.2	0.3
Aged 80 to 84	14,766	100.0	1.2	0.1	0.1	0.0	98.8	98.3	0.1	0.3
Aged 85 or older	14,726	100.0	0.8	0.1	0.1	0.0	99.2	98.7	0.2	0.2
OHIO										
State total	11,353,140	100.0	0.7	1.4	12.1	0.1	86.1	84.0	1.1	1.9
Total 55+	2,516,663	100.0	0.5	0.7	8.7	0.0	90.4	89.4	0.4	0.8
Aged 55 to 59	553,174	100.0	0.6	1.1	9.1	0.0	89.5	88.2	0.5	1.0
Aged 60 to 64	455,732	100.0	0.5	1.0	9.5	0.0	89.3	88.1	0.4	0.9
Total 65+	1,507,757	100.0	0.4	0.5	8.3	0.0	91.1	90.1	0.3	0.7
Aged 65 to 69	402,668	100.0	0.5	0.7	9.7	0.0	89.4	88.3	0.4	0.9
Aged 70 to 74	387,584	100.0	0.4	0.5	8.8	0.0	90.6	89.6	0.3	0.7
Aged 75 to 79	325,468	100.0	0.3	0.4	7.6	0.0	91.9	91.0	0.3	0.6
Aged 80 to 84	215,241	100.0	0.3	0.3	6.9	0.0	92.7	91.9	0.3	0.5
Aged 85 or older	176,796	100.0	0.3	0.3	7.1	0.0	92.5	91.8	0.3	0.4

OKLAHOMA	total number	percent	American Indian	Asian	black	Native Hawaiian	white total	white non-Hispanic	other	Hispanic
State total	3,450,654	100.0%	11.4%	1.7%	8.3%	0.1%	80.3%	74.1%	3.0%	5.2%
Total 55+	772,279	100.0	7.3	0.8	4.8	0.1	89.2	85.7	0.8	1.5
Aged 55 to 59	173,199	100.0	9.0	1.1	5.3	0.1	86.8	82.7	1.1	2.1
Aged 60 to 64	143,130	100.0	8.4	1.0	5.2	0.1	87.7	83.8	0.9	1.8
Total 65+	455,950	100.0	6.4	0.6	4.5	0.1	90.5	87.5	0.6	1.2
Aged 65 to 69	128,756	100.0	7.5	0.8	4.8	0.1	8.09	85.5	0.8	1.5
Aged 70 to 74	113,743	100.0	6.6	0.7	4.4	0.1	90.4	87.1	0.7	1.3
Aged 75 to 79	94,068	100.0	6.1	0.4	4.1	0.0	91.2	88.3	0.6	1.1
Aged 80 to 84	62,208	100.0	5.4	0.3	4.1	0.0	92.0	89.4	0.4	0.7
Aged 85 or older	57,175	100.0	4.9	0.3	4.7	0.1	91.8	89.4	0.4	0.7
OREGON										
State total	3,421,399	100.0	2.5	3.7	2.1	0.5	89.3	83.5	5.2	8.1
Total 55+	742,565	100.0	1.5	2.0	1.0	0.1	95.6	93.5	1.1	1.8
Aged 55 to 59	173,008	100.0	2.1	2.4	1.2	0.2	94.3	91.6	1.6	2.6
Aged 60 to 64	131,380	100.0	1.9	2.4	1.2	0.2	94.5	91.8	1.4	2.3
Total 65+	438,177	100.0	1.1	1.7	0.9	0.1	96.4	94.7	0.8	1.4
Aged 65 to 69	112,614	100.0	1.6	2.3	1.1	0.2	95.2	92.8	1.1	1.9
Aged 70 to 74	106,728	100.0	1.2	2.0	0.9	0.1	96.1	94.2	0.9	1.5
Aged 75 to 79	95,059	100.0	1.0	1.5	0.8	0.1	96.8	95.2	0.8	1.2
Aged 80 to 84	66,345	100.0	0.8	1.3	0.7	0.1	97.4	96.1	0.6	0.9
Aged 85 or older	57,431	100.0	0.7	0.9	0.7	0.1	97.8	96.6	0.6	0.8
PENNSYLVANIA										
State total	12,281,054	100.0	0.4	2.0	10.5	0.1	86.3	84.1	1.9	3.2
Total 55+	3,050,790	100.0	0.3	1.0	7.1	0.0	91.6	90.6	0.6	1.1
Aged 55 to 59	619,969	100.0	0.4	1.5	8.0	0.1	89.8	88.5	0.9	1.7
Aged 60 to 64	511,656	100.0	0.3	1.4	8.1	0.1	90.0	88.8	0.8	1.5
Total 65+	1,919,165	100.0	0.2	0.7	6.5	0.0	92.6	91.8	0.4	0.8
Aged 65 to 69	480,656	100.0	0.3	1.0	7.8	0.0	90.8	89.8	0.6	1.2
Aged 70 to 74	488,616	100.0	0.2	0.7	6.7	0.0	92.3	91.5	0.4	0.8
Aged 75 to 79	422,311	100.0	0.2	0.5	6.1	0.0	93.2	92.5	0.4	0.7
Aged 80 to 84	290,015	100.0	0.2	0.4	5.4	0.0	94.1	93.4	0.3	0.6
Aged 85 or older	237,567	100.0	0.2	0.4	5.5	0.0	94.0	93.3	0.3	0.5
RHODE ISLAND										
State total	1,048,319	100.0	1.0	2.7	5.5	0.2	86.9	81.9	6.6	8.7
Total 55+	241,391	100.0	0.6	1.1	2.6	0.1	94.5	92.4	2.4	2.6
Aged 55 to 59	49,982	100.0	0.7	1.6	3.1	0.1	92.8	90.2	3.3	4.0
Aged 60 to 64	39,007	100.0	0.8	1.7	3.5	0.1	92.3	89.6	3.3	3.7
Total 65+	152,402	100.0	0.5	0.8	2.2	0.1	95.6	93.9	2.0	1.9
Aged 65 to 69	36,023	100.0	0.7	1.3	3.2	0.1	93.3	91.1	2.9	3.0
Aged 70 to 74	37,661	100.0	0.5	0.9	2.5	0.1	95.1	93.4	2.1	2.1
Aged 75 to 79	34,076	100.0	0.4	0.7	2.0	0.1	96.3	94.8	1.6	1.5
Aged 80 to 84	23,745	100.0	0.4	0.5	1.5	0.1	97.0	95.6	1.6	1.4
Aged 85 or older	20,897	100.0	0.5	0.4	1.1	0.1	97.7	96.3	1.1	1.1

	total		American			Native	white			
	number	percent	Indian	Asian	black	Hawaiian	total	non-Hispanic	other	Hispanic
SOUTH CAROLINA										
State total	4,012,012	100.0%	0.7%	1.1%	29.9%	0.1%	68.0%	66.1%	1.3%	2.4%
Total 55+	858,244	100.0	0.5	0.6	21.9	0.1	77.2	76.4	0.3	0.7
Aged 55 to 59	206,762	100.0	0.6	0.8	22.6	0.1	76.1	75.1	0.4	0.9
Aged 60 to 64	166,149	100.0	0.5	0.8	22.2	0.1	76.7	75.8	0.3	0.8
Total 65+	485,333	100.0	0.4	0.4	21.6	0.1	77.9	77.2	0.2	0.6
Aged 65 to 69	145,599	100.0	0.5	0.6	21.5	0.1	77.7	76.9	0.2	0.7
Aged 70 to 74	124,449	100.0	0.4	0.5	21.1	0.1	78.3	77.6	0.2	0.6
Aged 75 to 79	101,445	100.0	0.4	0.3	20.4	0.1	79.1	78.5	0.2	0.5
Aged 80 to 84	63,571	100.0	0.3	0.3	22.1	0.0	77.6	77.0	0.2	0.5
Aged 85 or older	50,269	100.0	0.3	0.2	24.3	0.1	75.4	74.8	0.2	0.4
SOUTH DAKOTA										
State total	754,844	100.0	9.1	0.8	0.9	0.1	89.9	88.0	0.7	1.4
Total 55+	170,480	100.0	3.7	0.3	0.2	0.0	96.1	95.4	0.2	0.5
Aged 55 to 59	33,611	100.0	5.2	0.5	0.3	0.0	94.3	93.4	0.3	0.6
Aged 60 to 64	28,738	100.0	5.2	0.4	0.2	0.0	94.6	93.6	0.2	0.6
Total 65+	108,131	100.0	2.8	0.2	0.1	0.0	97.1	96.4	0.2	0.4
Aged 65 to 69	27,126	100.0	4.1	0.3	0.2	0.0	95.6	94.9	0.2	0.5
Aged 70 to 74	26,003	100.0	3.0	0.2	0.1	0.0	96.9	96.2	0.2	0.4
Aged 75 to 79	22,520	100.0	2.4	0.1	0.1	0.0	97.5	97.0	0.2	0.3
Aged 80 to 84	16,396	100.0	2.0	0.1	0.1	0.0	97.9	97.4	0.1	0.3
Aged 85 or older	16,086	100.0	1.7	0.1	0.1	0.0	98.3	97.8	0.1	0.3
TENNESSEE										
State total	5,689,283	100.0	0.7	1.2	16.8	0.1	81.2	79.2	1.3	2.2
Total 55+	1,236,562	100.0	0.6	0.6	10.8	0.0	88.4	87.5	0.2	0.6
Aged 55 to 59	293,942	100.0	0.7	0.8	11.0	0.0	87.7	86.7	0.3	0.8
Aged 60 to 64	239,309	100.0	0.6	0.8	11.0	0.0	88.0	87.0	0.3	0.7
Total 65+	703,311	100.0	0.5	0.4	10.7	0.0	88.8	87.9	0.2	0.5
Aged 65 to 69	204,571	100.0	0.6	0.6	11.0	0.0	88.3	87.3	0.2	0.5
Aged 70 to 74	178,281	100.0	0.5	0.5	10.6	0.0	88.8	88.0	0.2	0.5
Aged 75 to 79	144,848	100.0	0.5	0.3	10.0	0.0	89.6	88.8	0.2	0.4
Aged 80 to 84	94,146	100.0	0.5	0.3	10.2	0.0	89.4	88.6	0.2	0.4
Aged 85 or older	81,465	100.0	0.4	0.2	11.8	0.0	87.9	87.2	0.1	0.4
TEXAS										
State total	20,851,820	100.0	1.0	3.1	12.0	0.1	73.1	52.4	13.3	32.0
Total 55+	3,670,722	100.0	0.8	1.9	9.0	0.1	84.2	70.1	5.5	18.3
Aged 55 to 59	896,521	100.0	1.1	2.6	9.4	0.1	81.7	66.4	6.8	20.6
Aged 60 to 64	701,669	100.0	1.0	2.4	9.4	0.1	82.6	67.1	6.2	20.3
Total 65+	2,072,532	100.0	0.7	1.4	8.6	0.1	85.8	72.6	4.6	16.7
Aged 65 to 69	610,432	100.0	0.8	2.0	9.3	0.1	83.8	68.8	5.5	19.3
Aged 70 to 74	532,176	100.0	0.7	1.6	8.6	0.1	85.4	71.2	5.0	18.1
Aged 75 to 79	424,034	100.0	0.6	1.2	7.9	0.1	87.1	74.4	4.3	15.9
Aged 80 to 84	267,950	100.0	0.6	1.0	7.9	0.1	88.1	77.6	3.5	13.0
Aged 85 or older	237,940	100.0	0.5	0.8	9.0	0.1	87.4	77.0	3.4	12.8

	total		American			Native	white			
	number	percent	Indian	Asian	black	Hawaiian	total	non-Hispanic	other	Hispanic
UTAH										
State total	2,233,169	100.0%	1.8%	2.2%	1.1%	1.0%	91.1%	85.3%	5.1%	9.0%
Total 55+	332,730	100.0	0.9	1.5	0.5	0.4	95.8	93.0	1.8	3.7
Aged 55 to 59	80,053	100.0	1.2	1.7	0.5	0.5	94.6	91.3	2.4	4.7
Aged 60 to 64	62,455	100.0	1.1	1.6	0.5	0.5	95.1	91.8	2.1	4.5
Total 65+	190,222	100.0	0.7	1.4	0.4	0.3	96.5	94.1	1.4	3.0
Aged 65 to 69	53,734	100.0	0.9	1.5	0.4	0.4	95.8	92.8	1.7	3.9
Aged 70 to 74	47,814	100.0	0.9	1.4	0.4	0.3	96.2	93.7	1.5	3.3
Aged 75 to 79	39,745	100.0	0.6	1.4	0.5	0.2	96.7	94.4	1.2	2.8
Aged 80 to 84	27,178	100.0	0.5	1.2	0.3	0.2	97.2	95.6	1.1	2.0
Aged 85 or older	21,751	100.0	0.7	0.8	0.4	0.2	97.6	95.9	1.0	1.9
VERMONT										
State total	608,827	100.0	1.1	1.1	0.7	0.1	97.9	96.2	0.4	0.9
Total 55+	134,430	100.0	0.7	0.4	0.2	0.0	99.2	98.1	0.2	0.5
Aged 55 to 59	32,603	100.0	1.0	0.5	0.4	0.0	98.8	97.6	0.2	0.5
Aged 60 to 64	24,317	100.0	0.9	0.6	0.2	0.0	98.9	97.8	0.2	0.5
Total 65+	77,510	100.0	0.6	0.3	0.2	0.0	99.4	98.4	0.1	0.4
Aged 65 to 69	21,126	100.0	0.8	0.4	0.3	0.0	99.1	98.1	0.2	0.4
Aged 70 to 74	19,557	100.0	0.6	0.3	0.2	0.0	99.4	98.4	0.1	0.5
Aged 75 to 79	15,930	100.0	0.6	0.2	0.2	0.0	99.5	98.6	0.1	0.4
Aged 80 to 84	10,901	100.0	0.4	0.2	0.1	0.0	99.6	98.7	0.2	0.4
Aged 85 or older	9,996	100.0	0.4	0.2	0.2	0.0	99.7	98.8	0.2	0.5
VIRGINIA										
State total	7,078,515	100.0	0.7	4.3	20.4	0.1	73.9	70.2	2.7	4.7
Total 55+	1,423,944	100.0	0.5	2.6	15.6	0.1	81.4	79.8	0.6	1.5
Aged 55 to 59	358,442	100.0	0.7	3.5	15.2	0.1	80.7	78.7	0.9	2.1
Aged 60 to 64	273,169	100.0	0.6	3.3	16.2	0.1	80.0	78.2	0.8	1.8
Total 65+	792,333	100.0	0.5	2.0	15.6	0.1	82.1	80.8	0.5	1.2
Aged 65 to 69	229,553	100.0	0.5	2.9	16.5	0.1	80.3	78.7	0.6	1.5
Aged 70 to 74	202,903	100.0	0.4	2.1	15.8	0.1	81.8	80.4	0.5	1.3
Aged 75 to 79	166,178	100.0	0.4	1.6	15.1	0.1	83.2	82.0	0.4	1.0
Aged 80 to 84	106,433	100.0	0.4	1.3	14.8	0.1	83.7	82.6	0.4	0.9
Aged 85 or older	87,266	100.0	0.4	1.0	15.2	0.1	83.6	82.5	0.4	0.9
WASHINGTON										
State total	5,894,121	100.0	2.7	6.7	4.0	0.7	84.9	78.9	4.9	7.5
Total 55+	1,158,728	100.0	1.6	4.5	1.9	0.3	91.7	89.5	1.4	2.1
Aged 55 to 59	285,505	100.0	2.1	5.0	2.3	0.4	90.1	87.3	1.8	2.9
Aged 60 to 64	211,075	100.0	2.1	5.5	2.2	0.3	89.9	87.2	1.7	2.7
Total 65+	662,148	100.0	1.2	4.0	1.7	0.2	93.0	91.2	1.0	1.6
Aged 65 to 69	176,225	100.0	1.7	5.2	2.1	0.3	90.8	88.5	1.4	2.2
Aged 70 to 74	160,941	100.0	1.3	4.7	1.8	0.2	92.1	90.1	1.1	1.8
Aged 75 to 79	142,708	100.0	1.0	3.6	1.6	0.1	93.8	92.2	0.8	1.3
Aged 80 to 84	98,189	100.0	0.8	2.9	1.4	0.1	95.0	93.6	0.8	1.0
Aged 85 or older	84,085	100.0	0.8	2.3	1.2	0.1	95.8	94.4	0.7	1.1

	total		American			Native	white			
	number	percent	Indian	Asian	black	Hawaiian	total	non-Hispanic	other	Hispanic
WEST VIRGINIA										
State total	1,808,344	100.0%	0.6%	0.7%	3.5%	0.1%	95.9%	94.6%	0.3%	0.7%
Total 55+	461,711	100.0	0.5	0.4	2.5	0.0	97.1	96.2	0.1	0.4
Aged 55 to 59	98,916	100.0	0.7	0.6	2.2	0.0	97.0	96.0	0.1	0.5
Aged 60 to 64	85,900	100.0	0.6	0.5	2.2	0.0	97.1	96.2	0.1	0.5
Total 65+	276,895	100.0	0.5	0.2	2.6	0.0	97.1	96.2	0.1	0.4
Aged 65 to 69	75,863	100.0	0.5	0.3	2.2	0.0	97.3	96.5	0.1	0.4
Aged 70 to 74	72,600	100.0	0.4	0.3	2.7	0.0	97.0	96.2	0.1	0.4
Aged 75 to 79	58,802	100.0	0.5	0.2	2.6	0.0	97.2	96.2	0.1	0.4
Aged 80 to 84	37,851	100.0	0.5	0.2	2.7	0.0	97.0	96.2	0.1	0.3
Aged 85 or older	31,779	100.0	0.4	0.2	3.4	0.1	96.4	95.6	0.1	0.3
WISCONSIN										
State total	5,363,675	100.0	1.3	1.9	6.1	0.1	90.0	87.3	2.0	3.6
Total 55+	1,160,294	100.0	0.6	0.7	2.8	0.0	95.8	94.9	0.5	1.0
Aged 55 to 59	252,742	100.0	0.9	0.9	3.6	0.1	94.4	93.1	0.7	1.4
Aged 60 to 64	204,999	100.0	0.8	0.8	3.5	0.0	94.7	93.5	0.5	1.3
Total 65+	702,553	100.0	0.5	0.5	2.3	0.0	96.7	95.9	0.4	0.8
Aged 65 to 69	182,119	100.0	0.7	0.7	3.2	0.0	95.4	94.3	0.5	1.1
Aged 70 to 74	173,188	100.0	0.5	0.6	2.7	0.0	96.2	95.4	0.4	0.9
Aged 75 to 79	146,675	100.0	0.4	0.5	2.0	0.0	97.1	96.5	0.3	0.7
Aged 80 to 84	104,946	100.0	0.4	0.4	1.5	0.0	97.8	97.2	0.3	0.5
Aged 85 or older	95,625	100.0	0.3	0.3	1.4	0.0	98.0	97.4	0.3	0.4
WYOMING										
State total	493,782	100.0	3.0	0.8	1.0	0.1	93.7	88.9	3.2	6.4
Total 55+	102,283	100.0	1.7	0.5	0.4	0.1	96.9	93.8	1.4	3.4
Aged 55 to 59	24,935	100.0	2.3	0.6	0.4	0.1	96.2	93.0	1.6	3.6
Aged 60 to 64	19,655	100.0	2.2	0.6	0.5	0.0	96.2	92.9	1.5	3.9
Total 65+	57,693	100.0	1.3	0.4	0.4	0.0	97.4	94.5	1.3	3.1
Aged 65 to 69	16,598	100.0	1.7	0.5	0.5	0.1	96.8	93.6	1.4	3.7
Aged 70 to 74	14,745	100.0	1.4	0.5	0.5	0.0	97.2	94.3	1.2	3.3
Aged 75 to 79	11,808	100.0	1.2	0.4	0.3	0.0	97.6	94.7	1.2	3.0
Aged 80 to 84	7,807	100.0	1.1	0.2	0.5	0.0	98.2	95.4	1.1	2.5
Aged 85 or older	6,735	100.0	0.9	0.1	0.4	0.0	98.0	95.7	1.3	2.5

Note: Percentages will not add to 100 because each race includes those who identified themselves as being of the race alone and those who identified themselves as being of the race in combination with one or more other races, and because Hispanics may be of any race. Non-Hispanic whites include only those who identified themselves as "white alone" and non-Hispanic. American Indians include Alaska natives. Native Hawaiians include other Pacific Islanders.
Source: Bureau of the Census, Census 2000 Summary File 2, Internet site http://factfinder.census.gov/servlet/BasicFactsServlet; calculations by New Strategist

8

Spending

■ Householders aged 55 to 64 spent 10 percent more in 2002 than in 1997, after adjusting for inflation—double the 5 percent rise in spending by the average household during those years.

■ Households headed by retirees spent $27,535 in 2002, 3 percent more than they did in 1997, after adjusting for inflation. Retirees spent $1,136 more than their income—making up the difference with savings.

■ The spending of householders aged 55 to 64 was 9 percent above average in 2002. Behind their increasingly above-average spending is a change in lifestyle. A growing proportion of householders aged 55 to 64 are remaining in the labor force as early retirement prospects diminish.

■ In 2002, householders aged 65 or older spent $28,105, much less than the $40,677 spent by the average household. The spending of elderly householders is below average because their households are small and most are retired.

■ Householders aged 65 to 74 spent 79 percent as much as the average household in 2002. They spend more than the average household on full-service restaurant breakfasts and restaurant meals while on trips.

Older Householders Open Their Wallets

Householders aged 55 to 64 sharply increased their spending between 1997 and 2002.

Householders aged 55 to 64 spent 10 percent more in 2002 than in 1997, after adjusting for inflation—double the 5 percent rise in spending by the average household during those years. Householders aged 65 or older boosted their spending by 3 percent between 1997 and 2002.

Householders aged 55 to 64 are spending more because fewer are opting for early
retirement. As they stay in the labor force, their incomes are rising, allowing them to spend
more. The incomes of householders aged 55 or older rose 14 percent between 1997 and
2002, after adjusting for inflation. While the average household spent 6 percent more on
food away from home, householders aged 55 to 64 spent 12 percent more. The average
household boosted its spending on alcoholic beverages by 9 percent, while those aged 55 to
64 spent fully 33 percent more on this item. The average household spent 7 percent less on
furniture, while householders aged 55 to 64 spent 11 percent more. This is one of only two
age groups that spent more on women's clothes in 2002 than in 1997 (the other was under-
25-year-olds). And its spending on entertainment rose 8 percent.

The spending of householders aged 65 or older is more restrained, in part because the
small Depression-era generation is in the younger half of the age group. Consequently, a disproportionate share of people aged 65 or older are very old, with reduced spending. Nevertheless,
householders aged 65 or older increased spending on a number of items between 1997 and 2002,
including restaurant meals and alcoholic beverages.

■ The incomes and spending of older Americans will continue to rise as the labor force participation rate of older workers climbs steadily upward.

The spending of householders aged 55 to 64 grew 10 percent

(percent change in spending by age of householder, 1997 to 2002; in 2002 dollars)

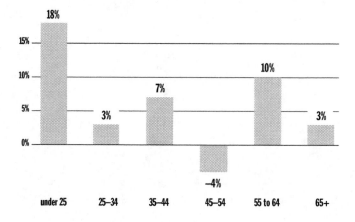

Table 8.1 Average Spending of Householders Aged 55 or Older, 1997 and 2002

(average annual spending of total consumer units and consumer units headed by people aged 55 or older, 1997 and 2002; percent change, 1997–2002; in 2002 dollars)

	total consumer units			aged 55 to 64			aged 65 or older		
	2002	1997	percent change 1997–02	2002	1997	percent change 1997–02	2002	1997	percent change 1997–02
Number of consumer units (in 000s)	112,108	105,576	6.2%	15,314	12,316	24.3%	21,983	21,936	0.2%
Average before-tax income	$49,430	$44,610	10.8	$53,162	$46,630	14.0	$29,711	$26,777	11.0
Average annual spending	40,677	38,904	4.6	44,330	40,172	10.4	28,105	27,277	3.0
FOOD	**$5,375**	**$5,364**	**0.2%**	**$5,559**	**$5,682**	**–2.2%**	**$3,910**	**$3,895**	**0.4%**
Food at home	3,099	3,218	–3.7	3,114	3,507	–11.2	2,548	2,562	–0.5
Cereals, bakery products	450	506	–11.1	423	525	–19.5	386	402	–4.0
Cereals and cereal products	154	180	–14.4	133	179	–25.6	120	132	–9.0
Bakery products	296	326	–9.3	290	346	–16.3	266	270	–1.6
Meats, poultry, fish, and eggs	798	830	–3.9	807	927	–13.0	641	648	–1.1
Beef	231	250	–7.7	216	258	–16.3	174	181	–3.9
Pork	167	175	–4.8	169	209	–19.1	144	149	–3.1
Other meats	101	107	–5.8	103	123	–16.2	84	86	–2.4
Poultry	144	162	–11.1	134	168	–20.1	110	124	–11.3
Fish and seafood	121	99	21.7	154	127	20.9	98	75	30.9
Eggs	34	37	–7.8	32	41	–22.6	30	34	–10.5
Dairy products	328	351	–6.5	325	363	–10.5	274	282	–2.7
Fresh milk and cream	127	143	–11.2	121	136	–11.2	107	118	–9.7
Other dairy products	201	208	–3.3	204	227	–10.1	167	163	2.4
Fruits and vegetables	552	532	3.8	591	613	–3.7	510	484	5.4
Fresh fruits	178	168	6.2	207	189	9.6	169	164	2.9
Fresh vegetables	175	160	9.5	191	207	–7.6	163	143	14.0
Processed fruits	116	114	1.8	113	121	–6.4	103	103	0.2
Processed vegetables	83	89	–7.1	81	97	–16.7	75	73	3.3
Other food at home	970	1,000	–3.0	967	1,078	–10.3	738	746	–1.1
Sugar and other sweets	117	127	–8.1	125	146	–14.6	108	107	0.7
Fats and oils	85	91	–6.1	90	111	–18.6	78	85	–8.1
Miscellaneous foods	472	450	4.8	434	450	–3.6	340	311	9.5
Nonalcoholic beverages	254	274	–7.2	265	298	–11.2	178	199	–10.5
Food prepared by household on trips	41	58	–29.4	54	73	–25.6	33	46	–28.0
Food away from home	**2,276**	**2,146**	**6.0**	**2,445**	**2,174**	**12.4**	**1,362**	**1,333**	**2.2**
ALCOHOLIC BEVERAGES	**376**	**345**	**8.9**	**420**	**316**	**32.8**	**237**	**220**	**7.7**
HOUSING	**13,283**	**12,594**	**5.5**	**13,831**	**12,391**	**11.6**	**9,176**	**9,030**	**1.6**
Shelter	**7,829**	**7,088**	**10.4**	**7,667**	**6,462**	**18.7**	**4,834**	**4,473**	**8.1**
Owned dwellings	5,165	4,397	17.5	5,595	4,535	23.4	3,162	2,918	8.3
Mortgage interest, charges	2,962	2,486	19.1	2,712	2,153	26.0	897	611	46.8

	total consumer units			aged 55 to 64			aged 65 or older		
	2002	**1997**	**percent change 1997–02**	**2002**	**1997**	**percent change 1997–02**	**2002**	**1997**	**percent change 1997–02**
Property taxes	$1,242	$1,085	14.5%	$1,540	$1,335	15.3%	$1,199	$1,184	1.2%
Maintenance, repairs, insurance, other expenses	960	825	16.4	1,343	1,046	28.4	1,066	1,124	–5.2
Rented dwellings	2,160	2,216	–2.5	1,303	1,279	1.9	1,259	1,174	7.2
Other lodging	505	476	6.1	770	647	19.0	413	380	8.7
Utilities, fuels, and public services	**2,684**	**2,695**	**–0.4**	**2,953**	**2,965**	**–0.4**	**2,371**	**2,410**	**–1.6**
Natural gas	330	336	–1.9	355	382	–7.1	338	378	–10.5
Electricity	981	1,016	–3.4	1,112	1,132	–1.8	894	937	–4.6
Fuel oil and other fuels	88	121	–27.1	127	141	–9.8	119	146	–18.7
Telephone services	957	904	5.9	981	941	4.3	689	616	11.9
Water, other public services	328	320	2.6	378	370	2.2	331	332	–0.3
Household services	**706**	**612**	**15.3**	**561**	**449**	**24.9**	**602**	**505**	**19.2**
Personal services	331	294	12.6	79	66	19.8	218	121	80.7
Other household services	375	318	17.8	481	383	25.5	384	383	0.2
Housekeeping supplies	**545**	**508**	**7.2**	**838**	**584**	**43.4**	**466**	**460**	**1.2**
Laundry and cleaning supplies	131	130	1.1	139	145	–4.3	110	101	9.4
Other household products	283	235	20.6	538	274	96.5	213	212	0.3
Postage and stationery	131	144	–9.1	161	165	–2.6	143	148	–3.0
Household furnishings and equipment	**1,518**	**1,689**	**–10.1**	**1,811**	**1,931**	**–6.2**	**903**	**1,183**	**–23.7**
Household textiles	136	88	54.1	183	112	63.8	106	60	75.7
Furniture	401	432	–7.3	484	436	11.1	186	212	–12.4
Floor coverings	40	87	–54.1	53	113	–53.0	30	139	–78.3
Major appliances	188	189	–0.4	220	275	–20.0	139	158	–11.8
Small appliances, misc. housewares	100	103	–2.7	134	137	–2.5	68	73	–6.4
Misc. household equipment	652	790	–17.5	738	858	–14.0	374	541	–30.8
APPAREL, SERVICES	**1,749**	**1,932**	**–9.5**	**1,791**	**1,850**	**–3.2**	**972**	**1,168**	**–16.8**
Men and boys	**409**	**455**	**–10.1**	**337**	**399**	**–15.5**	**208**	**245**	**–15.0**
Men, aged 16 or older	319	361	–11.6	297	355	–16.4	182	220	–17.3
Boys, aged 2 to 15	90	94	–4.1	40	44	–8.2	26	25	5.8
Women and girls	**704**	**760**	**–7.3**	**840**	**764**	**9.9**	**450**	**536**	**–16.1**
Women, aged 16 or older	587	641	–8.5	788	707	11.4	424	512	–17.1
Girls, aged 2 to 15	117	118	–1.2	52	57	–8.7	26	26	1.2
Children under age 2	**83**	**86**	**–3.5**	**49**	**38**	**29.0**	**21**	**25**	**–14.6**
Footwear	**313**	**352**	**–11.1**	**290**	**377**	**–23.0**	**160**	**211**	**–24.2**
Other apparel products and services	**240**	**279**	**–14.1**	**276**	**272**	**1.7**	**133**	**151**	**–11.8**
TRANSPORTATION	**7,759**	**7,215**	**7.5**	**8,449**	**7,495**	**12.7**	**4,481**	**4,259**	**5.2**
Vehicle purchases	**3,665**	**3,057**	**19.9**	**3,882**	**2,951**	**31.6**	**1,818**	**1,656**	**9.8**
Cars and trucks, new	1,753	1,373	27.7	2,080	1,535	35.5	1,038	868	19.6
Cars and trucks, used	1,842	1,636	12.6	1,763	1,416	24.5	761	767	–0.7
Gasoline and motor oil	**1,235**	**1,227**	**0.7**	**1,292**	**1,327**	**–2.7**	**777**	**724**	**7.3**

	total consumer units			aged 55 to 64			aged 65 or older		
	2002	1997	percent change 1997–02	2002	1997	percent change 1997–02	2002	1997	percent change 1997–02
Other vehicle expenses	**$2,471**	**$2,492**	**–0.8%**	**$2,735**	**$2,647**	**3.3%**	**$1,586**	**$1,537**	**3.2%**
Vehicle finance charges	397	327	21.3	370	291	27.4	153	106	44.1
Maintenance and repairs	697	762	–8.5	832	849	–2.0	482	549	–12.1
Vehicle insurance	894	844	6.0	991	951	4.2	666	613	8.6
Vehicle rental, leases, licenses, other charges	483	560	–13.7	542	558	–2.8	284	269	5.5
Public transportation	**389**	**439**	**–11.4**	**540**	**569**	**–5.1**	**300**	**341**	**–12.0**
HEALTH CARE	**2,350**	**2,057**	**14.2**	**3,007**	**2,444**	**23.1**	**3,586**	**3,190**	**12.4**
Health insurance	1,168	984	18.7	1,356	1,078	25.8	1,886	1,702	10.8
Medical services	590	593	–0.6	863	742	16.3	582	630	–7.6
Drugs	487	358	36.2	659	455	44.9	955	712	34.2
Medical supplies	105	121	–13.0	129	169	–23.5	163	145	12.2
ENTERTAINMENT	**2,079**	**2,026**	**2.6**	**2,297**	**2,123**	**8.2**	**1,139**	**1,232**	**–7.6**
Fees and admissions	542	526	3.0	584	504	15.9	301	331	–9.0
Television, radio, sound equipment	692	645	7.3	717	627	14.4	461	447	3.1
Pets, toys, and playground equipment	369	365	1.0	420	420	–0.0	200	210	–4.8
Other entertainment supplies, services	476	491	–3.0	577	572	0.9	177	245	–27.7
PERSONAL CARE PRODUCTS, SERVICES	**526**	**590**	**–10.8**	**557**	**605**	**–7.9**	**451**	**493**	**–8.5**
READING	**139**	**183**	**–24.1**	**181**	**221**	**–18.2**	**147**	**194**	**–24.4**
EDUCATION	**752**	**638**	**17.9**	**589**	**314**	**87.6**	**202**	**171**	**18.2**
TOBACCO PRODUCTS, SMOKING SUPPLIES	**320**	**295**	**8.5**	**361**	**326**	**10.6**	**152**	**174**	**–12.8**
MISCELLANEOUS	**792**	**946**	**–16.3**	**930**	**1,186**	**–21.6**	**686**	**692**	**–0.8**
CASH CONTRIBUTIONS	**1,277**	**1,118**	**14.2**	**1,520**	**1,350**	**12.6**	**1,679**	**1,482**	**13.3**
PERSONAL INSURANCE AND PENSIONS	**3,899**	**3,601**	**8.3**	**4,838**	**3,873**	**24.9**	**1,286**	**1,077**	**19.4**
Life, other personal insurance	406	424	–4.1	595	584	1.8	407	373	9.1
Pensions and Social Security	3,493	3,178	9.9	4,243	3,288	29.0	880	704	25.0
PERSONAL TAXES	**2,496**	**3,621**	**–31.1**	**2,856**	**3,911**	**–27.0**	**1,037**	**1,480**	**–30.0**
Federal income taxes	1,843	2,758	–33.2	2,136	2,975	–28.2	725	1,092	–33.6
State and local income taxes	506	721	–29.8	493	748	–34.1	144	193	–25.5
Other taxes	147	144	2.0	227	189	20.2	169	196	–13.6
GIFTS FOR NON-HOUSEHOLD MEMBERS	**1,036**	**1,183**	**–12.4**	**1,531**	**1,421**	**7.7**	**832**	**993**	**–16.2**
Food	**82**	**76**	**7.9**	**152**	**86**	**76.7**	**49**	**47**	**4.4**
Alcoholic beverages	**13**	**–**	**–**	**13**	**–**	**–**	**10**	**–**	**–**
Housing	**259**	**305**	**–15.1**	**334**	**367**	**–8.9**	**206**	**216**	**–4.5**
Housekeeping supplies	42	41	1.6	55	49	11.9	43	37	16.6
Household textiles	14	9	56.6	29	17	73.0	12	10	19.3

	total consumer units			aged 55 to 64			aged 65 or older		
	2002	1997	percent change 1997–02	2002	1997	percent change 1997–02	2002	1997	percent change 1997–02
Appliances and misc. housewares	$24	$30	−20.4%	$54	$62	−12.1%	$22	$21	3.6%
Major appliances	8	7	19.3	27	15	85.9	5	6	−10.5
Small appliances and misc. housewares	16	24	−31.8	27	46	−41.1	16	16	2.3
Misc. household equipment	65	74	−11.9	85	106	−19.9	53	50	5.4
Other housing	114	151	−24.4	111	133	−16.5	76	96	−20.9
Apparel and services	**237**	**282**	**−15.8**	**341**	**371**	**−8.1**	**193**	**226**	**−14.5**
Males, aged 2 or older	64	68	−6.1	74	97	−23.9	62	68	−9.0
Females, aged 2 or older	82	91	−9.4	158	113	40.0	77	85	−9.3
Children under age 2	40	37	8.5	41	36	14.7	20	22	−10.5
Other apparel products and services	52	86	−39.6	68	125	−45.7	33	50	−34.4
Jewelry and watches	24	55	−56.2	33	63	−47.3	11	32	−66.1
All other apparel products and services	28	32	−13.6	35	62	−43.1	23	18	28.7
Transportation	**44**	**64**	**−30.9**	**70**	**63**	**11.9**	**17**	**113**	**−84.9**
Health care	**33**	**34**	**−1.6**	**55**	**67**	**−18.0**	**39**	**44**	**−10.5**
Entertainment	**78**	**111**	**−29.5**	**107**	**154**	**−30.6**	**56**	**95**	**−41.0**
Toys, games, hobbies, and tricycles	30	46	−34.5	50	73	−31.2	27	40	−32.9
Other entertainment	48	65	−25.9	57	83	−31.1	29	55	−47.0
Personal care products and services	**21**	**–**	**–**	**17**	**–**	**–**	**21**	**–**	**–**
Reading	**1**	**–**	**–**	**2**	**–**	**–**	**3**	**–**	**–**
Education	**184**	**173**	**6.2**	**293**	**110**	**167.6**	**146**	**126**	**15.6**
All other gifts	**84**	**140**	**−39.9**	**145**	**205**	**−29.1**	**93**	**129**	**−27.6**

Note: The Bureau of Labor Statistics uses consumer units rather than households as the sampling unit in the Consumer Expenditure Survey. For the definition of consumer unit, see the glossary. Spending on gifts is included in the preceding product and service categories. (–) means sample is too small to make a reliable estimate or data are not available.
Source: Bureau of Labor Statistics, 1997 and 2002 Consumer Expenditure Surveys, Internet site http://www.bls.gov/cex/ ; calculations by New Strategist

Retirees Are Spending More

They spend more than their income, depending on their assets to make up the difference.

Households headed by retirees spent $27,535 in 2002, 3 percent more than they did in 1997, after adjusting for inflation. Retirees spent $1,136 more than their income—making up the difference with savings.

Retirees spent more in 2002 than in 1997 on many discretionary items, including food away from home, other lodging (such as hotels, motels, and vacation homes), new cars and trucks, public transportation (including airline and ship fares), fees and admissions to entertainment events, and cash contributions. Not surprisingly, they spent 14 percent more on health care—including a 37 percent increase in spending on prescription drugs.

Retirees spent less in 2002 than in 1997 on a variety of items such as food at home, alcoholic beverages, and apparel. They spent less on personal care products and services but much more on household personal services as a larger share of the aging retiree population required housekeeping, gardening, and adult day care services.

■ As Baby Boomers begin to retire, retiree spending patterns are likely to change, reflecting Boomer preferences.

Retirees spent more on many items in 2002

(percent change in spending by retirees on selected items, 1997 to 2002; in 2002 dollars)

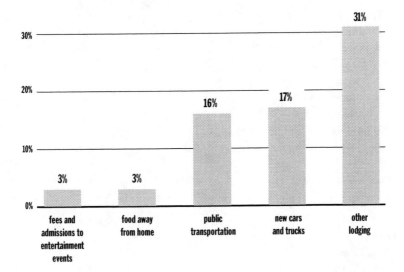

Table 8.2 Average Spending of Retirees, 1997 and 2002

(average annual spending of consumer units headed by retirees, 1997 and 2002; percent change, 1997–2002; in 2002 dollars)

	2002	1997	percent change 1997–02
Number of consumer units (in 000s)	19,204	19,145	0.3%
Average before-tax income	$26,399	$24,265	8.8
Average annual spending	27,535	26,837	2.6
FOOD	**$3,798**	**$3,954**	**–4.0%**
Food at home	**2,519**	**2,708**	**–7.0**
Cereals and bakery products	384	421	–8.8
Cereals and cereal products	117	143	–18.2
Bakery products	267	278	–4.0
Meats, poultry, fish, and eggs	616	708	–13.0
Beef	167	202	–17.4
Pork	144	155	–7.3
Other meats	82	94	–12.6
Poultry	102	135	–24.6
Fish and seafood	90	86	4.6
Eggs	30	36	–16.1
Dairy products	277	283	–2.0
Fresh milk and cream	108	118	–8.8
Other dairy products	168	164	2.3
Fruits and vegetables	501	496	1.0
Fresh fruits	165	167	–0.9
Fresh vegetables	160	149	7.7
Processed fruits	102	105	–2.9
Processed vegetables	74	76	–2.6
Other food at home	740	801	–7.6
Sugar and other sweets	104	113	–7.8
Fats and oils	79	89	–11.6
Miscellaneous foods	341	333	2.4
Nonalcoholic beverages	179	219	–18.3
Food prepared by household on trips	37	47	–21.2
Food away from home	**1,279**	**1,246**	**2.7**
ALCOHOLIC BEVERAGES	**208**	**249**	**–16.5**
HOUSING	**9,307**	**8,949**	**4.0**
Shelter	**4,871**	**4,311**	**13.0**
Owned dwellings	3,217	2,808	14.6
Mortgage interest and charges	891	627	42.1
Property taxes	1,247	1,135	9.8
Maintenance, repairs, insurance, other expenses	1,079	1,046	3.2

	2002	1997	percent change 1997–02
Rented dwellings	$1,219	$1,170	4.2%
Other lodging	435	332	31.1
Utilities, fuels, public services	**2,382**	**2,417**	**–1.4**
Natural gas	340	380	–10.5
Electricity	906	937	–3.4
Fuel oil and other fuels	123	134	–8.3
Telephone services	678	626	8.4
Water and other public services	335	339	–1.1
Household services	**616**	**464**	**32.8**
Personal services	244	114	114.1
Other household services	372	350	6.4
Housekeeping supplies	**477**	**464**	**2.9**
Laundry and cleaning supplies	108	107	0.7
Other household products	219	200	9.5
Postage and stationery	150	156	–4.1
Household furnishings and equipment	**962**	**1,294**	**–25.6**
Household textiles	99	63	58.2
Furniture	224	259	–13.6
Floor coverings	31	129	–75.9
Major appliances	144	174	–17.4
Small appliances, miscellaneous housewares	63	87	–27.7
Miscellaneous household equipment	402	583	–31.1
APPAREL AND SERVICES	**899**	**1,181**	**–23.9**
Men and boys	**196**	**209**	**–6.2**
Men, aged 16 or older	169	183	–7.8
Boys, aged 2 to 15	26	27	–3.0
Women and girls	**420**	**545**	**–23.0**
Women, aged 16 or older	395	499	–20.9
Girls, aged 2 to 15	25	46	–45.4
Children under age 2	**22**	**29**	**–24.3**
Footwear	**138**	**236**	**–41.5**
Other apparel products and services	**123**	**162**	**–24.1**
TRANSPORTATION	4,468	4,443	0.6
Vehicle purchases	**1,793**	**1,777**	**0.9**
Cars and trucks, new	1,068	910	17.4
Cars and trucks, used	714	867	–17.7
Gasoline and motor oil	**779**	**773**	**0.8**
Other vehicle expenses	**1,553**	**1,597**	**–2.7**
Vehicle finance charges	149	130	15.0
Maintenance and repairs	481	564	–14.8
Vehicle insurance	680	656	3.7
Vehicle rental, leases, licenses, other charges	243	247	–1.6
Public transportation	**343**	**295**	**16.3**

	2002	1997	percent change 1997–02
HEALTH CARE	**$3,482**	**$3,064**	**13.7%**
Health insurance	1,815	1,588	14.3
Medical services	594	650	–8.7
Drugs	925	676	36.8
Medical supplies	148	149	–0.4
ENTERTAINMENT	**1,254**	**1,293**	**–3.0**
Fees and admissions	330	320	3.3
Television, radio, sound equipment	490	431	13.6
Pets, toys, and playground equipment	212	226	–6.1
Other entertainment supplies, services	221	316	–30.1
PERSONAL CARE PRODUCTS AND SERVICES	**435**	**485**	**–10.3**
READING	**146**	**186**	**–21.3**
EDUCATION	**177**	**198**	**–10.5**
TOBACCO PRODUCTS AND SMOKING SUPPLIES	**163**	**191**	**–14.7**
MISCELLANEOUS	**657**	**638**	**3.0**
CASH CONTRIBUTIONS	**1,546**	**1,307**	**18.3**
PERSONAL INSURANCE AND PENSIONS	**995**	**702**	**41.8**
Life and other personal insurance	383	333	15.0
Pensions and Social Security	612	368	66.5
PERSONAL TAXES	**826**	**1,198**	**–31.0**
Federal income taxes	534	849	–37.1
State and local income taxes	93	178	–47.7
Other taxes	199	171	16.4
GIFTS FOR NON-HOUSEHOLD MEMBERS	**749**	**1,002**	**–25.3**
Food	**49**	**59**	**–17.3**
Alcoholic beverages	**8**	**–**	**–**
Housing	**191**	**225**	**–15.0**
Housekeeping supplies	46	40	14.4
Household textiles	13	9	45.4
Appliances and miscellaneous housewares	20	27	–25.4
Major appliances	8	9	–10.5
Small appliances and miscellaneous housewares	12	17	–28.4
Miscellaneous household equipment	50	58	–13.9
Other housing	62	92	–32.3
Apparel and services	**170**	**219**	**–22.4**
Males, aged 2 or older	56	59	–5.4
Females, aged 2 or older	67	79	–15.5
Children under age 2	20	26	–22.2
Other apparel products and services	27	56	–51.7
Jewelry and watches	8	32	–75.3
All other apparel products and services	19	24	–19.0

	2002	1997	percent change 1997–02
Transportation	$32	$87	−63.3%
Health care	30	58	−48.4
Entertainment	58	95	−38.9
Toys, games, hobbies, and tricycles	26	50	−48.3
Other entertainment	31	45	−30.6
Personal care products and services	11	–	–
Reading	2	–	–
Education	111	136	−18.6
All other gifts	87	123	−29.2

Note: The Bureau of Labor Statistics uses consumer units rather than households as the sampling unit in the Consumer Expenditure Survey. For the definition of consumer unit, see the glossary. Spending on gifts is included in the preceding product and service categories. (–) means sample is too small to make a reliable estimate or data are not available.
Source: Bureau of Labor Statistics, 1997 and 2002 Consumer Expenditure Surveys, Internet site http://www.bls.gov/cex/; calculations by New Strategist

The Spending of Householders Aged 55 to 64 Is above Average

Householders aged 55 to 64 spent $44,330 in 2002.

The spending of householders aged 55 to 64 was 9 percent above average in 2002 (with an index of 109). Behind the increasingly above-average spending of the age group is a change in its lifestyle. A growing proportion of householders aged 55 to 64 are remaining in the labor force as early retirement prospects diminish. They are enjoying peak earnings, which is reflected in their spending.

On many items, householders aged 55 to 64 spend well above average. They spend 26 to 27 percent more than the average household on lunches and dinners at full-service restaurants. They spend 40 percent more than average on roasted coffee because older Americans are the most devoted coffee drinkers. They spend 54 percent more on wine consumed at home. Householders aged 55 to 64 spend 84 percent more than average on owned vacation homes, 30 percent more on new cars, 36 percent more on airfares, twice the average on ship fares, and 68 percent more on motorized campers.

This age group spends significantly less than average on children's clothes, education, bicycles, and personal services such as day care. They spend only an average amount on computer online services and cell phone services.

■ Spending patterns among householders aged 55 to 64 will change as tech-savvy boomers move into the age group during the next decade. Expect to see spending on computers and cell phone service surge.

Householders aged 55 to 64 spend more than average on many items

(indexed spending of householders aged 55 to 64 on selected items, 2002)

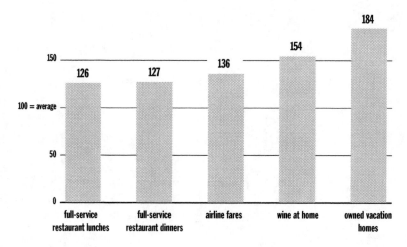

Table 8.3 Average and Indexed Spending of Householders Aged 55 to 64, 2002

(average annual spending of total consumer units (CUs) and average annual and indexed spending of consumer units headed by 55-to-64-year-olds, 2002)

	total consumer units	CUs headed by 55-to-64-year-olds	
		average spending	indexed spending
Number of consumer units (in 000s)	112,108	15,314	–
Average before-tax income	$49,430.00	$53,162.00	108
Average annual spending	40,676.60	44,330.04	109
FOOD	$5,374.80	$5,559.05	103
FOOD AT HOME	3,098.52	3,114.21	101
Cereals and bakery products	450.13	422.98	94
Cereals and cereal products	154.07	133.10	86
Flour	8.65	7.06	82
Prepared flour mixes	12.40	12.28	99
Ready-to-eat and cooked cereals	87.66	72.70	83
Rice	17.82	15.39	86
Pasta, cornmeal, and other cereal products	27.54	25.67	93
Bakery products	296.06	289.88	98
Bread	83.83	83.24	99
White bread	35.21	31.99	91
Bread, other than white	48.62	51.26	105
Crackers and cookies	70.67	69.12	98
Cookies	46.31	42.01	91
Crackers	24.36	27.11	111
Frozen and refrigerated bakery products	25.64	22.75	89
Other bakery products	115.92	114.76	99
Biscuits and rolls	41.04	42.71	104
Cakes and cupcakes	35.73	32.10	90
Bread and cracker products	3.50	3.48	99
Sweetrolls, coffee cakes, doughnuts	25.84	24.56	95
Pies, tarts, turnovers	9.82	11.91	121
Meats, poultry, fish, and eggs	798.42	807.14	101
Beef	231.17	215.90	93
Ground beef	86.29	75.01	87
Roast	40.99	45.74	112
Chuck roast	11.71	13.53	116
Round roast	10.23	12.16	119
Other roast	19.05	20.04	105
Steak	84.47	77.11	91
Round steak	13.29	11.63	88
Sirloin steak	26.62	25.89	97
Other steak	44.56	39.59	89
Pork	167.34	168.63	101
Bacon	28.45	27.29	96
Pork chops	38.43	36.20	94
Ham	37.16	41.79	112
Ham, not canned	35.66	40.08	112
Canned ham	1.50	1.71	114

	total consumer units	CUs headed by 55-to-64-year-olds	
		average spending	indexed spending
Sausage	$26.17	$27.31	104
Other pork	37.13	36.04	97
Other meats	101.08	102.59	101
Frankfurters	20.95	21.82	104
Lunch meats (cold cuts)	68.99	71.42	104
Bologna, liverwurst, salami	21.11	23.30	110
Lamb, organ meats, and others	11.14	9.35	84
Lamb and organ meats	7.99	6.16	77
Mutton, goat, and game	3.15	3.19	101
Poultry	144.13	133.57	93
Fresh and frozen chicken	113.25	104.65	92
Fresh and frozen whole chicken	32.08	29.66	92
Fresh and frozen chicken parts	81.17	74.99	92
Other poultry	30.88	28.92	94
Fish and seafood	120.97	154.23	127
Canned fish and seafood	16.13	17.87	111
Fresh fish and shellfish	69.31	89.43	129
Frozen fish and shellfish	35.53	46.93	132
Eggs	33.75	32.23	95
Dairy products	**328.34**	**325.44**	**99**
Fresh milk and cream	127.15	121.47	96
Fresh milk, all types	114.63	108.08	94
Cream	12.52	13.40	107
Other dairy products	201.19	203.96	101
Butter	18.48	19.33	105
Cheese	95.64	98.20	103
Ice cream and related products	58.74	59.50	101
Miscellaneous dairy products	28.33	26.94	95
Fruits and vegetables	**552.01**	**591.26**	**107**
Fresh fruits	178.20	206.58	116
Apples	32.59	36.07	111
Bananas	31.24	32.49	104
Oranges	20.34	20.25	100
Citrus fruits, excl. oranges	14.29	17.56	123
Other fresh fruits	79.74	100.22	126
Fresh vegetables	174.88	190.74	109
Potatoes	33.35	36.65	110
Lettuce	22.22	25.02	113
Tomatoes	33.71	35.41	105
Other fresh vegetables	85.60	93.65	109
Processed fruits	115.50	113.38	98
Frozen fruits and fruit juices	12.45	11.55	93
Frozen orange juice	6.31	5.00	79
Frozen fruits	2.79	3.60	129
Frozen fruit juices, excl. orange	3.35	2.95	88
Canned fruits	15.06	15.87	105
Dried fruits	6.06	7.23	119
Fresh fruit juice	22.20	22.93	103
Canned and bottled fruit juice	59.74	55.79	93

	total consumer units	CUs headed by 55-to-64-year-olds	
		average spending	indexed spending
Processed vegetables	$83.43	$80.56	97
Frozen vegetables	27.85	28.38	102
Canned and dried vegetables and juices	55.58	52.18	94
Canned beans	12.47	10.93	88
Canned corn	7.34	6.56	89
Canned miscellaneous vegetables	17.85	18.28	102
Dried peas	0.36	0.47	131
Dried beans	2.55	2.33	91
Dried miscellaneous vegetables	7.38	6.89	93
Dried processed vegetables	0.34	0.57	168
Frozen vegetable juices	0.06	–	–
Fresh and canned vegetable juices	7.23	6.13	85
Sugar and other sweets	**117.39**	**124.70**	**106**
Candy and chewing gum	75.44	83.45	111
Sugar	15.56	15.33	99
Artificial sweeteners	4.33	5.53	128
Jams, preserves, other sweets	22.06	20.39	92
Fats and oils	**85.16**	**89.59**	**105**
Margarine	9.86	12.35	125
Fats and oils	26.08	25.22	97
Salad dressings	27.01	28.43	105
Nondairy cream and imitation milk	9.33	11.46	123
Peanut butter	12.89	12.13	94
Miscellaneous foods	**471.92**	**434.23**	**92**
Frozen prepared foods	98.09	81.91	84
Frozen meals	29.88	25.65	86
Other frozen prepared foods	68.22	56.26	82
Canned and packaged soups	35.82	35.16	98
Potato chips, nuts, and other snacks	100.53	92.05	92
Potato chips and other snacks	76.37	62.05	81
Nuts	24.16	30.00	124
Condiments and seasonings	86.81	86.78	100
Salt, spices, and other seasonings	21.14	20.70	98
Olives, pickles, relishes	9.70	10.78	111
Sauces and gravies	37.78	34.60	92
Baking needs and miscellaneous products	18.19	20.72	114
Other canned/packaged prepared foods	150.67	138.32	92
Prepared salads	21.46	29.88	139
Prepared desserts	10.32	11.46	111
Baby food	31.57	17.39	55
Miscellaneous prepared foods	87.24	79.58	91
Nonalcoholic beverages	253.94	264.79	104
Cola	81.11	83.10	102
Other carbonated drinks	43.93	39.16	89
Coffee	41.59	55.69	134
Roasted coffee	27.38	38.44	140
Instant and freeze-dried coffee	14.21	17.25	121
Noncarbonated fruit-flavored drinks	18.95	14.24	75

	total consumer units	CUs headed by 55-to-64-year-olds	
		average spending	indexed spending
Tea	$15.86	$19.50	123
Nonalcoholic beer	0.64	0.67	105
Other nonalcoholic beverages and ice	51.85	52.43	101
Food prepared by CU on trips	41.20	54.09	131
FOOD AWAY FROM HOME	**2,276.29**	**2,444.84**	**107**
Meals at restaurants, carry-outs, other	**1,866.42**	**1,869.18**	**100**
Lunch	685.79	624.10	91
• At fast food, take-out, delivery, concession stands, buffet, and cafeteria (other than employer and school cafeteria)	377.71	299.43	79
• At full-service restaurants	224.82	283.36	126
• At vending machines, mobile vendors	5.50	4.17	76
• At employer and school cafeterias	77.76	37.14	48
Dinner	736.54	836.79	114
• At fast food, take-out, delivery, concession stands, buffet, and cafeteria (other than employer and school cafeteria)	213.33	170.82	80
• At full-service restaurants	518.02	659.86	127
• At vending machines, mobile vendors	1.87	4.09	219
• At employer and school cafeterias	3.32	2.03	61
Snacks and nonalcoholic beverages	262.67	224.31	85
• At fast food, take-out, delivery, concession stands, buffet, and cafeteria (other than employer and school cafeteria)	185.69	160.95	87
• At full-service restaurants	30.17	30.00	99
• At vending machines, mobile vendors	36.71	26.26	72
• At employer and school cafeterias	10.11	7.10	70
Breakfast and brunch	181.42	183.98	101
• At fast food, take-out, delivery, concession stands, buffet, and cafeteria (other than employer and school cafeteria)	87.83	66.27	75
• At full-service restaurants	87.08	113.04	130
• At vending machines, mobile vendors	1.40	1.89	135
• At employer and school cafeterias	5.11	2.77	54
Board (including at school)	**46.54**	**50.44**	**108**
Catered affairs	**69.00**	**184.76**	**268**
Food on trips	**211.49**	**303.24**	**143**
School lunches	**60.00**	**16.13**	**27**
Meals as pay	**22.86**	**21.09**	**92**
ALCOHOLIC BEVERAGES	**$375.95**	**$419.57**	**112**
At home	**228.08**	**242.66**	**106**
Beer and ale	112.34	84.48	75
Whiskey	13.90	11.94	86
Wine	77.75	119.39	154
Other alcoholic beverages	24.09	26.85	111

	total consumer units	CUs headed by 55-to-64-year-olds	
		average spending	indexed spending
Away from home	**$147.87**	**$176.91**	**120**
Beer and ale	52.86	59.40	112
• At fast food, take-out, delivery, concession stands, buffet, and cafeteria	7.99	7.41	93
• At full-service restaurants	41.95	51.82	124
• At vending machines, mobile vendors	0.32	0.16	50
• At catered affairs	2.59	–	–
Wine	25.85	34.36	133
• At fast food, take-out, delivery, concession stands, buffet and cafeteria	4.41	3.96	90
• At full-service restaurants	20.36	30.40	149
• At catered affairs	1.09	–	–
Other alcoholic beverages	69.16	83.16	120
• At fast food, take-out, delivery, concession stands, buffet, and cafeteria	3.50	1.71	49
• At full-service restaurants	28.94	41.74	144
• At catered affairs	3.94	–	–
Alcoholic beverages purchased on trips	32.78	39.70	121
HOUSING	**$13,283.08**	**$13,831.08**	**104**
SHELTER	**7,829.41**	**7,667.42**	**98**
Owned dwellings*	**5,164.96**	**5,594.55**	**108**
Mortgage interest and charges	2,962.16	2,711.96	92
Mortgage interest	2,811.49	2,502.25	89
Interest paid, home equity loan	88.61	102.17	115
Interest paid, home equity line of credit	61.88	107.54	174
Property taxes	1,242.36	1,539.97	124
Maintenance, repairs, insurance, other expenses	960.43	1,342.62	140
Homeowner's insurance	283.30	371.89	131
Ground rent	40.96	53.42	130
Maintenance and repair services	519.60	784.35	151
Painting and papering	55.58	98.33	177
Plumbing and water heating	46.63	59.19	127
Heat, air conditioning, electrical work	86.28	104.76	121
Roofing and gutters	71.20	76.58	108
Other repair and maintenance services	214.77	377.28	176
Repair, replacement of hard-surface flooring	43.54	66.88	154
Repair of built-in appliances	1.62	1.32	81
Maintenance and repair materials	83.75	93.26	111
Paints, wallpaper, and supplies	14.71	16.89	115
Tools, equipment for painting, wallpapering	1.58	1.81	115
Plumbing supplies and equipment	5.62	8.47	151
Electrical supplies, heating, cooling equip.	3.46	4.69	136
Hard-surface flooring, repair and replacement	8.72	7.08	81
Roofing and gutters	5.29	3.54	67
Plaster, paneling, siding, windows, doors, screens, awnings	13.92	21.79	157
Patio, walk, fence, driveway, masonry, brick, and stucco materials	1.29	1.03	80

	total consumer units	CUs headed by 55-to-64-year-olds	
		average spending	indexed spending
Landscape maintenance	$4.73	$4.67	99
Miscellaneous supplies and equipment	24.43	23.28	95
Insulation, other maintenance, repair	13.15	15.59	119
Finish basement, remodel rooms, build patios, walks, etc.	11.28	7.69	68
Property management and security	27.64	32.37	117
Property management	21.94	25.69	117
Management and upkeep services for security	5.71	6.68	117
Parking	5.17	7.33	142
Rented dwellings	**2,159.89**	**1,302.95**	**60**
Rent	2,104.66	1,259.94	60
Rent as pay	27.17	18.85	69
Maintenance, insurance, and other expenses	28.06	24.16	86
Tenant's insurance	8.90	7.19	81
Maintenance and repair services	11.16	13.26	119
Repair and maintenance services	10.58	12.06	114
Repair, replacement of hard-surface flooring	0.51	1.20	235
Repair of built-in appliances	0.07	–	–
Maintenance and repair materials	8.00	3.71	46
Paint, wallpaper, and supplies	1.01	0.93	92
Painting and wallpapering tools	0.11	0.10	91
Plastering, paneling, roofing, gutters, etc.	0.90	0.04	4
Plumbing supplies and equipment	0.80	0.38	48
Electrical supplies, heating, cooling equip.	0.30	0.02	7
Miscellaneous supplies and equipment	3.67	2.05	56
Insulation, other maintenance and repair	1.09	0.51	47
Materials for additions, finishing basements, remodeling rooms	2.43	1.41	58
Construction materials for jobs not started	0.15	0.14	93
Hard-surface flooring	0.73	0.03	4
Landscape maintenance	0.49	0.15	31
Other lodging	**504.56**	**769.91**	**153**
Owned vacation homes	171.55	314.87	184
Mortgage interest and charges	71.98	130.28	181
Property taxes	63.76	106.67	167
Maintenance, insurance and other expenses	35.81	77.91	218
Homeowner's insurance	9.70	10.07	104
Ground rent	2.93	6.04	206
Maintenance and repair services	16.76	42.46	253
Maintenance and repair materials	2.07	8.20	396
Property management and security	3.60	9.96	277
Property management	2.50	6.16	246
Management, upkeep services for security	1.10	3.80	345
Parking	0.76	1.18	155
Housing while attending school	80.14	87.50	109
Lodging on trips	252.87	367.54	145

	total consumer units	CUs headed by 55-to-64-year-olds	
		average spending	indexed spending
UTILITIES, FUELS, PUBLIC SERVICES	$2,684.32	$2,953.22	110
Natural gas	329.75	355.25	108
Natural gas (renter)	60.32	36.61	61
Natural gas (owner)	266.79	313.27	117
Natural gas (vacation)	2.54	5.22	206
Electricity	981.09	1,112.11	113
Electricity (renter)	223.26	152.81	68
Electricity (owner)	750.48	945.02	126
Electricity (vacation)	6.32	13.46	213
Fuel oil and other fuels	88.41	126.56	143
Fuel oil	45.98	65.68	143
Fuel oil (renter)	4.64	3.57	77
Fuel oil (owner)	40.98	60.65	148
Fuel oil (vacation)	0.36	1.46	406
Coal	0.07	0.21	300
Bottled/tank gas	35.27	51.67	146
Gas (renter)	5.09	4.29	84
Gas (owner)	27.19	42.75	157
Gas (vacation)	2.98	4.63	155
Wood and other fuels	7.09	8.99	127
Wood and other fuels (renter)	1.32	0.93	70
Wood and other fuels (owner)	5.68	8.07	142
Telephone services	956.74	980.99	103
Residential telephone and pay phones	641.00	696.51	109
Cellular phone service	293.76	265.65	90
Pager service	1.71	2.73	160
Phone cards	20.28	16.09	79
Water and other public services	328.33	378.30	115
Water and sewerage maintenance	237.16	267.38	113
Water and sewerage maintenance (renter)	32.76	23.61	72
Water and sewerage maintenance (owner)	201.79	239.51	119
Water and sewerage maintenance (vacation)	2.36	4.05	172
Trash and garbage collection	89.05	108.02	121
Trash and garbage collection (renter)	9.89	6.89	70
Trash and garbage collection (owner)	76.61	93.15	122
Trash and garbage collection (vacation)	2.53	7.98	315
Septic tank cleaning	2.12	2.90	137
HOUSEHOLD SERVICES	705.71	560.80	79
Personal services	331.02	79.43	24
Babysitting, child care in your own home	35.91	1.80	5
Babysitting, child care in someone else's home	27.48	6.00	22
Care for elderly, invalids, handicapped, etc.	50.07	31.90	64
Adult day care centers	6.81	3.06	45
Day care centers, nurseries, and preschools	210.74	36.67	17
Other household services	374.70	481.37	128
Housekeeping services	79.90	105.36	132
Gardening, lawn care service	72.38	114.50	158
Water softening service	3.15	3.22	102

	total consumer units	CUs headed by 55-to-64-year-olds	
		average spending	indexed spending
Nonclothing laundry, dry cleaning, sent out	$1.72	$2.19	127
Nonclothing laundry, dry cleaning, coin-operated	4.13	3.00	73
Termite/pest control services	13.25	17.13	129
Home security system service fee	17.40	20.17	116
Other home services	15.06	26.90	179
Termite/pest control products	0.68	0.99	146
Moving, storage, and freight express	33.13	30.61	92
Appliance repair, including service center	10.86	15.70	145
Reupholstering and furniture repair	7.40	21.69	293
Repairs/rentals of lawn/garden equipment, hand/power tools, etc.	3.62	5.34	148
Appliance rental	1.07	0.11	10
Rental of office equip., nonbusiness use	0.41	0.52	127
Repair of misc. household equip., furnishings	0.62	0.48	77
Repair of computer systems, nonbusiness use	2.53	2.87	113
Computer information services	107.29	110.59	103
HOUSEKEEPING SUPPLIES	**545.28**	**838.21**	**154**
Laundry and cleaning supplies	**130.57**	**138.95**	**106**
Soaps and detergents	72.89	69.99	96
Other laundry cleaning products	57.68	68.96	120
Other household products	**283.28**	**538.17**	**190**
Cleansing and toilet tissue, paper towels, and napkins	76.46	88.91	116
Miscellaneous household products	96.81	99.44	103
Lawn and garden supplies	110.01	349.82	318
Postage and stationery	**131.44**	**161.10**	**123**
Stationery, stationery supplies, giftwrap	60.20	65.63	109
Postage	69.12	91.75	133
Delivery services	2.12	3.73	176
HOUSEHOLD FURNISHINGS, EQUIPMENT	**1,518.36**	**1,811.44**	**119**
Household textiles	**135.52**	**183.06**	**135**
Bathroom linens	22.35	23.10	103
Bedroom linens	65.98	84.95	129
Kitchen and dining room linens	10.11	15.93	158
Curtains and draperies	16.65	17.90	108
Slipcovers and decorative pillows	7.40	19.99	270
Sewing materials for household items	11.44	20.12	176
Other linens	1.59	1.09	69
Furniture	**401.28**	**483.53**	**120**
Mattresses and springs	52.91	47.15	89
Other bedroom furniture	68.33	65.23	95
Sofas	85.33	98.27	115
Living room chairs	39.21	60.52	154
Living room tables	18.03	28.12	156
Kitchen and dining room furniture	61.28	98.92	161
Infants' furniture	6.46	2.37	37
Outdoor furniture	16.79	24.10	144
Wall units, cabinets, and other furniture	52.94	58.85	111

	total consumer units	CUs headed by 55-to-64-year-olds	
		average spending	indexed spending
Floor coverings	**$40.49**	**$53.35**	**132**
Wall-to-wall carpeting (renter)	0.65	0.46	71
Wall-to-wall carpet (replacement) (owner)	21.04	24.52	117
Floor coverings, nonpermanent	18.79	28.37	151
Major appliances	**188.47**	**219.72**	**117**
Dishwashers (built-in), garbage disposals, range hoods (renter)	1.24	0.53	43
Dishwashers (built-in), garbage disposals, range hoods (owner)	15.28	18.67	122
Refrigerators and freezers (renter)	5.58	1.81	32
Refrigerators and freezers (owner)	46.50	63.72	137
Washing machines (renter)	4.42	3.06	69
Washing machines (owner)	17.88	23.16	130
Clothes dryers (renter)	3.17	1.68	53
Clothes dryers (owner)	13.88	19.54	141
Cooking stoves, ovens (renter)	2.86	1.22	43
Cooking stoves, ovens (owner)	28.09	28.43	101
Microwave ovens (renter)	2.14	1.10	51
Microwave ovens (owner)	8.36	10.87	130
Portable dishwasher (renter)	0.25	–	–
Portable dishwasher (owner)	0.51	0.41	80
Window air conditioners (renter)	1.83	0.07	4
Window air conditioners (owner)	6.07	5.28	87
Electric floor-cleaning equipment	22.80	27.11	119
Sewing machines	4.79	6.53	136
Miscellaneous household appliances	**2.81**	**6.53**	**232**
Small appliances and misc. housewares	100.43	134.15	134
Housewares	77.55	105.58	136
Plastic dinnerware	1.57	1.74	111
China and other dinnerware	14.51	13.38	92
Flatware	3.79	5.62	148
Glassware	6.51	8.52	131
Silver serving pieces	4.05	5.86	145
Other serving pieces	1.44	3.16	219
Nonelectric cookware	24.25	24.38	101
Tableware, nonelectric kitchenware	21.44	42.93	200
Small appliances	22.89	28.57	125
Small electric kitchen appliances	17.18	21.86	127
Portable heating and cooling equipment	5.70	6.71	118
Miscellaneous household equipment	**652.17**	**737.62**	**113**
Window coverings	13.91	17.20	124
Infants' equipment	12.96	6.09	47
Laundry and cleaning equipment	15.15	16.24	107
Outdoor equipment	31.52	20.07	64
Clocks	5.87	5.53	94
Lamps and lighting fixtures	11.74	18.48	157
Other household decorative items	144.94	185.63	128
Telephones and accessories	32.73	37.45	114
Lawn and garden equipment	48.16	55.78	116

	total consumer units	CUs headed by 55-to-64-year-olds	
		average spending	indexed spending
Power tools	$33.27	$36.77	111
Office furniture for home use	10.57	13.40	127
Hand tools	8.05	8.74	109
Indoor plants and fresh flowers	49.78	68.69	138
Closet and storage items	9.98	10.46	105
Rental of furniture	4.60	2.50	54
Luggage	5.98	8.00	134
Computers and computer hardware, nonbusiness use	138.58	154.15	111
Computer software and accessories, nonbusiness use	17.67	17.43	99
Telephone answering devices	1.08	0.85	79
Calculators	1.44	0.61	42
Business equipment for home use	0.97	0.74	76
Other hardware	12.85	5.17	40
Smoke alarms (owner)	1.10	1.01	92
Smoke alarms (renter)	0.39	0.05	13
Other household appliances (owner)	8.00	10.23	128
Other household appliances (renter)	1.23	0.42	34
Misc. household equipment and parts	29.62	35.91	121
APPAREL AND SERVICES	**$1,749.22**	**$1,791.35**	**102**
Men's apparel	**319.48**	**297.25**	**93**
Suits	32.96	36.72	111
Sport coats and tailored jackets	10.65	14.34	135
Coats and jackets	33.86	23.10	68
Underwear	15.27	13.58	89
Hosiery	12.22	9.94	81
Nightwear	2.98	3.85	129
Accessories	22.41	22.84	102
Sweaters and vests	15.68	16.35	104
Active sportswear	15.13	14.17	94
Shirts	78.89	70.41	89
Pants	57.64	49.70	86
Shorts and shorts sets	12.22	12.41	102
Uniforms	3.21	2.18	68
Costumes	6.35	7.67	121
Boys' (aged 2 to 15) apparel	**89.98**	**40.19**	**45**
Coats and jackets	6.38	4.73	74
Sweaters	3.65	1.76	48
Shirts	19.50	6.09	31
Underwear	5.02	2.51	50
Nightwear	2.59	1.04	40
Hosiery	4.21	1.63	39
Accessories	4.12	1.27	31
Suits, sport coats, and vests	2.37	1.95	82
Pants	22.58	10.46	46
Shorts and shorts sets	8.66	3.38	39
Uniforms	3.35	1.44	43
Active sportswear	3.84	2.16	56
Costumes	3.72	1.77	48

	total consumer units	CUs headed by 55-to-64-year-olds	
		average spending	indexed spending
Women's apparel	**$586.91**	**$787.66**	**134**
Coats and jackets	50.06	70.61	141
Dresses	56.40	156.05	277
Sport coats and tailored jackets	6.48	7.49	116
Sweaters and vests	50.47	55.41	110
Shirts, blouses, and tops	103.24	150.43	146
Skirts	17.48	19.37	111
Pants	96.29	106.92	111
Shorts and shorts sets	16.09	14.23	88
Active sportswear	30.07	25.92	86
Nightwear	27.63	27.06	98
Undergarments	33.55	37.33	111
Hosiery	21.22	23.56	111
Suits	29.01	35.12	121
Accessories	33.37	42.79	128
Uniforms	6.12	7.13	117
Costumes	9.42	8.23	87
Girls' (aged 2 to 15) apparel	**117.21**	**52.31**	**45**
Coats and jackets	6.49	2.81	43
Dresses and suits	12.41	5.73	46
Shirts, blouses, and sweaters	29.33	12.29	42
Skirts and pants	24.07	11.94	50
Shorts and shorts sets	8.28	2.31	28
Active sportswear	9.32	2.14	23
Underwear and nightwear	7.63	4.27	56
Hosiery	4.30	2.45	57
Accessories	5.81	5.31	91
Uniforms	4.77	1.60	34
Costumes	4.80	1.47	31
Children under age 2	**82.60**	**48.56**	**59**
Coats, jackets, and snowsuits	2.43	2.49	102
Outerwear including dresses	23.71	22.80	96
Underwear	43.60	14.86	34
Nightwear and loungewear	4.07	5.26	129
Accessories	8.79	3.16	36
Footwear	**313.17**	**289.84**	**93**
Men's	102.90	72.84	71
Boys'	36.87	12.68	34
Women's	141.64	189.70	134
Girls'	31.76	14.61	46
Other apparel products and services	**239.87**	**275.54**	**115**
Material for making clothes	5.11	7.31	143
Sewing patterns and notions	8.20	17.74	216
Watches	13.62	12.42	91
Jewelry	89.65	113.82	127
Shoe repair and other shoe services	1.44	1.98	138
Coin-operated apparel laundry and dry cleaning	37.58	22.09	59
Apparel alteration, repair, and tailoring services	5.86	6.68	114
Clothing rental	2.66	1.51	57
Watch and jewelry repair	5.49	11.20	204
Professional laundry, dry cleaning	69.69	80.24	115
Clothing storage	0.55	0.56	102

	total consumer units	CUs headed by 55-to-64-year-olds average spending	CUs headed by 55-to-64-year-olds indexed spending
TRANSPORTATION	**$7,759.29**	**$8,448.62**	**109**
VEHICLE PURCHASES	**3,664.93**	**3,881.56**	**106**
Cars and trucks, new	**1,752.96**	**2,079.81**	**119**
New cars	883.08	1,151.52	130
New trucks	869.88	928.29	107
Cars and trucks, used	**1,842.29**	**1,763.01**	**96**
Used cars	1,113.46	1,143.17	103
Used trucks	728.82	619.84	85
Other vehicles	**69.68**	**38.74**	**56**
New motorcycles	36.26	18.46	51
Used motorcycles	33.42	20.28	61
GASOLINE AND MOTOR OIL	**1,235.06**	**1,292.37**	**105**
Gasoline	1,125.01	1,157.54	103
Diesel fuel	10.86	10.45	96
Gasoline on trips	88.24	113.71	129
Motor oil	10.05	9.51	95
Motor oil on trips	0.89	1.15	129
OTHER VEHICLE EXPENSES	**2,470.55**	**2,734.97**	**111**
Vehicle finance charges	**397.04**	**370.05**	**93**
Automobile finance charges	193.12	188.16	97
Truck finance charges	182.89	160.89	88
Motorcycle and plane finance charges	2.36	0.22	9
Other vehicle finance charges	18.67	20.78	111
Maintenance and repairs	**697.30**	**832.05**	**119**
Coolant, additives, brake, transmission fluids	3.82	3.27	86
Tires—purchased, replaced, installed	89.93	97.84	109
Parts, equipment, and accessories	41.70	49.43	119
Vehicle audio equipment, excl. labor	12.32	–	–
Vehicle products	4.92	10.05	204
Miscellaneous auto repair, servicing	43.69	93.30	214
Body work and painting	31.24	31.70	101
Clutch, transmission repair	48.68	40.63	83
Drive shaft and rear-end repair	6.51	9.07	139
Brake work	57.73	70.00	121
Repair to steering or front-end	16.91	21.18	125
Repair to engine cooling system	21.68	26.06	120
Motor tune-up	49.69	61.18	123
Lube, oil change, and oil filters	65.07	76.36	117
Front-end alignment, wheel balance, rotation	11.90	15.37	129
Shock absorber replacement	4.82	5.43	113
Gas tank repair, replacement	4.32	2.81	65
Tire repair and other repair work	39.83	56.21	141
Vehicle air conditioning repair	17.00	22.37	132
Exhaust system repair	12.56	12.04	96
Electrical system repair	28.42	30.93	109
Motor repair, replacement	76.62	80.83	105
Auto repair service policy	7.93	15.99	202

	total consumer units	CUs headed by 55-to-64-year-olds average spending	CUs headed by 55-to-64-year-olds indexed spending
Vehicle insurance	**$893.50**	**$991.15**	**111**
Vehicle rental, leases, licenses, other charges	**482.71**	**541.72**	**112**
Leased and rented vehicles	324.48	364.43	112
Rented vehicles	41.33	60.97	148
Auto rental	6.76	6.62	98
Auto rental on trips	28.28	49.23	174
Truck rental	2.21	1.14	52
Truck rental on trips	3.55	3.73	105
Leased vehicles	283.15	303.46	107
Car lease payments	149.63	170.20	114
Cash down payment (car lease)	11.13	17.62	158
Termination fee (car lease)	1.28	2.04	159
Truck lease payments	114.24	112.23	98
Cash down payment (truck lease)	4.92	0.42	9
Termination fee (truck lease)	1.94	0.97	50
Vehicle registration, state	72.82	85.51	117
Vehicle registration, local	7.76	8.25	106
Driver's license	6.26	6.82	109
Vehicle inspection	9.26	10.68	115
Parking fees	29.25	27.11	93
Parking fees in home city, excluding residence	24.24	21.18	87
Parking fees on trips	5.01	5.93	118
Tolls	10.59	11.55	109
Tolls on trips	3.94	4.95	126
Towing charges	5.60	5.06	90
Automobile service clubs	12.75	17.36	136
PUBLIC TRANSPORTATION	**388.75**	**539.72**	**139**
Airline fares	243.57	332.29	136
Intercity bus fares	11.48	15.54	135
Intracity mass transit fares	49.97	39.92	80
Local transportation on trips	10.91	15.39	141
Taxi fares and limousine service on trips	6.41	9.04	141
Taxi fares and limousine service	18.95	38.32	202
Intercity train fares	16.09	28.06	174
Ship fares	29.74	60.65	204
School bus	1.64	0.52	32
HEALTH CARE	**$2,350.32**	**$3,007.06**	**128**
HEALTH INSURANCE	**1,167.71**	**1,356.19**	**116**
Commercial health insurance	**217.53**	**303.33**	**139**
Traditional fee-for-service health plan (not BCBS)	68.27	113.73	167
Preferred-provider health plan (not BCBS)	149.26	189.60	127
Blue Cross, Blue Shield	**315.67**	**420.17**	**133**
Traditional fee-for-service health plan	53.76	92.77	173
Preferred-provider health plan	106.99	138.72	130
Health maintenance organization	101.53	139.72	138
Commercial Medicare supplement	47.35	41.18	87
Other BCBS health insurance	6.05	7.77	128

	total consumer units	CUs headed by 55-to-64-year-olds	
		average spending	indexed spending
Health maintenance plans (HMOs)	$280.47	$338.16	121
Medicare payments	186.87	129.48	69
Commercial Medicare supplements/			
other health insurance	167.18	165.06	99
Commercial Medicare supplement (not BCBS)	106.32	84.65	80
Other health insurance (not BCBS)	60.86	80.41	132
MEDICAL SERVICES	589.87	863.16	146
Physician's services	147.53	247.04	167
Dental services	226.99	316.55	139
Eye care services	34.20	32.76	96
Service by professionals other than physician	42.76	61.03	143
Lab tests, X-rays	26.79	43.38	162
Hospital room	36.57	54.91	150
Hospital services other than room	51.51	71.57	139
Care in convalescent or nursing home	12.46	22.77	183
Other medical services	9.46	13.14	139
DRUGS	487.43	658.75	135
Nonprescription drugs	64.45	63.67	99
Nonprescription vitamins	49.15	71.02	144
Prescription drugs	373.83	524.05	140
MEDICAL SUPPLIES	105.31	128.95	122
Eyeglasses and contact lenses	52.26	64.20	123
Hearing aids	14.98	22.22	148
Topicals and dressings	27.56	32.47	118
Medical equipment for general use	2.69	3.85	143
Supportive, convalescent medical equipment	5.21	3.96	76
Rental of medical equipment	1.06	0.79	75
Rental of supportive, convalescent			
medical equipment	1.55	1.46	94
ENTERTAINMENT	$2,078.99	$2,297.44	111
FEES AND ADMISSIONS	541.67	583.78	108
Recreation expenses on trips	25.64	32.02	125
Social, recreation, civic club membership	107.92	140.02	130
Fees for participant sports	75.05	78.97	105
Participant sports on trips	29.50	39.56	134
Movie, theater, opera, ballet	98.30	99.69	101
Movie, other admissions on trips	45.57	63.95	140
Admission to sports events	36.18	26.02	72
Admission to sports events on trips	15.19	21.31	140
Fees for recreational lessons	82.69	50.24	61
Other entertainment services on trips	25.64	32.02	125
TELEVISION, RADIO, SOUND EQUIPMENT	691.90	716.56	104
Television	543.66	600.70	110
Cable service and community antenna	382.28	439.91	115
Black-and-white TV	0.80	0.22	28
Color TV, console	38.63	55.92	145
Color TV, portable, table model	39.14	46.18	118

	total consumer units	CUs headed by 55-to-64-year-olds	
		average spending	indexed spending
VCRs and video disc players	$23.25	$21.22	91
Video cassettes, tapes, and discs	33.13	22.98	69
Video game hardware and software	23.46	10.51	45
Repair of TV, radio, and sound equipment	2.50	3.30	132
Rental of television sets	0.46	0.45	98
Radio and sound equipment	**148.25**	**115.86**	**78**
Radios	3.98	3.60	90
Tape recorders and players	5.31	3.22	61
Sound components and component systems	20.19	23.79	118
Miscellaneous sound equipment	3.18	–	–
Sound equipment accessories	5.97	4.72	79
Satellite dishes	1.00	1.01	101
Compact disc, tape, record, video mail order clubs	6.53	6.42	98
Records, CDs, audio tapes, needles	36.47	27.71	76
Rental of VCR, radio, sound equipment	0.25	0.48	192
Musical instruments and accessories	24.82	20.39	82
Rental and repair of musical instruments	1.22	0.54	44
Rental of video cassettes, tapes, discs, films	39.33	23.99	61
PETS, TOYS, PLAYGROUND EQUIPMENT	**369.12**	**419.90**	**114**
Pets	**248.25**	**315.36**	**127**
Pet food	102.56	141.06	138
Pet purchase, supplies, and medicines	52.29	74.99	143
Pet services	21.95	21.96	100
Veterinarian services	71.44	77.36	108
Toys, games, hobbies, and tricycles	**117.34**	**103.92**	**89**
Playground equipment	**3.54**	**0.62**	**18**
OTHER ENTERTAINMENT SUPPLIES, EQUIPMENT, SERVICES	**476.30**	**577.20**	**121**
Unmotored recreational vehicles	**47.14**	**86.74**	**184**
Boat without motor and boat trailers	16.15	49.41	306
Trailer and other attachable campers	30.99	37.33	120
Motorized recreational vehicles	**170.19**	**174.98**	**103**
Motorized camper	40.05	67.34	168
Other vehicle	35.47	46.31	131
Motorboats	94.67	61.32	65
Rental of recreational vehicles	**1.99**	**4.10**	**206**
Outboard motors	**0.71**	**3.61**	**508**
Docking and landing fees	**6.66**	**12.04**	**181**
Sports, recreation, exercise equipment	**150.33**	**209.54**	**139**
Athletic gear, game tables, exercise equipment	60.51	60.80	100
Bicycles	13.45	3.75	28
Camping equipment	9.59	6.11	64
Hunting and fishing equipment	35.68	105.82	297
Winter sports equipment	5.45	2.10	39
Water sports equipment	8.95	15.92	178
Other sports equipment	14.62	14.03	96
Rental and repair of misc. sports equipment	2.07	1.01	49

	total consumer units	CUs headed by 55-to-64-year-olds average spending	CUs headed by 55-to-64-year-olds indexed spending
Photographic equipment and supplies	**$90.48**	**$82.82**	**92**
Film	17.74	17.56	99
Other photographic supplies	2.27	1.75	77
Film processing	26.60	25.69	97
Repair and rental of photographic equipment	0.12	0.11	92
Photographic equipment	23.34	25.00	107
Photographer fees	20.42	12.71	62
Fireworks	**1.52**	**1.75**	**115**
Souvenirs	**1.25**	**0.16**	**13**
Visual goods	**1.19**	**1.23**	**103**
Pinball, electronic video games	**4.84**	**0.23**	**5**
PERSONAL CARE PRODUCTS AND SERVICES	**$525.80**	**$556.56**	**106**
Personal care products	**276.65**	**277.92**	**100**
Hair care products	53.57	42.17	79
Hair accessories	6.57	3.96	60
Wigs and hairpieces	1.32	1.73	131
Oral hygiene products	27.33	28.98	106
Shaving products	15.09	17.68	117
Cosmetics, perfume, and bath products	129.13	146.04	113
Deodorants, feminine hygiene, misc. products	30.29	25.49	84
Electric personal care appliances	13.34	11.88	89
Personal care services	**249.15**	**278.65**	**112**
READING	**$138.57**	**$181.44**	**131**
Newspaper subscriptions	43.88	66.74	152
Newspaper, nonsubscription	11.30	12.41	110
Magazine subscriptions	16.59	23.16	140
Magazines, nonsubscription	9.35	7.85	84
Books purchased through book clubs	6.62	6.32	95
Books not purchased through book clubs	50.38	64.63	128
Encyclopedia and other reference book sets	0.33	0.34	103
EDUCATION	**$751.95**	**$589.41**	**78**
College tuition	444.45	435.40	98
Elementary and high school tuition	128.94	29.53	23
Other school tuition	25.53	20.84	82
Other school expenses including rentals	25.77	16.07	62
Books, supplies for college	57.93	34.34	59
Books, supplies for elementary, high school	16.14	7.72	48
Books, supplies for day care, nursery school	3.39	0.84	25
Miscellaneous school expenses and supplies	49.80	44.67	90

	total consumer units	CUs headed by 55-to-64-year-olds	
		average spending	indexed spending
TOBACCO PRODUCTS AND SMOKING SUPPLIES	**$320.49**	**$360.52**	**112**
Cigarettes	291.89	327.02	112
Other tobacco products	26.27	32.04	122
Smoking accessories	2.33	1.45	62
FINANCIAL PRODUCTS, SERVICES	**$788.12**	**$929.83**	**118**
Miscellaneous fees	2.25	2.72	121
Lottery and gambling losses	46.94	39.85	85
Legal fees	132.99	206.21	155
Funeral expenses	77.91	112.44	144
Safe deposit box rental	3.84	5.50	143
Checking accounts, other bank service charges	25.91	20.90	81
Cemetery lots, vaults, and maintenance fees	16.05	19.71	123
Accounting fees	57.85	83.41	144
Miscellaneous personal services	39.77	28.59	72
Finance charges, except mortgage and vehicles	271.37	267.17	98
Occupational expenses	38.46	45.76	119
Expenses for other properties	65.99	86.16	131
Credit card memberships	2.82	3.40	121
Shopping club membership fees	5.97	7.89	132
CASH CONTRIBUTIONS	**$1,277.10**	**$1,520.18**	**119**
Support for college students	75.94	148.53	196
Alimony expenditures	21.18	47.14	223
Child support expenditures	190.75	65.31	34
Gifts to non-CU members of stocks, bonds, and mutual funds	24.23	32.85	136
Cash contributions to charities and other organizations	137.62	186.43	135
Cash contributions to church, religious organizations	557.29	710.09	127
Cash contributions to educational institutions	33.42	43.72	131
Cash contributions to political organizations	10.90	13.17	121
Other cash gifts	225.76	272.94	121
PERSONAL INSURANCE, PENSIONS	**$3,898.62**	**$4,837.93**	**124**
Life and other personal insurance	**406.11**	**594.98**	**147**
Life, endowment, annuity, other personal insurance	391.65	577.35	147
Other nonhealth insurance	14.46	17.63	122
Pensions and Social Security	**3,492.51**	**4,242.95**	**121**
Deductions for government retirement	69.48	96.39	139
Deductions for railroad retirement	2.21	1.92	87
Deductions for private pensions	390.38	453.85	116
Nonpayroll deposit to retirement plans	426.12	1,022.10	240
Deductions for Social Security	2,604.32	2,668.69	102

	total consumer units	CUs headed by 55-to-64-year-olds	
		average spending	indexed spending
PERSONAL TAXES	**$2,496.26**	**$2,855.85**	**114**
Federal income taxes	1,842.57	2,136.26	116
State and local income taxes	506.45	492.51	97
Other taxes	147.24	227.08	154
GIFTS FOR NON-HOUSEHOLD MEMBERS**	**$1,036.24**	**$1,530.65**	**148**
FOOD	**82.18**	**152.00**	**185**
Cakes and cupcakes	2.41	2.45	102
Other fresh fruits (excl. apples, bananas, citrus)	2.26	4.10	181
Candy and chewing gum	11.69	19.00	163
Board (including at school)	21.90	18.59	85
Catered affairs	26.19	89.36	341
ALCOHOLIC BEVERAGES	**13.42**	**13.22**	**99**
Beer and ale	4.73	4.80	101
Wine	5.84	6.02	103
HOUSING	**258.69**	**334.28**	**129**
Housekeeping supplies	**42.48**	**54.87**	**129**
Laundry and cleaning supplies	2.93	2.07	71
Other household products	11.69	20.59	176
Miscellaneous household products	5.85	8.28	142
Lawn and garden supplies	4.20	9.95	237
Postage and stationery	27.86	32.21	116
Stationery, stationery supplies, giftwrap	21.13	25.41	120
Postage	6.14	5.43	88
Household textiles	**13.72**	**28.81**	**210**
Bathroom linens	2.59	3.79	146
Bedroom linens	6.10	17.26	283
Appliances and miscellaneous housewares	**23.98**	**54.41**	**227**
Major appliances	8.41	27.23	324
Electric floor-cleaning equipment	2.77	11.10	401
Small appliances and miscellaneous housewares	15.57	27.18	175
China and other dinnerware	2.46	4.55	185
Nonelectric cookware	3.53	4.01	114
Tableware, nonelectric kitchenware	2.63	4.63	176
Small electric kitchen appliances	2.71	4.44	164
Miscellaneous household equipment	**64.70**	**84.91**	**131**
Infants' equipment	3.82	0.70	18
Outdoor equipment	2.07	1.33	64
Other household decorative items	25.76	37.24	145
Power tools	2.80	4.07	145
Indoor plants, fresh flowers	13.43	17.47	130
Computers and computer hardware	6.59	12.59	191
Miscellaneous household equipment	2.19	1.29	59
Other housing	**113.80**	**111.29**	**98**
Repair or maintenance services	4.51	1.87	41
Housing while attending school	39.93	54.26	136

	total consumer units	CUs headed by 55-to-64-year-olds	
		average spending	indexed spending
Natural gas (renter)	$3.62	$3.72	103
Electricity (renter)	14.67	15.55	106
Water, sewer maintenance (renter)	3.04	4.18	138
Day-care centers, nurseries, and preschools	23.81	6.03	25
APPAREL AND SERVICES	**237.13**	**341.33**	**144**
Men and boys, aged 2 or older	**63.74**	**74.00**	**116**
Men's coats and jackets	5.09	4.34	85
Men's accessories	4.45	2.43	55
Men's sweaters and vests	3.06	4.28	140
Men's active sportswear	2.76	1.69	61
Men's shirts	16.79	21.28	127
Men's pants	6.93	7.08	102
Boys' shirts	3.71	3.75	101
Boys' pants	3.76	5.69	151
Women and girls, aged 2 or older	**81.76**	**157.95**	**193**
Women's coats and jackets	5.62	13.86	247
Women's dresses	7.66	22.61	295
Women's vests and sweaters	8.50	17.06	201
Women's shirts, tops, blouses	9.06	14.27	158
Women's pants	6.62	18.39	278
Women's active sportswear	4.33	2.72	63
Women's sleepwear	6.45	7.58	118
Women's accessories	5.71	16.67	292
Girls' dresses and suits	2.98	4.12	138
Girls' shirts, blouses, sweaters	4.48	8.71	194
Girls' skirts and pants	3.32	5.14	155
Girls' accessories	2.38	3.22	135
Children under age 2	**39.99**	**41.40**	**104**
Infant dresses, outerwear	15.28	21.48	141
Infant underwear	16.91	9.99	59
Infant nightwear, loungewear	2.55	5.04	198
Infant accessories	3.93	2.59	66
Other apparel products and services	**51.63**	**67.99**	**132**
Jewelry and watches	24.01	32.97	137
Watches	2.16	2.72	126
Jewelry	21.85	30.25	138
Men's footwear	8.37	8.57	102
Boys' footwear	4.46	3.70	83
Women's footwear	8.82	11.99	136
Girls' footwear	3.30	5.40	164
TRANSPORTATION	**43.87**	**69.71**	**159**
New cars	7.09	7.02	99
Used cars	12.21	20.40	167
Airline fares	6.78	6.41	95
Ship fares	2.74	4.53	165

	total consumer units	CUs headed by 55-to-64-year-olds	
		average spending	indexed spending
HEALTH CARE	**$32.59**	**$55.16**	**169**
Physician's services	3.07	9.96	324
Dental services	4.03	6.44	160
Care in convalescent or nursing home	5.19	13.12	253
Nonprescription vitamins	3.93	2.63	67
Prescription drugs	2.38	3.71	156
ENTERTAINMENT	**78.24**	**107.30**	**137**
Toys, games, hobbies, and tricycles	29.98	49.82	166
Other entertainment	48.26	57.48	119
Fees for recreational lessons	7.88	10.88	138
Community antenna or cable TV	6.37	6.81	107
VCRs and videodisc players	2.26	3.14	139
Video game hardware and software	2.13	3.34	157
Athletic gear, game tables, exercise equipment	6.60	9.28	141
Hunting and fishing equipment	3.06	0.24	8
Photographer fees	3.19	6.66	209
PERSONAL CARE PRODUCTS, SERVICES	**21.15**	**16.94**	**80**
Cosmetics, perfume, bath preparation	12.53	9.48	76
Electric personal care appliances	3.31	3.19	96
EDUCATION	**183.88**	**292.98**	**159**
College tuition	127.83	244.04	191
Elementary and high school tuition	25.95	10.32	40
Other school tuition	4.44	10.41	234
Other school expenses including rentals	3.99	1.27	32
College books and supplies	11.93	15.56	130
Miscellaneous school supplies	7.38	9.62	130
ALL OTHER GIFTS	**83.76**	**145.43**	**174**
Gifts of trip expenses	44.40	75.41	170
Lottery and gambling losses	2.86	1.37	48
Legal fees	5.82	6.41	110
Funeral expenses	25.25	54.67	217
Miscellaneous personal services	2.16	1.00	46

* This figure does not include the amount paid for mortgage principle, which is considered an asset.
** Expenditures on gifts are also included in the preceding product and service categories. Food spending, for example, includes the amount spent on food gifts. Only gift categories with spending of $2.00 or more by the average consumer unit are shown.
Note: The Bureau of Labor Statistics uses consumer unit rather than household as the sampling unit in the Consumer Expenditure Survey. For the definition of consumer unit, see the glossary. (–) means not applicable or the sample is too small to make a reliable estimate.
Source: Bureau of Labor Statistics, unpublished data from the 2002 Consumer Expenditure Survey; calculations by New Strategist

Householders Aged 65 or Older Can Be Big Spenders

Those aged 65 or older spend 69 percent as much as the average household.

In 2002, householders aged 65 or older spent $28,105, much less than the $40,677 spent by the average household. The spending of elderly householders is below average because their households are small and most are retired.

Householders aged 65 to 74 spend 79 percent as much as the average household. They spend slightly more than the average household on full-service restaurant breakfasts and restaurant meals on trips. They spend 88 percent more than the average household on whiskey consumed at home. Their spending on travel lodging is 31 percent above average.

Householders aged 75 or older spend only 58 percent as much as the average household. Their spending is above average for items required by the frail elderly. These include adult day care centers, household services such as housekeeping and lawn care, and health care. They also spend more than average on postage. Householders aged 75 or older are the biggest spenders on newspaper subscriptions.

■ As better-educated generations age into their sixties and seventies, older Americans won't act so old anymore. Look for a revolution in the older market as Boomers enter the age group.

Today's older Americans prefer snail mail to e-mail

(indexed spending of householders aged 65 or older on postage and computer information services, 2002)

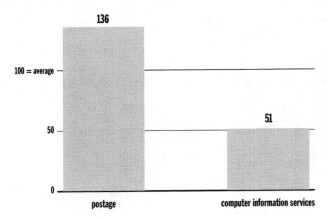

Table 8.4 Average and Indexed Spending of Householders Aged 65 or Older, 2002

(average annual spending of total consumer units (CUs) and average annual and indexed spending of consumer units headed by people aged 65 or older, 2002)

	total consumer units	CUs headed by people aged 65 or older average spending	indexed spending
Number of consumer units (in 000s)	112,108	21,983	–
Average before-tax income	$49,430.00	$29,711.00	60
Average annual spending	40,676.60	28,104.57	69
FOOD	$5,374.80	$3,910.20	73
FOOD AT HOME	3,098.52	2,548.02	82
Cereals and bakery products	450.13	386.24	86
Cereals and cereal products	154.07	120.23	78
Flour	8.65	8.52	98
Prepared flour mixes	12.40	11.05	89
Ready-to-eat and cooked cereals	87.66	69.76	80
Rice	17.82	11.92	67
Pasta, cornmeal, and other cereal products	27.54	18.98	69
Bakery products	296.06	266.01	90
Bread	83.83	81.98	98
White bread	35.21	30.90	88
Bread, other than white	48.62	51.08	105
Crackers and cookies	70.67	62.79	89
Cookies	46.31	41.07	89
Crackers	24.36	21.72	89
Frozen and refrigerated bakery products	25.64	19.99	78
Other bakery products	115.92	101.25	87
Biscuits and rolls	41.04	33.56	82
Cakes and cupcakes	35.73	27.59	77
Bread and cracker products	3.50	3.63	104
Sweetrolls, coffee cakes, doughnuts	25.84	25.09	97
Pies, tarts, turnovers	9.82	11.39	116
Meats, poultry, fish, and eggs	798.42	640.60	80
Beef	231.17	174.22	75
Ground beef	86.29	64.75	75
Roast	40.99	33.50	82
Chuck roast	11.71	9.10	78
Round roast	10.23	9.67	95
Other roast	19.05	14.74	77
Steak	84.47	59.73	71
Round steak	13.29	8.18	62
Sirloin steak	26.62	15.42	58
Other steak	44.56	36.14	81
Pork	167.34	143.82	86
Bacon	28.45	26.81	94
Pork chops	38.43	30.70	80
Ham	37.16	32.28	87
Ham, not canned	35.66	31.23	88
Canned ham	1.50	1.05	70

	total consumer units	CUs headed by people aged 65 or older	
		average spending	indexed spending
Sausage	$26.17	$22.59	86
Other pork	37.13	31.44	85
Other meats	101.08	84.19	83
Frankfurters	20.95	15.17	72
Lunch meats (cold cuts)	68.99	54.90	80
Bologna, liverwurst, salami	21.11	17.44	83
Lamb, organ meats, and others	11.14	14.12	127
Lamb and organ meats	7.99	11.42	143
Mutton, goat, and game	3.15	2.70	86
Poultry	144.13	110.17	76
Fresh and frozen chicken	113.25	84.93	75
Fresh and frozen whole chicken	32.08	25.37	79
Fresh and frozen chicken parts	81.17	59.56	73
Other poultry	30.88	25.24	82
Fish and seafood	120.97	97.77	81
Canned fish and seafood	16.13	16.43	102
Fresh fish and shellfish	69.31	56.58	82
Frozen fish and shellfish	35.53	24.76	70
Eggs	33.75	30.42	90
Dairy products	**328.34**	**273.64**	**83**
Fresh milk and cream	127.15	106.99	84
Fresh milk, all types	114.63	95.05	83
Cream	12.52	11.94	95
Other dairy products	201.19	166.66	83
Butter	18.48	17.19	93
Cheese	95.64	77.25	81
Ice cream and related products	58.74	51.12	87
Miscellaneous dairy products	28.33	21.09	74
Fruits and vegetables	**552.01**	**509.92**	**92**
Fresh fruits	178.20	168.87	95
Apples	32.59	26.28	81
Bananas	31.24	32.50	104
Oranges	20.34	17.47	86
Citrus fruits, excl. oranges	14.29	14.60	102
Other fresh fruits	79.74	78.02	98
Fresh vegetables	174.88	162.74	93
Potatoes	33.35	33.77	101
Lettuce	22.22	19.59	88
Tomatoes	33.71	29.92	89
Other fresh vegetables	85.60	79.46	93
Processed fruits	115.50	102.88	89
Frozen fruits and fruit juices	12.45	11.04	89
Frozen orange juice	6.31	6.44	102
Frozen fruits	2.79	2.75	99
Frozen fruit juices, excl. orange	3.35	1.85	55
Canned fruits	15.06	16.60	110
Dried fruits	6.06	8.50	140
Fresh fruit juice	22.20	21.71	98
Canned and bottled fruit juice	59.74	45.02	75

	total consumer units	CUs headed by people aged 65 or older average spending	CUs headed by people aged 65 or older indexed spending
Processed vegetables	$83.43	$75.44	90
Frozen vegetables	27.85	26.00	93
Canned and dried vegetables and juices	55.58	49.44	89
Canned beans	12.47	10.67	86
Canned corn	7.34	6.06	83
Canned miscellaneous vegetables	17.85	17.52	98
Dried peas	0.36	0.39	108
Dried beans	2.55	2.03	80
Dried miscellaneous vegetables	7.38	5.77	78
Dried processed vegetables	0.34	0.19	56
Frozen vegetable juices	0.06	0.02	33
Fresh and canned vegetable juices	7.23	6.79	94
Sugar and other sweets	**117.39**	**108.07**	**92**
Candy and chewing gum	75.44	66.77	89
Sugar	15.56	14.03	90
Artificial sweeteners	4.33	5.45	126
Jams, preserves, other sweets	22.06	21.84	99
Fats and oils	**85.16**	**78.40**	**92**
Margarine	9.86	10.69	108
Fats and oils	26.08	25.09	96
Salad dressings	27.01	21.29	79
Nondairy cream and imitation milk	9.33	9.03	97
Peanut butter	12.89	12.30	95
Miscellaneous foods	**471.92**	**339.52**	**72**
Frozen prepared foods	98.09	70.88	72
Frozen meals	29.88	27.01	90
Other frozen prepared foods	68.22	43.87	64
Canned and packaged soups	35.82	36.13	101
Potato chips, nuts, and other snacks	100.53	72.94	73
Potato chips and other snacks	76.37	45.04	59
Nuts	24.16	27.90	115
Condiments and seasonings	86.81	65.59	76
Salt, spices, and other seasonings	21.14	16.05	76
Olives, pickles, relishes	9.70	8.53	88
Sauces and gravies	37.78	25.18	67
Baking needs and miscellaneous products	18.19	15.82	87
Other canned/packaged prepared foods	150.67	93.98	62
Prepared salads	21.46	18.46	86
Prepared desserts	10.32	9.11	88
Baby food	31.57	5.55	18
Miscellaneous prepared foods	87.24	60.87	70
Nonalcoholic beverages	253.94	178.34	70
Cola	81.11	50.64	62
Other carbonated drinks	43.93	27.25	62
Coffee	41.59	41.10	99
Roasted coffee	27.38	23.33	85
Instant and freeze-dried coffee	14.21	17.77	125
Noncarbonated fruit-flavored drinks	18.95	9.62	51

	total consumer units	CUs headed by people aged 65 or older	
		average spending	indexed spending
Tea	$15.86	$15.20	96
Nonalcoholic beer	0.64	0.27	42
Other nonalcoholic beverages and ice	51.85	34.25	66
Food prepared by CU on trips	41.20	33.29	81
FOOD AWAY FROM HOME	**2,276.29**	**1,362.18**	**60**
Meals at restaurants, carry-outs, other	**1,866.42**	**1,162.92**	**62**
Lunch	685.79	396.49	58
• At fast food, take-out, delivery, concession stands, buffet, and cafeteria (other than employer and school cafeteria)	377.71	179.79	48
• At full-service restaurants	224.82	197.31	88
• At vending machines, mobile vendors	5.50	1.94	35
• At employer and school cafeterias	77.76	17.46	22
Dinner	736.54	511.60	69
• At fast food, take-out, delivery, concession stands, buffet, and cafeteria (other than employer and school cafeteria)	213.33	93.34	44
• At full-service restaurants	518.02	416.65	80
• At vending machines, mobile vendors	1.87	0.90	48
• At employer and school cafeterias	3.32	0.71	21
Snacks and nonalcoholic beverages	262.67	123.36	47
• At fast food, take-out, delivery, concession stands, buffet, and cafeteria (other than employer and school cafeteria)	185.69	84.09	45
• At full-service restaurants	30.17	27.16	90
• At vending machines, mobile vendors	36.71	10.37	28
• At employer and school cafeterias	10.11	1.75	17
Breakfast and brunch	181.42	131.47	72
• At fast food, take-out, delivery, concession stands, buffet, and cafeteria (other than employer and school cafeteria)	87.83	46.15	53
• At full-service restaurants	87.08	83.21	96
• At vending machines, mobile vendors	1.40	0.83	59
• At employer and school cafeterias	5.11	1.28	25
Board (including at school)	**46.54**	**13.53**	**29**
Catered affairs	**69.00**	**18.50**	**27**
Food on trips	**211.49**	**159.18**	**75**
School lunches	**60.00**	**4.00**	**7**
Meals as pay	**22.86**	**4.06**	**18**
ALCOHOLIC BEVERAGES	**$375.95**	**$236.89**	**63**
At home	**228.08**	**162.85**	**71**
Beer and ale	112.34	47.39	42
Whiskey	13.90	20.49	147
Wine	77.75	73.90	95
Other alcoholic beverages	24.09	21.07	87

	total consumer units	CUs headed by people aged 65 or older	
		average spending	indexed spending
Away from home	$147.87	$74.04	50
Beer and ale	52.86	27.27	52
• At fast food, take-out, delivery, concession stands, buffet, and cafeteria	7.99	2.85	36
• At full-service restaurants	41.95	23.75	57
• At vending machines, mobile vendors	0.32	0.09	28
• At catered affairs	2.59	0.57	22
Wine	25.85	13.87	54
• At fast food, take-out, delivery, concession stands, buffet and cafeteria	4.41	1.61	37
• At full-service restaurants	20.36	12.14	60
• At catered affairs	1.09	0.11	10
Other alcoholic beverages	69.16	32.90	48
• At fast food, take-out, delivery, concession stands, buffet, and cafeteria	3.50	0.90	26
• At full-service restaurants	28.94	13.53	47
• At catered affairs	3.94	0.25	6
Alcoholic beverages purchased on trips	32.78	18.23	56
HOUSING	**$13,283.08**	**$9,175.55**	**69**
SHELTER	**7,829.41**	**4,833.78**	**62**
Owned dwellings*	**5,164.96**	**3,162.27**	**61**
Mortgage interest and charges	2,962.16	897.07	30
Mortgage interest	2,811.49	812.25	29
Interest paid, home equity loan	88.61	53.41	60
Interest paid, home equity line of credit	61.88	31.40	51
Property taxes	1,242.36	1,199.35	97
Maintenance, repairs, insurance, other expenses	960.43	1,065.85	111
Homeowner's insurance	283.30	317.62	112
Ground rent	40.96	58.25	142
Maintenance and repair services	519.60	584.53	112
Painting and papering	55.58	54.38	98
Plumbing and water heating	46.63	70.83	152
Heat, air conditioning, electrical work	86.28	101.43	118
Roofing and gutters	71.20	112.16	158
Other repair and maintenance services	214.77	206.50	96
Repair, replacement of hard-surface flooring	43.54	37.12	85
Repair of built-in appliances	1.62	2.11	130
Maintenance and repair materials	83.75	57.00	68
Paints, wallpaper, and supplies	14.71	6.20	42
Tools, equipment for painting, wallpapering	1.58	0.67	42
Plumbing supplies and equipment	5.62	4.44	79
Electrical supplies, heating, cooling equip.	3.46	4.89	141
Hard-surface flooring, repair and replacement	8.72	6.84	78
Roofing and gutters	5.29	2.47	47
Plaster, paneling, siding, windows, doors, screens, awnings	13.92	10.91	78
Patio, walk, fence, driveway, masonry, brick, and stucco materials	1.29	1.06	82

	total consumer units	CUs headed by people aged 65 or older	
		average spending	indexed spending
Landscape maintenance	$4.73	$1.46	31
Miscellaneous supplies and equipment	24.43	18.05	74
Insulation, other maintenance, repair	13.15	11.18	85
Finish basement, remodel rooms, build patios, walks, etc.	11.28	6.87	61
Property management and security	27.64	40.40	146
Property management	21.94	30.97	141
Management and upkeep services for security	5.71	9.43	165
Parking	5.17	8.06	156
Rented dwellings	**2,159.89**	**1,258.81**	**58**
Rent	2,104.66	1,219.69	58
Rent as pay	27.17	18.23	67
Maintenance, insurance, and other expenses	28.06	20.88	74
Tenant's insurance	8.90	6.54	73
Maintenance and repair services	11.16	12.18	109
Repair and maintenance services	10.58	11.11	105
Repair, replacement of hard-surface flooring	0.51	1.03	202
Repair of built-in appliances	0.07	0.04	57
Maintenance and repair materials	8.00	2.15	27
Paint, wallpaper, and supplies	1.01	0.02	2
Painting and wallpapering tools	0.11	–	–
Plastering, paneling, roofing, gutters, etc.	0.90	–	–
Plumbing supplies and equipment	0.80	0.18	23
Electrical supplies, heating, cooling equip.	0.30	–	–
Miscellaneous supplies and equipment	3.67	1.82	50
Insulation, other maintenance and repair	1.09	0.43	39
Materials for additions, finishing basements, remodeling rooms	2.43	1.30	53
Construction materials for jobs not started	0.15	0.09	60
Hard-surface flooring	0.73	0.10	14
Landscape maintenance	0.49	0.03	6
Other lodging	**504.56**	**412.71**	**82**
Owned vacation homes	171.55	171.15	100
Mortgage interest and charges	71.98	29.43	41
Property taxes	63.76	97.07	152
Maintenance, insurance and other expenses	35.81	44.65	125
Homeowner's insurance	9.70	14.92	154
Ground rent	2.93	7.92	270
Maintenance and repair services	16.76	15.15	90
Maintenance and repair materials	2.07	2.10	101
Property management and security	3.60	3.64	101
Property management	2.50	2.69	108
Management, upkeep services for security	1.10	0.95	86
Parking	0.76	0.92	121
Housing while attending school	80.14	16.23	20
Lodging on trips	252.87	225.33	89

	total consumer units	CUs headed by people aged 65 or older	
		average spending	indexed spending
UTILITIES, FUELS, PUBLIC SERVICES	**$2,684.32**	**$2,370.52**	**88**
Natural gas	**329.75**	**337.54**	**102**
Natural gas (renter)	60.32	36.77	61
Natural gas (owner)	266.79	296.85	111
Natural gas (vacation)	2.54	3.80	150
Electricity	**981.09**	**894.37**	**91**
Electricity (renter)	223.26	98.57	44
Electricity (owner)	750.48	783.42	104
Electricity (vacation)	6.32	10.72	170
Fuel oil and other fuels	**88.41**	**118.69**	**134**
Fuel oil	45.98	63.50	138
Fuel oil (renter)	4.64	2.30	50
Fuel oil (owner)	40.98	60.80	148
Fuel oil (vacation)	0.36	0.40	111
Coal	0.07	–	–
Bottled/tank gas	35.27	43.33	123
Gas (renter)	5.09	4.46	88
Gas (owner)	27.19	36.45	134
Gas (vacation)	2.98	2.34	79
Wood and other fuels	7.09	11.85	167
Wood and other fuels (renter)	1.32	1.60	121
Wood and other fuels (owner)	5.68	10.18	179
Telephone services	**956.74**	**688.57**	**72**
Residential telephone and pay phones	641.00	554.93	87
Cellular phone service	293.76	125.13	43
Pager service	1.71	0.62	36
Phone cards	20.28	7.89	39
Water and other public services	**328.33**	**331.36**	**101**
Water and sewerage maintenance	237.16	232.98	98
Water and sewerage maintenance (renter)	32.76	14.13	43
Water and sewerage maintenance (owner)	201.79	213.58	106
Water and sewerage maintenance (vacation)	2.36	5.02	213
Trash and garbage collection	89.05	96.34	108
Trash and garbage collection (renter)	9.89	3.63	37
Trash and garbage collection (owner)	76.61	89.79	117
Trash and garbage collection (vacation)	2.53	2.88	114
Septic tank cleaning	2.12	2.03	96
HOUSEHOLD SERVICES	**705.71**	**602.47**	**85**
Personal services	**331.02**	**218.00**	**66**
Babysitting, child care in your own home	35.91	0.28	1
Babysitting, child care in someone else's home	27.48	0.51	2
Care for elderly, invalids, handicapped, etc.	50.07	175.86	351
Adult day care centers	6.81	26.49	389
Day care centers, nurseries, and preschools	210.74	14.86	7
Other household services	**374.70**	**384.47**	**103**
Housekeeping services	79.90	97.30	122
Gardening, lawn care service	72.38	116.47	161
Water softening service	3.15	2.78	88

	total consumer units	CUs headed by people aged 65 or older	
		average spending	indexed spending
Nonclothing laundry, dry cleaning, sent out	$1.72	$2.13	124
Nonclothing laundry, dry cleaning, coin-operated	4.13	2.13	52
Termite/pest control services	13.25	20.70	156
Home security system service fee	17.40	15.06	87
Other home services	15.06	19.98	133
Termite/pest control products	0.68	1.06	156
Moving, storage, and freight express	33.13	21.64	65
Appliance repair, including service center	10.86	14.90	137
Reupholstering and furniture repair	7.40	6.96	94
Repairs/rentals of lawn/garden equipment, hand/power tools, etc.	3.62	5.25	145
Appliance rental	1.07	0.25	23
Rental of office equipment, nonbusiness use	0.41	–	–
Repair of misc. household equip., furnishings	0.62	0.72	116
Repair of computer systems, nonbusiness use	2.53	1.94	77
Computer information services	107.29	55.20	51
HOUSEKEEPING SUPPLIES	**545.28**	**465.65**	**85**
Laundry and cleaning supplies	**130.57**	**109.53**	**84**
Soaps and detergents	72.89	57.85	79
Other laundry cleaning products	57.68	51.68	90
Other household products	**283.28**	**212.78**	**75**
Cleansing and toilet tissue, paper towels, and napkins	76.46	71.32	93
Miscellaneous household products	96.81	69.69	72
Lawn and garden supplies	110.01	71.77	65
Postage and stationery	**131.44**	**143.34**	**109**
Stationery, stationery supplies, giftwrap	60.20	48.17	80
Postage	69.12	94.12	136
Delivery services	2.12	1.05	50
HOUSEHOLD FURNISHINGS, EQUIPMENT	**1,518.36**	**903.13**	**59**
Household textiles	**135.52**	**106.06**	**78**
Bathroom linens	22.35	18.04	81
Bedroom linens	65.98	45.43	69
Kitchen and dining room linens	10.11	10.38	103
Curtains and draperies	16.65	13.75	83
Slipcovers and decorative pillows	7.40	8.57	116
Sewing materials for household items	11.44	8.89	78
Other linens	1.59	1.00	63
Furniture	**401.28**	**186.12**	**46**
Mattresses and springs	52.91	34.55	65
Other bedroom furniture	68.33	19.35	28
Sofas	85.33	46.65	55
Living room chairs	39.21	35.07	89
Living room tables	18.03	7.33	41
Kitchen and dining room furniture	61.28	13.62	22
Infants' furniture	6.46	1.66	26
Outdoor furniture	16.79	9.18	55
Wall units, cabinets, and other furniture	52.94	18.70	35

	total consumer units	CUs headed by people aged 65 or older	
		average spending	indexed spending
Floor coverings	**$40.49**	**$30.33**	**75**
Wall-to-wall carpeting (renter)	0.65	–	–
Wall-to-wall carpet (replacement) (owner)	21.04	21.60	103
Floor coverings, nonpermanent	18.79	8.73	46
Major appliances	**188.47**	**138.63**	**74**
Dishwashers (built-in), garbage disposals, range hoods (renter)	1.24	0.50	40
Dishwashers (built-in), garbage disposals, range hoods (owner)	15.28	9.93	65
Refrigerators and freezers (renter)	5.58	3.46	62
Refrigerators and freezers (owner)	46.50	40.92	88
Washing machines (renter)	4.42	2.39	54
Washing machines (owner)	17.88	15.49	87
Clothes dryers (renter)	3.17	0.75	24
Clothes dryers (owner)	13.88	7.24	52
Cooking stoves, ovens (renter)	2.86	1.38	48
Cooking stoves, ovens (owner)	28.09	23.18	83
Microwave ovens (renter)	2.14	1.25	58
Microwave ovens (owner)	8.36	8.32	100
Portable dishwasher (renter)	0.25	0.20	80
Portable dishwasher (owner)	0.51	–	–
Window air conditioners (renter)	1.83	1.18	64
Window air conditioners (owner)	6.07	5.34	88
Electric floor-cleaning equipment	22.80	9.39	41
Sewing machines	4.79	4.83	101
Miscellaneous household appliances	**2.81**	**2.86**	**102**
Small appliances and misc. housewares	100.43	68.28	68
Housewares	77.55	50.68	65
Plastic dinnerware	1.57	0.64	41
China and other dinnerware	14.51	10.51	72
Flatware	3.79	2.21	58
Glassware	6.51	3.47	53
Silver serving pieces	4.05	4.00	99
Other serving pieces	1.44	0.54	38
Nonelectric cookware	24.25	17.40	72
Tableware, nonelectric kitchenware	21.44	11.91	56
Small appliances	22.89	17.61	77
Small electric kitchen appliances	17.18	14.01	82
Portable heating and cooling equipment	5.70	3.60	63
Miscellaneous household equipment	**652.17**	**373.70**	**57**
Window coverings	13.91	10.43	75
Infants' equipment	12.96	2.10	16
Laundry and cleaning equipment	15.15	11.83	78
Outdoor equipment	31.52	7.52	24
Clocks	5.87	2.68	46
Lamps and lighting fixtures	11.74	5.37	46
Other household decorative items	144.94	100.93	70
Telephones and accessories	32.73	33.33	102
Lawn and garden equipment	48.16	33.64	70

	total consumer units	CUs headed by people aged 65 or older	
		average spending	indexed spending
Power tools	$33.27	$9.97	30
Office furniture for home use	10.57	4.57	43
Hand tools	8.05	4.30	53
Indoor plants and fresh flowers	49.78	43.25	87
Closet and storage items	9.98	5.30	53
Rental of furniture	4.60	0.74	16
Luggage	5.98	4.18	70
Computers and computer hardware, nonbusiness use	138.58	42.33	31
Computer software and accessories, nonbusiness use	17.67	8.29	47
Telephone answering devices	1.08	0.68	63
Calculators	1.44	0.31	22
Business equipment for home use	0.97	0.94	97
Other hardware	12.85	11.34	88
Smoke alarms (owner)	1.10	0.98	89
Smoke alarms (renter)	0.39	–	–
Other household appliances (owner)	8.00	6.13	77
Other household appliances (renter)	1.23	0.42	34
Miscellaneous household equipment and parts	29.62	22.15	75
APPAREL AND SERVICES	**$1,749.22**	**$972.38**	**56**
Men's apparel	**319.48**	**182.11**	**57**
Suits	32.96	17.00	52
Sport coats and tailored jackets	10.65	6.23	58
Coats and jackets	33.86	19.54	58
Underwear	15.27	10.45	68
Hosiery	12.22	6.47	53
Nightwear	2.98	2.16	72
Accessories	22.41	14.59	65
Sweaters and vests	15.68	9.54	61
Active sportswear	15.13	10.05	66
Shirts	78.89	38.99	49
Pants	57.64	37.67	65
Shorts and shorts sets	12.22	5.40	44
Uniforms	3.21	0.63	20
Costumes	6.35	3.38	53
Boys' (aged 2 to 15) apparel	**89.98**	**25.64**	**28**
Coats and jackets	6.38	1.16	18
Sweaters	3.65	1.23	34
Shirts	19.50	6.03	31
Underwear	5.02	1.40	28
Nightwear	2.59	1.95	75
Hosiery	4.21	1.16	28
Accessories	4.12	1.65	40
Suits, sport coats, and vests	2.37	0.96	41
Pants	22.58	6.23	28
Shorts and shorts sets	8.66	1.51	17
Uniforms	3.35	0.79	24
Active sportswear	3.84	0.52	14
Costumes	3.72	1.03	28

	total consumer units	CUs headed by people aged 65 or older average spending	indexed spending
Women's apparel	**$586.91**	**$424.17**	**72**
Coats and jackets	50.06	38.69	77
Dresses	56.40	36.46	65
Sport coats and tailored jackets	6.48	5.60	86
Sweaters and vests	50.47	34.54	68
Shirts, blouses, and tops	103.24	75.63	73
Skirts	17.48	9.44	54
Pants	96.29	66.31	69
Shorts and shorts sets	16.09	13.11	81
Active sportswear	30.07	20.88	69
Nightwear	27.63	26.28	95
Undergarments	33.55	23.03	69
Hosiery	21.22	20.00	94
Suits	29.01	20.22	70
Accessories	33.37	25.31	76
Uniforms	6.12	2.39	39
Costumes	9.42	6.29	67
Girls' (aged 2 to 15) apparel	**117.21**	**26.11**	**22**
Coats and jackets	6.49	2.09	32
Dresses and suits	12.41	2.18	18
Shirts, blouses, and sweaters	29.33	5.96	20
Skirts and pants	24.07	6.13	25
Shorts and shorts sets	8.28	2.35	28
Active sportswear	9.32	3.62	39
Underwear and nightwear	7.63	1.79	23
Hosiery	4.30	0.42	10
Accessories	5.81	0.46	8
Uniforms	4.77	0.38	8
Costumes	4.80	0.72	15
Children under age 2	**82.60**	**21.15**	**26**
Coats, jackets, and snowsuits	2.43	1.14	47
Outerwear including dresses	23.71	10.57	45
Underwear	43.60	5.74	13
Nightwear and loungewear	4.07	1.72	42
Accessories	8.79	1.98	23
Footwear	**313.17**	**159.71**	**51**
Men's	102.90	66.59	65
Boys'	36.87	6.43	17
Women's	141.64	80.94	57
Girls'	31.76	5.75	18
Other apparel products and services	**239.87**	**133.50**	**56**
Material for making clothes	5.11	8.49	166
Sewing patterns and notions	8.20	8.13	99
Watches	13.62	8.62	63
Jewelry	89.65	40.18	45
Shoe repair and other shoe services	1.44	1.25	87
Coin-operated apparel laundry and dry cleaning	37.58	18.46	49
Apparel alteration, repair, and tailoring services	5.86	4.46	76
Clothing rental	2.66	0.61	23
Watch and jewelry repair	5.49	6.63	121
Professional laundry, dry cleaning	69.69	35.77	51
Clothing storage	0.55	0.90	164

	total consumer units	CUs headed by people aged 65 or older	
		average spending	indexed spending
TRANSPORTATION	**$7,759.29**	**$4,480.51**	**58**
VEHICLE PURCHASES	**3,664.93**	**1,817.80**	**50**
Cars and trucks, new	**1,752.96**	**1,038.46**	**59**
New cars	883.08	641.32	73
New trucks	869.88	397.14	46
Cars and trucks, used	**1,842.29**	**761.50**	**41**
Used cars	1,113.46	550.71	49
Used trucks	728.82	210.78	29
Other vehicles	**69.68**	**17.84**	**26**
New motorcycles	36.26	17.84	49
Used motorcycles	33.42	–	–
GASOLINE AND MOTOR OIL	**1,235.06**	**776.53**	**63**
Gasoline	1,125.01	694.21	62
Diesel fuel	10.86	11.63	107
Gasoline on trips	88.24	65.16	74
Motor oil	10.05	4.88	49
Motor oil on trips	0.89	0.66	74
OTHER VEHICLE EXPENSES	**2,470.55**	**1,585.79**	**64**
Vehicle finance charges	**397.04**	**153.29**	**39**
Automobile finance charges	193.12	81.92	42
Truck finance charges	182.89	60.85	33
Motorcycle and plane finance charges	2.36	0.27	11
Other vehicle finance charges	18.67	10.25	55
Maintenance and repairs	**697.30**	**481.95**	**69**
Coolant, additives, brake, transmission fluids	3.82	1.88	49
Tires—purchased, replaced, installed	89.93	59.71	66
Parts, equipment, and accessories	41.70	27.76	67
Vehicle audio equipment, excl. labor	12.32	–	–
Vehicle products	4.92	2.04	41
Miscellaneous auto repair, servicing	43.69	22.10	51
Body work and painting	31.24	28.37	91
Clutch, transmission repair	48.68	30.42	62
Drive shaft and rear-end repair	6.51	1.85	28
Brake work	57.73	35.93	62
Repair to steering or front-end	16.91	13.04	77
Repair to engine cooling system	21.68	19.47	90
Motor tune-up	49.69	34.09	69
Lube, oil change, and oil filters	65.07	51.41	79
Front-end alignment, wheel balance, rotation	11.90	7.50	63
Shock absorber replacement	4.82	3.09	64
Gas tank repair, replacement	4.32	5.10	118
Tire repair and other repair work	39.83	29.81	75
Vehicle air conditioning repair	17.00	18.16	107
Exhaust system repair	12.56	11.58	92
Electrical system repair	28.42	26.87	95
Motor repair, replacement	76.62	49.10	64
Auto repair service policy	7.93	2.65	33

	total consumer units	CUs headed by people aged 65 or older average spending	CUs headed by people aged 65 or older indexed spending
Vehicle insurance	**$893.50**	**$666.24**	**75**
Vehicle rental, leases, licenses, other charges	**482.71**	**284.31**	**59**
Leased and rented vehicles	324.48	168.50	52
Rented vehicles	41.33	28.26	68
Auto rental	6.76	6.75	100
Auto rental on trips	28.28	16.99	60
Truck rental	2.21	1.79	81
Truck rental on trips	3.55	2.58	73
Leased vehicles	283.15	140.24	50
Car lease payments	149.63	95.51	64
Cash down payment (car lease)	11.13	5.23	47
Termination fee (car lease)	1.28	2.70	211
Truck lease payments	114.24	35.68	31
Cash down payment (truck lease)	4.92	–	–
Termination fee (truck lease)	1.94	1.13	58
Vehicle registration, state	72.82	58.78	81
Vehicle registration, local	7.76	6.14	79
Driver's license	6.26	5.16	82
Vehicle inspection	9.26	7.87	85
Parking fees	29.25	11.11	38
Parking fees in home city, excluding residence	24.24	7.79	32
Parking fees on trips	5.01	3.33	66
Tolls	10.59	4.35	41
Tolls on trips	3.94	2.74	70
Towing charges	5.60	2.45	44
Automobile service clubs	12.75	17.21	135
PUBLIC TRANSPORTATION	**388.75**	**300.40**	**77**
Airline fares	243.57	174.66	72
Intercity bus fares	11.48	13.18	115
Intracity mass transit fares	49.97	18.85	38
Local transportation on trips	10.91	10.62	97
Taxi fares and limousine service on trips	6.41	6.23	97
Taxi fares and limousine service	18.95	18.04	95
Intercity train fares	16.09	17.16	107
Ship fares	29.74	40.33	136
School bus	1.64	1.33	81
HEALTH CARE	**$2,350.32**	**$3,586.01**	**153**
HEALTH INSURANCE	**1,167.71**	**1,885.51**	**161**
Commercial health insurance	**217.53**	**138.90**	**64**
Traditional fee-for-service health plan (not BCBS)	68.27	82.73	121
Preferred-provider health plan (not BCBS)	149.26	56.17	38
Blue Cross, Blue Shield	**315.67**	**357.87**	**113**
Traditional fee-for-service health plan	53.76	63.99	119
Preferred-provider health plan	106.99	48.08	45
Health maintenance organization	101.53	70.17	69
Commercial Medicare supplement	47.35	167.47	354
Other BCBS health insurance	6.05	8.15	135

	total consumer units	CUs headed by people aged 65 or older	
		average spending	indexed spending
Health maintenance plans (HMOs)	$280.47	$186.57	67
Medicare payments	186.87	749.82	401
Commercial Medicare supplements/			
other health insurance	167.18	452.35	271
Commercial Medicare supplement (not BCBS)	106.32	346.06	325
Other health insurance (not BCBS)	60.86	106.29	175
MEDICAL SERVICES	589.87	582.48	99
Physician's services	147.53	121.03	82
Dental services	226.99	273.51	120
Eye care services	34.20	35.47	104
Service by professionals other than physician	42.76	33.49	78
Lab tests, X-rays	26.79	24.26	91
Hospital room	36.57	23.80	65
Hospital services other than room	51.51	35.87	70
Care in convalescent or nursing home	12.46	27.34	219
Other medical services	9.46	7.72	82
DRUGS	487.43	954.81	196
Nonprescription drugs	64.45	89.71	139
Nonprescription vitamins	49.15	61.10	124
Prescription drugs	373.83	804.00	215
MEDICAL SUPPLIES	105.31	163.21	155
Eyeglasses and contact lenses	52.26	51.27	98
Hearing aids	14.98	52.76	352
Topicals and dressings	27.56	33.36	121
Medical equipment for general use	2.69	4.19	156
Supportive, convalescent medical equipment	5.21	13.05	250
Rental of medical equipment	1.06	4.03	380
Rental of supportive, convalescent			
medical equipment	1.55	4.56	294
ENTERTAINMENT	$2,078.99	$1,139.18	55
FEES AND ADMISSIONS	541.67	300.80	56
Recreation expenses on trips	25.64	15.71	61
Social, recreation, civic club membership	107.92	73.96	69
Fees for participant sports	75.05	64.47	86
Participant sports on trips	29.50	19.01	64
Movie, theater, opera, ballet	98.30	46.33	47
Movie, other admissions on trips	45.57	26.15	57
Admission to sports events	36.18	15.08	42
Admission to sports events on trips	15.19	8.72	57
Fees for recreational lessons	82.69	15.66	19
Other entertainment services on trips	25.64	15.71	61
TELEVISION, RADIO, SOUND EQUIPMENT	691.90	460.68	67
Television	543.66	413.78	76
Cable service and community antenna	382.28	343.44	90
Black-and-white TV	0.80	0.15	19
Color TV, console	38.63	12.65	33
Color TV, portable, table model	39.14	27.08	69

	total consumer units	CUs headed by people aged 65 or older average spending	indexed spending
VCRs and video disc players	$23.25	$8.95	38
Video cassettes, tapes, and discs	33.13	14.71	44
Video game hardware and software	23.46	4.19	18
Repair of TV, radio, and sound equipment	2.50	2.53	101
Rental of television sets	0.46	0.07	15
Radio and sound equipment	**148.25**	**46.90**	**32**
Radios	3.98	3.74	94
Tape recorders and players	5.31	2.29	43
Sound components and component systems	20.19	7.43	37
Miscellaneous sound equipment	3.18	–	–
Sound equipment accessories	5.97	3.55	59
Satellite dishes	1.00	0.56	56
Compact disc, tape, record, video mail order clubs	6.53	3.25	50
Records, CDs, audio tapes, needles	36.47	10.78	30
Rental of VCR, radio, sound equipment	0.25	0.07	28
Musical instruments and accessories	24.82	7.89	32
Rental and repair of musical instruments	1.22	0.20	16
Rental of video cassettes, tapes, discs, films	39.33	7.14	18
PETS, TOYS, PLAYGROUND EQUIPMENT	**369.12**	**200.45**	**54**
Pets	**248.25**	**148.12**	**60**
Pet food	102.56	70.38	69
Pet purchase, supplies, and medicines	52.29	17.83	34
Pet services	21.95	14.81	67
Veterinarian services	71.44	45.10	63
Toys, games, hobbies, and tricycles	**117.34**	**51.86**	**44**
Playground equipment	**3.54**	**0.47**	**13**
OTHER ENTERTAINMENT SUPPLIES, EQUIPMENT, SERVICES	**476.30**	**177.25**	**37**
Unmotored recreational vehicles	**47.14**	**10.57**	**22**
Boat without motor and boat trailers	16.15	4.80	30
Trailer and other attachable campers	30.99	5.78	19
Motorized recreational vehicles	**170.19**	**78.62**	**46**
Motorized camper	40.05	1.13	3
Other vehicle	35.47	31.99	90
Motorboats	94.67	45.50	48
Rental of recreational vehicles	**1.99**	**0.53**	**27**
Outboard motors	**0.71**	**0.09**	**13**
Docking and landing fees	**6.66**	**3.74**	**56**
Sports, recreation, exercise equipment	**150.33**	**44.09**	**29**
Athletic gear, game tables, exercise equipment	60.51	28.03	46
Bicycles	13.45	2.13	16
Camping equipment	9.59	1.54	16
Hunting and fishing equipment	35.68	7.13	20
Winter sports equipment	5.45	0.79	14
Water sports equipment	8.95	0.29	3
Other sports equipment	14.62	2.98	20
Rental and repair of misc. sports equipment	2.07	1.20	58

	total consumer units	CUs headed by people aged 65 or older	
		average spending	indexed spending
Photographic equipment and supplies	**$90.48**	**$36.68**	**41**
Film	17.74	8.74	49
Other photographic supplies	2.27	1.39	61
Film processing	26.60	13.33	50
Repair and rental of photographic equipment	0.12	0.16	133
Photographic equipment	23.34	9.30	40
Photographer fees	20.42	3.78	19
Fireworks	**1.52**	–	–
Souvenirs	**1.25**	**0.31**	**25**
Visual goods	**1.19**	**0.16**	**13**
Pinball, electronic video games	**4.84**	**2.45**	**51**
PERSONAL CARE PRODUCTS AND SERVICES	**$525.80**	**$451.05**	**86**
Personal care products	**276.65**	**210.36**	**76**
Hair care products	53.57	33.42	62
Hair accessories	6.57	4.11	63
Wigs and hairpieces	1.32	0.84	64
Oral hygiene products	27.33	24.86	91
Shaving products	15.09	8.94	59
Cosmetics, perfume, and bath products	129.13	102.04	79
Deodorants, feminine hygiene, misc. products	30.29	25.27	83
Electric personal care appliances	13.34	10.88	82
Personal care services	**249.15**	**240.69**	**97**
READING	**$138.57**	**$147.39**	**106**
Newspaper subscriptions	43.88	73.97	169
Newspaper, nonsubscription	11.30	11.23	99
Magazine subscriptions	16.59	20.20	122
Magazines, nonsubscription	9.35	5.32	57
Books purchased through book clubs	6.62	7.78	118
Books not purchased through book clubs	50.38	28.74	57
Encyclopedia and other reference book sets	0.33	0.15	45
EDUCATION	**$751.95**	**$202.36**	**27**
College tuition	444.45	113.86	26
Elementary and high school tuition	128.94	35.03	27
Other school tuition	25.53	11.10	43
Other school expenses including rentals	25.77	4.01	16
Books, supplies for college	57.93	10.46	18
Books, supplies for elementary, high school	16.14	1.58	10
Books, supplies for day care, nursery school	3.39	0.74	22
Miscellaneous school expenses and supplies	49.80	25.59	51

	total consumer units	CUs headed by people aged 65 or older	
		average spending	indexed spending
TOBACCO PRODUCTS AND SMOKING SUPPLIES	**$320.49**	**$152.01**	**47**
Cigarettes	291.89	133.21	46
Other tobacco products	26.27	16.00	61
Smoking accessories	2.33	2.80	120
FINANCIAL PRODUCTS, SERVICES	**$788.12**	**$685.86**	**87**
Miscellaneous fees	2.25	0.92	41
Lottery and gambling losses	46.94	64.65	138
Legal fees	132.99	105.06	79
Funeral expenses	77.91	150.98	194
Safe deposit box rental	3.84	7.18	187
Checking accounts, other bank service charges	25.91	11.59	45
Cemetery lots, vaults, and maintenance fees	16.05	43.13	269
Accounting fees	57.85	67.56	117
Miscellaneous personal services	39.77	29.52	74
Finance charges, except mortgage and vehicles	271.37	134.04	49
Occupational expenses	38.46	6.85	18
Expenses for other properties	65.99	58.48	89
Credit card memberships	2.82	1.56	55
Shopping club membership fees	5.97	4.31	72
CASH CONTRIBUTIONS	**$1,277.10**	**$1,678.79**	**131**
Support for college students	75.94	41.48	55
Alimony expenditures	21.18	19.49	92
Child support expenditures	190.75	40.70	21
Gifts to non-CU members of stocks, bonds, and mutual funds	24.23	90.31	373
Cash contributions to charities and other organizations	137.62	220.96	161
Cash contributions to church, religious organizations	557.29	669.05	120
Cash contributions to educational institutions	33.42	58.09	174
Cash contributions to political organizations	10.90	26.43	242
Other cash gifts	225.76	512.28	227
PERSONAL INSURANCE, PENSIONS	**$3,898.62**	**$1,286.39**	**33**
Life and other personal insurance	**406.11**	**406.60**	**100**
Life, endowment, annuity, other personal insurance	391.65	389.85	100
Other nonhealth insurance	14.46	16.75	116
Pensions and Social Security	**3,492.51**	**879.79**	**25**
Deductions for government retirement	69.48	4.97	7
Deductions for railroad retirement	2.21	–	–
Deductions for private pensions	390.38	62.76	16
Nonpayroll deposit to retirement plans	426.12	199.47	47
Deductions for Social Security	2,604.32	612.60	24

	total consumer units	CUs headed by people aged 65 or older	
		average spending	indexed spending
PERSONAL TAXES	**$2,496.26**	**$1,037.29**	**42**
Federal income taxes	1,842.57	725.00	39
State and local income taxes	506.45	143.77	28
Other taxes	147.24	168.52	114
GIFTS FOR NON-HOUSEHOLD MEMBERS**	**$1,036.24**	**$831.92**	**80**
FOOD	**82.18**	**49.07**	**60**
Cakes and cupcakes	2.41	0.98	41
Other fresh fruits (excl. apples, bananas, citrus)	2.26	1.81	80
Candy and chewing gum	11.69	15.33	131
Board (including at school)	21.90	8.91	41
Catered affairs	26.19	7.81	30
ALCOHOLIC BEVERAGES	**13.42**	**10.01**	**75**
Beer and ale	4.73	2.73	58
Wine	5.84	5.53	95
HOUSING	**258.69**	**205.54**	**79**
Housekeeping supplies	**42.48**	**42.85**	**101**
Laundry and cleaning supplies	2.93	2.35	80
Other household products	11.69	8.09	69
Miscellaneous household products	5.85	3.77	64
Lawn and garden supplies	4.20	2.53	60
Postage and stationery	27.86	32.41	116
Stationery, stationery supplies, giftwrap	21.13	21.43	101
Postage	6.14	10.60	173
Household textiles	**13.72**	**11.60**	**85**
Bathroom linens	2.59	3.37	130
Bedroom linens	6.10	3.39	56
Appliances and miscellaneous housewares	**23.98**	**21.57**	**90**
Major appliances	8.41	5.40	64
Electric floor-cleaning equipment	2.77	0.74	27
Small appliances and miscellaneous housewares	15.57	16.17	104
China and other dinnerware	2.46	3.10	126
Nonelectric cookware	3.53	4.09	116
Tableware, nonelectric kitchenware	2.63	1.28	49
Small electric kitchen appliances	2.71	3.15	116
Miscellaneous household equipment	**64.70**	**53.06**	**82**
Infants' equipment	3.82	1.33	35
Outdoor equipment	2.07	0.59	29
Other household decorative items	25.76	19.17	74
Power tools	2.80	1.18	42
Indoor plants, fresh flowers	13.43	15.15	113
Computers and computer hardware	6.59	4.58	69
Miscellaneous household equipment	2.19	2.70	123
Other housing	**113.80**	**76.47**	**67**
Repair or maintenance services	4.51	4.19	93
Housing while attending school	39.93	15.30	38

	total consumer units	CUs headed by people aged 65 or older	
		average spending	indexed spending
Natural gas (renter)	$3.62	$4.18	115
Electricity (renter)	14.67	15.32	104
Water, sewer maintenance (renter)	3.04	3.12	103
Day-care centers, nurseries, and preschools	23.81	7.41	31
APPAREL AND SERVICES	**237.13**	**193.03**	**81**
Men and boys, aged 2 or older	**63.74**	**62.41**	**98**
Men's coats and jackets	5.09	1.80	35
Men's accessories	4.45	2.88	65
Men's sweaters and vests	3.06	2.50	82
Men's active sportswear	2.76	4.59	166
Men's shirts	16.79	14.36	86
Men's pants	6.93	8.34	120
Boys' shirts	3.71	5.23	141
Boys' pants	3.76	4.73	126
Women and girls, aged 2 or older	**81.76**	**77.13**	**94**
Women's coats and jackets	5.62	3.31	59
Women's dresses	7.66	8.30	108
Women's vests and sweaters	8.50	5.67	67
Women's shirts, tops, blouses	9.06	10.87	120
Women's pants	6.62	6.11	92
Women's active sportswear	4.33	5.66	131
Women's sleepwear	6.45	6.49	101
Women's accessories	5.71	3.97	70
Girls' dresses and suits	2.98	1.63	55
Girls' shirts, blouses, sweaters	4.48	4.20	94
Girls' skirts and pants	3.32	3.22	97
Girls' accessories	2.38	0.46	19
Children under age 2	**39.99**	**20.22**	**51**
Infant dresses, outerwear	15.28	10.08	66
Infant underwear	16.91	5.58	33
Infant nightwear, loungewear	2.55	1.49	58
Infant accessories	3.93	1.98	50
Other apparel products and services	**51.63**	**33.27**	**64**
Jewelry and watches	24.01	10.51	44
Watches	2.16	2.22	103
Jewelry	21.85	8.29	38
Men's footwear	8.37	5.92	71
Boys' footwear	4.46	3.62	81
Women's footwear	8.82	5.26	60
Girls' footwear	3.30	3.50	106
TRANSPORTATION	**43.87**	**17.43**	**40**
New cars	7.09	1.64	23
Used cars	12.21	2.70	22
Airline fares	6.78	5.50	81
Ship fares	2.74	3.09	113

	total consumer units	CUs headed by people aged 65 or older	
		average spending	indexed spending
HEALTH CARE	**$32.59**	**$38.70**	**119**
Physician's services	3.07	0.59	19
Dental services	4.03	4.92	122
Care in convalescent or nursing home	5.19	13.82	266
Nonprescription vitamins	3.93	2.02	51
Prescription drugs	2.38	4.36	183
ENTERTAINMENT	**78.24**	**55.99**	**72**
Toys, games, hobbies, and tricycles	29.98	26.80	89
Other entertainment	48.26	29.19	60
Fees for recreational lessons	7.88	2.71	34
Community antenna or cable TV	6.37	6.70	105
VCRs and videodisc players	2.26	1.05	46
Video game hardware and software	2.13	1.64	77
Athletic gear, game tables, exercise equipment	6.60	4.64	70
Hunting and fishing equipment	3.06	0.89	29
Photographer fees	3.19	0.77	24
PERSONAL CARE PRODUCTS, SERVICES	**21.15**	**20.62**	**97**
Cosmetics, perfume, bath preparation	12.53	12.01	96
Electric personal care appliances	3.31	2.54	77
EDUCATION	**183.88**	**146.10**	**79**
College tuition	127.83	90.21	71
Elementary and high school tuition	25.95	31.04	120
Other school tuition	4.44	2.18	49
Other school expenses including rentals	3.99	2.12	53
College books and supplies	11.93	7.70	65
Miscellaneous school supplies	7.38	11.87	161
ALL OTHER GIFTS	**83.76**	**92.66**	**111**
Gifts of trip expenses	44.40	49.47	111
Lottery and gambling losses	2.86	1.51	53
Legal fees	5.82	15.71	270
Funeral expenses	25.25	21.23	84
Miscellaneous personal services	2.16	2.48	115

* This figure does not include the amount paid for mortgage principle, which is considered an asset.
** Expenditures on gifts are also included in the preceding product and service categories. Food spending, for example, includes the amount spent on food gifts. Only gift categories with spending of $2.00 or more by the average consumer unit are shown.
Note: The Bureau of Labor Statistics uses consumer unit rather than household as the sampling unit in the Consumer Expenditure Survey. For the definition of consumer unit, see the glossary. (–) means not applicable or the sample is too small to make a reliable estimate.
Source: Bureau of Labor Statistics, unpublished data from the 2002 Consumer Expenditure Survey; calculations by New Strategist

Table 8.5 Average and Indexed Spending of Householders Aged 65 to 74, 2002

(average annual spending of total consumer units (CUs) and average annual and indexed spending of consumer units headed by 65-to-74-year-olds, 2002)

	total consumer units	CUs headed by people aged 65 to 74 average spending	CUs headed by people aged 65 to 74 indexed spending
Number of consumer units (in 000s)	**112,108**	**11,216**	**–**
Average before-tax income	**$49,430.00**	**$35,118.00**	**71**
Average annual spending	**40,676.60**	**32,242.52**	**79**
FOOD	**$5,374.80**	**$4,479.05**	**83**
FOOD AT HOME	**3,098.52**	**2,877.08**	**93**
Cereals and bakery products	**450.13**	**418.14**	**93**
Cereals and cereal products	154.07	128.14	83
Flour	8.65	9.25	107
Prepared flour mixes	12.40	12.16	98
Ready-to-eat and cooked cereals	87.66	71.24	81
Rice	17.82	14.45	81
Pasta, cornmeal, and other cereal products	27.54	21.04	76
Bakery products	296.06	290.00	98
Bread	83.83	93.10	111
White bread	35.21	34.89	99
Bread, other than white	48.62	58.21	120
Crackers and cookies	70.67	64.77	92
Cookies	46.31	43.12	93
Crackers	24.36	21.65	89
Frozen and refrigerated bakery products	25.64	21.79	85
Other bakery products	115.92	110.34	95
Biscuits and rolls	41.04	37.70	92
Cakes and cupcakes	35.73	31.62	88
Bread and cracker products	3.50	4.23	121
Sweetrolls, coffee cakes, doughnuts	25.84	24.61	95
Pies, tarts, turnovers	9.82	12.17	124
Meats, poultry, fish, and eggs	**798.42**	**744.65**	**93**
Beef	231.17	207.53	90
Ground beef	86.29	75.09	87
Roast	40.99	37.77	92
Chuck roast	11.71	11.00	94
Round roast	10.23	10.94	107
Other roast	19.05	15.83	83
Steak	84.47	75.76	90
Round steak	13.29	9.03	68
Sirloin steak	26.62	19.33	73
Other steak	44.56	47.40	106
Pork	167.34	168.57	101
Bacon	28.45	29.51	104
Pork chops	38.43	33.47	87
Ham	37.16	42.66	115
Ham, not canned	35.66	41.32	116
Canned ham	1.50	1.33	89

	total consumer units	CUs headed by people aged 65 to 74	
		average spending	indexed spending
Sausage	$26.17	$24.94	95
Other pork	37.13	38.00	102
Other meats	101.08	97.26	96
Frankfurters	20.95	15.84	76
Lunch meats (cold cuts)	68.99	65.02	94
Bologna, liverwurst, salami	21.11	17.70	84
Lamb, organ meats, and others	11.14	16.41	147
Lamb and organ meats	7.99	11.91	149
Mutton, goat, and game	3.15	4.50	143
Poultry	144.13	123.44	86
Fresh and frozen chicken	113.25	93.34	82
Fresh and frozen whole chicken	32.08	26.95	84
Fresh and frozen chicken parts	81.17	66.38	82
Other poultry	30.88	30.10	97
Fish and seafood	120.97	114.93	95
Canned fish and seafood	16.13	19.56	121
Fresh fish and shellfish	69.31	66.48	96
Frozen fish and shellfish	35.53	28.90	81
Eggs	33.75	32.92	98
Dairy products	**328.34**	**301.03**	**92**
Fresh milk and cream	127.15	111.56	88
Fresh milk, all types	114.63	98.49	86
Cream	12.52	13.07	104
Other dairy products	201.19	189.47	94
Butter	18.48	19.64	106
Cheese	95.64	92.71	97
Ice cream and related products	58.74	53.45	91
Miscellaneous dairy products	28.33	23.67	84
Fruits and vegetables	**552.01**	**555.66**	**101**
Fresh fruits	178.20	184.83	104
Apples	32.59	30.50	94
Bananas	31.24	32.29	103
Oranges	20.34	17.19	85
Citrus fruits, excl. oranges	14.29	17.24	121
Other fresh fruits	79.74	87.61	110
Fresh vegetables	174.88	175.87	101
Potatoes	33.35	35.16	105
Lettuce	22.22	21.48	97
Tomatoes	33.71	32.82	97
Other fresh vegetables	85.60	86.41	101
Processed fruits	115.50	108.04	94
Frozen fruits and fruit juices	12.45	10.49	84
Frozen orange juice	6.31	5.76	91
Frozen fruits	2.79	2.68	96
Frozen fruit juices, excl. orange	3.35	2.05	61
Canned fruits	15.06	17.71	118
Dried fruits	6.06	8.65	143
Fresh fruit juice	22.20	23.10	104
Canned and bottled fruit juice	59.74	48.08	80

	total consumer units	CUs headed by people aged 65 to 74 average spending	indexed spending
Processed vegetables	$83.43	$86.93	104
Frozen vegetables	27.85	27.60	99
Canned and dried vegetables and juices	55.58	59.33	107
Canned beans	12.47	12.03	96
Canned corn	7.34	6.90	94
Canned miscellaneous vegetables	17.85	21.39	120
Dried peas	0.36	0.54	150
Dried beans	2.55	2.52	99
Dried miscellaneous vegetables	7.38	6.46	88
Dried processed vegetables	0.34	0.36	106
Frozen vegetable juices	0.06	0.04	67
Fresh and canned vegetable juices	7.23	9.08	126
Sugar and other sweets	**117.39**	**124.81**	**106**
Candy and chewing gum	75.44	81.00	107
Sugar	15.56	13.76	88
Artificial sweeteners	4.33	5.54	128
Jams, preserves, other sweets	22.06	24.51	111
Fats and oils	**85.16**	**89.60**	**105**
Margarine	9.86	12.00	122
Fats and oils	26.08	30.18	116
Salad dressings	27.01	24.11	89
Nondairy cream and imitation milk	9.33	10.07	108
Peanut butter	12.89	13.24	103
Miscellaneous foods	**471.92**	**392.08**	**83**
Frozen prepared foods	98.09	76.30	78
Frozen meals	29.88	28.10	94
Other frozen prepared foods	68.22	48.20	71
Canned and packaged soups	35.82	38.54	108
Potato chips, nuts, and other snacks	100.53	88.47	88
Potato chips and other snacks	76.37	54.45	71
Nuts	24.16	34.02	141
Condiments and seasonings	86.81	81.28	94
Salt, spices, and other seasonings	21.14	19.86	94
Olives, pickles, relishes	9.70	10.38	107
Sauces and gravies	37.78	32.28	85
Baking needs and miscellaneous products	18.19	18.76	103
Other canned/packaged prepared foods	150.67	107.49	71
Prepared salads	21.46	20.43	95
Prepared desserts	10.32	10.06	97
Baby food	31.57	6.26	20
Miscellaneous prepared foods	87.24	70.74	81
Nonalcoholic beverages	253.94	206.59	81
Cola	81.11	62.25	77
Other carbonated drinks	43.93	34.06	78
Coffee	41.59	43.85	105
Roasted coffee	27.38	25.57	93
Instant and freeze-dried coffee	14.21	18.28	129
Noncarbonated fruit-flavored drinks	18.95	11.71	62

	total consumer units	CUs headed by people aged 65 to 74	
		average spending	indexed spending
Tea	$15.86	$17.42	110
Nonalcoholic beer	0.64	0.53	83
Other nonalcoholic beverages and ice	51.85	36.77	71
Food prepared by CU on trips	41.20	44.53	108
FOOD AWAY FROM HOME	**2,276.29**	**1,601.98**	**70**
Meals at restaurants, carry-outs, other	**1,866.42**	**1,328.81**	**71**
Lunch	685.79	444.48	65
• At fast food, take-out, delivery, concession stands, buffet, and cafeteria (other than employer and school cafeteria)	377.71	193.16	51
• At full-service restaurants	224.82	223.40	99
• At vending machines, mobile vendors	5.50	2.88	52
• At employer and school cafeterias	77.76	25.05	32
Dinner	736.54	599.46	81
• At fast food, take-out, delivery, concession stands, buffet, and cafeteria (other than employer and school cafeteria)	213.33	97.81	46
• At full-service restaurants	518.02	500.24	97
• At vending machines, mobile vendors	1.87	0.55	29
• At employer and school cafeterias	3.32	0.86	26
Snacks and nonalcoholic beverages	262.67	142.83	54
• At fast food, take-out, delivery, concession stands, buffet, and cafeteria (other than employer and school cafeteria)	185.69	98.43	53
• At full-service restaurants	30.17	29.47	98
• At vending machines, mobile vendors	36.71	12.45	34
• At employer and school cafeterias	10.11	2.47	24
Breakfast and brunch	181.42	142.05	78
• At fast food, take-out, delivery, concession stands, buffet, and cafeteria (other than employer and school cafeteria)	87.83	50.91	58
• At full-service restaurants	87.08	88.93	102
• At vending machines, mobile vendors	1.40	0.72	51
• At employer and school cafeterias	5.11	1.48	29
Board (including at school)	**46.54**	**18.15**	**39**
Catered affairs	**69.00**	**20.77**	**30**
Food on trips	**211.49**	**223.38**	**106**
School lunches	**60.00**	**6.24**	**10**
Meals as pay	**22.86**	**4.63**	**20**
ALCOHOLIC BEVERAGES	**$375.95**	**$323.56**	**86**
At home	**228.08**	**223.83**	**98**
Beer and ale	112.34	69.76	62
Whiskey	13.90	26.10	188
Wine	77.75	98.31	126
Other alcoholic beverages	24.09	29.66	123

	total consumer units	CUs headed by people aged 65 to 74 average spending	indexed spending
Away from home	$147.87	$99.73	67
Beer and ale	52.86	35.93	68
• At fast food, take-out, delivery, concession stands, buffet, and cafeteria	7.99	3.98	50
• At full-service restaurants	41.95	30.69	73
• At vending machines, mobile vendors	0.32	0.16	50
• At catered affairs	2.59	1.10	42
Wine	25.85	16.62	64
• At fast food, take-out, delivery, concession stands, buffet and cafeteria	4.41	1.97	45
• At full-service restaurants	20.36	14.43	71
• At catered affairs	1.09	0.22	20
Other alcoholic beverages	69.16	47.18	68
• At fast food, take-out, delivery, concession stands, buffet, and cafeteria	3.50	0.81	23
• At full-service restaurants	28.94	20.61	71
• At catered affairs	3.94	0.49	12
Alcoholic beverages purchased on trips	32.78	25.27	77
HOUSING	**$13,283.08**	**$10,052.07**	**76**
SHELTER	**7,829.41**	**5,298.58**	**68**
Owned dwellings*	**5,164.96**	**3,848.81**	**75**
Mortgage interest and charges	2,962.16	1,366.37	46
Mortgage interest	2,811.49	1,230.57	44
Interest paid, home equity loan	88.61	89.04	100
Interest paid, home equity line of credit	61.88	46.77	76
Property taxes	1,242.36	1,299.27	105
Maintenance, repairs, insurance, other expenses	960.43	1,183.16	123
Homeowner's insurance	283.30	356.77	126
Ground rent	40.96	49.56	121
Maintenance and repair services	519.60	638.00	123
Painting and papering	55.58	68.14	123
Plumbing and water heating	46.63	65.92	141
Heat, air conditioning, electrical work	86.28	123.49	143
Roofing and gutters	71.20	87.97	124
Other repair and maintenance services	214.77	243.09	113
Repair, replacement of hard-surface flooring	43.54	46.69	107
Repair of built-in appliances	1.62	2.71	167
Maintenance and repair materials	83.75	88.86	106
Paints, wallpaper, and supplies	14.71	9.03	61
Tools, equipment for painting, wallpapering	1.58	0.97	61
Plumbing supplies and equipment	5.62	5.80	103
Electrical supplies, heating, cooling equip.	3.46	8.04	232
Hard-surface flooring, repair, replacement	8.72	11.09	127
Roofing and gutters	5.29	4.80	91
Plaster, paneling, siding, windows, doors, screens, awnings	13.92	16.00	115
Patio, walk, fence, driveway, masonry, brick, and stucco materials	1.29	1.03	80

	total consumer units	CUs headed by people aged 65 to 74	
		average spending	indexed spending
Landscape maintenance	$4.73	$2.12	45
Miscellaneous supplies and equipment	24.43	29.97	123
Insulation, other maintenance, repair	13.15	17.62	134
Finish basement, remodel rooms, build patios, walks, etc.	11.28	12.36	110
Property management and security	27.64	41.25	149
Property management	21.94	30.31	138
Management and upkeep services for security	5.71	10.94	192
Parking	5.17	8.72	169
Rented dwellings	**2,159.89**	**905.16**	**42**
Rent	2,104.66	868.94	41
Rent as pay	27.17	18.40	68
Maintenance, insurance, and other expenses	28.06	17.82	64
Tenant's insurance	8.90	4.53	51
Maintenance and repair services	11.16	9.81	88
Repair and maintenance services	10.58	9.81	93
Repair, replacement of hard-surface flooring	0.51	–	–
Repair of built-in appliances	0.07	–	–
Maintenance and repair materials	8.00	3.49	44
Paint, wallpaper, and supplies	1.01	0.04	4
Painting and wallpapering tools	0.11	–	–
Plastering, paneling, roofing, gutters, etc.	0.90	–	–
Plumbing supplies and equipment	0.80	0.13	16
Electrical supplies, heating, cooling equip.	0.30	–	–
Miscellaneous supplies and equipment	3.67	3.25	89
Insulation, other maintenance and repair	1.09	0.53	49
Materials for additions, finishing basements, remodeling rooms	2.43	2.54	105
Construction materials for jobs not started	0.15	0.18	120
Hard-surface flooring	0.73	–	–
Landscape maintenance	0.49	0.07	14
Other lodging	**504.56**	**544.61**	**108**
Owned vacation homes	171.55	189.38	110
Mortgage interest and charges	71.98	37.86	53
Property taxes	63.76	95.78	150
Maintenance, insurance and other expenses	35.81	55.74	156
Homeowner's insurance	9.70	21.20	219
Ground rent	2.93	6.91	236
Maintenance and repair services	16.76	17.95	107
Maintenance and repair materials	2.07	3.59	173
Property management and security	3.60	4.48	124
Property management	2.50	3.38	135
Management, upkeep services for security	1.10	1.10	100
Parking	0.76	1.62	213
Housing while attending school	80.14	24.11	30
Lodging on trips	252.87	331.13	131

	total consumer units	CUs headed by people aged 65 to 74	
		average spending	indexed spending
UTILITIES, FUELS, PUBLIC SERVICES	**$2,684.32**	**$2,589.82**	**96**
Natural gas	**329.75**	**336.22**	**102**
Natural gas (renter)	60.32	29.55	49
Natural gas (owner)	266.79	303.08	114
Natural gas (vacation)	2.54	3.59	141
Electricity	**981.09**	**985.47**	**100**
Electricity (renter)	223.26	90.18	40
Electricity (owner)	750.48	881.11	117
Electricity (vacation)	6.32	12.20	193
Fuel oil and other fuels	**88.41**	**114.63**	**130**
Fuel oil	45.98	59.43	129
Fuel oil (renter)	4.64	2.27	49
Fuel oil (owner)	40.98	56.51	138
Fuel oil (vacation)	0.36	0.65	181
Coal	0.07	–	–
Bottled/tank gas	35.27	42.90	122
Gas (renter)	5.09	1.15	23
Gas (owner)	27.19	39.68	146
Gas (vacation)	2.98	1.95	65
Wood and other fuels	7.09	12.30	173
Wood and other fuels (renter)	1.32	1.43	108
Wood and other fuels (owner)	5.68	10.75	189
Telephone services	**956.74**	**793.94**	**83**
Residential telephone and pay phones	641.00	612.94	96
Cellular phone service	293.76	170.48	58
Pager service	1.71	1.05	61
Phone cards	20.28	9.47	47
Water and other public services	**328.33**	**359.55**	**110**
Water and sewerage maintenance	237.16	253.23	107
Water and sewerage maintenance (renter)	32.76	14.74	45
Water and sewerage maintenance (owner)	201.79	232.53	115
Water and sewerage maintenance (vacation)	2.36	5.73	243
Trash and garbage collection	89.05	104.09	117
Trash and garbage collection (renter)	9.89	3.59	36
Trash and garbage collection (owner)	76.61	97.05	127
Trash and garbage collection (vacation)	2.53	3.44	136
Septic tank cleaning	2.12	2.23	105
HOUSEHOLD SERVICES	**705.71**	**486.39**	**69**
Personal services	**331.02**	**78.93**	**24**
Babysitting, child care in your own home	35.91	0.22	1
Babysitting, child care in someone else's home	27.48	0.56	2
Care for elderly, invalids, handicapped, etc.	50.07	63.08	126
Adult day care centers	6.81	0.38	6
Day care centers, nurseries, and preschools	210.74	14.70	7
Other household services	**374.70**	**407.46**	**109**
Housekeeping services	79.90	88.16	110
Gardening, lawn care service	72.38	114.75	159
Water softening service	3.15	2.23	71

	total consumer units	CUs headed by people aged 65 to 74	
		average spending	indexed spending
Nonclothing laundry, dry cleaning, sent out	$1.72	$1.98	115
Nonclothing laundry, dry cleaning, coin-operated	4.13	1.80	44
Termite/pest control services	13.25	19.80	149
Home security system service fee	17.40	18.89	109
Other home services	15.06	21.98	146
Termite/pest control products	0.68	0.79	116
Moving, storage, and freight express	33.13	29.45	89
Appliance repair, including service center	10.86	16.19	149
Reupholstering and furniture repair	7.40	7.17	97
Repairs/rentals of lawn/garden equipment, hand/power tools, etc.	3.62	5.93	164
Appliance rental	1.07	0.36	34
Rental of office equip., nonbusiness use	0.41	–	–
Repair of misc. household equip., furnishings	0.62	1.39	224
Repair of computer systems, nonbusiness use	2.53	1.55	61
Computer information services	107.29	75.04	70
HOUSEKEEPING SUPPLIES	**545.28**	**546.71**	**100**
Laundry and cleaning supplies	**130.57**	**132.36**	**101**
Soaps and detergents	72.89	68.91	95
Other laundry cleaning products	57.68	63.45	110
Other household products	**283.28**	**250.43**	**88**
Cleansing and toilet tissue, paper towels, and napkins	76.46	72.54	95
Miscellaneous household products	96.81	85.39	88
Lawn and garden supplies	110.01	92.50	84
Postage and stationery	**131.44**	**163.92**	**125**
Stationery, stationery supplies, giftwrap	60.20	54.95	91
Postage	69.12	107.52	156
Delivery services	2.12	1.46	69
HOUSEHOLD FURNISHINGS, EQUIPMENT	**1,518.36**	**1,130.57**	**74**
Household textiles	**135.52**	**126.85**	**94**
Bathroom linens	22.35	21.99	98
Bedroom linens	65.98	59.45	90
Kitchen and dining room linens	10.11	12.42	123
Curtains and draperies	16.65	16.83	101
Slipcovers and decorative pillows	7.40	2.92	39
Sewing materials for household items	11.44	12.18	106
Other linens	1.59	1.07	67
Furniture	**401.28**	**242.47**	**60**
Mattresses and springs	52.91	45.32	86
Other bedroom furniture	68.33	29.24	43
Sofas	85.33	57.57	67
Living room chairs	39.21	39.06	100
Living room tables	18.03	11.16	62
Kitchen and dining room furniture	61.28	18.90	31
Infants' furniture	6.46	2.88	45
Outdoor furniture	16.79	15.37	92
Wall units, cabinets, and other furniture	52.94	22.95	43

	total consumer units	CUs headed by people aged 65 to 74	
		average spending	indexed spending
Floor coverings	**$40.49**	**$33.42**	**83**
Wall-to-wall carpeting (renter)	0.65	–	–
Wall-to-wall carpet (replacement) (owner)	21.04	23.93	114
Floor coverings, nonpermanent	18.79	9.49	51
Major appliances	**188.47**	**167.63**	**89**
Dishwashers (built-in), garbage disposals, range hoods (renter)	1.24	0.39	31
Dishwashers (built-in), garbage disposals, range hoods (owner)	15.28	9.20	60
Refrigerators and freezers (renter)	5.58	3.32	59
Refrigerators and freezers (owner)	46.50	48.40	104
Washing machines (renter)	4.42	1.87	42
Washing machines (owner)	17.88	21.14	118
Clothes dryers (renter)	3.17	0.74	23
Clothes dryers (owner)	13.88	8.61	62
Cooking stoves, ovens (renter)	2.86	2.70	94
Cooking stoves, ovens (owner)	28.09	31.71	113
Microwave ovens (renter)	2.14	1.38	64
Microwave ovens (owner)	8.36	10.03	120
Portable dishwasher (renter)	0.25	0.40	160
Portable dishwasher (owner)	0.51	–	–
Window air conditioners (renter)	1.83	0.87	48
Window air conditioners (owner)	6.07	4.99	82
Electric floor-cleaning equipment	22.80	12.17	53
Sewing machines	4.79	5.87	123
Miscellaneous household appliances	**2.81**	**3.85**	**137**
Small appliances and misc. housewares	100.43	92.72	92
Housewares	77.55	72.35	93
Plastic dinnerware	1.57	0.94	60
China and other dinnerware	14.51	15.75	109
Flatware	3.79	3.54	93
Glassware	6.51	5.18	80
Silver serving pieces	4.05	5.53	137
Other serving pieces	1.44	0.59	41
Nonelectric cookware	24.25	25.63	106
Tableware, nonelectric kitchenware	21.44	15.18	71
Small appliances	22.89	20.36	89
Small electric kitchen appliances	17.18	15.15	88
Portable heating and cooling equipment	5.70	5.21	91
Miscellaneous household equipment	**652.17**	**467.48**	**72**
Window coverings	13.91	15.58	112
Infants' equipment	12.96	3.60	28
Laundry and cleaning equipment	15.15	16.94	112
Outdoor equipment	31.52	7.60	24
Clocks	5.87	2.37	40
Lamps and lighting fixtures	11.74	8.29	71
Other household decorative items	144.94	115.74	80
Telephones and accessories	32.73	43.13	132
Lawn and garden equipment	48.16	42.44	88

	total consumer units	CUs headed by people aged 65 to 74	
		average spending	indexed spending
Power tools	$33.27	$16.27	49
Office furniture for home use	10.57	4.19	40
Hand tools	8.05	4.77	59
Indoor plants and fresh flowers	49.78	51.74	104
Closet and storage items	9.98	6.49	65
Rental of furniture	4.60	0.84	18
Luggage	5.98	5.87	98
Computers and computer hardware, nonbusiness use	138.58	53.96	39
Computer software and accessories, nonbusiness use	17.67	11.53	65
Telephone answering devices	1.08	0.84	78
Calculators	1.44	0.47	33
Business equipment for home use	0.97	1.01	104
Other hardware	12.85	19.33	150
Smoke alarms (owner)	1.10	0.37	34
Smoke alarms (renter)	0.39	–	–
Other household appliances (owner)	8.00	8.24	103
Other household appliances (renter)	1.23	0.63	51
Miscellaneous household equipment and parts	29.62	25.25	85
APPAREL AND SERVICES	**$1,749.22**	**$1,252.47**	**72**
Men's apparel	**319.48**	**251.65**	**79**
Suits	32.96	20.93	64
Sport coats and tailored jackets	10.65	9.11	86
Coats and jackets	33.86	32.88	97
Underwear	15.27	14.26	93
Hosiery	12.22	9.54	78
Nightwear	2.98	3.20	107
Accessories	22.41	22.93	102
Sweaters and vests	15.68	14.09	90
Active sportswear	15.13	9.74	64
Shirts	78.89	57.26	73
Pants	57.64	45.86	80
Shorts and shorts sets	12.22	6.41	52
Uniforms	3.21	0.75	23
Costumes	6.35	4.68	74
Boys' (aged 2 to 15) apparel	**89.98**	**33.25**	**37**
Coats and jackets	6.38	1.53	24
Sweaters	3.65	1.58	43
Shirts	19.50	7.35	38
Underwear	5.02	1.63	32
Nightwear	2.59	1.96	76
Hosiery	4.21	1.38	33
Accessories	4.12	2.58	63
Suits, sport coats, and vests	2.37	0.90	38
Pants	22.58	9.03	40
Shorts and shorts sets	8.66	2.17	25
Uniforms	3.35	1.33	40
Active sportswear	3.84	0.69	18
Costumes	3.72	1.12	30

	total consumer units	CUs headed by people aged 65 to 74	
		average spending	indexed spending
Women's apparel	**$586.91**	**$522.93**	**89**
Coats and jackets	50.06	48.46	97
Dresses	56.40	41.51	74
Sport coats and tailored jackets	6.48	5.06	78
Sweaters and vests	50.47	36.34	72
Shirts, blouses, and tops	103.24	90.19	87
Skirts	17.48	14.14	81
Pants	96.29	94.77	98
Shorts and shorts sets	16.09	17.19	107
Active sportswear	30.07	20.53	68
Nightwear	27.63	29.40	106
Undergarments	33.55	28.12	84
Hosiery	21.22	27.67	130
Suits	29.01	22.77	78
Accessories	33.37	34.38	103
Uniforms	6.12	3.94	64
Costumes	9.42	8.47	90
Girls' (aged 2 to 15) apparel	**117.21**	**34.74**	**30**
Coats and jackets	6.49	2.92	45
Dresses and suits	12.41	2.57	21
Shirts, blouses, and sweaters	29.33	6.03	21
Skirts and pants	24.07	8.29	34
Shorts and shorts sets	8.28	4.08	49
Active sportswear	9.32	6.48	70
Underwear and nightwear	7.63	2.08	27
Hosiery	4.30	0.33	8
Accessories	5.81	0.68	12
Uniforms	4.77	0.55	12
Costumes	4.80	0.74	15
Children under age 2	**82.60**	**26.80**	**32**
Coats, jackets, and snowsuits	2.43	1.75	72
Outerwear including dresses	23.71	14.91	63
Underwear	43.60	5.73	13
Nightwear and loungewear	4.07	2.55	63
Accessories	8.79	1.86	21
Footwear	**313.17**	**207.70**	**66**
Men's	102.90	98.92	96
Boys'	36.87	6.86	19
Women's	141.64	94.58	67
Girls'	31.76	7.34	23
Other apparel products and services	**239.87**	**175.40**	**73**
Material for making clothes	5.11	13.65	267
Sewing patterns and notions	8.20	13.24	161
Watches	13.62	12.07	89
Jewelry	89.65	54.73	61
Shoe repair and other shoe services	1.44	1.30	90
Coin-operated apparel laundry and dry cleaning	37.58	19.22	51
Apparel alteration, repair, and tailoring services	5.86	5.35	91
Clothing rental	2.66	1.19	45
Watch and jewelry repair	5.49	7.40	135
Professional laundry, dry cleaning	69.69	45.60	65
Clothing storage	0.55	1.64	298

	total consumer units	CUs headed by people aged 65 to 74	
		average spending	indexed spending
TRANSPORTATION	**$7,759.29**	**$5,730.69**	**74**
VEHICLE PURCHASES	**3,664.93**	**2,429.84**	**66**
Cars and trucks, new	**1,752.96**	**1,351.97**	**77**
New cars	883.08	769.17	87
New trucks	869.88	582.81	67
Cars and trucks, used	**1,842.29**	**1,042.90**	**57**
Used cars	1,113.46	789.66	71
Used trucks	728.82	253.24	35
Other vehicles	**69.68**	**34.97**	**50**
New motorcycles	36.26	34.97	96
Used motorcycles	33.42	–	–
GASOLINE AND MOTOR OIL	**1,235.06**	**969.76**	**79**
Gasoline	1,125.01	848.63	75
Diesel fuel	10.86	21.20	195
Gasoline on trips	88.24	92.77	105
Motor oil	10.05	6.24	62
Motor oil on trips	0.89	0.94	106
OTHER VEHICLE EXPENSES	**2,470.55**	**1,944.81**	**79**
Vehicle finance charges	**397.04**	**216.76**	**55**
Automobile finance charges	193.12	120.77	63
Truck finance charges	182.89	77.37	42
Motorcycle and plane finance charges	2.36	0.53	22
Other vehicle finance charges	18.67	18.08	97
Maintenance and repairs	**697.30**	**553.07**	**79**
Coolant, additives, brake, transmission fluids	3.82	2.28	60
Tires—purchased, replaced, installed	89.93	75.10	84
Parts, equipment, and accessories	41.70	36.27	87
Vehicle audio equipment, excl. labor	12.32	–	–
Vehicle products	4.92	2.14	43
Miscellaneous auto repair, servicing	43.69	27.26	62
Body work and painting	31.24	24.97	80
Clutch, transmission repair	48.68	31.03	64
Drive shaft and rear-end repair	6.51	2.62	40
Brake work	57.73	39.10	68
Repair to steering or front-end	16.91	19.38	115
Repair to engine cooling system	21.68	18.58	86
Motor tune-up	49.69	41.88	84
Lube, oil change, and oil filters	65.07	62.52	96
Front-end alignment, wheel balance, rotation	11.90	9.58	81
Shock absorber replacement	4.82	3.58	74
Gas tank repair, replacement	4.32	2.17	50
Tire repair and other repair work	39.83	35.43	89
Vehicle air conditioning repair	17.00	22.18	130
Exhaust system repair	12.56	10.47	83
Electrical system repair	28.42	32.28	114
Motor repair, replacement	76.62	49.48	65
Auto repair service policy	7.93	4.76	60

	total consumer units	CUs headed by people aged 65 to 74 average spending	CUs headed by people aged 65 to 74 indexed spending
Vehicle insurance	$893.50	$798.94	89
Vehicle rental, leases, licenses, other charges	482.71	376.04	78
Leased and rented vehicles	324.48	235.52	73
Rented vehicles	41.33	37.19	90
Auto rental	6.76	5.65	84
Auto rental on trips	28.28	25.11	89
Truck rental	2.21	1.72	78
Truck rental on trips	3.55	4.43	125
Leased vehicles	283.15	198.33	70
Car lease payments	149.63	129.20	86
Cash down payment (car lease)	11.13	6.30	57
Termination fee (car lease)	1.28	5.30	414
Truck lease payments	114.24	57.53	50
Cash down payment (truck lease)	4.92	–	–
Termination fee (truck lease)	1.94	–	–
Vehicle registration, state	72.82	72.47	100
Vehicle registration, local	7.76	7.19	93
Driver's license	6.26	5.60	89
Vehicle inspection	9.26	9.72	105
Parking fees	29.25	14.53	50
Parking fees in home city, excluding residence	24.24	10.01	41
Parking fees on trips	5.01	4.51	90
Tolls	10.59	5.43	51
Tolls on trips	3.94	4.44	113
Towing charges	5.60	2.88	51
Automobile service clubs	12.75	18.28	143
PUBLIC TRANSPORTATION	388.75	386.28	99
Airline fares	243.57	233.42	96
Intercity bus fares	11.48	16.82	147
Intracity mass transit fares	49.97	24.12	48
Local transportation on trips	10.91	11.79	108
Taxi fares and limousine service on trips	6.41	6.92	108
Taxi fares and limousine service	18.95	27.88	147
Intercity train fares	16.09	20.60	128
Ship fares	29.74	44.56	150
School bus	1.64	0.18	11
HEALTH CARE	$2,350.32	$3,588.05	153
HEALTH INSURANCE	1,167.71	1,920.75	164
Commercial health insurance	217.53	163.75	75
Traditional fee-for-service health plan (not BCBS)	68.27	88.01	129
Preferred-provider health plan (not BCBS)	149.26	75.73	51
Blue Cross, Blue Shield	315.67	359.40	114
Traditional fee-for-service health plan	53.76	55.25	103
Preferred-provider health plan	106.99	66.91	63
Health maintenance organization	101.53	73.06	72
Commercial Medicare supplement	47.35	157.14	332
Other BCBS health insurance	6.05	7.05	117

	total consumer units	CUs headed by people aged 65 to 74	
		average spending	indexed spending
Health maintenance plans (HMOs)	$280.47	$226.85	81
Medicare payments	186.87	740.76	396
Commercial Medicare supplements/ other health insurance	**167.18**	**429.98**	**257**
Commercial Medicare supplement (not BCBS)	106.32	305.45	287
Other health insurance (not BCBS)	60.86	124.53	205
MEDICAL SERVICES	**589.87**	**635.35**	**108**
Physician's services	147.53	132.38	90
Dental services	226.99	316.97	140
Eye care services	34.20	29.30	86
Service by professionals other than physician	42.76	33.52	78
Lab tests, X-rays	26.79	29.41	110
Hospital room	36.57	30.70	84
Hospital services other than room	51.51	39.97	78
Care in convalescent or nursing home	12.46	14.29	115
Other medical services	9.46	8.80	93
DRUGS	**487.43**	**884.02**	**181**
Nonprescription drugs	64.45	92.18	143
Nonprescription vitamins	49.15	64.15	131
Prescription drugs	373.83	727.69	195
MEDICAL SUPPLIES	**105.31**	**147.93**	**140**
Eyeglasses and contact lenses	52.26	58.91	113
Hearing aids	14.98	33.66	225
Topicals and dressings	27.56	30.61	111
Medical equipment for general use	2.69	4.95	184
Supportive, convalescent medical equipment	5.21	9.75	187
Rental of medical equipment	1.06	6.40	604
Rental of supportive, convalescent medical equipment	1.55	3.65	235
ENTERTAINMENT	**$2,078.99**	**$1,371.38**	**66**
FEES AND ADMISSIONS	**541.67**	**382.28**	**71**
Recreation expenses on trips	25.64	21.50	84
Social, recreation, civic club membership	107.92	91.28	85
Fees for participant sports	75.05	75.41	100
Participant sports on trips	29.50	27.28	92
Movie, theater, opera, ballet	98.30	59.63	61
Movie, other admissions on trips	45.57	34.30	75
Admission to sports events	36.18	19.47	54
Admission to sports events on trips	15.19	11.43	75
Fees for recreational lessons	82.69	20.49	25
Other entertainment services on trips	25.64	21.50	84
TELEVISION, RADIO, SOUND EQUIPMENT	**691.90**	**545.61**	**79**
Television	**543.66**	**473.50**	**87**
Cable service and community antenna	382.28	380.23	99
Black-and-white TV	0.80	0.29	36
Color TV, console	38.63	16.11	42
Color TV, portable, table model	39.14	31.17	80

	total consumer units	CUs headed by people aged 65 to 74	
		average spending	indexed spending
VCRs and video disc players	$23.25	$15.01	65
Video cassettes, tapes, and discs	33.13	23.45	71
Video game hardware and software	23.46	5.21	22
Repair of TV, radio, and sound equipment	2.50	1.95	78
Rental of television sets	0.46	0.09	20
Radio and sound equipment	**148.25**	**72.12**	**49**
Radios	3.98	7.22	181
Tape recorders and players	5.31	3.37	63
Sound components and component systems	20.19	10.95	54
Miscellaneous sound equipment	3.18	–	–
Sound equipment accessories	5.97	5.35	90
Satellite dishes	1.00	0.98	98
Compact disc, tape, record, video mail order clubs	6.53	3.83	59
Records, CDs, audio tapes, needles	36.47	15.38	42
Rental of VCR, radio, sound equipment	0.25	–	–
Musical instruments and accessories	24.82	14.45	58
Rental and repair of musical instruments	1.22	0.28	23
Rental of video cassettes, tapes, discs, films	39.33	10.31	26
PETS, TOYS, PLAYGROUND EQUIPMENT	**369.12**	**262.42**	**71**
Pets	**248.25**	**184.88**	**74**
Pet food	102.56	85.63	83
Pet purchase, supplies, and medicines	52.29	24.88	48
Pet services	21.95	20.03	91
Veterinarian services	71.44	54.35	76
Toys, games, hobbies, and tricycles	**117.34**	**76.79**	**65**
Playground equipment	**3.54**	**0.75**	**21**
OTHER ENTERTAINMENT SUPPLIES, EQUIPMENT, SERVICES	**476.30**	**181.07**	**38**
Unmotored recreational vehicles	**47.14**	**16.50**	**35**
Boat without motor and boat trailers	16.15	8.30	51
Trailer and other attachable campers	30.99	8.21	26
Motorized recreational vehicles	**170.19**	**46.65**	**27**
Motorized camper	40.05	2.22	6
Other vehicle	35.47	29.47	83
Motorboats	94.67	14.96	16
Rental of recreational vehicles	**1.99**	**1.04**	**52**
Outboard motors	**0.71**	**0.18**	**25**
Docking and landing fees	**6.66**	**5.31**	**80**
Sports, recreation, exercise equipment	**150.33**	**58.75**	**39**
Athletic gear, game tables, exercise equipment	60.51	35.51	59
Bicycles	13.45	2.89	21
Camping equipment	9.59	2.08	22
Hunting and fishing equipment	35.68	12.62	35
Winter sports equipment	5.45	0.91	17
Water sports equipment	8.95	0.56	6
Other sports equipment	14.62	3.86	26
Rental and repair of misc. sports equipment	2.07	0.33	16

	total consumer units	CUs headed by people aged 65 to 74 average spending	indexed spending
Photographic equipment and supplies	**$90.48**	**$50.98**	**56**
Film	17.74	12.18	69
Other photographic supplies	2.27	0.96	42
Film processing	26.60	18.98	71
Repair and rental of photographic equipment	0.12	0.01	8
Photographic equipment	23.34	14.41	62
Photographer fees	20.42	4.44	22
Fireworks	**1.52**	–	–
Souvenirs	**1.25**	**0.61**	**49**
Visual goods	**1.19**	**0.03**	**3**
Pinball, electronic video games	**4.84**	**1.02**	**21**
PERSONAL CARE PRODUCTS AND SERVICES	**$525.80**	**$508.65**	**97**
Personal care products	**276.65**	**257.03**	**93**
Hair care products	53.57	41.73	78
Hair accessories	6.57	4.50	68
Wigs and hairpieces	1.32	0.94	71
Oral hygiene products	27.33	28.20	103
Shaving products	15.09	11.97	79
Cosmetics, perfume, and bath products	129.13	131.45	102
Deodorants, feminine hygiene, misc. products	30.29	23.17	76
Electric personal care appliances	13.34	15.07	113
Personal care services	**249.15**	**251.63**	**101**
READING	**$138.57**	**$160.71**	**116**
Newspaper subscriptions	43.88	73.55	168
Newspaper, nonsubscription	11.30	13.76	122
Magazine subscriptions	16.59	21.76	131
Magazines, nonsubscription	9.35	7.70	82
Books purchased through book clubs	6.62	6.84	103
Books not purchased through book clubs	50.38	36.97	73
Encyclopedia and other reference book sets	0.33	0.12	36
EDUCATION	**$751.95**	**$288.58**	**38**
College tuition	444.45	140.10	32
Elementary and high school tuition	128.94	66.42	52
Other school tuition	25.53	20.27	79
Other school expenses including rentals	25.77	4.88	19
Books, supplies for college	57.93	15.30	26
Books, supplies for elementary, high school	16.14	2.76	17
Books, supplies for day care, nursery school	3.39	0.89	26
Miscellaneous school expenses and supplies	49.80	37.96	76

	total consumer units	CUs headed by people aged 65 to 74 average spending	indexed spending
TOBACCO PRODUCTS AND SMOKING SUPPLIES	**$320.49**	**$220.31**	**69**
Cigarettes	291.89	199.59	68
Other tobacco products	26.27	17.12	65
Smoking accessories	2.33	3.60	155
FINANCIAL PRODUCTS, SERVICES	**$788.12**	**$793.74**	**101**
Miscellaneous fees	2.25	1.63	72
Lottery and gambling losses	46.94	80.94	172
Legal fees	132.99	102.31	77
Funeral expenses	77.91	154.91	199
Safe deposit box rental	3.84	7.70	201
Checking accounts, other bank service charges	25.91	15.36	59
Cemetery lots, vaults, and maintenance fees	16.05	30.82	192
Accounting fees	57.85	75.96	131
Miscellaneous personal services	39.77	50.81	128
Finance charges, except mortgage and vehicles	271.37	195.92	72
Occupational expenses	38.46	9.70	25
Expenses for other properties	65.99	59.75	91
Credit card memberships	2.82	2.35	83
Shopping club membership fees	5.97	5.51	92
CASH CONTRIBUTIONS	**$1,277.10**	**$1,620.48**	**127**
Support for college students	75.94	65.10	86
Alimony expenditures	21.18	12.76	60
Child support expenditures	190.75	63.44	33
Gifts to non-CU members of stocks, bonds, and mutual funds	24.23	52.18	215
Cash contributions to charities and other organizations	137.62	227.83	166
Cash contributions to church, religious organizations	557.29	751.56	135
Cash contributions to educational institutions	33.42	86.83	260
Cash contributions to political organizations	10.90	7.22	66
Other cash gifts	225.76	353.57	157
PERSONAL INSURANCE, PENSIONS	**$3,898.62**	**$1,852.78**	**48**
Life and other personal insurance	**406.11**	**521.11**	**128**
Life, endowment, annuity, other personal insurance	391.65	505.50	129
Other nonhealth insurance	14.46	15.62	108
Pensions and Social Security	3,492.51	1,331.66	38
Deductions for government retirement	69.48	8.95	13
Deductions for railroad retirement	2.21	–	–
Deductions for private pensions	390.38	112.18	29
Nonpayroll deposit to retirement plans	426.12	284.88	67
Deductions for Social Security	2,604.32	925.65	36

	total consumer units	CUs headed by people aged 65 to 74	
		average spending	indexed spending
PERSONAL TAXES	**$2,496.26**	**$1,556.12**	**62**
Federal income taxes	1,842.57	1,110.82	60
State and local income taxes	506.45	229.85	45
Other taxes	147.24	215.45	146
GIFTS FOR NON-HOUSEHOLD MEMBERS**	**$1,036.24**	**$1,089.07**	**105**
FOOD	**82.18**	**60.51**	**74**
Cakes and cupcakes	2.41	0.74	31
Other fresh fruits (excl. apples, bananas, citrus)	2.26	3.04	135
Candy and chewing gum	11.69	18.71	160
Board (including at school)	21.90	14.57	67
Catered affairs	26.19	2.19	8
ALCOHOLIC BEVERAGES	**13.42**	**16.95**	**126**
Beer and ale	4.73	4.93	104
Wine	5.84	9.31	159
HOUSING	**258.69**	**268.07**	**104**
Housekeeping supplies	**42.48**	**55.87**	**132**
Laundry and cleaning supplies	2.93	3.34	114
Other household products	11.69	8.60	74
Miscellaneous household products	5.85	3.08	53
Lawn and garden supplies	4.20	3.96	94
Postage and stationery	27.86	43.93	158
Stationery, stationery supplies, giftwrap	21.13	27.10	128
Postage	6.14	16.34	266
Household textiles	**13.72**	**17.55**	**128**
Bathroom linens	2.59	5.12	198
Bedroom linens	6.10	5.65	93
Appliances and miscellaneous housewares	**23.98**	**31.56**	**132**
Major appliances	8.41	8.23	98
Electric floor-cleaning equipment	2.77	1.44	52
Small appliances and miscellaneous housewares	15.57	23.34	150
China and other dinnerware	2.46	4.07	165
Nonelectric cookware	3.53	6.58	186
Tableware, nonelectric kitchenware	2.63	1.79	68
Small electric kitchen appliances	2.71	3.72	137
Miscellaneous household equipment	**64.70**	**75.43**	**117**
Infants' equipment	3.82	2.44	64
Outdoor equipment	2.07	1.03	50
Other household decorative items	25.76	31.35	122
Power tools	2.80	2.29	82
Indoor plants, fresh flowers	13.43	17.73	132
Computers and computer hardware	6.59	5.31	81
Miscellaneous household equipment	2.19	3.04	139
Other housing	**113.80**	**87.66**	**77**
Repair or maintenance services	4.51	7.24	161
Housing while attending school	39.93	22.28	56

	total consumer units	CUs headed by people aged 65 to 74	
		average spending	indexed spending
Natural gas (renter)	$3.62	$2.12	59
Electricity (renter)	14.67	13.29	91
Water, sewer maintenance (renter)	3.04	4.24	139
Day-care centers, nurseries, and preschools	23.81	8.00	34
APPAREL AND SERVICES	**237.13**	**250.78**	**106**
Men and boys, aged 2 or older	**63.74**	**89.13**	**140**
Men's coats and jackets	5.09	2.76	54
Men's accessories	4.45	4.40	99
Men's sweaters and vests	3.06	3.65	119
Men's active sportswear	2.76	1.80	65
Men's shirts	16.79	22.87	136
Men's pants	6.93	15.72	227
Boys' shirts	3.71	6.05	163
Boys' pants	3.76	7.04	187
Women and girls, aged 2 or older	**81.76**	**88.37**	**108**
Women's coats and jackets	5.62	4.71	84
Women's dresses	7.66	4.95	65
Women's vests and sweaters	8.50	7.89	93
Women's shirts, tops, blouses	9.06	11.38	126
Women's pants	6.62	11.81	178
Women's active sportswear	4.33	4.30	99
Women's sleepwear	6.45	5.60	87
Women's accessories	5.71	4.70	82
Girls' dresses and suits	2.98	2.53	85
Girls' shirts, blouses, sweaters	4.48	5.42	121
Girls' skirts and pants	3.32	3.99	120
Girls' accessories	2.38	0.68	29
Children under age 2	**39.99**	**25.68**	**64**
Infant dresses, outerwear	15.28	14.23	93
Infant underwear	16.91	5.73	34
Infant nightwear, loungewear	2.55	2.12	83
Infant accessories	3.93	1.86	47
Other apparel products and services	**51.63**	**47.60**	**92**
Jewelry and watches	24.01	14.54	61
Watches	2.16	3.61	167
Jewelry	21.85	10.93	50
Men's footwear	8.37	11.44	137
Boys' footwear	4.46	1.52	34
Women's footwear	8.82	6.79	77
Girls' footwear	3.30	6.34	192
TRANSPORTATION	**43.87**	**11.17**	**25**
New cars	7.09	–	–
Used cars	12.21	–	–
Airline fares	6.78	5.45	80
Ship fares	2.74	2.29	84

	total consumer units	CUs headed by people aged 65 to 74 average spending	CUs headed by people aged 65 to 74 indexed spending
HEALTH CARE	**$32.59**	**$39.97**	**123**
Physician's services	3.07	1.00	33
Dental services	4.03	4.50	112
Care in convalescent or nursing home	5.19	10.47	202
Nonprescription vitamins	3.93	3.90	99
Prescription drugs	2.38	5.30	223
ENTERTAINMENT	**78.24**	**73.48**	**94**
Toys, games, hobbies, and tricycles	29.98	38.33	128
Other entertainment	48.26	35.15	73
Fees for recreational lessons	7.88	2.21	28
Community antenna or cable TV	6.37	6.11	96
VCRs and videodisc players	2.26	1.44	64
Video game hardware and software	2.13	2.19	103
Athletic gear, game tables, exercise equipment	6.60	7.42	112
Hunting and fishing equipment	3.06	1.68	55
Photographer fees	3.19	0.90	28
PERSONAL CARE PRODUCTS, SERVICES	**21.15**	**30.81**	**146**
Cosmetics, perfume, bath preparation	12.53	18.80	150
Electric personal care appliances	3.31	3.68	111
EDUCATION	**183.88**	**194.24**	**106**
College tuition	127.83	96.43	75
Elementary and high school tuition	25.95	58.60	226
Other school tuition	4.44	4.25	96
Other school expenses including rentals	3.99	1.88	47
College books and supplies	11.93	10.29	86
Miscellaneous school supplies	7.38	21.00	285
ALL OTHER GIFTS	**83.76**	**140.28**	**167**
Gifts of trip expenses	44.40	70.78	159
Lottery and gambling losses	2.86	2.07	72
Legal fees	5.82	30.79	529
Funeral expenses	25.25	28.88	114
Miscellaneous personal services	2.16	4.55	211

* This figure does not include the amount paid for mortgage principle, which is considered an asset.

** Expenditures on gifts are also included in the preceding product and service categories. Food spending, for example, includes the amount spent on food gifts. Only gift categories with spending of $2.00 or more by the average consumer unit are shown.

Note: The Bureau of Labor Statistics uses consumer unit rather than household as the sampling unit in the Consumer Expenditure Survey. For the definition of consumer unit, see the glossary. (–) means not applicable or the sample is too small to make a reliable estimate.

Source: Bureau of Labor Statistics, unpublished data from the 2002 Consumer Expenditure Survey; calculations by New Strategist

Table 8.6 Average and Indexed Spending of Householders Aged 75 or Older, 2002

(average annual spending of total consumer units (CUs) and average annual and indexed spending of consumer units headed by people aged 75 or older, 2002)

	total consumer units	CUs headed by people aged 75 or older	
		average spending	indexed spending
Number of consumer units (in 000s)	112,108	10,767	–
Average before-tax income	$49,430.00	$23,890.00	48
Average annual spending	40,676.60	23,758.89	58
FOOD	**$5,374.80**	**$3,302.10**	**61**
Food at Home	3,098.52	2,195.04	71
Cereals and bakery products	450.13	351.99	78
Cereals and cereal products	154.07	111.74	73
Flour	8.65	7.74	89
Prepared flour mixes	12.40	9.87	80
Ready-to-eat and cooked cereals	87.66	68.16	78
Rice	17.82	9.20	52
Pasta, cornmeal, and other cereal products	27.54	16.77	61
Bakery products	296.06	240.26	81
Bread	83.83	70.05	84
White bread	35.21	26.62	76
Bread, other than white	48.62	43.43	89
Crackers and cookies	70.67	60.67	86
Cookies	46.31	38.87	84
Crackers	24.36	21.81	90
Frozen and refrigerated bakery products	25.64	18.05	70
Other bakery products	115.92	91.49	79
Biscuits and rolls	41.04	29.11	71
Cakes and cupcakes	35.73	23.25	65
Bread and cracker products	3.50	2.98	85
Sweetrolls, coffee cakes, doughnuts	25.84	25.60	99
Pies, tarts, turnovers	9.82	10.54	107
Meats, poultry, fish, and eggs	**798.42**	**528.87**	**66**
Beef	231.17	138.46	60
Ground beef	86.29	53.65	62
Roast	40.99	28.92	71
Chuck roast	11.71	7.06	60
Round roast	10.23	8.29	81
Other roast	19.05	13.57	71
Steak	84.47	42.52	50
Round steak	13.29	7.26	55
Sirloin steak	26.62	11.21	42
Other steak	44.56	24.05	54
Pork	167.34	117.25	70
Bacon	28.45	23.90	84
Pork chops	38.43	27.73	72
Ham	37.16	21.13	57
Ham, not canned	35.66	20.39	57
Canned ham	1.50	0.74	49

	total consumer units	CUs headed by people aged 75 or older	
		average spending	indexed spending
Sausage	$26.17	$20.08	77
Other pork	37.13	24.40	66
Other meats	101.08	70.15	69
Frankfurters	20.95	14.46	69
Lunch meats (cold cuts)	68.99	44.03	64
Bologna, liverwurst, salami	21.11	17.17	81
Lamb, organ meats, and others	11.14	11.67	105
Lamb and organ meats	7.99	10.90	136
Mutton, goat, and game	3.15	0.77	24
Poultry	144.13	95.92	67
Fresh and frozen chicken	113.25	75.90	67
Fresh and frozen whole chicken	32.08	23.67	74
Fresh and frozen chicken parts	81.17	52.23	64
Other poultry	30.88	20.02	65
Fish and seafood	120.97	79.34	66
Canned fish and seafood	16.13	13.07	81
Fresh fish and shellfish	69.31	45.95	66
Frozen fish and shellfish	35.53	20.32	57
Eggs	33.75	27.74	82
Dairy products	**328.34**	**244.24**	**74**
Fresh milk and cream	127.15	102.08	80
Fresh milk, all types	114.63	91.35	80
Cream	12.52	10.73	86
Other dairy products	201.19	142.16	71
Butter	18.48	14.57	79
Cheese	95.64	60.65	63
Ice cream and related products	58.74	48.63	83
Miscellaneous dairy products	28.33	18.31	65
Fruits and vegetables	**552.01**	**460.80**	**83**
Fresh fruits	178.20	151.74	85
Apples	32.59	21.74	67
Bananas	31.24	32.72	105
Oranges	20.34	17.78	87
Citrus fruits, excl. oranges	14.29	11.76	82
Other fresh fruits	79.74	67.73	85
Fresh vegetables	174.88	148.64	85
Potatoes	33.35	32.27	97
Lettuce	22.22	17.56	79
Tomatoes	33.71	26.81	80
Other fresh vegetables	85.60	71.99	84
Processed fruits	115.50	97.34	84
Frozen fruits and fruit juices	12.45	11.63	93
Frozen orange juice	6.31	7.17	114
Frozen fruits	2.79	2.83	101
Frozen fruit juices, excl. orange	3.35	1.63	49
Canned fruits	15.06	15.42	102
Dried fruits	6.06	8.33	137
Fresh fruit juice	22.20	20.22	91
Canned and bottled fruit juice	59.74	41.73	70

	total consumer units	average spending	indexed spending
Processed vegetables	$83.43	$63.09	76
Frozen vegetables	27.85	24.28	87
Canned and dried vegetables and juices	55.58	38.81	70
Canned beans	12.47	9.20	74
Canned corn	7.34	5.15	70
Canned miscellaneous vegetables	17.85	13.38	75
Dried peas	0.36	0.23	64
Dried beans	2.55	1.51	59
Dried miscellaneous vegetables	7.38	5.03	68
Dried processed vegetables	0.34	–	–
Frozen vegetable juices	0.06	–	–
Fresh and canned vegetable juices	7.23	4.33	60
Sugar and other sweets	**117.39**	**90.11**	**77**
Candy and chewing gum	75.44	51.48	68
Sugar	15.56	14.31	92
Artificial sweeteners	4.33	5.34	123
Jams, preserves, other sweets	22.06	18.97	86
Fats and oils	**85.16**	**66.36**	**78**
Margarine	9.86	9.29	94
Fats and oils	26.08	19.61	75
Salad dressings	27.01	18.26	68
Nondairy cream and imitation milk	9.33	7.91	85
Peanut butter	12.89	11.28	88
Miscellaneous foods	**471.92**	**283.09**	**60**
Frozen prepared foods	98.09	65.07	66
Frozen meals	29.88	25.85	87
Other frozen prepared foods	68.22	39.22	57
Canned and packaged soups	35.82	33.54	94
Potato chips, nuts, and other snacks	100.53	56.26	56
Potato chips and other snacks	76.37	34.94	46
Nuts	24.16	21.32	88
Condiments and seasonings	86.81	48.73	56
Salt, spices, and other seasonings	21.14	11.96	57
Olives, pickles, relishes	9.70	6.55	68
Sauces and gravies	37.78	17.56	46
Baking needs and miscellaneous products	18.19	12.66	70
Other canned/packaged prepared foods	150.67	79.49	53
Prepared salads	21.46	16.35	76
Prepared desserts	10.32	8.09	78
Baby food	31.57	4.78	15
Miscellaneous prepared foods	87.24	50.27	58
Nonalcoholic beverages	253.94	148.00	58
Cola	81.11	38.18	47
Other carbonated drinks	43.93	19.94	45
Coffee	41.59	38.14	92
Roasted coffee	27.38	20.92	76
Instant and freeze-dried coffee	14.21	17.22	121
Noncarbonated fruit-flavored drinks	18.95	7.38	39

	total consumer units	CUs headed by people aged 75 or older	
		average spending	indexed spending
Tea	$15.86	$12.81	81
Nonalcoholic beer	0.64	–	–
Other nonalcoholic beverages and ice	51.85	31.55	61
Food prepared by CU on trips	41.20	21.58	52
FOOD AWAY FROM HOME	**2,276.29**	**1,107.06**	**49**
Meals at restaurants, carry-outs, other	**1,866.42**	**984.79**	**53**
Lunch	685.79	344.96	50
• At fast food, take-out, delivery, concession stands, buffet, and cafeteria (other than employer and school cafeteria)	377.71	165.44	44
• At full-service restaurants	224.82	169.29	75
• At vending machines, mobile vendors	5.50	0.93	17
• At employer and school cafeterias	77.76	9.31	12
Dinner	736.54	417.25	57
• At fast food, take-out, delivery, concession stands, buffet, and cafeteria (other than employer and school cafeteria)	213.33	88.54	42
• At full-service restaurants	518.02	326.88	63
• At vending machines, mobile vendors	1.87	1.28	68
• At employer and school cafeterias	3.32	0.55	17
Snacks and nonalcoholic beverages	262.67	102.47	39
• At fast food, take-out, delivery, concession stands, buffet, and cafeteria (other than employer and school cafeteria)	185.69	68.68	37
• At full-service restaurants	30.17	24.68	82
• At vending machines, mobile vendors	36.71	8.14	22
• At employer and school cafeterias	10.11	0.96	9
Breakfast and brunch	181.42	120.11	66
• At fast food, take-out, delivery, concession stands, buffet, and cafeteria (other than employer and school cafeteria)	87.83	41.03	47
• At full-service restaurants	87.08	77.07	89
• At vending machines, mobile vendors	1.40	0.95	68
• At employer and school cafeterias	5.11	1.06	21
Board (including at school)	**46.54**	**8.72**	**19**
Catered affairs	**69.00**	**16.13**	**23**
Food on trips	**211.49**	**92.30**	**44**
School lunches	**60.00**	**1.66**	**3**
Meals as pay	**22.86**	**3.46**	**15**
ALCOHOLIC BEVERAGES	**$375.95**	**$144.05**	**38**
At home	**228.08**	**97.37**	**43**
Beer and ale	112.34	23.37	21
Whiskey	13.90	14.46	104
Wine	77.75	47.69	61
Other alcoholic beverages	24.09	11.85	49

	total consumer units	CUs headed by people aged 75 or older	
		average spending	indexed spending
Away from home	**$147.87**	**$46.68**	**32**
Beer and ale	52.86	17.96	34
• At fast food, take-out, delivery, concession stands, buffet, and cafeteria	7.99	1.65	21
• At full-service restaurants	41.95	16.29	39
• At vending machines, mobile vendors	0.32	0.02	6
• At catered affairs	2.59	–	–
Wine	25.85	10.91	42
• At fast food, take-out, delivery, concession stands, buffet and cafeteria	4.41	1.23	28
• At full-service restaurants	20.36	9.68	48
• At catered affairs	1.09	–	–
Other alcoholic beverages	69.16	17.81	26
• At fast food, take-out, delivery, concession stands, buffet, and cafeteria	3.50	1.00	29
• At full-service restaurants	28.94	5.92	20
• At catered affairs	3.94	–	–
Alcoholic beverages purchased on trips	32.78	10.89	33
HOUSING	**$13,283.08**	**$8,257.08**	**62**
SHELTER	**7,829.41**	**4,349.62**	**56**
Owned dwellings*	**5,164.96**	**2,447.13**	**47**
Mortgage interest and charges	2,962.16	408.21	14
Mortgage interest	2,811.49	376.51	13
Interest paid, home equity loan	88.61	16.30	18
Interest paid, home equity line of credit	61.88	15.40	25
Property taxes	1,242.36	1,095.27	88
Maintenance, repairs, insurance, other expenses	960.43	943.64	98
Homeowner's insurance	283.30	276.85	98
Ground rent	40.96	67.29	164
Maintenance and repair services	519.60	528.82	102
Painting and papering	55.58	40.04	72
Plumbing and water heating	46.63	75.94	163
Heat, air conditioning, electrical work	86.28	78.46	91
Roofing and gutters	71.20	137.36	193
Other repair and maintenance services	214.77	168.39	78
Repair, replacement of hard-surface flooring	43.54	27.15	62
Repair of built-in appliances	1.62	1.48	91
Maintenance and repair materials	83.75	23.81	28
Paints, wallpaper, and supplies	14.71	3.24	22
Tools, equipment for painting, wallpapering	1.58	0.35	22
Plumbing supplies and equipment	5.62	3.03	54
Electrical supplies, heating, cooling equip.	3.46	1.62	47
Hard-surface flooring, repair and replacement	8.72	2.42	28
Roofing and gutters	5.29	0.04	1
Plaster, paneling, siding, windows, doors, screens, awnings	13.92	5.62	40
Patio, walk, fence, driveway, masonry, brick, and stucco materials	1.29	1.09	84

	total consumer units	CUs headed by people aged 75 or older	
		average spending	indexed spending
Landscape maintenance	$4.73	$0.77	16
Miscellaneous supplies and equipment	24.43	5.63	23
Insulation, other maintenance, repair	13.15	4.47	34
Finish basement, remodel rooms, build patios, walks, etc.	11.28	1.16	10
Property management and security	27.64	39.51	143
Property management	21.94	31.64	144
Management and upkeep services for security	5.71	7.87	138
Parking	5.17	7.36	142
Rented dwellings	**2,159.89**	**1,627.19**	**75**
Rent	2,104.66	1,585.05	75
Rent as pay	27.17	18.06	66
Maintenance, insurance, and other expenses	28.06	24.08	86
Tenant's insurance	8.90	8.65	97
Maintenance and repair services	11.16	14.66	131
Repair and maintenance services	10.58	12.47	118
Repair, replacement of hard-surface flooring	0.51	2.10	412
Repair of built-in appliances	0.07	0.09	129
Maintenance and repair materials	8.00	0.77	10
Paint, wallpaper, and supplies	1.01	–	–
Painting and wallpapering tools	0.11	–	–
Plastering, paneling, roofing, gutters, etc.	0.90	–	–
Plumbing supplies and equipment	0.80	0.22	28
Electrical supplies, heating, cooling equip.	0.30	–	–
Miscellaneous supplies and equipment	3.67	0.33	9
Insulation, other maintenance and repair	1.09	0.33	30
Materials for additions, finishing basements, remodeling rooms	2.43	–	–
Construction materials for jobs not started	0.15	–	–
Hard-surface flooring	0.73	0.21	29
Landscape maintenance	0.49	–	–
Other lodging	**504.56**	**275.31**	**55**
Owned vacation homes	171.55	152.16	89
Mortgage interest and charges	71.98	20.65	29
Property taxes	63.76	98.40	154
Maintenance, insurance and other expenses	35.81	33.10	92
Homeowner's insurance	9.70	8.38	86
Ground rent	2.93	8.97	306
Maintenance and repair services	16.76	12.24	73
Maintenance and repair materials	2.07	0.55	27
Property management and security	3.60	2.77	77
Property management	2.50	1.97	79
Management, upkeep services for security	1.10	0.80	73
Parking	0.76	0.19	25
Housing while attending school	80.14	8.03	10
Lodging on trips	252.87	115.12	46

	total consumer units	CUs headed by people aged 75 or older	
		average spending	indexed spending
UTILITIES, FUELS, PUBLIC SERVICES	$2,684.32	$2,142.10	80
Natural gas	329.75	338.90	103
Natural gas (renter)	60.32	44.29	73
Natural gas (owner)	266.79	290.37	109
Natural gas (vacation)	2.54	4.02	158
Electricity	981.09	799.47	81
Electricity (renter)	223.26	107.31	48
Electricity (owner)	750.48	681.66	91
Electricity (vacation)	6.32	9.18	145
Fuel oil and other fuels	88.41	122.92	139
Fuel oil	45.98	67.75	147
Fuel oil (renter)	4.64	2.35	51
Fuel oil (owner)	40.98	65.26	159
Fuel oil (vacation)	0.36	0.14	39
Coal	0.07	–	–
Bottled/tank gas	35.27	43.79	124
Gas (renter)	5.09	7.91	155
Gas (owner)	27.19	33.09	122
Gas (vacation)	2.98	2.75	92
Wood and other fuels	7.09	11.38	161
Wood and other fuels (renter)	1.32	1.79	136
Wood and other fuels (owner)	5.68	9.60	169
Telephone services	956.74	578.81	60
Residential telephone and pay phones	641.00	494.50	77
Cellular phone service	293.76	77.89	27
Pager service	1.71	0.18	11
Phone cards	20.28	6.25	31
Water and other public services	328.33	301.99	92
Water and sewerage maintenance	237.16	211.88	89
Water and sewerage maintenance (renter)	32.76	13.49	41
Water and sewerage maintenance (owner)	201.79	193.84	96
Water and sewerage maintenance (vacation)	2.36	4.28	181
Trash and garbage collection	89.05	88.28	99
Trash and garbage collection (renter)	9.89	3.67	37
Trash and garbage collection (owner)	76.61	82.22	107
Trash and garbage collection (vacation)	2.53	2.30	91
Septic tank cleaning	2.12	1.83	86
HOUSEHOLD SERVICES	705.71	723.36	103
Personal services	331.02	362.87	110
Babysitting, child care in your own home	35.91	0.35	1
Babysitting, child care in someone else's home	27.48	0.46	2
Care for elderly, invalids, handicapped, etc.	50.07	293.34	586
Adult day care centers	6.81	53.69	788
Day care centers, nurseries, and preschools	210.74	15.03	7
Other household services	374.70	360.50	96
Housekeeping services	79.90	106.83	134
Gardening, lawn care service	72.38	118.27	163
Water softening service	3.15	3.36	107

	total consumer units	CUs headed by people aged 75 or older	
		average spending	indexed spending
Nonclothing laundry, dry cleaning, sent out	$1.72	$2.28	133
Nonclothing laundry, dry cleaning, coin-operated	4.13	2.47	60
Termite/pest control services	13.25	21.63	163
Home security system service fee	17.40	11.06	64
Other home services	15.06	17.90	119
Termite/pest control products	0.68	1.34	197
Moving, storage, and freight express	33.13	13.51	41
Appliance repair, including service center	10.86	13.55	125
Reupholstering and furniture repair	7.40	6.73	91
Repairs/rentals of lawn/garden equipment, hand/power tools, etc.	3.62	4.53	125
Appliance rental	1.07	0.14	13
Rental of office equip., nonbusiness use	0.41	–	–
Repair of misc. household equip., furnishings	0.62	–	–
Repair of computer systems, nonbusiness use	2.53	2.35	93
Computer information services	107.29	34.54	32
HOUSEKEEPING SUPPLIES	**545.28**	**378.61**	**69**
Laundry and cleaning supplies	**130.57**	**85.01**	**65**
Soaps and detergents	72.89	45.96	63
Other laundry cleaning products	57.68	39.04	68
Other household products	**283.28**	**172.35**	**61**
Cleansing and toilet tissue, paper towels, and napkins	76.46	70.01	92
Miscellaneous household products	96.81	52.84	55
Lawn and garden supplies	110.01	49.51	45
Postage and stationery	**131.44**	**121.25**	**92**
Stationery, stationery supplies, giftwrap	60.20	40.89	68
Postage	69.12	79.74	115
Delivery services	2.12	0.61	29
HOUSEHOLD FURNISHINGS, EQUIPMENT	**1,518.36**	**663.39**	**44**
Household textiles	**135.52**	**83.94**	**62**
Bathroom linens	22.35	13.79	62
Bedroom linens	65.98	30.38	46
Kitchen and dining room linens	10.11	8.18	81
Curtains and draperies	16.65	10.53	63
Slipcovers and decorative pillows	7.40	14.65	198
Sewing materials for household items	11.44	5.47	48
Other linens	1.59	0.94	59
Furniture	**401.28**	**127.43**	**32**
Mattresses and springs	52.91	23.33	44
Other bedroom furniture	68.33	9.04	13
Sofas	85.33	35.27	41
Living room chairs	39.21	30.92	79
Living room tables	18.03	3.35	19
Kitchen and dining room furniture	61.28	8.13	13
Infants' furniture	6.46	0.40	6
Outdoor furniture	16.79	2.73	16
Wall units, cabinets, and other furniture	52.94	14.27	27

	total consumer units	CUs headed by people aged 75 or older	
		average spending	indexed spending
Floor coverings	**$40.49**	**$27.12**	**67**
Wall-to-wall carpeting (renter)	0.65	–	–
Wall-to-wall carpet (replacement) (owner)	21.04	19.18	91
Floor coverings, nonpermanent	18.79	7.94	42
Major appliances	**188.47**	**108.30**	**57**
Dishwashers (built-in), garbage disposals, range hoods (renter)	1.24	0.62	50
Dishwashers (built-in), garbage disposals, range hoods (owner)	15.28	10.70	70
Refrigerators and freezers (renter)	5.58	3.62	65
Refrigerators and freezers (owner)	46.50	33.14	71
Washing machines (renter)	4.42	2.94	67
Washing machines (owner)	17.88	9.61	54
Clothes dryers (renter)	3.17	0.77	24
Clothes dryers (owner)	13.88	5.82	42
Cooking stoves, ovens (renter)	2.86	–	–
Cooking stoves, ovens (owner)	28.09	14.30	51
Microwave ovens (renter)	2.14	1.11	52
Microwave ovens (owner)	8.36	6.53	78
Portable dishwasher (renter)	0.25	–	–
Portable dishwasher (owner)	0.51	–	–
Window air conditioners (renter)	1.83	1.51	83
Window air conditioners (owner)	6.07	5.71	94
Electric floor-cleaning equipment	22.80	6.41	28
Sewing machines	4.79	3.74	78
Miscellaneous household appliances	**2.81**	**1.79**	**64**
Small appliances and misc. housewares	100.43	42.19	42
Housewares	77.55	27.45	35
Plastic dinnerware	1.57	0.32	20
China and other dinnerware	14.51	4.89	34
Flatware	3.79	0.82	22
Glassware	6.51	1.64	25
Silver serving pieces	4.05	2.34	58
Other serving pieces	1.44	0.48	33
Nonelectric cookware	24.25	8.57	35
Tableware, nonelectric kitchenware	21.44	8.40	39
Small appliances	22.89	14.73	64
Small electric kitchen appliances	17.18	12.82	75
Portable heating and cooling equipment	5.70	1.92	34
Miscellaneous household equipment	**652.17**	**274.41**	**42**
Window coverings	13.91	5.07	36
Infants' equipment	12.96	0.49	4
Laundry and cleaning equipment	15.15	6.33	42
Outdoor equipment	31.52	7.42	24
Clocks	5.87	3.01	51
Lamps and lighting fixtures	11.74	2.32	20
Other household decorative items	144.94	85.02	59
Telephones and accessories	32.73	22.80	70
Lawn and garden equipment	48.16	24.48	51

	total consumer units	CUs headed by people aged 75 or older	
		average spending	indexed spending
Power tools	$33.27	$3.21	10
Office furniture for home use	10.57	4.97	47
Hand tools	8.05	3.82	47
Indoor plants and fresh flowers	49.78	34.41	69
Closet and storage items	9.98	4.03	40
Rental of furniture	4.60	0.63	14
Luggage	5.98	2.41	40
Computers and computer hardware, nonbusiness use	138.58	30.22	22
Computer software and accessories, nonbusiness use	17.67	4.92	28
Telephone answering devices	1.08	0.50	46
Calculators	1.44	0.13	9
Business equipment for home use	0.97	0.87	90
Other hardware	12.85	2.76	21
Smoke alarms (owner)	1.10	1.61	146
Smoke alarms (renter)	0.39	–	–
Other household appliances (owner)	8.00	3.92	49
Other household appliances (renter)	1.23	0.21	17
Miscellaneous household equipment and parts	29.62	18.82	64
APPAREL AND SERVICES	**$1,749.22**	**$673.79**	**39**
Men's apparel	**319.48**	**107.88**	**34**
Suits	32.96	12.91	39
Sport coats and tailored jackets	10.65	3.24	30
Coats and jackets	33.86	5.22	15
Underwear	15.27	6.36	42
Hosiery	12.22	3.17	26
Nightwear	2.98	1.08	36
Accessories	22.41	5.64	25
Sweaters and vests	15.68	4.80	31
Active sportswear	15.13	10.38	69
Shirts	78.89	19.37	25
Pants	57.64	28.88	50
Shorts and shorts sets	12.22	4.31	35
Uniforms	3.21	0.50	16
Costumes	6.35	2.02	32
Boys' (aged 2 to 15) apparel	**89.98**	**17.63**	**20**
Coats and jackets	6.38	0.78	12
Sweaters	3.65	0.86	24
Shirts	19.50	4.63	24
Underwear	5.02	1.15	23
Nightwear	2.59	1.95	75
Hosiery	4.21	0.92	22
Accessories	4.12	0.66	16
Suits, sport coats, and vests	2.37	1.03	43
Pants	22.58	3.32	15
Shorts and shorts sets	8.66	0.82	9
Uniforms	3.35	0.23	7
Active sportswear	3.84	0.35	9
Costumes	3.72	0.94	25

	total consumer units	CUs headed by people aged 75 or older	
		average spending	indexed spending
Women's apparel	**$586.91**	**$318.30**	**54**
Coats and jackets	50.06	28.20	56
Dresses	56.40	31.04	55
Sport coats and tailored jackets	6.48	6.17	95
Sweaters and vests	50.47	32.60	65
Shirts, blouses, and tops	103.24	59.99	58
Skirts	17.48	4.39	25
Pants	96.29	35.76	37
Shorts and shorts sets	16.09	8.73	54
Active sportswear	30.07	21.24	71
Nightwear	27.63	22.94	83
Undergarments	33.55	17.57	52
Hosiery	21.22	11.76	55
Suits	29.01	17.56	61
Accessories	33.37	15.57	47
Uniforms	6.12	0.77	13
Costumes	9.42	4.01	43
Girls' (aged 2 to 15) apparel	**117.21**	**17.00**	**15**
Coats and jackets	6.49	1.22	19
Dresses and suits	12.41	1.77	14
Shirts, blouses, and sweaters	29.33	5.89	20
Skirts and pants	24.07	3.89	16
Shorts and shorts sets	8.28	0.55	7
Active sportswear	9.32	0.54	6
Underwear and nightwear	7.63	1.50	20
Hosiery	4.30	0.53	12
Accessories	5.81	0.22	4
Uniforms	4.77	0.20	4
Costumes	4.80	0.69	14
Children under age 2	**82.60**	**15.27**	**18**
Coats, jackets, and snowsuits	2.43	0.50	21
Outerwear including dresses	23.71	6.05	26
Underwear	43.60	5.75	13
Nightwear and loungewear	4.07	0.86	21
Accessories	8.79	2.11	24
Footwear	**313.17**	**108.17**	**35**
Men's	102.90	31.88	31
Boys'	36.87	5.96	16
Women's	141.64	66.30	47
Girls'	31.76	4.04	13
Other apparel products and services	**239.87**	**89.52**	**37**
Material for making clothes	5.11	2.95	58
Sewing patterns and notions	8.20	2.65	32
Watches	13.62	5.03	37
Jewelry	89.65	25.02	28
Shoe repair and other shoe services	1.44	1.20	83
Coin-operated apparel laundry and dry cleaning	37.58	17.67	47
Apparel alteration, repair, and tailoring services	5.86	3.53	60
Clothing rental	2.66	–	–
Watch and jewelry repair	5.49	5.82	106
Professional laundry, dry cleaning	69.69	25.52	37
Clothing storage	0.55	0.13	24

	total consumer units	CUs headed by people aged 75 or older	
		average spending	indexed spending
TRANSPORTATION	**$7,759.29**	**$3,177.83**	**41**
VEHICLE PURCHASES	**3,664.93**	**1,180.26**	**32**
Cars and trucks, new	**1,752.96**	**711.89**	**41**
New cars	883.08	508.15	58
New trucks	869.88	203.74	23
Cars and trucks, used	**1,842.29**	**468.37**	**25**
Used cars	1,113.46	301.81	27
Used trucks	728.82	166.56	23
Other vehicles	**69.68**	**–**	**–**
New motorcycles	36.26	–	–
Used motorcycles	33.42	–	–
GASOLINE AND MOTOR OIL	**1,235.06**	**575.24**	**47**
Gasoline	1,125.01	533.36	47
Diesel fuel	10.86	1.66	15
Gasoline on trips	88.24	36.40	41
Motor oil	10.05	3.46	34
Motor oil on trips	0.89	0.37	42
OTHER VEHICLE EXPENSES	**2,470.55**	**1,211.70**	**49**
Vehicle finance charges	**397.04**	**87.18**	**22**
Automobile finance charges	193.12	41.45	21
Truck finance charges	182.89	43.63	24
Motorcycle and plane finance charges	2.36	–	–
Other vehicle finance charges	18.67	2.09	11
Maintenance and repairs	697.30	407.80	58
Coolant, additives, brake, transmission fluids	3.82	1.47	38
Tires—purchased, replaced, installed	89.93	43.69	49
Parts, equipment, and accessories	41.70	18.91	45
Vehicle audio equipment, excl. labor	12.32	–	–
Vehicle products	4.92	1.94	39
Miscellaneous auto repair, servicing	43.69	16.56	38
Body work and painting	31.24	31.92	102
Clutch, transmission repair	48.68	29.78	61
Drive shaft and rear-end repair	6.51	1.04	16
Brake work	57.73	32.62	57
Repair to steering or front-end	16.91	6.45	38
Repair to engine cooling system	21.68	20.40	94
Motor tune-up	49.69	25.98	52
Lube, oil change, and oil filters	65.07	39.83	61
Front-end alignment, wheel balance, rotation	11.90	5.33	45
Shock absorber replacement	4.82	2.58	54
Gas tank repair, replacement	4.32	8.24	191
Tire repair and other repair work	39.83	23.95	60
Vehicle air conditioning repair	17.00	13.97	82
Exhaust system repair	12.56	12.74	101
Electrical system repair	28.42	21.25	75
Motor repair, replacement	76.62	48.71	64
Auto repair service policy	7.93	0.45	6

	total consumer units	CUs headed by people aged 75 or older	
		average spending	indexed spending
Vehicle insurance	**$893.50**	**$528.01**	**59**
Vehicle rental, leases, licenses, other charges	**482.71**	**188.72**	**39**
Leased and rented vehicles	324.48	98.69	30
Rented vehicles	41.33	18.95	46
Auto rental	6.76	7.90	117
Auto rental on trips	28.28	8.54	30
Truck rental	2.21	1.87	85
Truck rental on trips	3.55	0.65	18
Leased vehicles	283.15	79.73	28
Car lease payments	149.63	60.41	40
Cash down payment (car lease)	11.13	4.11	37
Termination fee (car lease)	1.28	–	–
Truck lease payments	114.24	12.91	11
Cash down payment (truck lease)	4.92	–	–
Termination fee (truck lease)	1.94	2.31	119
Vehicle registration, state	72.82	44.52	61
Vehicle registration, local	7.76	5.04	65
Driver's license	6.26	4.70	75
Vehicle inspection	9.26	5.95	64
Parking fees	29.25	7.56	26
Parking fees in home city, excluding residence	24.24	5.47	23
Parking fees on trips	5.01	2.09	42
Tolls	10.59	3.19	30
Tolls on trips	3.94	0.98	25
Towing charges	5.60	2.00	36
Automobile service clubs	12.75	16.09	126
PUBLIC TRANSPORTATION	**388.75**	**210.62**	**54**
Airline fares	243.57	113.46	47
Intercity bus fares	11.48	9.38	82
Intracity mass transit fares	49.97	13.36	27
Local transportation on trips	10.91	9.39	86
Taxi fares and limousine service on trips	6.41	5.52	86
Taxi fares and limousine service	18.95	7.48	39
Intercity train fares	16.09	13.58	84
Ship fares	29.74	35.91	121
School bus	1.64	2.53	154
HEALTH CARE	**$2,350.32**	**$3,583.79**	**152**
HEALTH INSURANCE	**1,167.71**	**1,848.81**	**158**
Commercial health insurance	**217.53**	**113.02**	**52**
Traditional fee-for-service health plan (not BCBS)	68.27	77.22	113
Preferred-provider health plan (not BCBS)	149.26	35.80	24
Blue Cross, Blue Shield	**315.67**	**356.27**	**113**
Traditional fee-for-service health plan	53.76	73.09	136
Preferred-provider health plan	106.99	28.47	27
Health maintenance organization	101.53	67.16	66
Commercial Medicare supplement	47.35	178.24	376
Other BCBS health insurance	6.05	9.30	154

	total consumer units	CUs headed by people aged 75 or older	
		average spending	indexed spending
Health maintenance plans (HMOs)	$280.47	$144.62	52
Medicare payments	186.87	759.25	406
Commercial Medicare supplements/ other health insurance	167.18	475.64	285
Commercial Medicare supplement (not BCBS)	106.32	388.36	365
Other health insurance (not BCBS)	60.86	87.28	143
MEDICAL SERVICES	**589.87**	**527.41**	**89**
Physician's services	147.53	109.20	74
Dental services	226.99	228.24	101
Eye care services	34.20	41.90	123
Service by professionals other than physician	42.76	33.45	78
Lab tests, X-rays	26.79	18.89	71
Hospital room	36.57	16.61	45
Hospital services other than room	51.51	31.59	61
Care in convalescent or nursing home	12.46	40.93	328
Other medical services	9.46	6.60	70
DRUGS	**487.43**	**1,028.36**	**211**
Nonprescription drugs	64.45	87.05	135
Nonprescription vitamins	49.15	57.83	118
Prescription drugs	373.83	883.48	236
MEDICAL SUPPLIES	**105.31**	**179.21**	**170**
Eyeglasses and contact lenses	52.26	43.32	83
Hearing aids	14.98	72.65	485
Topicals and dressings	27.56	36.30	132
Medical equipment for general use	2.69	3.39	126
Supportive, convalescent medical equipment	5.21	16.48	316
Rental of medical equipment	1.06	1.57	148
Rental of supportive, convalescent medical equipment	1.55	5.50	355
ENTERTAINMENT	**$2,078.99**	**$896.01**	**43**
FEES AND ADMISSIONS	**541.67**	**215.92**	**40**
Recreation expenses on trips	25.64	9.68	38
Social, recreation, civic club membership	107.92	55.92	52
Fees for participant sports	75.05	53.07	71
Participant sports on trips	29.50	10.39	35
Movie, theater, opera, ballet	98.30	32.49	33
Movie, other admissions on trips	45.57	17.66	39
Admission to sports events	36.18	10.51	29
Admission to sports events on trips	15.19	5.89	39
Fees for recreational lessons	82.69	10.63	13
Other entertainment services on trips	25.64	9.68	38
TELEVISION, RADIO, SOUND EQUIPMENT	**691.90**	**372.01**	**54**
Television	**543.66**	**351.58**	**65**
Cable service and community antenna	382.28	305.13	80
Black-and-white TV	0.80	–	–
Color TV, console	38.63	9.06	23
Color TV, portable, table model	39.14	22.83	58

	total consumer units	CUs headed by people aged 75 or older	
		average spending	indexed spending
VCRs and video disc players	$23.25	$2.63	11
Video cassettes, tapes, and discs	33.13	5.61	17
Video game hardware and software	23.46	3.13	13
Repair of TV, radio, and sound equipment	2.50	3.14	126
Rental of television sets	0.46	0.06	13
Radio and sound equipment	**148.25**	**20.43**	**14**
Radios	3.98	–	–
Tape recorders and players	5.31	1.13	21
Sound components and component systems	20.19	3.76	19
Miscellaneous sound equipment	3.18	–	–
Sound equipment accessories	5.97	1.63	27
Satellite dishes	1.00	0.12	12
Compact disc, tape, record, video mail order clubs	6.53	2.65	41
Records, CDs, audio tapes, needles	36.47	5.98	16
Rental of VCR, radio, sound equipment	0.25	0.15	60
Musical instruments and accessories	24.82	1.06	4
Rental and repair of musical instruments	1.22	0.11	9
Rental of video cassettes, tapes, discs, films	39.33	3.84	10
PETS, TOYS, PLAYGROUND EQUIPMENT	**369.12**	**135.19**	**37**
Pets	**248.25**	**109.12**	**44**
Pet food	102.56	54.01	53
Pet purchase, supplies, and medicines	52.29	10.27	20
Pet services	21.95	9.37	43
Veterinarian services	71.44	35.47	50
Toys, games, hobbies, and tricycles	**117.34**	**25.90**	**22**
Playground equipment	**3.54**	**0.17**	**5**
OTHER ENTERTAINMENT SUPPLIES, EQUIPMENT, SERVICES	**476.30**	**172.89**	**36**
Unmotored recreational vehicles	**47.14**	**4.39**	**9**
Boat without motor and boat trailers	16.15	1.15	7
Trailer and other attachable campers	30.99	3.24	10
Motorized recreational vehicles	**170.19**	**111.93**	**66**
Motorized camper	40.05	–	–
Other vehicle	35.47	34.62	98
Motorboats	94.67	77.31	82
Rental of recreational vehicles	**1.99**	**–**	**–**
Outboard motors	**0.71**	**–**	**–**
Docking and landing fees	**6.66**	**2.10**	**32**
Sports, recreation, exercise equipment	**150.33**	**28.39**	**19**
Athletic gear, game tables, exercise equipment	60.51	20.00	33
Bicycles	13.45	1.34	10
Camping equipment	9.59	0.97	10
Hunting and fishing equipment	35.68	1.23	3
Winter sports equipment	5.45	0.67	12
Water sports equipment	8.95	0.02	0
Other sports equipment	14.62	2.07	14
Rental and repair of misc. sports equipment	2.07	2.11	102

	total consumer units	CUs headed by people aged 75 or older	
		average spending	indexed spending
Photographic equipment and supplies	**$90.48**	**$21.80**	**24**
Film	17.74	5.15	29
Other photographic supplies	2.27	1.84	81
Film processing	26.60	7.44	28
Repair and rental of photographic equipment	0.12	0.31	258
Photographic equipment	23.34	3.97	17
Photographer fees	20.42	3.08	15
Fireworks	**1.52**	–	–
Souvenirs	**1.25**	–	–
Visual goods	**1.19**	**0.29**	**24**
Pinball, electronic video games	**4.84**	**3.98**	**82**
PERSONAL CARE PRODUCTS AND SERVICES	**$525.80**	**$389.55**	**74**
Personal care products	**276.65**	**160.24**	**58**
Hair care products	53.57	24.49	46
Hair accessories	6.57	3.69	56
Wigs and hairpieces	1.32	0.73	55
Oral hygiene products	27.33	21.27	78
Shaving products	15.09	5.69	38
Cosmetics, perfume, and bath products	129.13	70.46	55
Deodorants, feminine hygiene, misc. products	30.29	27.53	91
Electric personal care appliances	13.34	6.38	48
Personal care services	**249.15**	**229.31**	**92**
READING	**$138.57**	**$133.51**	**96**
Newspaper subscriptions	43.88	74.41	170
Newspaper, nonsubscription	11.30	8.60	76
Magazine subscriptions	16.59	18.57	112
Magazines, nonsubscription	9.35	2.83	30
Books purchased through book clubs	6.62	8.75	132
Books not purchased through book clubs	50.38	20.17	40
Encyclopedia and other reference book sets	0.33	0.18	55
EDUCATION	**$751.95**	**$112.15**	**15**
College tuition	444.45	86.52	19
Elementary and high school tuition	128.94	2.33	2
Other school tuition	25.53	1.55	6
Other school expenses including rentals	25.77	3.11	12
Books, supplies for college	57.93	5.41	9
Books, supplies for elementary, high school	16.14	0.35	2
Books, supplies for day care, nursery school	3.39	0.58	17
Miscellaneous school expenses and supplies	49.80	12.30	25

	total consumer units	CUs headed by people aged 75 or older	
		average spending	indexed spending
TOBACCO PRODUCTS AND SMOKING SUPPLIES	**$320.49**	**$80.83**	**25**
Cigarettes	291.89	64.05	22
Other tobacco products	26.27	14.84	56
Smoking accessories	2.33	1.94	83
FINANCIAL PRODUCTS, SERVICES	**$788.12**	**$572.27**	**73**
Miscellaneous fees	2.25	0.15	7
Lottery and gambling losses	46.94	47.16	100
Legal fees	132.99	107.92	81
Funeral expenses	77.91	146.89	189
Safe deposit box rental	3.84	6.64	173
Checking accounts, other bank service charges	25.91	7.66	30
Cemetery lots, vaults, and maintenance fees	16.05	55.95	349
Accounting fees	57.85	58.82	102
Miscellaneous personal services	39.77	6.66	17
Finance charges, except mortgage and vehicles	271.37	69.58	26
Occupational expenses	38.46	3.88	10
Expenses for other properties	65.99	57.15	87
Credit card memberships	2.82	0.74	26
Shopping club membership fees	5.97	3.07	51
CASH CONTRIBUTIONS	**$1,277.10**	**$1,739.54**	**136**
Support for college students	75.94	16.87	22
Alimony expenditures	21.18	26.51	125
Child support expenditures	190.75	17.01	9
Gifts to non-CU members of stocks, bonds, and mutual funds	24.23	130.02	537
Cash contributions to charities and other organizations	137.62	213.82	155
Cash contributions to church, religious organizations	557.29	583.11	105
Cash contributions to educational institutions	33.42	28.15	84
Cash contributions to political organizations	10.90	46.44	426
Other cash gifts	225.76	677.61	300
PERSONAL INSURANCE, PENSIONS	**$3,898.62**	**$696.41**	**18**
Life and other personal insurance	**406.11**	**287.31**	**71**
Life, endowment, annuity, other personal insurance	391.65	269.38	69
Other nonhealth insurance	14.46	17.93	124
Pensions and Social Security	**3,492.51**	**409.09**	**12**
Deductions for government retirement	69.48	0.82	1
Deductions for railroad retirement	2.21	–	–
Deductions for private pensions	390.38	11.27	3
Nonpayroll deposit to retirement plans	426.12	110.50	26
Deductions for Social Security	2,604.32	286.50	11

	total consumer units	CUs headed by people aged 75 or older	
		average spending	indexed spending
PERSONAL TAXES	**$2,496.26**	**$478.66**	**19**
Federal income taxes	1,842.57	309.57	17
State and local income taxes	506.45	51.09	10
Other taxes	147.24	117.99	80
GIFTS FOR NON-HOUSEHOLD MEMBERS**	**$1,036.24**	**$559.82**	**54**
FOOD	**82.18**	**36.79**	**45**
Cakes and cupcakes	2.41	1.25	52
Other fresh fruits (excl. apples, bananas, citrus)	2.26	0.49	22
Candy and chewing gum	11.69	11.71	100
Board (including at school)	21.90	3.02	14
Catered affairs	26.19	13.67	52
ALCOHOLIC BEVERAGES	**13.42**	**2.56**	**19**
Beer and ale	4.73	0.37	8
Wine	5.84	1.46	25
HOUSING	**258.69**	**138.96**	**54**
Housekeeping supplies	**42.48**	**28.86**	**68**
Laundry and cleaning supplies	2.93	1.29	44
Other household products	11.69	7.53	64
Miscellaneous household products	5.85	4.52	77
Lawn and garden supplies	4.20	0.99	24
Postage and stationery	27.86	20.05	72
Stationery, stationery supplies, giftwrap	21.13	15.34	73
Postage	6.14	4.44	72
Household textiles	**13.72**	**5.25**	**38**
Bathroom linens	2.59	1.50	58
Bedroom linens	6.10	0.95	16
Appliances and miscellaneous housewares	**23.98**	**10.88**	**45**
Major appliances	8.41	2.37	28
Electric floor-cleaning equipment	2.77	–	–
Small appliances and miscellaneous housewares	15.57	8.51	55
China and other dinnerware	2.46	2.06	84
Nonelectric cookware	3.53	1.43	41
Tableware, nonelectric kitchenware	2.63	0.73	28
Small electric kitchen appliances	2.71	2.56	94
Miscellaneous household equipment	**64.70**	**29.16**	**45**
Infants' equipment	3.82	0.14	4
Outdoor equipment	2.07	0.12	6
Other household decorative items	25.76	6.09	24
Power tools	2.80	–	–
Indoor plants, fresh flowers	13.43	12.47	93
Computers and computer hardware	6.59	3.81	58
Miscellaneous household equipment	2.19	2.34	107
Other housing	**113.80**	**64.81**	**57**
Repair or maintenance services	4.51	1.02	23
Housing while attending school	39.93	8.03	20

	total consumer units	CUs headed by people aged 75 or older	
		average spending	indexed spending
Natural gas (renter)	$3.62	$6.33	175
Electricity (renter)	14.67	17.43	119
Water, sewer maintenance (renter)	3.04	1.96	64
Day-care centers, nurseries, and preschools	23.81	6.80	29
APPAREL AND SERVICES	**237.13**	**131.60**	**55**
Men and boys, aged 2 or older	**63.74**	**33.93**	**53**
Men's coats and jackets	5.09	0.78	15
Men's accessories	4.45	1.25	28
Men's sweaters and vests	3.06	1.30	42
Men's active sportswear	2.76	7.58	275
Men's shirts	16.79	5.21	31
Men's pants	6.93	0.42	6
Boys' shirts	3.71	4.34	117
Boys' pants	3.76	2.33	62
Women and girls, aged 2 or older	**81.76**	**65.12**	**80**
Women's coats and jackets	5.62	1.81	32
Women's dresses	7.66	11.89	155
Women's vests and sweaters	8.50	3.29	39
Women's shirts, tops, blouses	9.06	10.34	114
Women's pants	6.62	–	–
Women's active sportswear	4.33	7.12	164
Women's sleepwear	6.45	7.45	116
Women's accessories	5.71	3.18	56
Girls' dresses and suits	2.98	0.66	22
Girls' shirts, blouses, sweaters	4.48	2.89	65
Girls' skirts and pants	3.32	2.41	73
Girls' accessories	2.38	0.22	9
Children under age 2	**39.99**	**14.54**	**36**
Infant dresses, outerwear	15.28	5.75	38
Infant underwear	16.91	5.41	32
Infant nightwear, loungewear	2.55	0.83	33
Infant accessories	3.93	2.11	54
Other apparel products and services	**51.63**	**18.02**	**35**
Jewelry and watches	24.01	6.31	26
Watches	2.16	0.77	36
Jewelry	21.85	5.54	25
Men's footwear	8.37	–	–
Boys' footwear	4.46	5.88	132
Women's footwear	8.82	3.61	41
Girls' footwear	3.30	0.44	13
TRANSPORTATION	**43.87**	**23.96**	**55**
New cars	7.09	3.35	47
Used cars	12.21	5.50	45
Airline fares	6.78	5.55	82
Ship fares	2.74	3.91	143

	total consumer units	CUs headed by people aged 75 or older	
		average spending	indexed spending
HEALTH CARE	**$32.59**	**$37.24**	**114**
Physician's services	3.07	0.16	5
Dental services	4.03	5.35	133
Care in convalescent or nursing home	5.19	17.30	333
Nonprescription vitamins	3.93	–	–
Prescription drugs	2.38	3.37	142
ENTERTAINMENT	**78.24**	**37.66**	**48**
Toys, games, hobbies, and tricycles	29.98	14.78	49
Other entertainment	48.26	22.88	47
Fees for recreational lessons	7.88	3.23	41
Community antenna or cable TV	6.37	7.31	115
VCRs and videodisc players	2.26	0.64	28
Video game hardware and software	2.13	1.07	50
Athletic gear, game tables, exercise equipment	6.60	1.66	25
Hunting and fishing equipment	3.06	0.04	1
Photographer fees	3.19	0.63	20
PERSONAL CARE PRODUCTS, SERVICES	**21.15**	**9.68**	**46**
Cosmetics, perfume, bath preparation	12.53	4.73	38
Electric personal care appliances	3.31	1.33	40
EDUCATION	**183.88**	**95.65**	**52**
College tuition	127.83	83.73	66
Elementary and high school tuition	25.95	2.33	9
Other school tuition	4.44	0.03	1
Other school expenses including rentals	3.99	2.36	59
College books and supplies	11.93	5.00	42
Miscellaneous school supplies	7.38	2.06	28
ALL OTHER GIFTS	**83.76**	**42.97**	**51**
Gifts of trip expenses	44.40	27.27	61
Lottery and gambling losses	2.86	0.90	31
Legal fees	5.82	–	–
Funeral expenses	25.25	13.27	53
Miscellaneous personal services	2.16	0.25	12

* This figure does not include the amount paid for mortgage principle, which is considered an asset.
** Expenditures on gifts are also included in the preceding product and service categories. Food spending, for example, includes the amount spent on food gifts. Only gift categories with spending of $2.00 or more by the average consumer unit are shown.
Note: The Bureau of Labor Statistics uses consumer unit rather than household as the sampling unit in the Consumer Expenditure Survey. For the definition of consumer unit, see the glossary. (–) means not applicable or the sample is too small to make a reliable estimate.
Source: Bureau of Labor Statistics, unpublished data from the 2002 Consumer Expenditure Survey; calculations by New Strategist

9

Wealth

■ Among householders aged 65 to 74, net worth rose 68 percent between 1989 and 2001, to $176,300. The 55-to-64 age group has the highest net worth, at $181,500.

■ The financial assets of householders aged 55 to 64 rose 57 percent between 1989 and 2001, to $56,630, the highest of any age group. Behind the rise in financial assets was the soaring stock market of the 1990s.

■ Householders aged 55 to 64 saw only a small increase in the value of their nonfinancial assets between 1989 and 2001—a gain of just 14 percent after adjusting for inflation. The nonfinancial assets of those aged 65 or older rose by a much larger 72 percent.

■ Householders aged 55 to 64 saw their debt more than double between 1989 and 2001— the largest increase of any age group. In contrast, the debt of householders aged 75 or older grew more slowly than those of any other age group. It rose 30 percent to $5,000.

■ Only 31 percent of men 65 or older receive a company or union pension, and the figure is a much smaller 17 percent among women. Fully 90 to 92 percent of people aged 65 or older receive Social Security income.

Net Worth of Older Americans Is Growing

The biggest increase has been among householders aged 65 to 74.

Since 1989, the median net worth (assets minus debts) of the average household rose 33 percent after adjusting for inflation, from $64,600 in 1989 to $86,100 in 2001. The net worth of Americans aged 65 or older rose much faster during those years. Among householders aged 65 to 74, net worth rose an enormous 68 percent, to $176,300, while that of household-ers aged 75 or older rose 52 percent to $151,400. Despite these gains, the net worth of house-holders aged 65 or older was less than that of householders aged 55 to 64, which stood at $181,500 in 2001.

Behind the rising wealth of older Americans is the aging of a more affluent generation into the older age groups. Also playing a role is the sharp rise in home values during the past few decades. While the debt of older Americans has grown since 1989, financial and nonfinancial assets have grown even faster, more than making up the difference.

In contrast to the gains made by older householders, those under age 55 have seen little growth in their net worth since 1989, and the net worth of those aged 45 to 54 has actually declined. Postponed homeownership by those under age 55 is behind this lacklus-ter showing. As homeownership rates climb, the net worth of younger householders may rise.

■ Older Americans are likely to see their net worth continue to grow as real estate values climb.

Net worth peaks in the older age groups

(median net worth of total householders and householders aged 55 or older, 2001)

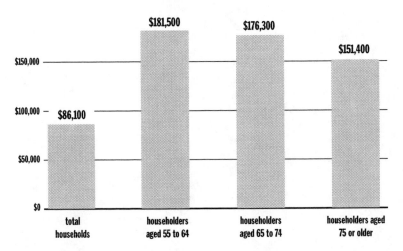

Table 9.1 Net Worth of Households by Age of Householder, 1989 to 2001

(median net worth of households by age of householder, 1989 to 2001; percent change, 1989–2001 and 1998–2001; in 2001 dollars)

	2001	1998	1995	1992	1989	percent change 1998–01	percent change 1989–01
Total households	**$86,100**	**$78,000**	**$66,400**	**$61,200**	**$64,600**	**10.4%**	**33.3%**
Under age 35	11,600	9,900	13,900	11,400	10,700	17.2	8.4
Aged 35 to 44	77,600	69,000	60,300	55,100	77,000	12.5	0.8
Aged 45 to 54	132,900	114,800	107,500	96,800	135,900	15.8	–2.2
Aged 55 to 64	181,500	139,200	133,200	141,100	134,700	30.4	34.7
Aged 65 to 74	176,300	159,500	128,000	121,700	105,000	10.5	67.9
Aged 75 or older	151,400	136,700	107,500	107,500	99,700	10.8	51.9

Source: Federal Reserve Board, results from the Survey of Consumer Finances; Internet site http://www.federalreserve.gov/pubs/oss/oss2/2001/scf2001home.html; calculations by New Strategist

Financial Assets Peak among 55-to-74-Year-Olds

But financial assets are worth much less than nonfinancial assets in every age group.

As the stock market boomed, the financial assets of American households rose a substantial 80 percent between 1989 and 2001—to $28,000, after adjusting for inflation. The financial assets of householders aged 65 to 74 rose an even greater 92 percent, to $51,400. Householders aged 55 to 64 saw their assets rise a smaller 57 percent, but the value was higher than that for any other age group, at $56,630. The oldest householders were the only ones to see the value of their financial assets decline between 1989 and 2001, falling 1 percent to $40,000.

Behind the rise in financial assets was the soaring stock market. Fifty-seven percent of householders aged 55 to 64 own stock, as do 39 percent of those aged 65 to 74 and 34 percent of those aged 75 or older. The value of stock owned by older householders more than doubled between 1989 and 2001. It's likely that those values are lower today because of the stock market decline.

Householders aged 57 or older account for 27 percent of the nation's equity owners, according to the Investment Company Institute and the Securities Industry Association. Among stock-owning householders aged 57 or older, 54 percent own individual stocks and 88 percent own stocks through mutual funds.

■ Despite the rapid rise in financial assets over the past few years, nonfinancial assets still account for the bulk of net worth. In particular, housing equity remains the most important asset to most Americans.

Financial assets peak in older age groups

(median value of financial assets of total householders and householders aged 55 or older, 2001)

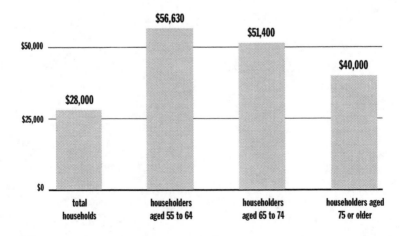

Table 9.2 Financial Assets of Households by Age of Householder, 1989 to 2001

(percentage of households owning financial assets and median value of assets for owners, by age of householder, 1989 to 2001; percentage point change in ownership and percent change in value of asset, 1989–2001 and 1998–2001; in 2001 dollars)

						percentage point change	
	2001	1998	1995	1992	1989	1998–01	1989–01
PERCENT OWNING ANY FINANCIAL ASSET							
Total households	**93.1%**	**92.9%**	**91.0%**	**90.2%**	**88.7%**	**0.2**	**4.4**
Under age 35	89.2	88.6	86.9	85.7	84.8	0.6	4.4
Aged 35 to 44	90.2	91.0	91.8	93.3	93.3	–0.8	–3.1
Aged 45 to 54	94.4	94.9	92.8	92.5	90.6	–0.5	3.8
Aged 55 to 64	94.8	95.6	90.8	92.5	87.5	–0.8	7.3
Aged 65 to 74	94.6	95.6	92.6	91.2	92.0	–1.0	2.6
Aged 75 or older	95.1	92.1	94.2	92.1	91.4	3.0	3.7

						percent change	
	2001	1998	1995	1992	1989	1998–01	1989–01
MEDIAN VALUE OF FINANCIAL ASSET							
Total households	**$28,000**	**$24,498**	**$17,992**	**$14,230**	**$15,554**	**14.3%**	**80.0%**
Under age 35	6,250	5,002	6,242	4,578	3,716	25.0	68.2
Aged 35 to 44	26,900	24,890	15,922	12,374	19,339	8.1	39.1
Aged 45 to 54	45,700	41,127	32,363	23,634	25,052	11.1	82.4
Aged 55 to 64	56,630	49,634	37,911	35,265	35,981	14.1	57.4
Aged 65 to 74	51,400	49,852	24,504	31,553	26,772	3.1	92.0
Aged 75 or older	40,000	39,882	26,469	26,047	40,537	0.3	–1.3

Source: Federal Reserve Board, results from the Survey of Consumer Finances; Internet site http://www.federalreserve.gov/pubs/oss/oss2/2001/scf2001home.html; calculations by New Strategist

Table 9.3 Financial Assets of Households by Type of Asset and Age of Householder, 2001

(percent of household owning selected financial assets, and median value of asset for owners, by type of asset and age of householder, 2001)

	total	under 35	35 to 44	45 to 54	55 to 64	65 to 74	75 or older
PERCENT OWNING ASSET							
Any financial asset	93.1%	89.2%	93.3%	94.4%	94.8%	94.6%	95.1%
Transaction accounts	90.9	86.0	90.7	92.2	93.6	93.8	93.7
Certificates of deposit	15.7	6.3	9.8	15.2	14.4	29.7	36.5
Savings bonds	16.7	12.7	22.6	21.0	14.3	11.3	12.5
Bonds	3.0	–	2.1	2.8	6.1	3.9	5.7
Stocks	21.3	17.4	21.6	22.0	26.7	20.5	21.8
Mutual funds	17.7	11.5	17.5	20.2	21.3	19.9	19.5
Retirement accounts	52.2	45.1	61.4	63.4	59.1	44.0	25.7
Life insurance	28.0	15.0	27.0	31.1	35.7	36.7	33.3
Other managed assets	6.6	2.1	3.1	6.4	13.0	11.8	11.2
Other financial assets	9.3	10.4	9.5	8.5	10.6	8.5	7.3
MEDIAN VALUE OF ASSET							
Total financial assets	**$28,000**	**$6,300**	**$26,900**	**$45,700**	**$56,600**	**$51,400**	**$40,000**
Transaction accounts	4,000	1,800	3,400	4,600	5,500	8,000	7,300
Certificates of deposit	15,000	4,000	6,000	12,000	19,000	20,000	25,000
Savings bonds	1,000	300	1,000	1,000	2,500	2,000	3,000
Bonds	43,500	–	13,600	60,000	60,000	71,400	35,000
Stocks	20,000	5,700	15,000	15,000	37,500	85,000	60,000
Mutual funds	35,000	9,000	17,500	38,500	60,000	70,000	70,000
Retirement accounts	29,000	6,600	28,500	48,000	55,000	60,000	46,000
Life insurance	10,000	10,000	9,000	11,000	10,000	8,800	7,000
Other managed assets	70,000	40,000	50,000	60,000	55,000	120,000	100,000
Other financial assets	4,000	1,300	2,000	5,000	10,000	8,000	17,500

Note: (–) means sample is too small to make a reliable estimate.
Source: Federal Reserve Board, results from the Survey of Consumer Finances; Internet site http://www.federalreserve.gov/pubs/oss/oss2/2001/scf2001home.html

Table 9.4 Stock Ownership of Households by Age of Householder, 1989 to 2001

(percentage of householders owning stocks directly or indirectly, median value of stocks for owners, and share of total household financial assets accounted for by stock holdings, by age of householder, 1989 to 2001; percent and percentage point change, 1989–2001 and 1998–2001; in 2001 dollars)

						percentage point change	
	2001	1998	1995	1992	1989	1998–01	1989–01
PERCENT OWNING STOCK							
Total households	**51.9%**	**48.9%**	**40.4 %**	**36.7%**	**31.7%**	**3.0**	**20.2**
Under age 35	48.9	40.8	36.6	28.4	22.4	8.1	26.5
Aged 35 to 44	59.5	56.7	46.4	42.4	39.0	2.8	20.5
Aged 45 to 54	59.2	58.6	48.9	46.4	41.8	0.6	17.4
Aged 55 to 64	57.1	55.9	40.0	45.3	36.2	1.2	20.9
Aged 65 to 74	39.2	42.7	34.4	30.2	26.7	–3.5	12.5
Aged 75 or older	34.2	29.4	27.9	25.7	25.9	4.8	8.3

						percent change	
	2001	1998	1995	1992	1989	1998–01	1989–01
MEDIAN VALUE OF STOCK							
Total households	**$34,250**	**$27,212**	**$16,875**	**$12,992**	**$11,700**	**54.6%**	**240.0%**
Under age 35	7,000	7,619	5,895	4,331	4,129	–8.1	69.5
Aged 35 to 44	27,500	21,769	11,558	9,280	7,089	26.3	287.9
Aged 45 to 54	50,000	41,362	29,986	18,561	18,100	20.9	176.2
Aged 55 to 64	81,200	51,158	35,831	30,934	25,327	58.7	220.6
Aged 65 to 74	150,000	60,954	39,298	19,798	27,942	146.1	436.8
Aged 75 or older	120,000	65,308	23,117	30,934	34,412	83.7	248.7

						percentage point change	
	2001	1998	1995	1992	1989	1998–01	1989–01
STOCK AS SHARE OF FINANCIAL ASSETS							
Total households	**56.0%**	**53.9%**	**39.9%**	**33.7%**	**27.8%**	**2.1**	**28.2**
Under age 35	52.6	44.8	27.2	24.8	20.2	7.8	32.4
Aged 35 to 44	57.3	54.6	39.5	31.0	29.2	2.7	28.1
Aged 45 to 54	59.1	55.7	42.6	40.8	33.5	3.4	25.6
Aged 55 to 64	56.1	58.4	44.2	37.3	27.6	-2.3	28.5
Aged 65 to 74	55.1	51.3	35.8	31.6	26.0	3.8	29.1
Aged 75 or older	51.4	48.7	39.8	25.5	25.0	2.7	26.4

Source: Federal Reserve Board, results from the Survey of Consumer Finances; Internet site http://www.federalreserve.gov/pubs/oss/oss2/2001/scf2001home.html; calculations by New Strategist

Table 9.5 Characteristics of Equity Owners by Generation, 2002

(selected characteristics of equity owners by generation, 2002)

	total	Generation X (born 1965 or later)	Baby Boom (born between 1946 and 1964)	Silent or GI (born in 1945 or earlier)
Percent of all equity investors	100%	25%	48%	27%
Median age*	47	30	46	65
Median household income	$62,500	$60,000	$70,000	$50,000
Median household financial assets**	100,000	35,000	125,000	350,000
Median household financial assets in equities	50,000	25,000	51,000	69,600
Median number of individual stocks and stock mutual funds owned	4	3	5	5
Percent of equity-owning households				
Married or living with partner*	71%	66%	76%	66%
College or postgraduate degree*	50	52	49	48
Employed*	77	93	91	38
Own individual stock (net)***	49	43	49	54
Inside employer-sponsored retirement plans	17	18	20	11
Outside employer-sponsored retirement plans	41	34	41	48
Stock mutual funds (net)***	89	86	92	88
Inside employer-sponsored retirement plans	66	69	76	43
Outside employer-sponsored retirement plans	56	48	53	68

* Refers to the household's responding financial decisionmaker for investments.
** Includes assets in employer-sponsored retirement plans but excludes value of primary residence.
*** Multiple responses included.
Note: Number of respondents varies.
Source: Investment Company Institute and the Securities Industry Association, Equity Ownership in America, 2002; Internet sites http://www.ici.org and http://www.sia.com

Nonfinancial Assets of Older Householders Rose Sharply

The value of nonfinancial assets peaks in the 65-to-74 age group.

For the average American household, the median value of nonfinancial assets amounted to $113,500 in 2001, a gain of 22 percent since 1989, after adjusting for inflation. The value of nonfinancial assets held by householders aged 65 or older rose much faster than average during those years—up 72 percent. In contrast, householders aged 55 to 64 saw a below-average increase in the value of their nonfinancial assets between 1989 and 2001—a gain of just 14 percent.

The value of the primary residence accounts for the bulk of the average household's nonfinancial assets. The rapid rise in home prices over the past few years has boosted the value of the nonfinancial assets owned by older householders—who are most likely to be homeowners. The percentage of householders who own their home peaks in the 55-to-74 age group at 83 percent. The value of nonfinancial assets peaks in the 65-to-74 age group at $149,211. With nonfinancial assets of $147,863, those aged 55 to 64 are not far behind. The value of nonfinancial assets falls in the oldest age group as people downsize by moving into smaller homes.

■ Expect to see a continued rise in the value of the nonfinancial assets owned by older Americans as boomers, with their oversized homes, move into the age group.

Nonfinancial assets peak in the 65-to-74 age group

(median value of nonfinancial assets of total householders and householders aged 55 or older, 2001)

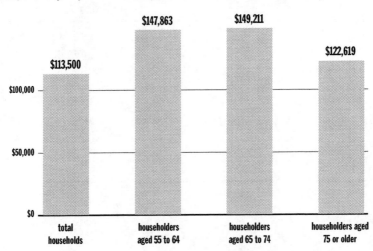

Table 9.6 Nonfinancial Assets of Households by Age of Householder, 1989 to 2001

(percentage of households owning nonfinancial assets and median value of assets for owners, by age of house-holder, 1989 to 2001; percentage point change in ownership and percent change in value of asset, 1989–2001 and 1998–2001; in 2001 dollars)

	2001	1998	1995	1992	1989	percentage point change 1998–01	percentage point change 1989–01
PERCENT OWNING ANY NONFINANCIAL ASSET							
Total households	**90.7%**	**89.9%**	**90.9%**	**90.8%**	**89.3%**	**0.8**	**1.4**
Under age 35	83.0	83.3	87.1	85.6	83.9	–0.3	–0.9
Aged 35 to 44	93.2	92.1	90.6	92.3	91.8	1.1	1.4
Aged 45 to 54	95.2	92.9	93.6	94.4	93.2	2.3	2.0
Aged 55 to 64	95.4	93.8	93.9	92.7	91.2	1.6	4.2
Aged 65 to 74	91.6	92.0	92.6	91.6	92.7	–0.4	–1.1
Aged 75 or older	86.4	87.2	89.9	91.3	85.4	–0.8	1.0

	2001	1998	1995	1992	1989	percent change 1998–01	percent change 1989–01
MEDIAN VALUE OF NONFINANCIAL ASSET							
Total households	**$113,500**	**$106,398**	**$96,050**	**$85,379**	**$92,911**	**6.7%**	**22.2%**
Under age 35	30,538	24,654	25,486	21,468	23,606	23.9	29.4
Aged 35 to 44	117,806	112,602	111,211	102,003	116,035	4.6	1.5
Aged 45 to 54	141,558	137,991	130,593	116,777	148,554	2.6	–4.7
Aged 55 to 64	147,863	138,154	124,830	131,687	129,249	7.0	14.4
Aged 65 to 74	149,211	119,568	109,631	97,474	86,717	24.8	72.1
Aged 75 or older	122,619	104,575	91,311	86,090	71,129	17.3	72.4

Source: Federal Reserve Board, results from the Survey of Consumer Finances; Internet site http://www.federalreserve.gov/pubs/oss/oss2/2001/scf2001home.html; calculations by New Strategist

Table 9.7 Nonfinancial Assets of Households by Type of Asset and Age of Householder, 2001

(percent of household owning selected nonfinancial assets, and median value of asset for owners, by type of asset and age of householder, 2001)

	total	under 35	35 to 44	45 to 54	55 to 64	65 to 74	75 or older
PERCENT OWNING ASSET							
Any nonfinancial asset	**90.7%**	**83.0%**	**93.2%**	**95.2%**	**95.4%**	**91.6%**	**86.4%**
Vehicles	84.8	78.8	88.9	90.5	90.7	81.3	73.9
Primary residence	67.7	39.9	67.8	76.2	83.2	82.5	76.2
Other residential property	11.3	3.4	9.2	14.7	18.3	13.7	15.2
Equity in nonresidential property	8.3	2.8	7.6	10.0	12.3	12.9	8.3
Business equity	11.8	7.0	14.2	17.1	15.6	11.6	2.4
Other nonfinancial assets	7.6	6.9	8.0	7.2	7.9	9.7	6.2
MEDIAN VALUE OF ASSET							
Total nonfinancial assets	**$113,200**	**$30,500**	**$117,800**	**$140,300**	**$147,900**	**$149,200**	**$122,600**
Vehicles	13,500	11,300	14,800	15,700	15,100	13,600	8,800
Primary residence	122,000	95,000	125,000	135,000	130,000	129,000	111,000
Other residential property	80,000	75,000	75,000	65,000	80,000	145,000	80,000
Equity in nonresidential property	49,000	33,300	39,500	56,400	78,500	50,000	28,000
Business equity	100,000	50,000	100,000	102,000	100,000	100,000	510,900
Other nonfinancial assets	12,000	10,000	9,000	11,000	30,000	20,000	15,000

Source: Federal Reserve Board, results from the Survey of Consumer Finances; Internet site http://www.federalreserve.gov/pubs/oss/oss2/2001/scf2001home.html

Table 9.8 Household Ownership of Primary Residence by Age of Householder, 1989 to 2001

(percentage of households owning primary residence, median value of asset for owners, and median value of home-secured debt for owners, by age of householder, 1989 to 2001; percentage point change in ownership and percent change in value of asset, 1989–2001 and 1998–2001; in 2001 dollars)

	2001	1998	1995	1992	1989	percentage point change 1998–01	percentage point change 1989–01
PERCENT OWNING PRIMARY RSESIDENCE							
Total households	**67.7%**	**66.2%**	**64.7%**	**63.9%**	**63.9%**	**1.5**	**3.8**
Under age 35	39.9	38.9	37.9	36.9	39.4	1.0	0.5
Aged 35 to 44	67.8	67.1	64.7	64.5	66.1	0.7	1.7
Aged 45 to 54	76.2	74.4	75.3	75.4	76.5	1.8	−0.3
Aged 55 to 64	83.2	80.3	82.0	77.5	80.1	2.9	3.1
Aged 65 to 74	82.5	81.5	79.5	79.3	77.7	1.0	4.8
Aged 75 or older	76.2	77.0	72.8	77.2	69.9	−0.8	6.3

	2001	1998	1995	1992	1989	percent change 1998–01	percent change 1989–01
MEDIAN VALUE OF PRIMARY RESIDENCE							
Total households	**$123,000**	**$108,847**	**$104,025**	**$98,990**	**$96,352**	**1.3%**	**27.7%**
Under age 35	95,000	91,431	87,843	85,379	83,964	3.9	13.1
Aged 35 to 44	125,000	109,935	109,804	111,363	110,117	13.7	13.5
Aged 45 to 54	135,000	130,616	115,583	111,363	116,999	3.4	15.4
Aged 55 to 64	130,000	119,732	100,557	105,053	103,234	8.6	25.9
Aged 65 to 74	129,000	103,405	98,246	85,379	75,705	24.8	70.4
Aged 75 or older	111,000	92,520	92,467	86,616	75,625	20.0	46.8

	2001	1998	1995	1992	1989	percent change 1998–01	percent change 1989–01
MEDIAN VALUE OF HOME-SECURED DEBT							
Total households	**$70,000**	**$67,485**	**$59,119**	**$53,207**	**$44,047**	**3.7%**	**58.9%**
Under age 35	77,000	77,281	71,662	63,106	60,564	−0.4	27.1
Aged 35 to 44	80,000	76,193	69,350	68,055	55,058	5.0	45.3
Aged 45 to 54	75,000	74,016	56,636	49,495	35,788	1.3	109.6
Aged 55 to 64	55,000	52,247	42,766	37,121	27,529	5.3	99.8
Aged 65 to 74	39,000	28,300	21,961	21,035	12,527	37.8	211.3
Aged 75 or older	44,800	23,106	13,523	34,646	9,635	93.9	365.0

Source: Federal Reserve Board, results from the Survey of Consumer Finances; Internet site http://www.federalreserve.gov/pubs/oss/oss2/2001/scf2001home.html; calculations by New Strategist

Older Americans Have More Debt

The debt load more than doubled for 55-to-64-year-olds between 1989 and 2001.

The debt of the average American household grew 88 percent between 1989 and 2001, to $38,775. For some older Americans, debt grew much faster. The median amount of money owed by householders aged 55 to 64 grew 163 percent between 1989 and 2001, after adjusting for inflation, to $34,615. The debt of householders aged 65 to 74 rose 90 percent to $13,100, while that of householders aged 75 or older rose just 30 percent to $5,000. Between 1998 and 2001, debt fell for householders aged 55 to 64 and aged 75 or older.

The percentage of households with debt peaks in the 35-to-44 age group at 89 percent, then declines with age. The 75 percent majority of householders aged 55 to 64 have debts, as do 57 percent of those aged 65 to 74. But among householders aged 75 or older, only 29 percent are in debt.

Fewer than half of people aged 55 or older hold mortgage debt. The fact that many have paid off their mortgages is the primary reason their debts are so much lower than those of middle-aged adults. Only 10 percent of householders aged 75 or older have mortgage debt, while the figure is 32 percent among 65-to-74-year-olds and 49 percent among those aged 55 to 64. Older householders are also less likely to have other types of debt. Fewer than half carry a balance on their credit card or have an installment loan.

■ The net worth of older Americans is higher than that of younger adults because their debts are much less.

Debt declines with age

(median amount of debt owed by total householders and householders aged 55 or older, 2001)

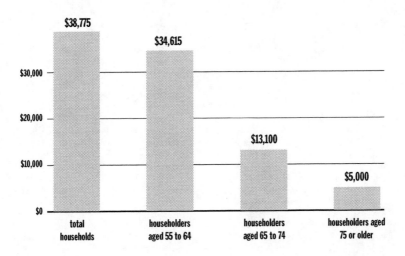

Table 9.9 Debt of Households by Age of Householder, 1989 to 2001

(percentage of households with debts and median amount of debt for debtors, by age of householder, 1989 to 2001; percentage point change in households with debt and percent change in amount of debt, 1989–2001 and 1998–2001; in 2001 dollars)

	2001	1998	1995	1992	1989	percentage point change	
						1998–01	1989–01
PERCENT WITH DEBT							
Total households	**75.1%**	**74.1%**	**74.5%**	**73.3%**	**72.3%**	**1.0**	**2.8**
Under age 35	82.7	81.2	83.5	81.5	80.0	1.5	2.7
Aged 35 to 44	88.6	87.6	87.0	86.4	88.6	1.0	0.0
Aged 45 to 54	84.6	87.0	86.3	85.4	85.3	–2.4	–0.7
Aged 55 to 64	75.4	76.4	73.7	70.1	70.8	–1.0	4.6
Aged 65 to 74	56.8	51.4	53.4	51.5	49.6	5.4	7.2
Aged 75 or older	29.2	24.6	28.4	31.6	21.0	4.6	8.2

	2001	1998	1995	1992	1989	percent change	
						1998–01	1989–01
MEDIAN AMOUNT OF DEBT							
Total households	**$38,775**	**$35,368**	**$24,987**	**$21,163**	**$20,647**	**9.6%**	**87.8%**
Under age 35	24,898	20,942	17,373	12,876	15,692	18.9	58.7
Aged 35 to 44	61,539	60,577	42,841	44,125	41,412	1.6	48.6
Aged 45 to 54	54,255	52,225	45,221	33,409	32,562	3.9	66.6
Aged 55 to 64	34,615	37,204	24,273	23,681	13,170	–7.0	162.8
Aged 65 to 74	13,100	12,964	8,146	5,974	6,882	1.1	90.3
Aged 75 or older	5,000	8,761	2,196	2,908	3,839	–42.9	30.2

Source: Federal Reserve Board, results from the Survey of Consumer Finances; Internet site http://www.federalreserve.gov/pubs/oss/oss2/2001/scf2001home.html; calculations by New Strategist

Table 9.10 Debt of of Households by Type of Debt and Age of Householder, 2001

(percent of householders with debt, and median value of debt for those with debts, by type of debt and age of householder, 2001)

	total	under 35	35 to 44	45 to 54	55 to 64	65 to 74	75 or older
PERCENT WITH DEBT							
Any debt	**75.1%**	**82.7%**	**88.6%**	**84.6%**	**75.4%**	**56.8%**	**29.2%**
Mortgage and home equity	44.6	35.7	59.6	59.8	49.0	32.0	9.5
Other residential property	4.7	2.7	4.9	6.5	8.0	3.4	2.0
Installment loans	45.2	63.8	57.1	45.9	39.3	21.1	9.5
Credit card balances	44.4	49.6	54.1	50.4	41.6	30.0	18.4
Other lines of credit	1.5	1.7	1.7	1.5	3.1	–	–
Other debt	7.2	8.8	8.0	7.4	7.4	5.0	3.6
MEDIAN VALUE OF DEBT FOR DEBTOR HOUSEHOLDS							
Total debt	**$38,800**	**$24,900**	**$61,500**	**$54,300**	**$34,600**	**$13,100**	**$5,000**
Mortgage, home equity	70,000	77,000	80,000	75,000	55,000	39,000	44,800
Other residential property	40,000	52,000	45,500	33,500	40,000	77,000	42,000
Installment loans	9,700	9,500	11,100	9,600	9,000	7,000	5,800
Credit card balances	1,900	2,000	2,000	2,300	1,900	1,000	700
Other lines of credit	3,900	500	700	5,300	20,500	–	–
Other debt	3,000	2,000	3,100	5,000	5,000	2,500	2,500

Note: (–) means sample is too small to make a reliable estimate.
Source: Federal Reserve Board, results from the Survey of Consumer Finances; Internet site http://www.federalreserve.gov/pubs/oss/oss2/2001/scf2001home.html

Social Security Dominates Retirement Funding

A minority of older Americans receives pension income.

With fewer than half of American workers participating in a pension plan, it's no surprise that a minority of people aged 65 or older receive pension income. Only 30 percent of men aged 65 or older receive a company or union pension, and the figure is a much smaller 13 percent among women. Fully 90 to 92 percent of people aged 65 or older receive Social Security income. In second place is interest income, 57 percent of men and 53 percent of women receive. The median amount of interest income received by people aged 65 or older was less than $2,000 in 2002. Only 22 percent of men and 13 percent of women aged 65 or older earn money from a job.

With retirement approaching, most of the nation's older workers are confident in having enough money to live comfortably throughout retirement, according to the Employee Benefit Research Institute's 2003 Retirement Confidence Survey. Fully 64 percent of workers aged 58 or older say they are "very" or "somewhat" confident in having enough money. Perhaps contributing to their confidence is the fact that 65 percent expect to work for pay in retirement.

Inheritances are helping to fund the retirement of some older Americans. Twenty-four percent of people aged 56 or older in 2001 had already received an inheritance and 6 percent expected to receive one. Among those who had received an inheritance, the median value was $108,885.

■ Older Americans depend on a variety of income sources to fund their retirement, the most important being Social Security.

Most older Americans receive Social Security and interest income

(percent of people aged 65 or older receiving income by source and sex, 2002)

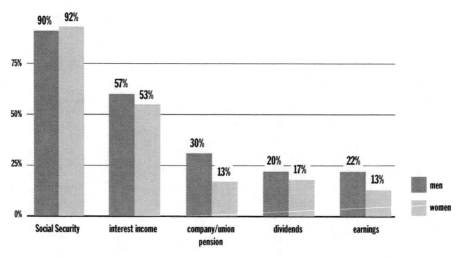

Table 9.11 Pension Coverage by Sex and Age, 2001

(total number of workers, number and percent whose employer offer a pension plan, and number and percent included in the plan, by sex and age, 2001; numbers in thousands)

	total	with employer offered plan		included in plan	
		number	percent	number	percent
Total workers	**151,608**	**84,059**	**55.4%**	**65,445**	**43.2%**
Aged 15 to 24	24,593	8,597	35.0	3,135	12.7
Aged 25 to 44	71,281	41,904	58.8	33,534	47.0
Aged 45 to 64	50,230	31,462	62.6	27,476	54.7
Aged 65 or older	5,504	2,096	38.1	1,301	23.6
Men	**80,300**	**44,358**	**55.2**	**35,916**	**44.7**
Aged 15 to 24	12,816	4,375	34.1	1,732	13.5
Aged 25 to 44	38,048	22,223	58.4	18,417	48.4
Aged 45 to 64	26,313	16,579	63.0	14,990	57.0
Aged 65 or older	3,123	1,181	37.8	776	24.9
Women	**71,308**	**39,701**	**55.7**	**29,529**	**41.1**
Aged 15 to 24	11,777	4,223	35.9	1,403	11.9
Aged 25 to 44	33,232	19,680	59.2	15,117	45.5
Aged 45 to 64	23,917	14,883	62.2	12,485	52.2
Aged 65 or older	2,382	915	38.4	525	22.0

Source: Bureau of the Census, 2002 Current Population Survey Annual Demographic Supplement, Internet site http:// ferret.bls.census.gov/macro/032002/noncash/nc8_000.htm

Table 9.12 Retirement Income of People Aged 65 or Older by Sex, 2002

(number and percent distribution of people aged 65 or older receiving income, and median income received by those with income, by sex and type of income, 2002; ranked by percent receiving income; numbers in thousands)

	people receiving income		median income of
	number	percent	those with income
Men aged 65 or older	**14,273**	**100.0%**	**$19,436**
Social Security	12,873	90.2	11,714
Interest	8,093	56.7	1,733
Retirement income	6,500	45.5	10,470
Company or union retirement	4,459	31.2	7,963
State or local government retirement	918	6.4	15,778
Federal government retirement	659	4.6	20,889
Military retirement	359	2.5	17,877
IRA, KEOGH, or 401(k)	100	0.7	5,734
Railroad retirement	100	0.7	16,249
Annuities	90	0.6	4,486
Pension income	6,231	43.7	10,549
Company or union retirement	4,331	30.3	8,057
State or local government retirement	887	6.2	15,951
Federal government retirement	627	4.4	21,171
Military retirement	358	2.5	17,920
Railroad retirement	90	0.6	15,524
Earnings	3,184	22.3	19,677
Dividends	2,887	20.2	1,745
Rents, royalties, estates, and trusts	1,286	9.0	2,665
Women aged 65 or older	**19,061**	**100.0**	**11,406**
Social Security	17,518	91.9	8,439
Interest	10,045	52.7	1,679
Retirement income	5,385	28.3	5,955
Company or union retirement	3,272	17.2	3,955
State or local government retirement	1,303	6.8	9,420
Federal government retirement	498	2.6	11,376
Annuities	171	0.9	3,721
Military retirement	115	0.6	7,537
IRA, KEOGH, or 401(k)	108	0.6	2,774
Railroad retirement	94	0.5	9,757
Pension income	4,163	21.8	5,831
Company or union retirement	2,529	13.3	3,897
State or local government retirement	1,182	6.2	9,857
Federal government retirement	324	1.7	13,037
Railroad retirement	62	0.3	–
Military retirement	23	0.1	–
Dividends	3,295	17.3	1,761
Earnings	2,496	13.1	11,282
Rents, royalties, estates, and trusts	1,463	7.7	1,986

Note: (–) means sample is too small to make a reliable estimate.
Source: Bureau of the Census, 2003 Current Population Survey, Annual Social and Economic Supplement, Internet site ttp:// ferret.bls.census.gov/macro/032003/perinc/new08_000.htm

Table 9.13 Retirement Confidence by Generation, 2003

(percent responding by generation, 2003)

	total	Gen X	younger Boomers	older Boomers	pre-retirees
Overall confidence in having enough money to live comfortably throughout retirement					
Very confident	21%	19%	23%	19%	29%
Somewhat confident	45	49	49	39	35
Not too confident	17	17	16	18	21
Not at all confident	16	15	12	23	14
Have saved for retirement					
Self	68	64	74	66	64
Household	71	68	78	69	68
Have done a retirement savings needs calculation					
Self	37	36	38	37	39
Household	43	41	45	41	42
Contribute to a retirement savings plan at work					
Yes	78	78	78	78	72
No	22	22	22	21	28
Expected retirement age					
Less than 55	6	8	7	4	–
Aged 55 to 59	10	11	10	11	0
Aged 60 to 64	21	19	22	22	24
Aged 65	25	28	28	21	17
Aged 66 or older	24	23	22	24	28
Never retire	6	4	5	7	10
Percentage expecting to work for pay in retirement	70	68	73	70	65

Note: Pre-retirees were born in 1945 or earlier; older Boomers were born between 1946 and 1954; younger Boomers were born between 1955 and 1964; Generation Xers were born in 1965 to 1978; (–) means data not available.
Source: 2003 Retirement Confidence Survey, EBRI/ASEC/Greenwald, Internet site http://www.ebri.org/

Table 9.14 Inheritance Receipt and Expectations by Generation, 1989 to 2001

(percent responding by generation and year, 1989 to 2001)

	pre-Boomers	Boomers	post-Boomers
Percent of households that have received at least one inheritance			
2001	24.0%	17.3%	11.0%
1998	29.1	16.9	11.8
1995	27.7	18.0	11.8
1992	27.1	15.5	9.9
1989	29.1	17.4	12.4
Percent of households that expect to receive an inheritance			
2001	5.8	14.9	18.4
1998	6.2	16.4	19.3
1995	6.4	18.1	20.7
1992	8.4	19.3	24.6
1989	10.8	26.9	20.6
Percent of households by amount inherited			
Total	**100.0**	**100.0**	**100.0**
No inheritance	76.0	82.7	89.0
$1 to $20,000	3.2	5.2	4.9
$20,001 to $50,000	3.8	3.6	2.4
$50,001 to $100,000	4.2	3.1	1.7
$100,000 or more	12.8	5.4	2.0
Median value of inheritances received (in 2002 dollars)			
2001	$108,885	$47,909	$22,167
1998	79,849	49,062	24,844
1995	78,499	41,833	20,325
1992	89,831	44,654	17,232
1989	105,165	44,692	27,635

Note: Pre-Boomers were born before 1946; Boomers were born from 1946 through 1964; post-Boomers were born after 1964.
Source: © 2003, AARP. Reprinted with permission. "Pennies from Heaven: Will Inheritances Bail Out the Boomers?" Mitja Ng-Baumhackl, John Gist, and Carlos Figueiredo, Data Digest, DD Number 90, AARP Public Policy Institute

For More Information

The federal government is a rich source of data on almost every aspect of American life. Below are the Internet addresses of federal and other agencies collecting the demographic data analyzed in this book. Also shown are phone numbers of the agencies and of the subject specialists at the Census Bureau and the Bureau of Labor Statistics, organized alphabetically by name of agency or specialty topic. A list of State Data Centers and Small Business Development Centers is also below to help you track down demographic and economic information for your state or local area. E-mail addresses are shown when available. Note: Telephone numbers at the Census Bureau change regularly. If the numbers below do not allow you to reach the specialists you need, go to http://www. census.gov/contacts/www/contacts.html for the most up-to-date lists.

Internet Addresses

- AARP, http://www.aarp.org
- Agency for Healthcare Research and Quality, www.meps.ahrq.gov/Data_Public.htm
- Behavioral Risk Factor Surveillance System, http://apps.nccd.cdc.gov/brfss/index.asp
- Bureau of the Census, www.census.gov
- Bureau of Labor Statistics, www.bls.gov
- Centers for Disease Control and Prevention,www .cdc.gov
- Consumer Expenditure Survey, www.bls.gov/cex/
- Current Population Survey, www.bls.census.gov/cps/ cpsmain.htm
- Employee Benefit Research Institute, www.ebri.org
- Federal Interagency Forum on Child and Family Statistics, http://childstats.gov/
- Higher Education Research Institute, www.gseis.ucla.edu/heri/heri.html
- Institute for Social Research, University of Michigan, http://monitoringthefuture.org
- Investment Company Institute, http://www.ici.org
- National Center for Education Statistics, http:// nces.ed.gov
- National Center for Health Statistics, www.cdc.gov/ nchs
- National Sporting Goods Association, www.nsga.org
- Securities Industry Association, www.sia.com
- Sourcebook of Criminal Justice Statistics,www .albany.edu/sourcebook/

- Sporting Goods Manufacturers Association, www.sgma.com
- Survey of Consumer Finances, www.federalreserve .gov/pubs/oss/oss2/scfindex.html
- U.S. Substance Abuse and Mental Health Services Administrations, www.samhsa.gov
- U.S. Citizenship and Immigration Services, http:// uscis.gov/graphics/shared/aboutus/statistics/index.htm
- Youth Risk Behavior Surveillance System, www.cdc .gov/nccdphp/dash/yrbs/results.htm

Subject Specialists

Absences from work, Staff 202-691-6378
Aging population, Staff 301-763-2378
American Community Survey/C2SS Results,
    Larry McGinn 301-763-8050
Ancestry, Staff 301-763-2403
Apportionment, Edwin Byerly 301-763-2381
Apportionment and redistricting,
    Cathy McCully 301-763-4039
Business expenditures, Sheldon Ziman 301-763-3315
Business investment, Charles Funk 301-763-3324
Business owners, characteristics of,
    Valerie Strang 301-763-3316
Census 1990 and earlier, Staff 301-763-2422
Census 2000
- American Factfinder, Staff 301-763-INFO (4636)
- Annexations/boundary changes,
    Joe Marinucci 301-763-1099
- Apportionment, Edwin Byerly 301-763-2381
- Census 2000 Briefs, Staff 301-763-2437
- Census 2000 tabulations, Staff 301-763-2422
- Census 2010, Ed Gore 301-763-3998
- Census history, Dave Pemberton 301-763-1167
- Citizenship, Staff 301-763-2411
- Commuting and place of work, Clara Reschovsky/ Celia Boertlein 301-763-2454
- Confidentiality and privacy, Jerry Gates 301-763-2515
- Count question resolution, Staff 866-546-0527
- Count review, Paul Campbell 301-763-2381
- Data dissemination, Staff 301-763-INFO (4636)
- Disability, Staff 301-763-3242
- Education, Staff 301-763-2464
- Employment/unemployment, Staff 301-763-3230
- Foreign born, Staff 301-763-2411

- Geographic entities, Staff 301-763-1099
- Grandparents as caregivers, Staff 301-763-2416
- Group quarters population, Denise Smith 301-763-2378
- Hispanic origin, ethnicity, ancestry, Staff 301-763-2403
- Homeless, Annetta Clark 301-763-2378
- Housing, Staff 301-763-3237
- Immigration/emigration, Staff 301-763-2411
- Income, Staff 301-763-3243
- Island areas, Idabelle Hovland 301-763-8443
- Labor force status/work experience, Staff 301-763-3230
- Language spoken in home, Staff 301-763-2464
- Living arrangements, Staff 301-763-2416
- Maps, customer services 301-763-INFO (4636)
- Marital status, Staff 301-763-2416
- Metropolitan areas, concepts and standards, Michael Ratcliffe 301-763-2419
- Microdata files, Amanda Shields 301-763-1326
- Migration, Carol Faber 301-763-2454
- Occupation/industry, Staff 301-763-3239
- Place of birth/native born, Carol Faber 301-763-2454
- Population (general information), Staff 301-763-2422
- Poverty, Alemayehu Bishaw 301-763-3213
- Race, Staff 301-763-2402
- Redistricting, Cathy McCully 301-763-4039
- Residence rules, Karen Mills 301-763-2381
- Small area income and poverty estimates, David Waddington 301-763-3195
- Special censuses, Mike Stump 301-763-3577
- Special populations, Staff 301-763-2378
- Special tabulations, Linda Showalter 301-763-2429
- Undercount, Phil Gbur 301-763-4206
  - Demographic analysis, Greg Robinson 301-763-2110
- Unmarried partners, Staff 301-763-2416
- Urban/rural, Ryan Short 301-763-1099
- U.S. citizens abroad, Staff 301-763-2422
- Veteran status, Staff 301-763-3230
- Voting districts, John Byle 301-763-1099
- Women, Renee Spraggins 301-763-2378
- ZIP codes, Staff 301-763-2422

Census Bureau customer service, Staff 301-763-INFO (4636)

Child care, Martin O'Connell/Kristin Smith 301-763-2416

Children, Staff 301-763-2416

Citizenship status, Staff 301-763-2411

Communications and Utilities
- Current programs, Ruth Bramblett 301-763-2787
- Economic census, Jim Barron 301-763-2786

Commuting, means of transportation, and place of work, Clara Reschovsky/Celia Boertlein 301-763-2454

Construction
- Building permits, Staff 301-763-5160
- Economic census, Susan Bucci, Staff 301-763-4680
- Housing starts and completions, Staff 301-763-5160
- Manufactured housing, Lisa Feldman 301-763-1605
- Residential characteristics, price index, and sales, Staff 301-763-5160
- Residential improvements and repairs, Joe Huesman 301-763-1605
- Value of new construction, Mike Davis 301-763-1605

Consumer Expenditure Survey, Staff 202-691-6900, cexinfo@bls.gov

Contingent workers, Staff 202-691-6378

County Business Patterns, Phillip Thompson 301-763-2580

County populations, Staff 301-763-2422

Crime, Marilyn Monahan 301-763-5315

Current Population Survey, general information, Staff, 301-763-3806

Demographic surveys, demographic statistics, Staff 301-763-2422

Disability, Staff 301-763-3242

Discouraged workers, Staff 202-691-6378

Displaced workers, Staff 202-691-6378

Economic census 1997
- Accommodations and food services, Fay Dorsett 301-763-2687
- Construction, Staff 301-763-4680
- Finance and insurance, Faye Jacobs 301-763-2824
- General information, Robert Marske 301-763-2547
- Internet dissemination, Paul Zeisset 301-763-4151
- Manufacturing:
  - Consumer goods industries, Robert Reinard 301-763-4810
  - Investment goods industries, Kenneth Hansen 301-763-4755
  - Primary goods industries, Nat Shelton 301-763-6614
- Mining, Susan Bocci 301-763-4680
- Minority/women-owned businesses, Valerie Strang 301-763-3316
- North American Industry Class. System, Wanda Dougherty 301-763-2790
- Puerto Rico and the Island Areas, Irma Harahush 301-763-3319
- Real estate and rental/leasing, Pam Palmer 301-763-2824
- Retail trade, Fay Dorsett 301-763-2687
- Services:
  - Administrative, waste management, remediation, Dan Wellwood 301-763-5181

- Arts, entertainment, and recreation, Tara Dryden 301-763-5181
- Educational services, Kim Casey 301-763-5181
- Health care and social assistance, Laurie Davis 301-763-5181
- Information, Joyce Kiessling/Joy Pierson/ Steve Cornell 301-763-5181
- Management of companies and enterprises, Julie Ishman 301-763-5181
- Other services (except public administration), Patrice Norman 301-763-5181
- Professional, scientific, and technical services, Karen Dennison/John Goodenough 301-763-5181
- Transportation and utilities:
  - Commodity Flow Survey, John Fowler 301-763-2108
  - Establishments, James Barron 301-763-2786
  - Vehicle Inventory and Use Survey, Thomas Zabelsky 301-763-5175
- Wholesale trade, Donna Hambric 301-763-2725
- Zip codes:
  - Accommodation and food services, Fay Dorsett 301-763-5180
  - Retail trade, Fay Dorsett 301-763-5180

Economic studies, Arnold Reznek 301-763-1856

Education surveys, Steve Tourkin 301-763-3791

Educational attainment, Staff 301-763-2464

Emigration, Staff 301-763-2422

Employee Benefits Survey, Staff 202-691-6199; ocltinfo@bls.gov

Employment and Earnings periodical, John Stinson 202-691-6373

Employment and unemployment trends, Staff 202-691-6378

Employment projections, demographics, Mitra Toosi 202-691-5721

Enterprise statistics, Melvin Cole 301-763-3321

Equal employment opportunity data, Staff 301-763-3242

Fertility, Barbara Downs 301-763-2416

Finance and insurance, Faye Jacobs 301-763-2824

Flexitime and shift work, Staff 202-691-6378

Foreign born:
- General information, Staff 301-763-2422
- Concepts and analysis, Staff 301-763-2411

Geographic concepts:
- American Indian and Alaska Native areas, Vince Osier 301-763-1099
- Annexations and boundary changes, Dorothy Stroz 301-763-1099
- Area measurement:
  - Land, Jim Davis 301-763-1099
  - Water, Dave Aultman 301-763-1099

- Census blocks, Barbara Saville 301-763-1099
- Census county divisions, Pat Ream 301-763-1099
- Census designated places, Pat Ream 301-763-1099
- Census geographic concepts, Staff 301-763-1099
- Census maps, 1990 and 2000, Staff 301-763-INFO (4636)
- Census tracts, Dan Flynn 301-763-1099
- Centers of population, Staff 301-763-1128
- Congressional districts, boundaries, Donna Zorn 301-763-1099
- Island areas, Jim Davis 301-763-1099
- Metropolitan areas, Michael Ratcliffe 301-763-2419
- Postal geography, Dan Sweeney 301-763-1106
- School districts, Dave Aultman 301-763-1099
- Traffic analysis zones, Carrie Saunders 301-763-1099
- Urban/rural concepts, Ryan Short 301-763-1099
- Urban areas, Ryan Short 301-763-1099
- Voting districts, John Byle 301-763-1099
- Zip code tabulation areas, Andy Flora 301-763-1100
- Zip codes:
  - Demographic data, Staff 301-763-INFO (4636)
  - Economic data, Andy Hait 301-763-6747
  - Geography, Andy Flora 301-763-1100

Governments
- Census of governments, Donna Hirsch 301-763-5154
- Criminal and juvenile justice, Charlene Sebold 301-763-1591
- Education
  - Education and library statistics, Johnny Monaco 301-763-2584
  - Elementary and secondary, Staff 301-763-1563
- Employment, Ellen Thompson 301-763-1531
- Federal expenditure data, Gerard Keffer 301-763-1522
- Government finance, Stephen Poyta/David Kellerman 301-763-1580/7242
- Government information, Staff 301-763-1580
- Governmental organization, Stephen Owens 301-763-5149
- Public retirement systems, Sandra Reading 301-763-7248

Group quarters population, Denise Smith 301-763-2378

Health insurance statistics, Staff 301-763-3242

Health surveys, Adrienne Oneto 301-763-3891

Hispanic statistics
- General information, Staff 301-763-2422
- Concepts and analysis, Staff 301-763-2403

Home-based work, Staff 202-691-6378

Homeless, Annetta Clark 301-763-2378

Household wealth, Staff 301-763-3242

Households and families, Staff 301-763-2416

Housing
- American Housing Survey data, Paul Harble
  301-763-3235
- Census, Staff 301-763-3237
- Homeownership, vacancy data, Linda Cavanaugh/
  Robert Callis 301-763-3199
- Housing affordability, Howard Savage 301-763-3199
- Market absorption, Alan Friedman/Mary Schwartz
  301-763-3199
- New York City Housing and Vacancy Survey,
  Alan Friedman/Robert Callis 301-763-3199
- Residential finance, Howard Savage 301-763-3199

Immigration and Emigration
- General information, Staff 301-763-2422
- Concepts and analysis, Staff 301-763-2411

Income statistics, Staff 301-763-3243

Industry and commodity classification, James Kristoff
  301-763-5179

International Statistics:
- Africa, Asia, Latin Am., North Am., and Oceania,
  Staff 301-763-1358
- Aging population, Staff 301-763-1371
- China, People's Republic, Staff 301-763-1360
- Europe, former Soviet Union, Staff 301-763-1360
- Health, Staff 301-763-1433
- International data base, Pat Dickerson/Peter Johnson
  301-763-1351/1410
- Technical assistance and training, Staff 301-763-1444
- Women in development, Victoria Velkoff
  301-763-1371

Job tenure, Staff 202-691-6378

Journey to work, Phil Salopek/Celia Boertlein
  301-763-2454

Labor force concepts, Staff 202-691-6378

Language, Staff 301-763-2464

Longitudinal surveys, Ron Dopkowski 301-763-3801

Manufacturing and mining:
- Concentration, Patrick Duck 301-763-4699
- Exports from manufacturing establishments, John Gates
  301-763-4589
- Financial statistics (Quarterly Financial Report),
  Yolando St. George 301-763-3343
- Foreign direct investment, Julius Smith 301-763-4683
- Fuels, electric energy consumed and prod. index,
  Susan Bucci 301-763-4680
- General information and data requests, Nishea Quash
  301-763-4673
- Industries:
  - Electrical and trans. equip., instruments, machinery,
    Kenneth Hansen 301-763-4755

- Food, textiles, and apparel, Robert Reinard
  301-763-4810
- Furniture, printing, and misc., Robert Reinard
  301-763-4810
- Metals, Nat Shelton 301-763-6614
- Wood, paper, chemicals, petroleum prod., rubber,
  plastics, Nat Shelton 301-763-6614
- Mining, Susan Bucci 301-763-4680
- Monthly shipments, inventories, and orders,
  Dan Sansbury 301-763-4832
- Plant capacity utilization, Julius Smith 301-763-4683
- Research and development, Julius Smith 301-763-4683

Marital and family characteristics of workers,
  Staff 202-691-6378

Metropolitan areas, Staff 301-763-2422

Metropolitan standards, Michael Ratcliffe 301-763-2419

Migration
- General information, Staff 301-763-2422
- Domestic/internal, Carol Faber 301-763-2454
- International, Staff 301-763-2411

Minimum wage data, Steven Haugen 202-691-6378

Minority/women-owned businesses, Valerie Strang
  301-763-3316

Minority workers, Staff 202-691-6378

Multiple jobholders, Staff 202-691-6373

National Center for Education Statistics,
  Staff 202-502-7300

National Center for Health Statistics, Staff 301-458-4000

National Compensation Survey, Staff 202-691-6199;
  ocltinfo@bls.gov

National Opinion Research Center, Staff 773-256-6000;
  norcinfo@norcmail.uchicago.edu

Nonemployer statistics, Staff 301-763-5184

North Am. Industry Class. System (NAICS),
  Wanda Dougherty 301-763-2790

Occupational and industrial statistics, Staff 301-763-3239

Occupational data, Staff 202-691-6378

Occupational employment statistics, Staff 202-691-6569;
  oesinfo@bls.gov

Occupational Outlook Quarterly, Kathleen Green
  202-691-5717

Occupational projections:
- College graduate outlook, Arlene Dohm/Ian Wyatt
  202-691-5727/5690
- Education and training, Chet Levine/Jon Sargent
  202-691-5715/5722
- General information, Chet Levine/Jon Sargent
  202-691-5715/5722
- Industry-occupation matrix, David Frank 202-691-5708

- Projections:
  - Computer, Chet Levine/Roer Moncarz
    202-691-5715/5694
  - Construction, Doug Braddock/William Lawhorn
    202-691-5695/5093
  - Education, Arlene Dohm 202-691-5727
  - Engineering, Doug Braddock 202-691-5695
  - Food and lodging, Theresa Cosca/Jon Kelinson
    202-691-5712/5688
  - Health, Theresa Cosca/Alan Lacey/Terry Schau
    202-601-5712/5731/5720
  - Legal, Tamara Dillon 202-691-5733
  - Mechanics and repairers, Theresa Cosca
    202-691-5712
  - Sales, Doug Braddock/Andrew Alpert
    202-691-5695/5754
  - Scientific, Henry Kasper 292-691-5696
- Replacement and separation rates, Alan Lacey/
  Lynn Shniper 202-691-5731/5732
Older workers, Staff 202-691-6378
Outlying areas, Michael Levin 301-763-1444
Part-time workers, Staff 202-691-6378
Place of birth, Staff 301-763-2422
Population estimates and projections, Staff 301-763-2422
Population information, Staff 301-763-2422
Poverty statistics, Staff 301-763-3242
Prisoner surveys, Marilyn Monahan 301-763-5315
Puerto Rico, Idabelle Hovland 301-763-8443
Quarterly Financial Report, Yolando St. George
  301-763-3343
Race, concepts and interpretation, Staff 301-763-2402
Race statistics, Staff 301-763-2422
Retail trade
- Advance monthly, Scott Scheleur 301-763-2713;
  svsd@census.gov
- Annual retail, Scott Scheleur 301-763-2713;
  svsd@census.gov
- Economic census, Fay Dorsett 301-763-5180;
  rcb@census.gov
- Monthly sales and inventory, Nancy Piesto
  301-763-2747; retail.trade@census.gov
- Quarterly Financial Report, Yolando St. George
  301-763-3343; cad@census.gov
School enrollment, Staff 301-763-2464
Seasonal adjustment methodology, Richard Tiller/Thomas
  Evans 202-691-6370/6354
Services
- Current Reports, Ruth Bramblett 301-763-2787;
  svsd@census.gov
- Economic census, Jack Moody 301-763-5181;
  scb@census.gov

- General information, Staff 1-800-541-8345;
  scb@census.gov
Small area income and poverty estimates, Staff
  301-763-3193
Special censuses, Mike Stump 301-763-3577
Special surveys, Ron Dopkowski 301-763-3801
Special tabulations, Linda Showalter 301-763-2429
State population estimates, Staff 301-763-2422
Statistics of U.S. businesses, Melvin Cole 301-763-3321
Survey of Income and Program Participation (SIPP),
  Staff 301-763-3242
Transportation
- Commodity Flow Survey, John Fowler 301-763-2108;
  svsd@census.gov
- Establishments, James Barron 301-763-2786;
  ucb@census.gov
- Vehicle inventory and use survey, Thomas Zabelsky
  301-763-5175; vius@census.gov
- Wholesale trade, Donna Hambric 301-763-2725;
  svsd@census.gov
Undercount, demographic analysis, Gregg Robinson
  301-763-2110
Union membership, Staff 202-691-6378
Urban/rural population, Michael Ratcliff 301-763-2419
Veterans in labor force, Staff 202-691-6378
Veterans' status, Staff 301-763-3230
Voters, characteristics, Staff 301-763-2464
Voting age population, Staff 301-763-2464
Weekly earnings, Staff 202-691-6378
Wholesale trade
- Annual wholesale, Scott Scheleur 301-763-2713;
  svsd@census.gov
- Current sales and inventories, Scott Scheleur
  301-763-2713; svsd@census.gov
- Economic census, Donna Hambric 301-763-2725;
  wcb@census.gov
- Quarterly Financial Report, Yolando St. George
  301-763-3343; csd@census.gov
Women, Renee Spraggins 301-763-2378
Women in the labor force, Staff 202-691-6378
Work experience, Staff 202-691-6378
Working poor, Staff 202-691-6378
Youth, students, and dropouts in labor force,
  Staff 202-691-6378

Census Regional Offices

Information specialists in the Census Bureau's 12
regional offices answer thousands of questions each year.
If you have questions about the Census Bureau's products
and services, contact the regional office serving your

state. The states served by each regional office are listed in parentheses.

- Atlanta (AL, FL, GA) 404-730-3833
  www.census.gov/atlanta
- Boston, MA (CT, MA, ME, NH, NY, RI, VT)
  617-424-0510; www.census.gov/boston
- Charlotte (KY, NC, SC, TN, VA) 704-424-6430
  www.census.gov/charlotte
- Chicago (IL, IN, WI) 708-562-1350
  www.census.gov/chicago
- Dallas (LA, MS, TX) 214-253-4481
  www.census.gov/dallas
- Denver (AZ, CO, MT, NE, ND, NM, NV, SD, UT, WY)
  303-969-7750; www.census.gov/denver
- Detroit (MI, OH, WV) 313-259-1875
  www.census.gov/detroit
- Kansas City (AR, IA, KS, MN, MO, OK)
  913-551-6711; www.census.gov/kansascity
- Los Angeles (southern CA, HI) 818-904-6339
  www.census.gov/losangeles
- New York (NY, NJ-selected counties) 212-264-4730
  www.census.gov/newyork
- Philadelphia (DE, DC, MD, NJ-selected counties, PA)
  215-656-7578; www.census.gov/philadelphia
- Seattle (northern CA, AK, ID, OR, WA) 206-553-5835
  www.census.gov/seattle
- Puerto Rico and the U.S. Virgin Islands are serviced by the Boston regional office. All other outlying areas are serviced by the Los Angeles regional office.

State Data Centers and Business and Industry Data Centers

For demographic and economic information about states and local areas, contact your State Data Center (SDC) or Business and Industry Data Center (BIDC). Every state has a State Data Center. Below are listed the leading centers for each state-usually a state government agency, university, or library that heads a network of affiliate centers. Asterisks (*) identify states that also have BIDCs. In some states, one agency serves as the lead for both the SDC and the BIDC. The BIDC is listed separately if a separate agency serves as the lead.

- Alabama, Annette Watters, University of Alabama
  205-348-6191; awatters@cba.ua.edu
- Alaska, Kathryn Lizik, Department of Labor
  907-465-2437; kathryn_lizik@labor.state.ak.us
- American Samoa, Vaitoelau Filiga, Department of Commerce 684-633-5155; vfiliga@doc.asg.as
- Arizona*, Betty Jeffries, Dept of Economic Security
  602-542-5984; betty.jeffries@de.state.az.us

- Arkansas, Sarah Breshears, University of Arkansas/ Little Rock 501-569-8530; sgbreshears@ualr.edu
- California, Julie Hoang, Department of Finance
  916-323-4086; fijhoang@dof.ca.gov
- Colorado, Rebecca Picaso, Department of Local Affairs
  303-866-3120; rebecca.picaso@state.co.us
- Connecticut, Bill Kraynak, Office of Policy and
  Mgmt., 860-418-6230; william.kraynak@po.state.ct.us
- Delaware*, Mike Helmer, Economic Development
  Office 302-672-6848; michael.helmer@state.de.us
- District of Columbia, Herb Bixhorn, Mayor's Office of
  Planning 202-442-7603; herb.bixhorn@dc.gov
- Florida*, Pam Schenker, Florida Agency for Workforce
  Innovation 850-488-1048;
  pamela.schenker@awi.state.fl.us
- Georgia, Robert Giacomini, Office of Planning and
  Budget 404-656-6505;
  girt@mail.opb.state.ga.us
- Guam, Isabel Lujan, Bureau of Statistics and Plans
  671-472-4201; idlujan@mail.gov.gu
- Hawaii, Jan Nakamoto, Dept. of Business, Ec. Dev.,
  and Tourism 808-586-2493;
  jnakamot@dbedt.hawaii.gov
- Idaho, Alan Porter, Department of Commerce
  208-334-2470; aporter@idoc.state.id.us
- Illinois*, Suzanne Ebetsch, Dept. of Commerce and
  Community Affairs
  217-782-1381; sue_ebetsch@commerce.state.il.us
- Illinois BIDC, Ed Taft, Dept. of Commerce and
  Community Affairs
  217-785-7545; ed_taft@commerce.state.il.us
- Indiana*, Roberta Brooker, State Library
  317-232-3733; rbrooker@statelib.lib.in.us
- Indiana BIDC, Carol Rogers, Business Research Center
  317-274-2205; rogersc@iupui.edu
- Iowa, Beth Henning, State Library 515-281-4350;
  beth.henning@lib.state.ia.us
- Kansas, Marc Galbraith, State Library 785-296-3296;
  marcg@kslib.info
- Kentucky*, Ron Crouch, University of Louisville
  502-852-7990; rtcrou01@gwise.louisville.edu
- Louisiana, Karen Paterson, Office of Planning and
  Budget 225-219-5987; kpaters@doa.state.la.us
- Maine*, Eric VonMagnus, State Planning Office
  207-287-3261; eric.vonmagnus@state.me.us
- Maryland*, Jane Traynham, Office of Planning
  410-767-4450; jtraynham@mdp.state.md.us
- Massachusetts*, John Gaviglio, Institute for Social and
  Econ. Research 413-545-3460; miser@miser.umass.edu

- Michigan, Daarren Warner, Library of Michigan 517-373-2548; warnerd@michigan.gov
- Minnesota*, Dona Ronningen, State Demographer's Office 651-296-4886; barbara.ronningen@state.mn.us
- Mississippi*, Rachel McNeely, University of Mississippi 662-915-7288; rmcneely@olemiss.edu
- Mississippi BIDC, Deloise Tate, Dept. of Ec. and Comm. Dev. 601-359-3593; dtate@mississippi.org
- Missouri*, Debra Pitts, State Library 573-526-7648; pittsd@sosmail.state.mo.us
- Missouri BIDC, Cathy Frank, Small Business Research Information Center 573-341-6484; cfrank@umr.edu
- Montana*, Pam Harris, Department of Commerce 406-841-2740; paharris@state.mt.us
- Nebraska, Jerome Deichert, University of Nebraska at Omaha 402-554-2134; jerome_deichert@unomaha.edu
- Nevada, Ramona Reno, State Library and Archives 775-684-3326; rlreno@clan.lib.nv.us
- New Hampshire, Thomas Duffy, Office of State Planning 603-271-2155; t_duffy@osp.state.nh.us
- New Jersey*, David Joye, Department of Labor 609-984-2595; djoye@dol.state.nj.us
- New Mexico*, Kevin Kargacin, University of New Mexico 505-277-6626; kargacin@unm.edu
- New Mexico BIDC, Beth Davis, Economic Development Dept. 505-827-0264; edavis@edd.state.nm.us
- New York*, Staff, Department of Economic Development 518-292-5300; rscardamalia@empire.state.ny.us
- North Carolina*, Staff, State Library 919-733-3270; francine.stephenson@ncmail.net
- North Dakota, Richard Rathge, North Dakota State University 701-231-8621; richard.rathge@ndsu.nodak.edu
- Northern Mariana Islands, Diego A. Sasamoto, Dept. of Commerce 670-664-3033; csd@itecnmi.com
- Ohio*, Steve Kelley, Department of Development 614-466-2116; skelley@odod.state.oh.us
- Oklahoma*, Jeff Wallace, Department of Commerce 405-815-5184; jeff_wallace@odoc.state.ok.us
- Oregon, George Hough, Portland State University. 503-725-5159; houghg@mail.pdx.edu
- Pennsylvania*, Sue Copella, Pennsylvania State Univ./ Harrisburg 717-948-6336; sdc3@psu.edu
- Puerto Rico, Lillian Torres Aguirre, Planning Bd. 787-727-4444; torres_l@jp.gobierno.pr
- Rhode Island, Mark Brown, Department of Administration 401-222-6183; mbrown@planning.state.ri.us
- South Carolina, Mike MacFarlane, Budget and Control Board 803-734-3780; mmacfarl@drss.state.sc.us
- South Dakota, Nancy Nelson, University of South Dakota 605-677-5287; nnelson@usd.edu
- Tennessee, Betty Vickers, University of Tennessee, Knoxville 865-974-5441; bvickers@utk.edu
- Texas*, Steve Murdock, Texas A&M University 979-845-5115/5332; smurdock@rsocsun.tamu.edu
- Texas BIDC, Ann Griffith, Dept. of Economic Dev. 512-936-0550; bidc@txed.state.tx.us
- Utah*, Sophia DiCaro, Governor's Office of Planning and Budget 801-537-9013; sdicaro@utah.gov
- Vermont, William Sawyer, Center for Rural Studies 802-656-3021; william.sawyer@uvm.edu
- Virgin Islands, Frank Mills, University of the Virgin Islands 340-693-1027; fmills@uvi.edu
- Virginia*, Don Lillywhite, Virginia Employment Commission 804-786-7496; dlillywhite@vec.state.va.us
- Washington*, Yi Zhao, Office of Financial Management 360-902-0592; yi.zhao@ofm.wa.gov
- West Virginia*, Delphine Coffey, West Virginia Dev. Office 304-558-4010; dcoffey@wvdo.org
- West Virginia BIDC, Randy Childs, Bureau of Business & Economic Research 304-293-7832; randy.childs@mail.wvu.edu
- Wisconsin*, Robert Naylor, Demographic Services Center 608-266-1927; bob.naylor@doa.state.wi.us
- Wisconsin BIDC, Dan Veroff, University of Wisconsin 608-265-9545; dlveroff@facstaff.wisc.edu
- Wyoming, Wenlin Liu, Dept. of Administration and Information 307-777-7504; wliu@missc.state.wy.us

Glossary

adjusted for inflation Income or a change in income that has been adjusted for the rise in the cost of living, or the consumer price index (CPI-U-RS).

American Housing Survey (AHS) The AHS collects national and metropolitan-level data on the nation's housing, including apartments, single-family homes, and mobile homes. The nationally representative survey, with a sample of 55,000 homes, is conducted by the Census Bureau for the Department of Housing and Urban Development every other year.

American Indians In this book, American Indians include Alaska Natives (Eskimos and Aleuts). In tables showing 2000 census data, the term "American Indian" may include those who identified themselves as American Indian and no other race (called "American Indian alone") or those who identified themselves as American Indian and some other race (called "American Indian in combination").

Asian The term "Asian" is defined differently depending on whether census or survey data are shown. In tables showing 2000 census data, Asians do not include Native Hawaiians or other Pacific Islanders unless noted. The term "Asian" may include those who identified themselves as Asian and no other race (called "Asian alone") or those who identified themselves as Asian and some other race (called "Asian in combination"). Asian estimates from the 2003 Current Population Survey include both those who identified themselves as Asian alone and those who identified themselves as Asian in combination. Asian estimates in earlier survey data do not include the multiracial option. Also, in surveys and other noncensus data collections, Asian figures include Native Hawaiians and other Pacific Islanders.

Baby Boom Americans born between 1946 and 1964.

Baby Bust Americans born between 1965 and 1976, also known as Generation X.

Behavioral Risk Factor Surveillance System (BRFSS) The BRFSS is a collaborative project of the Centers for Disease Control and Prevention and U.S. states and territories. It is an ongoing data collection program designed to measure behavioral risk factors in the adult population aged 18 or older. All 50 states, three territories, and the District of Columbia take part in the survey, making the BRFSS the primary source of information on the health-related behaviors of Americans.

black The black racial category includes those who identified themselves as "black or African American." The term "black" is defined differently depending on whether census or survey data are shown. In tables showing 2000 census data, the term "black" may include those who identified themselves as black and no other race (called "black alone") or those who identified themselves as black and some other race (called "black in combination"). Black estimates from the 2003 Current Population Survey include both those who identified themselves as black alone and those who identified themselves as black in combination. Black estimates in earlier survey data do not include the multiracial option.

central cities The largest city in a metropolitan area is called the central city. The balance of the metropolitan area outside the central city is regarded as the "suburbs."

Consumer Expenditure Survey (CEX) The Consumer Expenditure Survey is an ongoing study of the day-to-day spending of American households administered by the Bureau of Labor Statistics. The survey is used to update prices for the Consumer Price Index. The CEX includes an interview survey and a diary survey. The average spending figures shown in this book are the integrated data from both the diary and interview components of the survey. Two separate, nationally representative samples are used for the interview and diary surveys. For the interview survey, about 7,500 consumer units are interviewed on a rotating panel basis each quarter for five consecutive quarters. For the diary survey, 7,500 consumer units keep weekly diaries of spending for two consecutive weeks.

consumer unit *(on spending tables only)* For convenience, the term consumer unit and households are used interchangeably in the spending section of this book, although consumer units are somewhat different from the Census Bureau's households. Consumer units are all related members of a household, or financially independent members of a household. A household may include more than one consumer unit.

disability *(1997 Current Population Survey data)* People aged 15 or older were identified as having a disability if they met any of the following criteria: 1) used a wheelchair, cane, crutches, or walker; 2) had difficulty performing one or more functional activities (seeing, hearing, speaking, lifting/carrying, climbing stairs, walking, or grasping small objects); 3) had difficulty with one or more activities of daily living (or ADL, which include getting around inside the home, getting in or out of bed or a chair, bathing, dressing, eating, and toileting); 4) had difficulty with one or more instrumental activities of daily living (or IADL, which include going outside the home, keeping track of money and bills, preparing meals, doing light housework, taking prescription medicines, and using the telephone); 5) had one or more specified conditions such as a learning disability, mental retardation, or another developmental disability, Alzheimer's disease, or some other type of mental or emotional condition; 6) had any other mental or emotional condition that seriously interfered with everyday activities (frequently depressed or anxious, trouble getting along with others, trouble concentrating, or trouble coping with day-to-day stress); 7) had a condition that limited the ability to work around the house; 8) if age 16 to 67, had a condition that made it difficult to work at a job or business; or 9) received federal benefits based on an inability to work. People were considered to have a severe disability if they met criteria 1, 6, or 9, or had Alzheimer's disease, mental retardation, or another developmental disability, or were unable to perform or needed help to perform one or more activities in criteria 2, 3, 4, 7, or 8. Children under age 5 were identified as disabled if they had a developmental delay or a condition that limited the ability to use arms or legs or a condition that limited walking, running, or playing. Children aged 6 to 14 were identified as severely disabled if they met any of the following criteria: 1) had a mental retardation or some other developmental disability; 2) had a developmental condition for which they had received therapy or diagnostic services; 3) used an ambulatory aid; 4) had a severe limitation in the ability to see, hear, or speak; or 5) needed personal assistance for an activity of daily living.

disability *(2000 Census data)* The 2000 Census defined the disabled as those who were blind, deaf, or had severe vision or hearing impairments, and/or had a condition that substantially limited one or more basic physical activities such as walking, climbing stairs, reaching, lifting, or carrying. It also included people who, because of a physical, mental, or emotional condition lasting six months or more, have difficulty learning, remembering, concentrating, dressing, bathing, getting around inside the home, going outside the home alone to shop or visit a doctor's office, or working at a job or business.

disability *(2001 National Health Interview Survey data)* This survey estimated the number of people aged 18 or older who had difficulty in physical and/or social functioning, probing whether respondents could perform 12 activities by themselves without using special equipment. Physical functioning questions were grouped in two categories: mobility, and flexibility/strength. The mobility category comprised difficulties in performing the following activities: walking a quarter of a mile, standing for two hours, or walking up 10 steps without resting. The flexibility/strength category comprised difficulties in performing the following activities: stooping, bending, kneeling, reaching over one's head, grasping or handling small objects, carrying a 10-pound object, or pushing/pulling a large object. Social functioning questions probed the following: difficulty in sitting for two hours, going shopping, going to movies, attending sporting events, visiting friends, attending clubs or meetings, going to parties, reading, watching television, sewing, or listening to music. Adults who indicated that the activities were "only a little difficult" or "somewhat difficult" were considered to have a moderate difficulty, and those who indicated that the activities were "very difficult" or "can't do this activity" were considered to have severe difficulty.

disability, work *(2003 Current Population Survey data)* A work disability is a specific physical or mental condition that prevents an individual from working. The disability must be so severe that it completely incapacitates the individual and prevents him/her from doing any kind of work for at least the next six months.

Current Population Survey (CPS) The CPS is a nationally representative survey of the civilian noninstitutional population aged 15 or older. It is taken monthly by the Census Bureau for the Bureau of Labor Statistics, collecting information from more than 50,000 households on employment and unemployment. In March of each year, the survey includes the Annual Social and Economic Supplement (formerly called the Annual Demographic Survey), which is the source of most national data on the characteristics of Americans, such as educational attainment, living arrangements, and incomes.

dual-earner couple A married couple in which both the householder and the householder's spouse are in the labor force.

earnings A type of income, earnings is the amount of money a person receives from his or her job. *See also* Income.

employed All civilians who did any work as a paid employee or farmer/self-employed worker, or who worked 15 hours or more as an unpaid farm worker or in a family-owned business, during the reference period. All those who have jobs but who are temporarily absent from their jobs due to illness, bad weather, vacation, labor management dispute, or personal reasons are considered employed.

expenditure The transaction cost including excise and sales taxes of goods and services acquired during the survey period. The full cost of each purchase is recorded even though full payment may not have been made at the date of purchase. Average expenditure figures may be artificially low for infrequently purchased items such as cars because figures are calculated using all consumer units within a demographic segment rather than just purchasers. Expenditure estimates include money spent on gifts for others.

family A group of two or more people (one of whom is the householder) related by birth, marriage, or adoption and living in the same household.

family household A household maintained by a householder who lives with one or more people related to him or her by blood, marriage, or adoption.

female/male householder A woman or man who maintains a household without a spouse present. May head family or nonfamily households.

foreign-born population People who are not U.S. citizens at birth.

full-time employment Full-time is 35 or more hours of work per week during a majority of the weeks worked.

full-time, year-round Indicates 50 or more weeks of full-time employment during the previous calendar year.

Generation X Americans born between 1965 and 1976, also known as the baby-bust generation.

group quarters population The group quarters population includes all people not living in households. Two general categories of people in group quarters are recognized: 1) the institutionalized population, which includes people under formally authorized, supervised care or custody in institutions at the time of enumeration such as correctional institutions, nursing homes, and juvenile institutions; and 2) the noninstitutionalized population, which includes all people who live in group quarters other than institutions such as college dormitories, military quarters, and group homes.

Hispanic Hispanic origin is self-reported in a question separate from race. Because Hispanic is an ethnic origin rather than a race, Hispanics may be of any race. While most Hispanics are white, there are black, Asian, American Indian, and even Native Hawaiian Hispanics. On the 2000 census, many Hispanics identified their race as "other" rather than white, black, and so on. In fact, 90 percent of people identifying their race as "other" also identified themselves as Hispanic. The 2000 census count of Hispanics differs from estimates in the Current Population Survey and other noncensus data collections in part due to methodological differences.

household All the persons who occupy a housing unit. A household includes the related family members and all the unrelated persons, if any, such as lodgers, foster children, wards, or employees who share the housing unit. A person living alone is counted as a household. A group of unrelated people who share a housing unit as roommates or unmarried partners is also counted as a household. Households do not include group quarters such as college dormitories, prisons, or nursing homes.

household, race/ethnicity of Households are categorized according to the race or ethnicity of the householder only.

householder The householder is the person (or one of the persons) in whose name the housing unit is owned or rented or, if there is no such person, any adult member. With married couples, the householder may be either the husband or wife. The householder is the reference person for the household.

householder, age of The age of the householder is used to categorize households into age groups such as those used in this book. Married couples, for example, are classified according to the age of either the husband or wife, depending on which one identified him or herself as the householder.

housing unit A housing unit is a house, an apartment, a group of rooms, or a single room occupied or intended for occupancy as separate living quarters. Separate living quarters are those in which the occupants do not live and eat with any other persons in the structure and that have direct access from the outside of the building or through a common hall that is used or intended for use by the occupants of another unit or by the general public. The occupants may be a single family, one person living alone, two or more families living together, or any other group of related or unrelated persons who share living arrangements.

Housing Vacancy Survey The AHS is a supplement to the Current Population Survey, providing quarterly and annual data on rental and homeowner vacancy rates, characteristics of units available for occupancy, and homeownership rates by age, household type, region, state, and metropolitan area. The Current Population Survey sample includes 51,000 occupied housing units and 9,000 vacant units.

housing value The respondent's estimate of how much his or her house and lot would sell for if it were for sale.

immigration The relatively permanent movement (change of residence) of people into the country of reference.

in-migration The relatively permanent movement (change of residence) of people into a subnational geographic entity, such as a region, division, state, metropolitan area, or county.

income Money received in the preceding calendar year by each person aged 15 or older from each of the following sources: (1) earnings from longest job (or self-employment); (2) earnings from jobs other than longest job; (3) unemployment compensation; (4) workers' compensation; (5) Social Security; (6) Supplemental Security income; (7) public assistance; (8) veterans' payments; (9) survivor benefits; (10) disability benefits; (11) retirement pensions; (12) interest; (13)

dividends; (14) rents and royalties or estates and trusts; (15) educational assistance; (16) alimony; (17) child support; (18) financial assistance from outside the household, and other periodic income. Income is reported in several ways in this book. Household income is the combined income of all household members. Income of persons is all income accruing to a person from all sources. Earnings are the money a person receives from his or her job.

industry Refers to the industry in which a person worked longest in the preceding calendar year.

institutionalized population *See* Group quarters population.

job tenure The length of time a person has been employed continuously by the same employer.

labor force The labor force tables in this book show the civilian labor force only. The labor force includes both the employed and the unemployed (people who are looking for work). People are counted as in the labor force if they were working or looking for work during the reference week in which the Census Bureau fields the Current Population Survey.

labor force participation rate The percent of the civilian noninstitutional population that is in the civilian labor force, which includes both the employed and the unemployed.

married couples with or without children under age 18 Refers to married couples with or without own children under age 18 living in the same household. Couples without children under age 18 may be parents of grown children who live elsewhere, or they could be childless couples.

median The median is the amount that divides the population or households into two equal portions: one below and one above the median. Medians can be calculated for income, age, and many other characteristics.

median income The amount that divides the income distribution into two equal groups, half having incomes above the median, half having incomes below the median. The medians for households or families are based on all households or families. The median for persons are based on all persons aged 15 or older with income.

Medical Expenditure Panel Survey MEPS is a nationally representative survey that collects detailed information on the health status, access to care, health care use and expenses and health insurance coverage of the civilian noninstitutionalized population of the U.S. and nursing home residents. MEPS comprises four component surveys: the Household Component, the Medical Provider Component, the Insurance Component, and the Nursing Home Component. The Household Component is the core survey and is conducted each year, and includes 15,000 households and 37,000 people.

metropolitan statistical area (MSA) To be defined as a metropolitan statistical area (or MSA), an area must include a city with 50,000 or more inhabitants, or a Census Bureau-defined urbanized area of at least 50,000 inhabitants and a total metropolitan population of at least 100,000 (75,000 in New England). The county (or counties) that contains the largest city becomes the "central county" (counties), along with any adjacent counties that have at least 50 percent of their population in the urbanized area surrounding the largest city. Additional "outlying counties" are included in the MSA if they meet specified requirements of commuting to the central counties and other selected requirements of metropolitan character (such as population density and percent urban). In New England, MSAs are defined in terms of cities and towns rather than counties. For this reason, the concept of NECMA is used to define metropolitan areas in the New England division.

Millennial generation Americans born between 1977 and 1994.

mobility status People are classified according to their mobility status on the basis of a comparison between their place of residence at the time of the March Current Population Survey and their place of residence in March of the previous year. Nonmovers are people living in the same house at the end of the period as at the beginning of the period. Movers are people living in a different house at the end of the period than at the beginning of the period. Movers from abroad are either citizens or aliens whose place of residence is outside the United States at the beginning of the period, that is, in an outlying area under the jurisdiction of the United States or in a foreign country. The mobility status for children is fully allocated from the mother if she is in the household; otherwise it is allocated from the householder.

Monitoring the Future Project (MTF) The MTF survey is conducted by the University of Michigan Survey Research Center. The survey is administered to approximately 50,000 students in 420 public and private secondary schools every year. High school seniors have been surveyed annually since 1975. Students in 8th and 10th grade have been surveyed annually since 1991.

National Ambulatory Medical Care Survey (NAMCS) The NAMCS is an annual survey of visits to nonfederally employed office-based physicians who are primarily engaged in direct patient care. Data are collected from physicians rather than patients, with each physician assigned a one-week reporting period. During that week, a systematic random sample of visit characteristics are recorded by the physician or office staff.

National Health Interview Survey (NHIS) The NHIS is a continuing nationwide sample survey of the civilian noninstitutional population of the U.S. conducted by the Census Bureau for the National Center for Health Statistics. Each year, data are collected from more than 100,000 people about their illnesses, injuries, impairments, chronic and acute conditions, activity limitations, and the use of health services.

National Home and Hospice Care Survey These are a series of surveys of a nationally representative sample of home and hospice care agencies in the U.S., sponsored by the National Center for Health Statistics. Data on the characteristics of patients and services provided are collected through personal interviews with administrators and staff.

National Hospital Discharge Survey This survey has been conducted annually since 1965, sponsored by the National Center for Health Statistics, to collect nationally representative information on the characteristics of inpatients discharged from nonfederal, short-stay hospitals in the U.S. The survey collects data from a sample of approximately 270,000 inpatient records acquired from a national sample of about 500 hospitals.

National Household Education Survey (NHES) The NHES, sponsored by the National Center for Education Statistics, provides descriptive data on the educational activities of the U.S. population, including after-school care and adult education. The NHES is a system of telephone surveys of a representative sample of 45,000 to 60,000 households in the U.S. It has been conducted in 1991, 1993, 1995, 1996, 1999, 2001, and 2003.

National Nursing Home Survey This is a series of national sample surveys of nursing homes, their residents, and staff conducted at various intervals since 1973–74 and sponsored by the National Center for Health Statistics. The latest survey was taken in 1999. data for the survey are obtained through personal interviews with administrators and staff, and occasionally with self-administered questionnaires, in a sample of about 1,500 facilities.

National Survey on Drug Use and Health *(formerly called the National Household Survey on Drug Abuse)* This survey, sponsored by the Substance Abuse and Mental Health Services Administration, has been conducted since 1971. It is the primary source of information on the use of illegal drugs by the U.S. population. Each year, a nationally representative sample of about 70,000 individuals aged 12 or older are surveyed in the 50 states and the District of Columbia.

Native Hawaiian and other Pacific Islander The 2000 census, for the first time, identified this group as a separate racial category from Asians. The term "Native Hawaiian and other Pacific Islander" may include those who identified themselves as Native Hawaiian and other Pacific Islander and no other race (called "Native Hawaiian and other Pacific Islander alone") or those who identified themselves as Native Hawaiian and other Pacific Islander and some other race (called "Native Hawaiian and other Pacific Islander in combination").

net migration Net migration is the result of subtracting out-migration from in-migration for an area. Another way to derive net migration is to subtract natural increase (births minus deaths) from total population change in an area.

net worth The amount of money left over after a household's debts are subtracted from its assets.

nonfamily household A household maintained by a householder who lives alone or who lives with people to whom he or she is not related.

nonfamily householder A householder who lives alone or with nonrelatives.

non-Hispanic People who do not identify themselves as Hispanic are classified as non-Hispanic. Non-Hispanics may be of any race.

non-Hispanic white People who identify their race as white and who do not indicate a Hispanic origin. The 2000 census classified people as non-Hispanic white if they identified their race as "white alone" and did not indicate their ethnicity as Hispanic. This definition is close to the one used in the Current Population Survey and other government data collection efforts.

noninstitutionalized population *See* Group quarters population.

nonmetropolitan area Counties that are not classified as metropolitan areas.

occupation Occupational classification is based on the kind of work a person did at his or her job during the previous calendar year. If a person changed jobs during the year, the data refer to the occupation of the job held the longest during that year.

occupied housing units A housing unit is classified as occupied if a person or group of people is living in it or if the occupants are only temporarily absent—on vacation, example. By definition, the count of occupied housing units is the same as the count of households.

other race The 2000 census included "other race" as a racial category. The category was meant to capture the few Americans, such as Creoles, who may not consider themselves as belonging to the other five racial groups. In fact, more than 18 million Americans identified themselves as "other race," including 42 percent of the nation's Hispanics. Among the 18 million people who claim to be of "other" race, 90 percent also identified themselves as Hispanic. The government considers Hispanic to be an ethnic identification rather than a race since there are white, black, American Indian, and Asian Hispanics. But many Hispanics consider their ethnicity to be a separate race.

outside central city The portion of a metropolitan county or counties that falls outside of the central city or cities; generally regarded as the suburbs.

own children Own children are sons and daughters, including stepchildren and adopted children, of the householder. The totals include never-married children living away from home in college dormitories.

owner occupied A housing unit is "owner occupied" if the owner lives in the unit, even if it is mortgaged or not fully paid for. A cooperative or condominium unit is "owner occupied" only if the owner lives in it. All other occupied units are classified as "renter occupied."

part-time employment Part-time is less than 35 hours of work per week in a majority of the weeks worked during the year.

percent change The change (either positive or negative) in a measure that is expressed as a proportion of the starting measure. When median income changes from $20,000 to $25,000, for example, this is a 25 percent increase.

percentage point change The change (either positive or negative) in a value which is already expressed as a percentage. When a labor force participation rate changes from 70 percent of 75 percent, for example, this is a 5 percentage point increase.

poverty level The official income threshold below which families and people are classified as living in poverty. The threshold rises each year with inflation and varies depending on family size and age of householder.

proportion or share The value of a part expressed as a percentage of the whole. If there are 4 million people aged 25 and 3 million of them are white, then the white proportion is 75 percent.

race Race is self-reported and defined differently depending on the data source. On the 2000 census, respondents identified themselves as belonging to one or more of six racial groups: American Indian and Alaska Native, Asian, black, Native Hawaiian and other Pacific Islander, white, and other. In publishing the results, the Census Bureau created three new terms to distinguish one group from another. The "race alone" population is people who identified themselves as only one race. The "race in combination" population is people who identified themselves as more than one race, such as white and black. The "race, alone or in combination" population includes both those who identified themselves as one race and those who identified themselves as more than one race. Other government data collection efforts included the multira-

cial option beginning in 2003. The tables in this book that include race data from government surveys or from censuses prior to 2000 do not include the multiracial option.

regions The four major regions and nine census divisions of the United States are the state groupings as shown below:

Northeast:
—New England: Connecticut, Maine, Massachusetts, New Hampshire, Rhode Island, and Vermont
—Middle Atlantic: New Jersey, New York, and Pennsylvania

Midwest:
—East North Central: Illinois, Indiana, Michigan, Ohio, and Wisconsin
—West North Central: Iowa, Kansas, Minnesota, Missouri, Nebraska, North Dakota, and South Dakota

South:
—South Atlantic: Delaware, District of Columbia, Florida, Georgia, Maryland, North Carolina, South Carolina, Virginia, and West Virginia
—East South Central: Alabama, Kentucky, Mississippi, and Tennessee
—West South Central: Arkansas, Louisiana, Oklahoma, and Texas

West:
—Mountain: Arizona, Colorado, Idaho, Montana, Nevada, New Mexico, Utah, and Wyoming
—Pacific: Alaska, California, Hawaii, Oregon, and Washington

renter occupied *See* Owner occupied.

rounding Percentages are rounded to the nearest tenth of a percent; therefore, the percentages in a distribution do not always add exactly to 100.0 percent. The totals, however, are always shown as 100.0. Moreover, individual figures are rounded to the nearest thousand without being adjusted to group totals, which are independently rounded; percentages are based on the unrounded numbers.

self-employment A person is categorized as self-employed if he or she was self-employed in the job held longest during the reference period. Persons who report self-employment from a second job are excluded, but those who report wage-and-salary income from a second job are included. Unpaid workers in family businesses are excluded. Self-employment statistics include only nonagricultural workers and exclude people who work for themselves in incorporated business.

sex ratio The number of men per 100 women.

suburbs *See* Outside central city.

Survey of Consumer Finances The Survey of Consumer Finances is a triennial survey taken by the Federal Reserve Board. It collects data on the assets, debts, and net worth of American households. For the 2001 survey, the Federal Reserve Board interviewed more than 4,000 households.

Survey of Income and Program Participation (SIPP) SIPP is a longitudinal survey conducted at four-month intervals by the Census Bureau. The main focus of SIPP is information on labor force participation, jobs, income, and participation in federal assistance programs. Information on other topics is collected in topical modules on a rotating basis.

two or more races People who identified themselves as belonging to two or more racial groups on the 2000 Census. *See* Race.

unemployed Unemployed people are those who, during the survey period, had no employment but were available and looking for work. Those who were laid off from their jobs and were waiting to be recalled are also classified as unemployed.

white The term "white" is defined differently depending on whether census or survey data are shown. In tables showing 2000 census data, the term "white" may include those who identified themselves as white and no other race (called "white alone") or those who identified themselves as white and some other race (called "white in combination"). White estimates from the 2003 Current Population Survey include both those who identified themselves as white alone and those who identified themselves as white in combination. White estimates in earlier survey data do not include the multiracial option.

Youth Risk Behavior Surveillance System (YRBSS) The YRBSS was created by the Centers for Disease Control to monitor health risks being taken by young people at the national, state, and local level. The national survey is taken every two years based on a nationally representative sample of 16,000 students in 9th through 12th grade in public and private schools.

Bibliography

AARP
>   Internet site http://www.aarp.org
>   —*Boomers at Midlife: The AARP Life Stage Study*, A National Survey Conducted by Princeton Survey Research Associates, November 2002
>   —"Pennies from Heaven: Will Inheritances Bail Out the Boomers?" Mitja Ng-Baumhackl, John Gist, and Carlos Figueiredo, *Data Digest*, No. 90, AARP Public Policy Institute
>   —*Staying Ahead of the Curve 2003: The AARP Working in Retirement Study*

Agency for Healthcare Research and Quality
>   Internet site http://www.meps.ahrq.gov/Data_Public.htm
>   —Medical Expenditure Panel Survey, 2000

Bureau of Labor Statistics
>   Internet site http://www.bls.gov
>   —1997 and 2002 Consumer Expenditure Surveys, Internet site http://www.bls.gov/cex/
>   —2002 Consumer Expenditure Survey, unpublished data
>   —2003 Current Population Survey, unpublished data
>   —*Characteristics of Minimum Wage Workers, 2002*, Internet site http://www.bls.gov/cps/minwage2002.htm
>   —*Contingent and Alternative Employment Arrangements*, February 2001, USDL 01-153, Internet site http://www.bls.gov/news.release/conemp.toc.htm
>   —*Employee Tenure in 2002*, Internet site http://www.bls.gov/news.release/tenure.toc.htm
>   —Employment Projections, 2002–2012, Internet site http://www.bls.gov/emp/emplab1.htm
>   —Labor force participation rates, historical, Public Query Data Tool, Internet site http://www.bls.gov/data
>   —*Workers on Flexible and Shift Schedules in 2001*, USDL 02-225, Internet site http://www.bls.gov/news.release/flex.toc.htm

Bureau of the Census
>   Internet site http://www.census.gov
>   —2003 Current Population Survey Annual Social and Economic Supplement, Internet site http://www.census.gov/hhes/income/dinctabs.html
>   —*Age: 2000*, Census 2000 Brief, 2001
>   —*American Housing Survey for the United States in 2001*, Internet site http://www.census.gov/hhes/www/ahs.html
>   —Census 2000, Internet site http://factfinder.census.gov/servlet/BasicFactsServlet
>   —*Children's Living Arrangements and Characteristics: March 2002*, detailed tables for Current Population Report P20-547, Internet site http://www.census.gov/population/www/socdemo/hh-fam/cps2002.html
>   —Current Population Surveys, historical data, Internet site http://www.census.gov/hhes/income/histinc/histinctb.html

—*Disability Status: 2000*, Census 2000 Brief, 2003

—*Educational Attainment in the United States: March 2002*, detailed tables (PPL-169), Internet site http://www.census.gov/population/www/socdemo/education/ppl-169.html

—*Foreign-Born Population of the United States, Current Population Survey—March 2002*, detailed tables (PPL-162), Internet site http://www.census.gov/population/www/socdemo/foreign/ppl-162.html

—*Geographic Mobility: 2003*, detailed tables for P20-549, Internet site http://www.census.gov/population/www/socdemo/migrate/p20-549.html

—Housing Vacancy Surveys, Internet site http://www.census.gov/hhes/www/housing/hvs/annual03/ann03ind.html

—National Population Estimates, Internet site http://eire.census.gov/popest/

—*School Enrollment—Social and Economic Characteristics of Students: October 2002*, detailed tables; Internet site http://www.census.gov/population/www/socdemo/school/cps2002.html

—*U.S. Interim Projections by Age, Sex, Race, and Hispanic Origin*, Internet site http://www.census.gov/ipc/www/usinterimproj/

Centers for Disease Control and Prevention

Internet site http://www.cdc.gov

—Behavioral Risk Factor Surveillance System Prevalence Data, Internet site http://apps.nccd .cdc.gov/brfss/index.asp

Employee Benefit Research Institute

Internet site http://www.ebri.org

—2003 Retirement Confidence Survey, EBRI/ASEC/Greenwald, Internet site http://www .ebri.org/

Federal Reserve Board

Internet site http://www.federalreserve.gov

—2001 Survey of Consumer Finances; Internet site http://www.federalreserve.gov/pubs/oss/oss2/2001/scf2001home.html

Investment Company Institute and Securities Industry Association

Internet sites http://www.ici.org and http://www.sia.com

—*Equity Ownership in America, 2002*; Internet sites http://www.ici.org and http://www.sia.com

National Center for Education Statistics

Internet site http://nces.ed.gov

—Adult Education and Lifelong Learning Survey of the National Household Education Surveys Program, Internet site http://nces.ed.gov/programs/coe/2003/section1/tables/t08_2.asp

National Center for Health Statistics

Internet site http://www.cdc.gov/nchs

—Deaths: Final Data for 2001, *National Vital Statistics Report*, Vol. 52, No. 3, 2003

—Deaths: Leading Causes for 2001, *National Vital Statistics Report*, Vol. 52, No. 9, 2003

—Deaths: Preliminary Data for 2002, *National Vital Statistics Report*, Vol. 52, No. 13, 2004

—Health Behaviors of Adults: United States, 1999–2001, *Vital and Health Statistics*, Series 10, No. 219, 2004

—*Health, United States, 2003*, Internet site http://www.cdc.gov/nchs/hus.htm

—National Ambulatory Medical Care Survey: 2001 Summary, *Advance Data* No. 337, 2003

—National Hospital Ambulatory Medical Care Survey: 2001 Emergency Department Summary, *Advance Data* No. 335, 2003

—National Hospital Ambulatory Medical Care Survey: 2001 Outpatient Department Summary, *Advance Data* No. 338, 2003

—*Summary Health Statistics for U.S. Adults: National Health Interview Survey, 2001*, Series 10, No. 218, 2004

Sporting Goods Manufacturers Association
Internet site http://www.sgma.com

U.S. Citizenship and Immigration Services
—*2002 Yearbook of Immigration Statistics*, Internet site http://uscis.gov/graphics/shared/aboutus/statistics/index.htm

U.S. Substance Abuse and Mental Health Services Administration, Office of Applied Studies
Internet site http://www.samhsa.gov/
—National Survey on Drug Use and Health, 2002

Index

abdominal machine, number using, 30

accidents, as cause of death, 59–66

accounts, financial, 364

activity limitations, 22, 24, 45–48

adult education, 5, 19–20

AIDS, 45, 49

air conditioning, houses with, 71, 91–92

alcoholic beverages:
  consumer spending by detailed category, 276, 280–281, 294, 297, 301–302, 315, 321–322, 335, 341–342, 355
  consumer spending trends, 266–267, 271–272
  consumption, 31, 33

alimony, as source of income, 155–160

Alzheimer's disease, as cause of death, 59–62, 65–66

amenities in housing, 71, 91–92

American Indians:
  by state, 251–263
  homeownership of, 78–79
  population, 238–239, 251–263

apartments:
  living in, 71, 83–85
  nearby, 96–97

apparel and services:
  consumer spending by detailed category, 276, 286–287, 295, 307–308, 316, 327–328, 336, 347–348, 356
  consumer spending trends, 266, 268, 270–271, 273–274

anxiety, 40–42

arthritis, 21, 39–42

Asian-American men:
  educational attainment, 5, 12–13
  employment status, 168–169
  full-time workers, 135
  income, 133, 135
  living alone, 203
  marital status, 222–223

Asian-American women:
  educational attainment, 12, 14
  employment status, 168, 170
  full-time workers, 141
  income, 139, 141
  living alone, 202–203
  marital status, 219, 222–223

Asian Americans:
  by state, 251–263
  educational attainment, 12–14
  homeownership of, 71, 78–79

household income, 116–117

household type, 199, 202–203, 209, 211

households with children, 209, 211

in poverty, 161–162

population, 238–239, 251–263

assets:
  financial, 359, 362–366
  nonfinancial, 359, 367–370

asthma, 40–42

attitudes towards retirement, 195, 197, 374, 377

back pain, 40–42

bathrooms, number of, 83, 86

bedrooms, number of, 83, 86

Black-American men:
  educational attainment, 5, 12–13
  employment status, 168–169
  full-time workers, 136
  income, 133, 136
  living alone, 204
  marital status, 224–225

Black-American women:
  educational attainment, 12, 14
  employment status, 168, 170
  full-time workers, 142
  income, 139, 142
  living alone, 202, 204
  marital status, 219, 224–225

Black Americans:
  by state, 251–263
  educational attainment, 12–14
  homeownership of, 78–79
  household income, 116, 118
  household types, 199, 202, 204, 209, 212
  households with children, 209, 212
  in poverty, 161–162
  population, 237–239, 251–263

bonds, 364

bowling, number participating, 30

breast cancer, 40–42, 54, 58

bronchitis, 40–42

business equity, 369

calisthenics, number participating, 30

cancer:
  as cause of death, 59–66
  as reason for home health care, 56

as reason for hospice care, 55, 58
by type, 40–42, 54
hospital patients with, 50, 54
cash contributions:
consumer spending by detailed category, 293, 314, 334, 354
consumer spending trends, 269, 274
central cities, homeownership in, 80, 82
cerebrovascular disease:
as cause of death, 60–66
as reason for home health care, 56
hospital patients with, 50, 54
certificates of deposit, 364
child support, as source of income, 155–160
children, presence of in households, 199, 209–214
cholesterol, high, 39, 43
cigarette smoking, 31–32. *See also* Tobacco products.
citizens, 241–242
climate, as a reason for moving, 105, 108–110
college, as a reason for moving, 108–110
college enrollment, 17–18
contractors. *See* Independent contractors.
coronary, 40–42, 54
credit card debt, 371, 373
crime, as neighborhood problem, 96, 98

death, causes of, 59–66
debt, household, 359, 371–373
deck, houses with, 71, 91–92
dental:
problems, 40–42
services, 37–38
depression, 40–42
diabetes:
as cause of death, 60–66
as reason for home health care, 56
health condition, 40–42
hospital patients with, 50, 54
dieting, 25, 27
dining room, houses with, 92
disability:
benefits, as source of income, 155–160
by education, 45, 48
by type, 45–47
of nursing home residents, 55, 57
percent with, 21, 45–48
work, 45, 48
dishwashers, houses with, 71, 91–92
dividends, as source of income, 155–160, 374, 376
divorce, 219–229
down payment for house, source of, 104
drinking, alcoholic beverages, 31, 33

drugs:
consumer spending by detailed category, 290, 296, 311, 317, 331, 337, 351, 357
consumer spending trends, 269, 271, 274
illicit, use of, 31, 34
prescription, 21, 37–38, 269, 271, 274, 290, 296, 311, 317, 331, 337, 351, 357
dryers, houses with, 91–92
dual-income couples, 171–172

earnings:
as source of income, 154–160, 374, 376
by educational attainment, 145–153
minimum wage, 191–192
of full-time workers, 145–153
eating away from home. *See* Food.
education:
adult, 5, 19–20
consumer spending by detailed category, 276, 292, 296, 313, 317, 333, 337, 353, 357
consumer spending trends, 269–270, 274–275
disability status by, 45, 48
earnings by, 145–153
educational assistance, as source of income, 155–160
educational attainment:
by race and Hispanic origin, 5, 12–14
by sex, 5–14
electricity: *See also* Utilities, fuels, and public services.
as heating fuel, 89–90.
cost of, monthly, 101
emergency departments, 21, 37–38, 50, 52
emphysema, 40–42
employment-based health insurance, 35–36
employment, long-term, 183, 185
employment status:
by race and Hispanic origin, 168–170
by sex, 163, 166–170
entertainment:
consumer spending by detailed category, 290–292, 296, 311–313, 317, 331–333, 338, 351–353, 358
consumer spending trends, 266, 269–271, 274–275
exercise, participation in, 28–30

face pain, 40–42
families. *See* Households.
family, as a reason for moving, 108–110
female-headed household. *See* Households, female-headed.
financial services, spending on, 293, 314, 334, 354
fireplace, houses with, 91–92
fishing, number participating, 30

food:
    at home, 267, 271–272, 276–280, 298–301, 318–321, 338–341
    away from home, 265–267, 271–272, 276, 280, 297, 301, 321, 341
    consumer spending by detailed category, 276–280, 294, 297–301, 315, 318–321, 335, 338–341, 355
    consumer spending trends, 265–267, 271–272
foreign-born population, 231, 241–243
fractures, 54, 56
free weights, number using, 28, 30
fuel oil. *See also* Utilities, fuels, and public services.
    as heating fuel, 89–90
    cost of, monthly, 101
full-time workers, 133–153, 179–180
furnishings and equipment:
    consumer spending by detailed category, 284–286, 305–307, 325–327, 345–347
    consumer spending trends, 268, 273

garage, houses with, 91–92
gas: *See also* Transportation *and* Utilities, fuels, and public services.
    as heating fuel, 89–90
    cost of, monthly, 101
geographic mobility:
    rate, 105–107
    reason for, 108–110
gifts:
    consumer spending by detailed category, 294–296, 315–317, 335–337, 355–357
    consumer spending trends, 269–270, 274–275
golf, number participating, 28, 30

hay fever, 40–42
headaches, 40–42
health, as a reason for moving, 105, 108–110
health care:
    consumer spending by detailed category, 289–290, 296–297, 310–311, 317, 330–331, 337, 350–351, 357
    consumer spending trends, 269–271, 274–275
    home, 37–38, 55–56
    spending by source of payment, 37–38
health conditions, 21, 39–48, 54–58
health insurance:
    consumer spending by detailed category, 289–290, 296, 310–311, 317, 330–331, 337, 350–351, 357
    consumer spending trends, 269, 274
    coverage, 35–38

health problems:
    mental, 22, 24, 40–42, 45–46, 54
    physical, 22, 24, 39–48, 54–58
health status, 21–24
hearing impairments, 39–42
heart disease:
    as cause of death, 59–66
    as reason for home health care, 56
    as reason for hospice care, 58
    health condition, 40–42
    hospital patients with, 50, 54
heating fuel, 89–90
high blood pressure. *See* Hypertension.
high cholesterol, 39, 43
hiking, number participating, 28, 30
Hispanic-American men:
    educational attainment, 5, 12–13
    employment status, 168–169
    full-time workers, 137
    income, 133, 137
    living alone, 205
    marital status, 226–227
Hispanic-American women:
    educational attainment, 12, 14
    employment status, 168, 170
    full-time workers, 143
    income, 139, 143
    living alone, 202, 205
    marital status, 219, 226–227
Hispanic Americans:
    by state, 251–263
    educational attainment, 12–14
    homeownership of, 78–79
    household income, 116, 119
    household types, 199, 202, 205, 209, 213
    households with children, 209, 213
    in poverty, 161–162
    population, 237–239, 251–263
home health care, 37–38, 55–56
homeowners:
    amenities in housing unit, 91–92
    by heating fuel used, 89–90
    by household type, 76–77
    by metropolitan status, 80, 82
    by opinion of home, 93–94
    by opinion of neighborhood, 93, 95
    by race and Hispanic origin, 71, 78–79
    by region, 80–81
    by size of housing unit, 83, 86
    by type of structure, 83, 85
    by value of home, 102–104
    housing costs of, 99–101
    in new housing, 87–88

sinusitis, 40–42
smoking, 31–32
Social Security, as source of income, 111, 154–160, 374, 376
spending:
    by detailed product category, 265, 276–357
    of retirees, 265, 271–275
    on medical services, 37–38
    on housing, monthly, 99–101
    trends, 265–275
states:
    moving between, 105–107
    population of, 231, 246, 249–263
stationary cycling, number participating, 28, 30
stock ownership, 359, 362, 364–366
stretching, number participating, 28, 30
stroke, 40–42
suburbs, homeownership in, 82
suicide, as cause of death, 59–63

taxes, personal:
    consumer spending by detailed category, 294, 315, 335, 355
    consumer spending trends, 269, 274
telephone, houses with, 92. *See also* Utilities, fuels, and public services.
temporary help workers, 186–187
tobacco products.
    consumer spending by detailed category, 293, 314, 334, 354
    consumer spending trends, 269, 274
transportation:
    consumer spending by detailed category, 276, 288–289, 295, 309–310, 316, 329–330, 336, 349–350, 356
    consumer spending trends, 268–271, 273–275
trash removal, monthly cost of, 101. *See also* Utilities, fuels, and public services.
treadmill, number using, 28, 30

ulcers, 40–42, 56
unemployment:
    compensation, as source of income, 155–160
    rate, 167, 169–170
union membership, 193–194
utilities, fuels, and public services:
    consumer spending by detailed category, 283, 295, 304, 316, 324, 336, 344, 356
    consumer spending trends, 268, 273

vehicle purchases:
    consumer spending by detailed category, 276, 288, 295, 309, 316, 329, 336, 349, 356
    consumer spending trends, 268, 271, 273
vehicles, as nonfinancial assets, 369
veteran's benefits, as source of income, 155–160
vision:
    impairments, 39–42
    services, 37–38
vitamins, spending on, 290, 311, 331, 351

wages and salaries, as source of income, 154–160, 374, 376
walking for fitness, number participating, 28, 30
washers, houses with, 91–92
water, monthly cost of, 101. *See also* Utilities, fuels, and public services.
wealth, household, 359–378
weight loss, 25, 27
welfare. *See* Public assistance.
White-American men, employment status, 168–169
White-American women, employment status, 168, 170
White Americans:
    by state, 251–263
    population, 238–239, 251–263
White non-Hispanic American men:
    educational attainment, 5, 12–13
    full-time workers, 138
    income, 133, 138
    living alone, 206
    marital status, 228–229
White, non-Hispanic American women:
    educational attainment, 12, 14
    full-time workers, 144
    income, 139, 144
    living alone, 202, 206
    marital status, 219, 228–229
White, non-Hispanic Americans:
    by state, 246, 251–263
    educational attainment, 12–14
    homeownership of, 71, 78–79
    household income, 116, 120
    household types, 199, 202, 206, 209, 214
    households with children, 209, 214
    in poverty, 161–162
    population, 231, 237–239, 246, 251–263
widowhood, 199, 219–229
women:
    disabled, 46
    drinking, 31, 33
    earnings by educational attainment, 145, 150–153
    educational attainment, 5–7, 10–11, 12, 14